RELIGION IN POLITICS

RELIGION IN POLITICS

Secularism and National Integration in Modern Nigeria

edited by
Julius O. Adekunle

Africa World Press, Inc.

P.O. Box 1892
Trenton, NJ 08607

P.O. Box 48
Asmara, ERITREA

Africa World Press, Inc.

P.O. Box 1892
Trenton, NJ 08607

P.O. Box 48
Asmara, ERITREA

First Printing 2009

Book design: Saverance Publishing Services
Cover design: Ashraful Haque

Library of Congress Cataloging-in-Publication Data

Religion in politics : secularism and national integration in modern Nigeria / edited by Julius O. Adekunle.

p. cm.

Includes bibliographical references and index.

ISBN 1-59221-722-2 (hard cover) -- ISBN 1-59221-723-0 (pbk.) 1. Religion and politics--Nigeria. 2. Nigeria--Religion. 3. Nigeria--Politics and government. 4. Secularism--Nigeria. 5. Nationalism--Nigeria. 6. Democracy--Nigeria. 7. Nigeria--Ethnic relations--Political aspects. 8. Nigeria--Social conditions. 9. Social conflict--Nigeria. 10. Islamic law--Nigeria. I. Adekunle, Julius.

BL2470.N5R4335 2009

201'.7209669--dc22

2009031353

Dedicated to Esther, an inestimable gem, for her invaluable support

TABLE OF CONTENTS

FOREWORD

Plural societies are hard and complicated to manage. Their component units, as in the case of Nigeria, are structured and defined by identities. Such identities can be framed by ethnicity and religion. It does matter, as the contributors to this fascinating volume have done, to point out the religious elements in the formation of these identities, but also how they affect the management of politics—a point that is very well articulated in this important study. Both issues—the religious foundation of identity and the intersection between religion and politics—are part of the fundamental issues in political pluralism. As fundamentals, not only must we understand them, we also have to seek solutions to the problems that do generate.

The contributors note the contradictions in the affirmation of the secular nature of the constitution and the reality of religious controversies and conflicts. Professor Adekunle and his contributors recognize the various distinctions between wishes and reality, between the political statements of political leaders and the misguided nature of their approaches, between the peace affirming nature of the World religions and the competitions unleashed by their practices, between the rhetoric of faith and the polemics of war, and between the gentility of faces in mosques and churches and the lionized behavior of mobs. Such contradictions, expressed in the narratives in many chapters, open up Nigeria as a book that has to be read, analyzed and digested.

The book has a sympathetic tone. While appreciative of the contributions that Islam and Christianity have made, they are critical of the conflicts that they have generated. We are reminded of the intricate relationship between religion and politics in the precolonial and colonial era, but how these were carefully blended to produce cohesion and progress. The arguments in the second and third sections on religion, politics and ethnicity demonstrate the linkages as they impact upon democracy, intergroup relations, and violence. A separate section devoted to associations reveal the intricacies of religious movements and how they are connected to capacity building. As associations develop the concerns and ambitions of individuals to promote personal religious values, they tend to do so within groups that can also be shaped by ideologies and practical politics. As citizens and religious people, Nigerians face the challenge of aligning issues of faith with those of politics and justice, as the last section makes very clear.

In totality, this interesting book carefully foregrounds a set of interlocking interactions between religion and democracy, religion and ethnicity, and religion and the intricate web of political pluralism, thereby revealing an analytical grid that enables us to understand and track the intensity of religion in the Nigerian space over time. We are exposed to a clear and clever understanding of the distinctive quality of Nigeria as a complicated state as well as the challenges of unifying its various identities. The contributors have a positive political agenda: the possibility of creating a knowledge base to rebrand Nigeria. They deserve our gratitude.

Toyin Falola
The Frances Higginbotham Nalle Centennial Professor in History
Fellow of the Nigerian Academy of Letters
Fellow of the Historical Society of Nigeria

Preface

The interplay of religion and politics is not a new development in Nigeria. Historically, religion has been a major part of politics and this situation has not radically changed. Although Nigeria is an ethnically plural and multi-faith society, the idea of severing religion from politics is reflected in the secular nature of the country. Being a secular country does not preclude the practice of religion, but it does not encourage the interference of religion in politics. While many Nigerians strongly support the secular clause of the constitution, successive governments have not remained totally neutral in order to ensure fair treatment to all religious groups. Nigeria, with its complex ethno-cultural composition, grapples with several crises and conflicts, many of which are associated with religion. In some cases, the causes of the conflicts and violence are either remotely related or not related at all to religion, but because of the sharp religious divide, the country is vulnerable to religious violence. Since 1999 when Nigeria returned to a democratic rule, there have been many instances of religious riots, which have claimed thousands of lives.

This book is only an attempt to examine the role that religion played, continues to play, or should play in Nigerian politics. The emphasis is on the two universal religions: Christianity and Islam. While traditional religions had been a force to reckon with in the precolonial political system, a significant change occurred, first when Islam arrived, and second when the British imposed their colonial rule on all the societies that now compose Nigeria. As traditional religions and politics were inseparable, Islam also dominated the palaces of rulers, and Christianity penetrated the colonial office. In the justice system, Islam and colonialism conflicted because of the implementation of the Shari'a legal law and the British legal system.

Associations are formed to promote or defend the rights of each religion and their adherents. The participation of the successive governments of Nigeria on religious matters lends credence to how religion is interjected into politics. While it is not possible to eliminate any religion, it is important to note that the interference of religion in politics may be more hurtful than helpful. The many religious crises with their attendant human loss and destruction of property are testaments to how people in Nigeria are misusing religion. Using religion to foster partisan politics or to fester division is not compatible with the national aspiration of unity and it does not support nation building. Maintaining national unity is fundamental for development and Nigerians should not wait for national tragedies to force national unity on them. Religion should not be used as a tool to destroy and divide, but to unite and promote national development and political stability.

Julius O. Adekunle
Monmouth University
July 2009

Acknowledgement

In May 2005, I attended a conference on world religions in Tokyo, Japan and presented a paper on religion and politics in Nigeria. That conference and the paper presented provided a stimulus for this book. The consideration of the role that religion plays in Nigerian politics cannot be overlooked. More than before, religion is taking a more prominent position in politics.

Returning from Tokyo, I discussed my plan of a book with Dr. Saliba Sarsar who strongly supported the idea and offered some very useful suggestions. For this, I am indebted to Saliba for his encouragement and help in seeing the project through. I am also thankful to Dr. Toyin Falola for his support, suggestions, and for writing the foreword. I thank all contributors who have worked very hard to make the publication of the book possible. The road was long and hard, but we have gotten to the point of reaching lovers of religion and politics with ideas that can lead to peace and sustainable democracy in modern Nigeria.

Many other people assisted me and they deserve my appreciation. I thank Sherri Xie of the Interlibrary Loan, Guggenheim Library, Monmouth University, for her assistance in finding books and articles on interlibrary loan. I am indebted to Robert Grasso and Kathy Shapiro who helped in proofreading the entire manuscript. Both of them did an invaluable job in making this book readable. I am grateful to Roderick Erickson for the maps. I thank Professor Biodun Adediran of Obafemi Awolowo University, Ile-Ife, and all members of the Department of History and Anthropology, Monmouth University for their support and understanding while writing this book. I appreciate Drs. Brian Greenberg, Bill Mitchell, Datta Naik, Saliba Sarsar, and Ken Stunkel for being my mentors. My appreciation also goes to Monmouth University for granting my mini-sabbatical to complete this project.

I received tremendous help and support from my wife, Esther, and our dear children (Wumi, Toyin, Femi, and Funmi). They all shared their different but useful ideas about religion and politics with me, and they patiently tolerated my habit of staying late at the office to write. Their support was a strong encouragement to me.

It has been a pleasant experience editing a book on religion in politics in Nigeria. Each contributor comes from different perspectives and they have done an excellent by expressing their opinions on how religion and politics can cohabit without encroaching on each other, especially because Nigeria is considered a secular country. The central idea is that religion can be and should be used to promote peace and sustain democracy but not to divide the Nigerian polity.

This book is peer-reviewed and every attempt was made to present accurate ideas and analysis, but there are possible misinterpretations. Authors may have analyzed their views in different ways, none of the sources used are responsible for the inaccuracy that may be found and therefore as the editor, I accept responsibility for all the flaws in this book.

Maps

Nigerian States Today

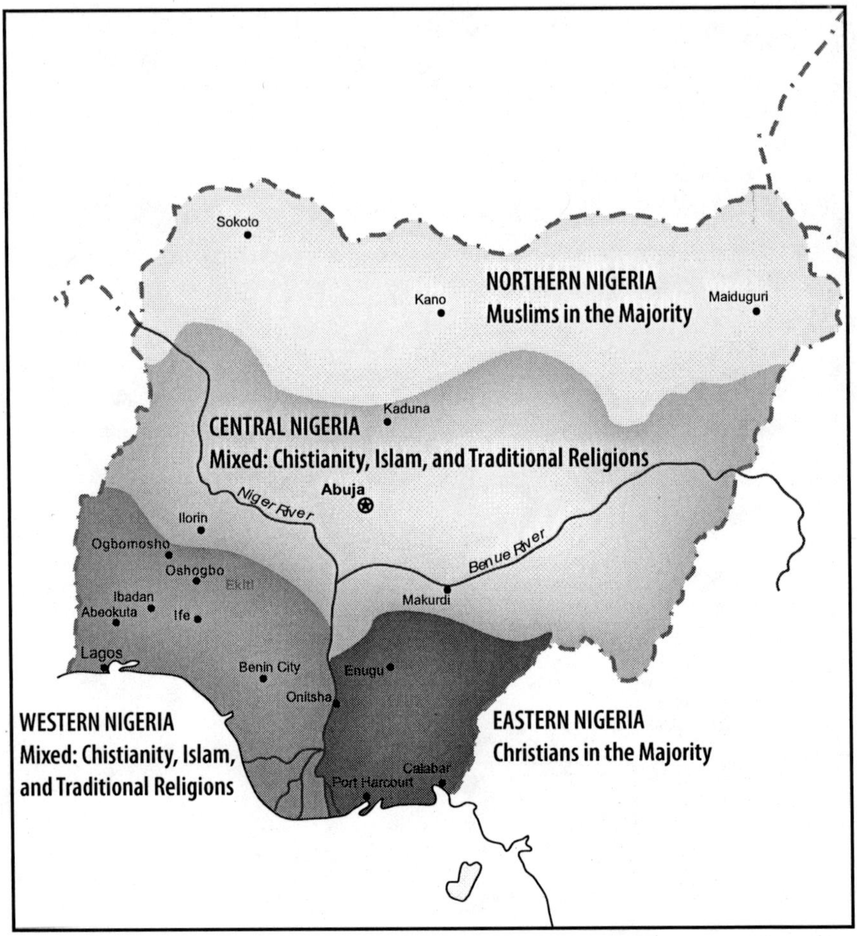

NIGERIA SHOWING RELIGIOUS GROUPINGS

NIGERIAN SHARI'A STATES

List of Abbreviations

CDC	Constitutional Drafting Committee
ATR	African Traditional Religion
SAP	Structural Adjustment Program
NPRC	National Political Reform Conference
CAN	Christian Association of Nigeria
FOMWAN	Federation of Muslim Women's Associations of Nigeria
NRMs	New Religious Movements
SDP	Social Democratic Party
NRC	National Republican Convention
JNI	Jama'atu Nasril Islamiyya
SCIA	Supreme Council of Islamic Affairs
ANPP	All Nigerian People's Party
AC	Action Congress
FDP	Fresh Democratic Party
OPC	Oodua People's Congress
BBA	Bakassi Boys of Africa
MASSOB	Movement for the Actualization of the Sovereign State of Biafra
MBF	Middle Belt Forum
IYC	Ijaw Youth Council
ACF	Arewa Consultative Forum
NCNC	National Council of Nigerian Citizens
NADECO	National Democratic Coalition
NPN	National Party of Nigeria

UPN	Unity Party of Nigeria
APP	All People's Party
PDP	People's Democratic Party
CMS	Church Missionary Society
RCM	Roman Catholic Mission
AAC	Archbishops Advisory Committee
RNC	Royal Niger Company
WAI	War Against Indiscipline
AFRC	The Armed Forces Ruling Council
NTA	Nigerian Television Authority
SCSN	Supreme Council for Shari'a in Nigeria
IDB	Islamic Development Bank
IMF	International Monetary Fund
OAU	Organization for African Unity
NCA	Northern Christians Association
CCN	Christian Council of Nigeria
CSM	Christian Social Movement
BLP	Better Life Programme
FSP	Family Support Programme
TMG	Transition Monitoring Group
DFID	Department for International Development
INEC	Independent National Electoral Commission
OSIWA	Open Society for West Africa
NEMG	Nigerian Election Monitoring Group
EMP	Election Monitoring Programme
CLO	Civil Liberties Organization
MULAG	Muslim League for Accountability
CEDPA	Centre for Development and Population Activities
NDI	National Democratic Institute
ERN	Election Reform Network
JDPC	Justice, Development and Peace Commission

LEMT	Labour Election Monitoring Team
ECWA	Evangelical Churches of West Africa
COCIN	Church of Christ in Central Nigeria
OIC	Organization of Islamic Conference
NTA	National Television Authority
S.A.W.	*Sallalahu Alaihi Wasallam*
CAC	Christ Apostolic Church
NASFAT	Nasrul-Lahi-il-Faithi
AIC	African Initiated Churches
BMJ	British Medical Journal
JP	Justice Party
ACF	The Arewa Consultative Forum
ANUNSA	All-Nigeria United Nations Youth and Students
SSG	Secretary to the State Government

INTRODUCTION

Introduction

Religion and Politics in Transition

Julius O. Adekunle

Nigeria is diverse in multi-dimensional ways: culture, ethnicity, language, and religion. The three main religions practiced in Nigeria – traditional or indigenous religions, Christianity, and Islam – have always had a profound impact on the social, political, and public life of the people. The interactions between religion and politics have been that of the spiritual and the secular, and they have also been that of transition from precolonial to the colonial and to the post colonial. The level of interference by religious groups in politics may differ from one period to another, but religion has continuously and powerfully played a profound role in politics. In the traditional societies of Nigeria, two of the most influential components of unity and togetherness were religion and politics. While religion offers a sense of brotherhood, which promotes understanding and harmony, politics provides an administrative structure, an identity and a consciousness of belonging. Both religion and politics work toward securing peace and stability for the community.

Historically, there has been a lot of discourse on the separation of Church and State, especially in Europe. As two powerful institutions, the overlap of authority and functions did not allow each of the institutions to operate as independent bodies and the growing powers of rulers called for the removal of the church from state matters. Generally in Africa but particularly in Nigeria, religion and politics were closely related. Even in contemporary discourse, religion and politics do not operate as completely parallel bodies. Both deal with the daily, moral, and social activities of the citizens in a country. Members of religious groups constitute the secular society that is governed by a political body. This indicates that the relationship between politics and religion is very strong, and both work together to promote the unity and growth of the nation. Both have the ability to foster democracy in spite of the secular nature of the state. Democracy is a political process in which religion can be used as one of the means to reach its destination. Religion has the transforming power over individuals and societies and if used wisely, it is a potent force to transform politics. Hence, both religion and politics are considered important vehicles through which peace, stability, and nation building are facilitated.

Nigeria has a long history of interpenetration of religion with politics. In precolonial times, religion was an integral part of politics. Some Nigerian societies had divine or sacred kingship where kings held both religious and political authority. The alaafin of Oyo, the oba of Benin, and the sultan of Sokoto held dual positions as religious and political leaders. They led their people in religious festivals and ceremonies and performed rituals and sacrifices. Hence, rulers were not only symbols of political power; they were also defenders of religion and traditions. Basil Davidson indicated that among the Yoruba, "politics was mixed up with religion" and the system of government not only "rested on the political power of appointed rulers among leading families, but also on their religious power."[1] N. A. Fadipe, a Yoruba sociologist, indicated:

> The elaborate religious ritual surrounding the creation of a king has for its object the passing on to him in direct continuity with his earliest predecessor what is believed to be the source of authority. This was brought about either by making the new king partake of a part of the flesh of his predecessor (the heart) or by keeping among his principal objects of worship the head of the predecessor. As in the case of nearly every *orisa* worshipped by the Yoruba, additional measures were taken to impart to the new king, on his installation, special magical powers as a means of reinforcing the attitude of awe toward him by the people.[2]

For the Yoruba people religion was not only the foundation of political authority, but it was also a source of empowerment. This made it paramount for them to devise sacred mechanisms for continuity. In Omisade Awolalu's view:

> Religion and political authority were inter-dependent. The king or ruler promoted religion – built places of worship, enforced doctrine and ritual observances for the good of the whole land and its inhabitants. For example, in Yorubaland, the *oba* who was the political head of his community was also the chief priest on festival occasions. Hence the Yoruba say *Oba ni olori awon aworo* ("the king is the leader among the cultic functionaries").[3]

The culture of the Yoruba people is replete with the intermingling of religion and politics. The performance of rituals and sacrifices by rulers for both spiritual as well as political reasons indicate that there was no defined separation between religion and politics. It was traditional for kingmakers to consult the oracle for spiritual guidance before any king was proclaimed. When consulting the oracle, pieces of kola nuts were usually used for divination. It was believed that when the nuts fell face up the oracle approved of the candidate. Failure of the kingmakers to abide by the choice of the oracle often resulted in anarchy. A new king would rely on the dictate and guidance of the oracle if he wanted his reign to be peaceful, prosperous, and successful.

Among the Igbo and Ogoni, where centralized rule did not exist in precolonial times, political institutions, which recognized the oracles, allowed rulers to perform multi-faceted functions. Oracles were important instruments in oath taking and in judicial matters. They were consulted for mediation when conflicts arose between two communities and they were consulted before going to war. In *Things Fall Apart*, Chinua Achebe asserted that Umuofia would never go to war without it being approved by the Oracle of the Hills and the Caves, and "there were indeed occasions when the oracle had forbidden Umuofia to wage a war."[4] This suggests that spirituality played important roles in the military and political practices of the Igbo. For the many years that Christianity has prevailed in Igboland, it has not been able to eliminate the power and the belief in oracles. The Igbo people still believe that oracles possess supernatural powers to punish offenders.

Until the religious revolution of 1804, the Habe rulers of the Hausa states used traditional religion as the basis of their authority to rule. Islam was the first of the foreign religions to infiltrate Nigeria. It was introduced through trade and since its penetration Islam has established a relationship with the people and their culture. Some aspects of Islam agreed with the cultural beliefs and practices of the Nigerian societies, and assimilated well into their pre-Islamic political system. Thus Islam appealed to some rulers and gradually became a major influence on politics. It displaced the

Habe indigenous rulers and installed a religiously based political system. The establishment of the Sokoto Caliphate in 1808 under the leadership of Usman dan Fodio brought about a political and religious reconfiguration of the Hausa states.

Christianity and colonialism went hand in hand, beginning from the second half of the nineteenth century. Colonial authority deliberately allowed Christianity to thrive in the southern part of Nigeria, but prohibited its penetration into Muslim dominated areas, which allowed Islam to flourish in the North. The reason for this was to preserve and protect the British system of Indirect Rule and to make it more successful. This was another way of enforcing their divide and rule policy over the people of Nigeria. Since colonial times, religious dichotomy has featured prominently in Nigerian history. While the southern states are predominantly Christian, a larger part of the northern states are essentially Muslim, and traditional, indigenous worshippers are scattered all over the country.

Within the two main religious groups, there are different categorizations of sects. Among the Muslims there are the Sunni, who make up approximately 99 percent and Shi'ites who are about 1 percent of the Muslim population. There are different groups and denominations in Christianity (the Catholic, Protestant, and Pentecostal) and they are found largely in the southern states. Catholicism is dominant in the East, especially among the Igbo and Pentecostalism is widespread in the West among the Yoruba. This means that Nigeria is an example a conglomerate religious society. For Nigerians, therefore, religion is extremely important in everything, and it is of little surprise that it has been deeply intertwined with politics.

Some of the political roles, which indigenous religions used to play in precolonial times, have been reduced or have become hidden traditions as a result of outright increasing influence of Christianity and Islam, change, or gradual transition from one period to the other. As Christianity and Islam gained converts and their population soared, the number of traditional worshippers dwindled. Colonization, modernization, and democracy have accounted for the changes. In the colonial period, European missionaries supplanted traditional religious leaders while Christianity appeared to go hand in hand with colonialism at the government level. Although traditional religions remained a factor to reckon with in local politics, they did not wield considerable influence on the colonial administration. Gradually, some of the African indigenous cultural and religious practices were eradicated. Although traditional rulers continued to engage in some religious rituals as part of their investiture, many of the rites were no longer performed openly. For example, human sacrifice, which used to be part of the burial tradition of an Alaafin of Oyo, was prohibited during the colonial period.

Nigeria gained independence from Britain in October 1960, but the rhetoric of religion in politics continued. This was very evident in Northern Nigeria where Sir Ahmadu Bello embodied religious and political leadership, much like Usman dan Fodio, his great-great-grandfather, who combined religious and political functions. Ahmadu Bello was the Sultan, the Premier of Northern Nigeria, and the leader of the Northern Peoples Congress (NPC). Even while serving as the Premier of Northern Nigeria, Ahmadu Bello aggressively promoted Islam. While visiting Mecca in 1965, he declared that he was able to convert 60,000 non-Muslims to Islam within five months. He also remarked that, "the Government of Northern Nigeria of which I am the head, has made arrangements whereby religion is taught in all government schools." He created an Islamic Advisory Committee to advise him and his government "on the means of promoting Islamic religion, our culture and unity amongst the people."[5] He believed that "a ruler is responsible to God for all his actions."[6] He firmly believed that his religious leadership would advance his political cause, especially the northernization policy, which he aggressively pursued. Ahmadu Bello's dual role was terminated in 1966 in the first coup that ushered in a military government.

In many respects, the north is profoundly different from the south; religion only represents an example of the differences. The Muslims in northern Nigeria regard Islam as a mark of identity while the southerners identify more with Western education and political astuteness rather than Christianity. However, Christianity dominates in the southern states. This difference in religion and identity are reflections in the way the British handled their colonial administration in the two regions. For example, the British set up Islamic political and judicial systems, which promoted Islamic education and permitted the adoption of the Shari'a, which had been in place in northern Nigeria since the establishment of the Sokoto Caliphate. This collaboration between Islam and politics was a deliberate action on the part of the British for the expediency of their administration. In the early 1930s, a Muslim Court of Appeal was created in later renamed the Shari'a Court of Appeal. In order to avoid conflict between the Shari'a and the State, the operations of the Shari'a Court of Appeal were limited to civil cases for Muslims.[7] During the process of decolonization, after WWII, well-educated southerners (mainly Christians), dominated nationalist politics to the chagrin of Muslim northerners. Many of the first Nigerian nationalists were Christians and southerners who received sound Western education. Upon independence, both northerners and southerners agreed to work together as a political unit agreeing that religion was not to be used to divide or unite.

As reflected in the Nigerian pledge of allegiance and the national anthem, it is difficult to ignore the influence of religion on politics, and the interaction between the two has not always been peaceful: there have been occasions of friction. What happens when religion and politics clash? Since independence, Nigeria has witnessed several cases of ethnic rivalry (between the majority and minority groups) as well as religious conflicts (between Christians and Muslims), making political stability and national integration very difficult to achieve and sustain.

The National Pledge of Allegiance

I pledge to Nigeria my country
To be faithful, loyal and honest
To serve Nigeria with all my strength
To defend her unity and uphold her honor and glory
So help me God.

Nigerian National Anthem

Arise, O compatriots, Nigeria's call obey
To serve our fatherland
With love and strength and faith
The labor of our heroes past
Shall never be in vain
To serve with heart and might
One nation bound in freedom, peace and unity.

Oh God of creation, direct our noble cause
Guide our leaders right
Help our youth the truth to know
In love and honesty to grow
And living just and true
Great lofty heights attain
To build a nation where peace and justice shall reign.

Although no specific religion is referred to in the pledge and anthem, there is enough evidence that the early leaders of Nigeria believed in the influence of religion on politics. No one in Nigeria has opposed the insertion of religious words in the national symbols.

Human Rights places emphasis on the freedom of religion and the Draft Constitution of 1976 in Nigeria recommended: "There shall be a Federal Sharia Court of Appeal which shall be an intermediate court of appeal between the States' Sharia Courts of Appeal and the Supreme Court of Nigeria."[8] To this end, David Laitin pointed out:

> Although religious issues had not previously dominated the agenda of Nigeria-wide politics, [the recommendation of the Draft Constitution] looked like an issue which would divide all Nigerians on the basis of their religious affiliations. The political climate was hot. Many commentators of the Nigerian scene foresaw bloody religious conflict in Nigeria that would rival the Biafran war in its devastation.[9]

Nigeria has often been referred to as a secular state, and the constitution provides for freedom of thought, conscience, and religion or belief. Secularism, however, does not mean the total absence of religion from the lives of the people; it simply refers to a position where religion is not used to influence public and political decisions. This was the basis of the separation of church and state. In spite of the secular clause, it would appear that religion has not yet been totally severed from politics in modern Nigeria. According to G. A. Akinola, "The country [Nigeria], though officially secular, now features religious rituals in public offices, institutions and functions. Churches and chapels compete with mosques in government houses and students' college hostels."[10] Successive governments since independence have sponsored, from time to time, either religious activities or programs, especially pilgrimages to either Jerusalem or Mecca. The government financially supports the building of churches and mosques and declares some religious festivals as public holidays. The argument behind the government's actions is to use religion for the purpose of promoting national unity. Plausible as this purpose might be, the Committee on Constituting A New Sustainable Democratic Order in Nigeria, in 2005, supported banning the use of public funds for religious purposes.[11]

Religion has the potential to bring peace and stability to a country. It is, however, disturbing that in Nigeria religion has created untold havoc and conflict, leaving the government to engage in political and religious conflict resolution. Many people have been killed and several churches and mosques have been destroyed in the wake of various religious conflicts. For example, following Pope John Paul II's visit to Nigeria in 1980, violence erupted in the northern states where churches were burned down. More religious riots followed in 1982, 1985, and 1987.[12] Reacting to the religious violence that erupted in Kaduna in 1987, Yakubu Mohammed, Managing

Editor of *Newswatch* magazine, questioned what had occurred since both Christianity and Islam preach peace. He asked:

> If the two religions preach peaceful co-existence, love and harmony, what went wrong in Kaduna State, where so many lives were lost and inestimable property including such holy places like mosques and churches were desecrated and torched during the unprecedented display of intolerance and fanaticism? What went wrong?[13]

What went wrong was religious intolerance, misuse of religion, and taking advantage of a dispute that could have been easily resolved. What went wrong was an act of fanaticism. The Kaduna riot occurred when President Babangida was grappling with the problem of Nigeria's membership in the Organization of Islamic Conference (OIC).

Religion did not play a major divisive role in 1999 when Olusegun Obasanjo was elected president in sharp contrast to the political milieu, which was occasioned by Babangida's annulment of the 1993 election results. As the military was preparing to relinquish power to a civilian government, the Yoruba and their supporters were asking for the "actualization of June 12," that is, they wanted M. K. O. Abiola to be recognized as the president of Nigeria. The annulment was devastating to the Yoruba who believed that the northerners have held power for a long time and it was time for a change of leadership. Therefore electing a Yoruba in the 1999 presidential election seemed to be a reasonable compromise. Indeed, the two presidential candidates (Obasanjo and Olu Falae) were Yoruba. While in power, Obasanjo was identified with three things: the southern region, the Yoruba ethnic group, and Christianity. However, since returning to democratic rule in May 1999, religion has continued to penetrate the fabric of partisan politics to the extent that politicians not only openly declare their faith, but also hinge each of their political activities and policies on God or Allah. On the one hand, politicians carry politics to churches or mosques where people are being mobilized to support either a candidate or government policy, and on the other hand, religious leaders no longer regard politics as dirty business. Instead, they encourage their followers to participate in politics. In many cases, politicians engage the services of religious leaders not only for prayers, but also to win the support of the electorate because they (religious leaders) have tremendous influence on their congregants.

The reintroduction of the Shari'a caused a major uproar in the year 2000. The Shari'a (Islamic Law or the right path) is based on the Qur'an and the Hadith. It is an amalgamation of laws and regulations found all over the Qur'an. The Shari'a is important to the Muslims because the Qur'an and the Hadith do not answer all the questions one might have regarding Islam. Thus the Shari'a fills the gaps, especially the legal matters. However, in many parts of the world, the Shari'a is only partially enforced if at all. In Egypt, Morocco, Tunisia, and Turkey, for example, the Shari'a has been reframed and is used only for civil law, while criminal law remains under the secular authorities. Additionally, the Shari'a takes Christians and Jews (People of the Book) into account, recognizing their status as unbelievers, and therefore the laws do not apply to them.[14] During the colonial period in 1959, the British permitted the use of the Shari'a in northern Nigeria, but disallowed punishments such as amputation of the hand and capital punishment. Since the Shari'a is a strong part of Islam, it is surprising that it was not strictly enforced in Nigeria until 2000. Henceforth, the Shari'a became an issue of political and religious debate and a cause of violence.

The political climate changed in both the 2003 and 2007 elections because ethnicity, regional affiliation, and religion became prominent in the ensuing campaigns. While Obasanjo was seeking re-election, some northerners claimed that the southerners and Christians had already had their turn and it was necessary to install a northern Muslim as president. Almost all the politicians employed the services of religious groups for support. They often claim that their getting to that political position was "an act of God." Princess Mordi, the only female presidential aspirant in the 2003 primary elections, did not hide her religious desire to move Nigeria closer to God. She declared that, "It is for every Nigerian to go back to God. If we all turn back to God I think most of our problems in this country will be solved."[15]

Even though Mordi was not referring to a particular religion, the statement failed to recognize the secular nature of Nigeria. Like Mordi, Nigerians identify with religion more than anything else because they understand religion more than the political system. The government also encourages this type of identity. As Jibrin Ibrahim points out, "most official forms have been constructed in a way that encourages Nigerians to identify themselves as either Muslims or Christians."[16] In more recent times the argument has been made that Nigeria's poor economy has given rise to poverty and has become a driving force for people to identify with and to use religion, not politics, as a means of comfort. In a survey conducted in October 2006, 91 percent Muslim and 76 percent Christian respondents claimed that religion was the most important issue to them.[17] The high number of adherents of the two religions often makes the outbreak of religious riots very catastrophic. Religion, as many argue, should be used to unite, but not to divide. As Hank Eso argues, "nothing is as divisive as religion -- especially when it is used as a tool of politics."[18] But when used in the proper way, religion can promote political unity.

The spate of political assassinations between 1999 and 2007 became a matter of concern for all Nigerians. Strong candidates for various political positions were being targeted and brutally murdered. Acts of intolerance, inordinate ambition, and political immaturity led to loss of many lives. To mention a few, Odunayo Olagbaju was killed on December 19, 2001, Bola Ige on December 23, 2001, Funso Williams on July 27, 2006, and Ayodele Daramola on August 14, 2006. Many religious leaders condemn such actions by political cowards. For example, when Funso Williams was brutally murdered in his home in 2006, president of North-Western Union Mission of the Adventist church, Pastor Joseph Ola, observed that the development of political killings was creating fear in both Nigerians and foreigners.[19] It was a political problem that the government had to confront.

Given the fact that the combination of religion and politics has been a dangerous and "deadly mix in Nigeria,"[20] some fundamental questions arise: Because of the secular clause in the constitution, is it possible to sever religion from politics? Is religion an essential partner of politics? Are religious groups, irrespective of their faith not allowed to express their views or participate in the affairs of their own country? Or, to what extent should religion be allowed to influence politics? How can religion be used to promote peace, justice, equity, national integration, national development, and political stability? And, as G. A. Akinola asked, "Is religion, especially in the context of what looks like an emergent neo-Christian culture, becoming some kind of alibi or hypocritical garb, particularly for people in power?"[21] These are some of the questions that this book attempts to answer.

Structure and Content of the Book

This book is divided into five sections to show the intersection of religion and politics in Nigeria from the precolonial to the contemporary period. Nigeria has experienced a political transformation and transition, from dictatorship to democracy, but the influence of religion on politics has remained constant and strong. The three religions (Traditional or Indigenous, Islam, and Christianity) have in different ways dictated or determined political activities and policies. Religion has contributed to the political development of Nigeria, and it has been a means of identity and an agency for the achievement of national integration. The seventeen essays in the five sections are perspectives on how religion and politics have interacted and how they have influenced the Nigerian societies for centuries.

Section One: The Precolonial and Colonial Times

Akeem Oladiti indicates in Chapter One that religion and politics were inseparable in the precolonial times. As the basis of authority and power, religion played a major role in the political systems by providing guidance for political leaders and by contributing to national development. Traditional rulers or institutions among the different ethnic groups that make up Nigeria relied on religion for peace and political stability. There is a continuing trend of interaction between religion and politics in the colonial period as Funso Afolayan explains in Chapter Two. Using the activities of Dr. Walter Miller as an example, Afolayan describes how the Christian missionaries utilized their position and influence to work hand in hand with colonial officers for mutual goals. Dr. Miller, a Church Missionary Society (CMS) missionary was determined to make a difference in northern Nigeria through Christianity and education. In the process, Miller came into conflict with the traditional rulers, but his influence remained strong in Zaria and Kano.

Section Two: Religion, Politics, and Ethnicity

In precolonial times, there were few instances of inter-religious conflict in Nigeria. Aside from the Sokoto Jihad that began in 1804 under the leadership of Usman dan Fodio, there were no other major religious conflicts. Philip Akpen argues in Chapter Three that religious and ethnic conflicts became prevalent in modern Nigeria and that it undermined national integration and hindered the achievement of sustainable democracy. The argument that Nigeria is a secular state is made, but Shola Omotola, in Chapter Four, critically examines the shadowy nature of religion in the Nigerian democratic system. He argues that the interjection of religion into politics is counter-productive and therefore the role of religion in politics should be minimized. This, according to him, calls for the political institutionalization of democratic forces, including political parties and civil society, in a way that strengthen their capability to generate sustainable social capital, and in turn, a generalized sense of trust among the citizenry.

As a pluralistic society, Nigeria has been confronted with the problems of ethnicity and power politics. There is constant conflict between the majority and minority groups, with the latter claiming marginalization by the former. In Chapter Five, Lateef Adeniran discusses the countervailing forces of politics and religion. He argues that Nigeria is surviving because of its resilience in spite of many political and religious challenging situations.

The politics in the church, especially with the struggle for an indigene to be chosen and recognized as a leader, and the adoption of the indigenous language in the Benin City diocese is what Uyilawa Usuanlele considers in Chapter Six. He points out that ethnic minorities and ethno-nationalism penetrated the church. Uyilawa traces the source of the conflict to the colonial period when non-Benin bishops were imposed on the people of Benin City, thereby creating ethnic and language problems. As demonstrated in the Catholic Church in Benin City, power politics within the church undermined the unity of the Benin diocese.

Section Three: The Shari'a and the Politics of Religion

The Shari'a issue dominated politics in the two-term Olusegun Obasanjo administration between 1999 and 2007. Mukhtar Bunza traces the history of Islam and the Shari'a in northern Nigeria and examines its political development in Chapter Seven. He argues that Shari'a had been part of Islamic obligation and practice. Hence, it is impossible to separate the Shari'a from Islam. He points out that the colonial officers recognized that the Shari'a was an integral part of Islam and allowed it to be practiced in northern Nigeria. In the same way, Saadatu Hasaan Liman, in Chapter Eight, argues that the Shari'a should not cause any conflict in modern Nigeria since it had been a long time practice in Islam. She points out that the many and complex conflicts in modern Nigeria are not exclusively religious or ethnic; they are a mixture of the two. She dismisses the fact that Nigeria is a secular state because of the extensive role that religion plays in politics. She also points out that the Shari'a does not separate religion from politics. It is apparent that, whether deliberately or inadvertently, the issue of the Shari'a led to acts of violence between 2000 and 2007. In Chapter Nine, Julius Adekunle examines the violence that engulfed Nigeria as a result of religion in politics, focusing mainly on the Shari'a. He argues that rather than being used as a divisive factor, religion should be employed as an instrument of integration.

Section Four: Religious Associations and Politics

Religious and gender associations have been formed to foster the cause of each religion. The Christian Association of Nigeria (CAN), the Organization of Islamic Conference (OIC) of which Nigeria is a member, the Federation of Muslim Women's Association of Nigeria (FOMWAN), and the Pentecostal movements are all discussed in this section. Adeyemi Oyeniyi explores Nigeria's membership in the OIC in Chapter Ten. The issue of Nigerian membership in the OIC has moved from one political leader to the next since 1976. As Oyeniyi argues, Ibrahim Babangida used his power and position as the president of the country to unilaterally change Nigeria's position from observer status to permanent membership in the IOC for political reasons.

In Chapter Eleven, Olayemi Akinwumi and Ibrahim Umaru are of the opinion that CAN, formed in 1976, provides a religious identity and serves as an umbrella association for all Nigerian Christians. CAN has continuously opposed the marginalization and political victimization of its members and rejects any attempt to turn Nigeria into an Islamic state. From CAN's perspective, the government is politicizing religion and is favoring one religion against the others. The role of women in religion and politics cannot be waved away easily. Hence, Olufunke Adeboye, in Chapter Twelve, analyzes the formation of the FOMWAN as an avenue to express women's political activism in a civil and democratic society. Although the FOMWAN has a religious base, it operates in other dimensions that help in achieving political ends. Chapters Thirteen and Fourteen are on religious movements. Adoyi Onoja traces the involvement of the Pentecostal movement in politics, arguing that the Pentecostal churches have deviated from the orthodox methods of worship, especially during periods of economic instability, by their establishment of commercial businesses and their emphasis on prosperity. The failing performance of the government drives people to religion to find support. Adoyi Onoja considers the exploitation of the political situation by the leaders of the Pentecostal movement to be excessive. Olujide Gbadegesin, in Chapter Fourteen, evaluates the roles of New Religious Movements (NRMs) in providing religious identity and in contributing to nation building in modern Nigeria. He examines the impact and influence of NRMs on the socio-political milieu that is Nigerian society, arguing that their emergence is a milestone in Nigerian religious history.

Section Five: Religion and the Justice System

The justice system is not only a political matter, but it is also connected with religion, since Nigeria provides for the freedom of religion. Akin Alao, in Chapter Fifteen, articulates the secular nature of Nigeria as guaranteed by the constitution. He discusses the judicial attitude to religious freedom. He uses the provisions in the Nigerian Constitution and various judicial case studies to support his argument on the secular nature of the country. The Shari'a and the case of Amina Lawal is the focus of Chapter Sixteen in which Teresa A. Booker argues that the Amina case would have been judged differently had it been under the indigenous judicial systems.

She points out that spirituality shapes the lives of various groups and each society that makes up Nigeria evolved a judicial system that was closely connected with politics and religion.

In Chapter Seventeen, Julius Adekunle describes the various strategies the government employs to resolve or stop religious conflicts and violence. He argues that although the government is trying to stop all acts of violence, more stringent and prompt action should be taken. He also mentions that the government needs to develop prevention strategies in order to reduce the incidences of religious and ethnic violence.

As Nigeria advances in the democratic system, the delimitation between religion and politics would take better shape. The secular clause in the constitution does not mean a complete absence of religion; it only refers to the separation of religion from politics. In politics, religion is not supposed to take the center stage, but it should help in facilitating a peaceful process for a successful democratic system. Religion, in its public role, should help in good governance when political leaders apply the good principles of their religions for the general benefit of the people they govern. The misunderstanding or misinterpretation of secularism tends to present secularism as a threat to the existence of religions. As Jan H. Boer puts it, "Secularism tends to suck the lifeblood out of spirituality and imposes too many restrictive blindfolds to be viable over the long haul."[22] While religion plays important roles in the search for peace, unity, and political stability, the acts of violence should be eliminated. We live in a global and diverse world. Therefore, every effort should be geared toward securing a peaceful environment. After a long period of military rule, Nigeria deserves a more stable and peaceful political system that promotes socio-economic growth for its steadily increasing population.

Notes

1. Basil Davidson, *West Africa before the Colonial Era: A History to 1850* (London: Longman, 1998), 112-113.
2. N. A. Fadipe, *The Sociology of the Yoruba* (Ibadan, Nigeria: Ibadan University Press, 1970), 206.
3. J. Omisade Awolalu, "Christianity in a New Nigerian Political Order," in *Christianity and Socio-Political Order in Nigeria*, ed. S. A. Adewale (Ibadan, Nigeria: The Nigerian Association for Christian Studies, 1987), 11.
4. Chinua Achebe, *Things Fall Apart* (Oxford: Heinemann Educational Publishers, 1958), 9.

5. A good source on the life and career of Ahamdu Bello is John N. Paden, *Ahmadu Bello, Sardauna of Sokoto: Values and Leadership in Nigeria* (London: Hodder and Stoughton, 1986).
6. Ibid., 364.
7. David D. Laitin, *Hegemony and Culture: Politics and Change among the Yoruba* (Chicago: University of Chicago Press, 1986), 2.
8. Ibid., 3.
9. Ibid.
10. G. A. Akinola, "Religion and the Obasanjo Administration," *The Guardian*, March 19, 2006.
11. "Seks Ban on Govt. Funding of Pilgrimage," http://www.thisdayonline.com/nview.php?id=14224
12. Toyin Falola, *Violence in Nigeria: The Crisis of Religious Politics and Secular Ideologies* (Rochester, NY: University of Rochester Press, 2001).
13 Yakubu Mohammed, "In the Name of God," *Newswatch* March 30, 1987, 4.
14. Discussion with my colleague, Dr. Mustafa Aksakal, Department of History and Anthropology, Monmouth University, February 9, 2005.
15. Tony Edike & Emma Aziken, "PDP Names 6 Presidential Aspirants for Jan 3-5 Battle," *Vanguard*, Lagos, http://allafrica.com/stories/200301020571.html, January 1, 2003
16. Jibrin Ibraim, "Religion and Political Turbulence in Nigeria," *The Journal of Modern African Studies*, Vol. 29, No. 1, 1991, 115-136.
17. Robert Ruby and Timothy Samuel Shah, "Nigeria's Presidential Election: The Christian-Muslim Divide," *Pew Forum on Religion and Public Life*, March 21, 2007, pewforum.org/docs/?DocID=182
18. Hank Eso, "Nigeria: Religion as a Tool of Politics," www.kwenu.com/publications/hankeso/religion_politics.htm
19. "Church Mourns Williams, urges end to Killings," *The Guardian*, August 7, 2006, 7.
20. Lydia Polgreen, "Religion and politics a deadly mix in Nigeria," February 24, 2006, www.iht.com/articles/2006/02/23/news/lagos.php
21. Akinola, "Religion and the Obasanjo Administration," *The Guardian*, March 19, 2006.
22. Jan H. Boer, "Christian-Muslim Relations in Nigeris," http://www.aspecten.org/customers/srw.webadres.nu/documents/Archief/JanHdeBoer_Studies_MuslimChristianRelations.doc

THE PRECOLONIAL AND COLONIAL TIMES

Chapter One

Religion and Politics in Precolonial Nigeria

Abiodun Akeem Oladiti

This chapter examines the place of religion as an instrument of maintaining peace and stability in the precolonial political history of Nigeria. Although limited information exists on the role of religion in maintaining peace, there is sufficient evidence on the interaction of religion and politics. Before the advent of colonialism, political power was a sacred trust, exercised for the common good of the society.[1] Institutions such as kings, age-grades, guilds, associations, secret societies, and open societies were religious organizations as well as political agencies that helped to maintain law and order by suppressing tension and clashes of interest among the people.[2]

Traditional religion and Islam predated colonialism, but Christianity became a force to reckon with at the end of the nineteenth century when the Europeans penetrated several parts of Nigeria. Before the introduction of Islam and Christianity, traditional religion was fully integrated into the political systems of all Nigerian societies.[3] In the Yoruba, Hausa, and Benin communities, the ruler, chief priest, and elders of the town usually decided how to improve the life of the community through consultation with the oracle. Among the Yoruba people, the *Oba* (ruler) usually sought the advice of the *babalawo* (*Ifa* priest) on how to improve the well being of his people.[4] Traditional religion became an instrument used as a check and balance in the political system. The priests often mediated in the rights and claims of various individuals and groups in the society by ensuring that political leaders did not abuse their power.[5] In the Yoruba tradition, if an alaafin used his political power arbitrarily, he could be removed. The process began with the Oyo Mesi (Council of Chiefs) in consultation with the Ogboni society. The alaafin would be presented with a white calabash with the words: "the earth rejects you, the gods reject you, and the people reject you." The implication was that the Alaafin had to commit suicide, which happened on a number of occasions.

For their part, the people ensured that security of lives and property were protected, law and order was upheld, and peaceful co-existence was maintained with neighbors.[6] Traditional religion also provided a theology that linked local beliefs to the central government and its sovereignty.[7] Since religion was partly utilized to legitimize political power, the ruler and the ancestors were responsible for the welfare of the entire population in the town.[8]

Traditional religion and Islam contributed to the political processes of the Nigerian societies. In the case of Islam, T. G. O. Gbadamosi pointed out that during the initial contact with Islam in Yorubaland and Hausaland, Muslims were few and barely organized. He further stated that Muslims worshipped privately and secretly. In the course of time, their number grew and their position became stronger. The conversion of influential people, who were close to political power, helped in the rapid spread of Islam.[9]

The earliest manifestation of Islam in political affairs was in the role played by Muslim *mallams* and the *parakoyi*. In Oyo and Hausaland, *mallams* first patronized the rulers for permission to live in the town, to pray for the people, and to preach. *Mallams* often served as advisors to the ruler or as administrators and judges. The *parakoyi* were the spokesmen of the Muslims in Yorubaland. They led the Muslim prayers, and acted as liaison officers between the Muslims and political authorities. They were also in charge of commerce, collecting taxes, and maintained fair treatment and orderliness in market places.[10]

By the end of the nineteenth century, Christianity was not only introduced to Nigeria, but it also intermixed with colonial politics as Christian missionaries collaborated with colonial authorities for mutual benefits. Many Nigerians embraced Christianity not only because it provided an alternative religion and new doctrines, but also because it offered and promoted literacy opportunities. The support of the colonial authorities made it possible for Christianity to penetrate many societies in Nigeria.

Religions in Precolonial Nigeria

Approximately 250 distinct ethnic groups exist in Nigeria with the Yoruba, the Igbo, the Hausa, and the Fulani as the largest and politically dominant. Others include the Edo, the Ibiobio, the Tiv, the Nupe, the Kanuri, the Ijaw, the Itsekiri, and the Kalabari. They all have distinct customs, traditions, and languages, but they all adopted traditional religious beliefs and practices in precolonial times.

In Hausaland, the traditional religion was organized on a clan basis. A hereditary chief priest maintained each shrine on behalf of the town. The *Kano Chronicle* shows that the traditional priests performed the various rituals and sacrifices, especially of food and animals. Through the sacrifices, the people believed that the community would have and maintain peace and stability. The Hausa religion was centered on a cult, which represented a belief system on a single deity, the god of Tsumburburai, also known as Randaya.[11]

The Hausa religious practices transcended animal sacrifices.It also entailed the veneration of shrines located in groves and the use of charms for protection. Shobana Shankar[12] described the Hausa religion as a synthesis of many religious traditions, generally known as *bori*. With Islam gaining ground, the practice of *bori* was not only discouraged, but it was also denounced. Islam's objection to *bori* led to the outbreak of the jihad of Uthman dan Fodio in 1804.

In Igboland, there was a strong belief in ancestral worship, animal sacrifices, and ritual worship in groves. Sacrifices in the Igbo religion were performed in the town purposely to ward off evil spirits, for petition, expiation, and thanksgiving. The Igbo people believed in a supernatural being who was worshipped through various deities or spirits such as *anyanwu* (the god of the sun), *Igwe*, (the god of the sky), and *ale* or *ane* (the god of the earth). Ancestors were believed to be contributing to the maintenance of solidarity in the community.[13]

The Igbo religion was a mixture of human and spiritual beings. The human category consisted of the priests, diviners, and ritual elders who conducted religious worship and sacrifice to the gods and goddesses. The divinities included ancestral spirits, and spirits of national heroes, and other deities. The revered gods and goddesses varied from one society to the other, and the shrines could be found in rivers, trees, road junctions, and on mountains and hills. They were regarded as the guardian spirits, who could be benevolent or mischievous, lovable or fearful.[14]

Although the Yoruba believe in the existence of a Supreme Being called Olodumare or Olorun, *orisa* is the general name for the large number of deities in their religion. These include *Ifa* (the oracle of palm nuts); *Esu*, often referred to as the trickster and a divinity of mischief. Esu in the Yoruba religion possesses protective and benevolent powers and should not be mistaken for the devil or Satan in other religions; others include Obatala, also known as Oduduwa; *Ogun* the god of iron and war; and *Sonpona* associated with small pox. There are also *Sango,* the god of lightening; *Oya* Sango's wife and the goddess of thunderstorms; and *Orisa Oko* the patron of hunters.

Ifa was consulted on every social and political event. It was important to do so for its unifying force. The *Ifa* was usually consulted on matters concerning the choice of a new ruler and in important political decisions such as going to war, and in marriage. The oracle was the court of the people, and its judgment was binding on the people.[24] Ifa and all other orisas were propitiated for peace, progress, stability, and success.[25]

Aside from the Supreme Being there were numerous divinities. Natural phenomena such as rivers, trees, mountains, hills, iron, thunder and lightening, were venerated in the traditional belief system but not in Islam and Christianity. There was the belief in an afterlife, which the people viewed as an extension of life itself. Many societies held the belief that the spirits of the departed had great power of intervention in the affairs of the living. The practice of each ethnic group was supervised by an organized priesthood, which could mediate between humans and the deities.[15]

A wind of change occurred with the penetration of Islam and Christianity. First, Islam was established in Hausaland in the eleventh century and had flourished by the fifteenth century. At its inception, Islam found its way into the palace and Muslims gradually wielded political influence. By the early nineteenth century, Islam had dominated the whole of northern Nigeria. The role of Islam in politics became apparent with the jihad of Usman dan Fodio in 1804. Although the jihad's initial motive was to purify Islam, politics became a major factor with the overthrow of the Habe traditional rulers of Hausaland and the establishment of a theocratic state. By the time the jihad was concluded, the Sokoto Caliphate had been established and Usman dan Fodio emerged as the religious and political leader. By the middle of the nineteenth century, Islam had spread southward to Yorubaland, but it did not have the same influence on politics as it had in northern Nigeria. The Yoruba were reputed for their traditional religion, which they did not want to give up for Islam. That was partly why a coalition of Yoruba and Borgu forces fought the jihadists during the Ilorin War between 1830 and 1835. It was only with the military assistance of Ibadan that the Oyo-Yoruba forces were able to halt the further spread of Islam at the battle of Osogbo in 1840.

The Portuguese were the first Europeans to introduce Christianity in West Africa, particularly in Nigeria. During the Age of Discovery in the fifteenth century, the Portuguese, in their quest to find a sea route to India in order to participate in the lucrative spice trade, established economic, religious, and political relations with some rulers along the West African coast. The Benin and Warri kingdoms benefited from this contact. To facilitate their economic interests, the Portuguese introduced Catholicism to the Benin and Warri kingdoms. This served as the first current of Christianity, which did not extend beyond the palace confines. The Portuguese relations with the rulers were short-lived because of a clash of economic interests. The collapse of the economic arrangements led to the breakdown in religious and political relations. The Portuguese failed to send missionaries and very soon, all vestiges of Christianity were removed from both kingdoms. Since Christianity did not penetrate the interior, the Yoruba and Hausa people did not experience the religion. Hence, Christianity did not play any role in their politics until the nineteenth century when a more effective introduction occurred. However, Samuel Johnson noted that the missionaries in Yorubaland contributed in terms of a provision of military arms and ammunitions to ensure that the Egba people defeated other neighboring towns during the civil wars. This partly explains why Oba Sodeke allowed Christianity to flourish in Abeokuta.[16]

Following explorers such as Mungo Park, Hugh Clapperton, and the Lander brothers (in the early nineteenth century) who penetrated the interior of Nigeria were Christian missionaries. Samuel Ajayi Crowther (1807-1891) a Yoruba clergy, along with European missionaries, spread Christianity into the interior through the Niger Expedition in 1845. Many Nigerian communities initially resisted Christianity because of some of its anti-African cultural practices. However, the support of the colonial authorities led to an effective evangelization, especially in the south. In Yorubaland, the missionaries were welcomed because they served as mediators and peacemakers in a civil war that engulfed the whole region. The missionaries became peacemakers because of the support shown to traditional rulers in helping them fight neighboring towns during the Yoruba civil wars. The missionaries envisaged that the civil unrest would prevent evangelical activities. Hence, they decided to intervene and organize peace accord treaties and agreements with various communities. The missionaries were most successful in this regard.[17]

Religious and Political Organizations

In several Nigerian communities, individuals, lineages, and family units had their own deities through which they communicated with the Supreme Being.[18] Sacrifices of different kinds were offered and annual festivals were held. Each divinity had its food preferences for sacrifices and worshippers ensured that their deities were well served. In times of serious trouble such as epidemics, famine, or drought, members of the community, including political leaders, came together to appease the gods.[19] Priests, rulers, and political office holders presided over religious matters and made pronouncements that were backed up by religious regulations.[20]

Various ethnic groups created political institutions, such as, the *ogboni*, the *osugbo*, the *ilari*, *age-grades*, the *guilds*, and *ekpe* primarily for maintaining peace and law and order.[21] The *ogboni* cult was a powerful religious-political institution among the Yoruba. S. O. Biobaku asserted that the *ogboni* was a secret society to which prominent chiefs and elders of the town sought initiation in order to promote social harmony, peace, and cooperation for the social, religious, and political affairs of the people. Members of the cult took an oath of secrecy.[22] Although traditional religion did not have a written sacred book like Islam and Christianity, there was an unwritten code of conduct, which had been transmitted from one generation to another. S. A. Adewale described actions of disobedience to the rules and regulations of the *ogboni* as a breach of contract to the society, resulting in serious sanctions to the offender.[23] Similar to the *ogboni* in the Oyo-Yoruba group was the *osugbo* among the Ijebu. The *osugbo* and *ogboni* performed the same religious, political, and social functions.

The *ilari* was an important religious institution among the Oyo-Yoruba people. According to O. Adewoye, the *ilari* performed the religious function of administering the oath to the plaintiff at the chief court in the palace.[24] The *ilari* served as the king's bodyguard, intelligence officer, land arbitrator, and ambassador to vassal states. Each *ilari* had a special name, which expressed either the divine power of the king, his intention, or his disposition on a particular issue. It was the responsibility of the *ilari* to carry the King's staff of office when going on important interstate functions or when representing the king at coronation ceremonies in other parts of Yorubaland.[25]

The guild system was used as a religious means geared toward strict obedience to law and order by way of punishment and the reporting of offences to the appropriate authority. Examples of guilds included hunters, warriors, women political associations, occupational, and mutual aid associations. Market women also formed guilds with their leader being addressed as *iyaloja* ("head of the market women").[26] These guilds usually regulated matters relating to members' professional interests, mutual help, the taking of disciplinary measures against members who violated professional and fraternal obligations, as well as ensured the fulfillment of common religious obligations, which included the observance of funeral rites for their members.

Age-grades existed as religious, social, and political institutions. They acted as watchdogs of public ethics and etiquette, and the guardian of public morality. They participated in various public works assigned to them by the political authorities. Their leaders arranged the tasks such as renovating the king's palace and constructing public roads and bridges. During public occasions such as the installation of a new king, people were arranged according to their age-grades. Age-grades served as vehicles through which people were acculturated and socialized. Members of each age-grade had the right to discuss social and political matters, and they could present matters of concern to the political authorities. There was a provision for exchange and coordination of views by sectional groups of the same age in large towns. On the whole, age grades were important in the society for the performance of their duties as citizens of the community in which they resided.

P. A. Talbolt described the *Ekpe* among the Ibibio to have been anchored on ancestral worship.[27] He opined that the religious aspect was of more consequence even in those clubs where political activities now predominate. The Idiong were a cult of sorcerers and diviners. Members of this society were believed to have the power to see the unseen, to know the unknown, and to be able to communicate effectively with the spirits and the ancestors. Hence, anyone who had a misfortune sought a remedy from the ancestors. Some diviners combined divination with cure.[28] Hausa communities were organized on a clan basis and each clan recognized particular divinities or shrines. Hereditary chief priests interceded between the divinity and the worshippers and maintained the shrines.

Nature of Political System

Political systems in pre –colonial Nigeria varied from one ethnic group to another. Before the introduction of colonialism, kingdoms such as Benin, Oyo, Kanem-Bornu, Hausa states, Nupe, and Jukun developed important centralized political structures.[29] Politics was the affair of the rulers and his appointed officials. The society was run through an unwritten constitution, but guided by religious sanctions. This shows that in the precolonial times, religion and politics were inseparable.

Two major forms of political organization existed in the precolonial period: the monarchical system and gerontocracy. The monarchial system, which operated among the Yoruba, Hausa, and Benin, was a centralized form of government. J. A. Atanda, a Yoruba historian, pointed out that a king, selected from the royal family and whose right to rule was divinely ordained, headed the monarchical system.[30] The king was assisted by an institutionalized council of chiefs such as the *ijoye, igbimo* or *ilu* among the Yoruba, the *sarakuma* among the Hausa, and the *uzama* in Benin. In theory, the ruler held absolute powers, but in practice, there were certain checks and balances.

Gerontocracy, adopted by the Igbo, Niger Delta, and Benue people, was a non-centralized political system. Anthropologists refer to this system as stateless or acepahalous because the elders and lineage heads performed religious and political functions since there was no institutionalized political authority.[31] W. Oyemakinde remarked that gerontocracy was a village democracy where the general will of the people was taken into consideration.[32] Instead of royal courts and palaces, market centers were used for religious and political activities such as debate, and decisions on vital issues of public interest were taken there as well.

Political power in both systems described above was not absolute because there was divine intervention and people participation. E. E. Osaghae contended that political power was divine and almost mystical. It epitomized the unity of the people and was held in trust for the people by the ruler and elders of the community. The ruler could not enforce his personal will on the people indiscriminately. Osaghae further mentioned that there were two sources of political power. First, the concept of "divine right of kings," made the ruler a representative of the ancestors as well as the spiritual symbol for the people. Second, the people were a source of political power since they selected the ruler. This indicated that religion and people constituted primary sources of political empowerment for the ruler.[33]

Interconnected with religion and politics was the formation of associations geared towards promoting and protecting the common interests of the people. Fadipe and Fajana agreed that the tradition of having associations was common to all precolonial Nigerian societies.[34] Associations were used as social-religious agencies for enforcing political policies and for maintaining law and order; they were sources of political empowerment.[35]

Religion in Traditional Political System

Religion played an important role in the judicial systems of early Nigerian societies. According to J. R. W. Haffenden, rulers possessed supernatural attributes and they were invested with magico-religious powers in order to perform their political and judicial functions effectively.[36] Powerful traditional fetishes were used for detecting and punishing criminals. Religion was employed as an instrument of providing and legitimizing security for the people. Individuals and families were expected to be loyal not only to the king, but also to religious regulations and societal norms. A breach of religious or societal laws was punishable with sanctions, punishment by ordeal, banishment, or imprisonment.[37] Actions of disobedience or deviant behavior in the community were considered anti-sacred and not secular; whatever religion disapproved, the society also condemned.

Religious and political laws were interwoven. For the purpose of peace, everyone in the society was required to obey the law and to respect constituted authorities. Violators of religious or societal laws received heavy penalties such as an affliction with a terrible disease, financial ruin (on an individual or collective basis through poor harvests), or barrenness for women, or even death. There is a strong belief among the people that the ancestors and gods often rewarded good behavior or compliance with the law with longevity, peace, prosperity, and freedom from sickness. Because rulers and their subjects wanted peace and prosperity, emphasis was placed on satisfying the ancestors and gods through regular and annual sacrifices. In this respect, religion not only regulated the people's behavior, it also served as the bedrock of peaceful co-existence. In *The Rationale of Punishment*, H. Oppenheimer stated that:

> Offences are viewed as affronts to the deities or the ancestral spirits, who will bring disaster to the entire community or tribe if violations are not appropriately dealt with? Death and expulsion from the group are common mode of punishment for the serious crimes as sorcery, witchcraft, sacrilege and other magico-religious offences. Responsibility is often viewed as communicable for action of its Members; criminal guilt may contaminate the offenders associates, his relatives and even his possession.[38]

The above confirms J. H. Driberg's argument that there was collective punishment for crime and offences in precolonial Nigeria.[39] Driberg asserts that only appropriate rituals could cleanse the community of the wrath or penalty since the ancestors or gods dictated the punishments for offences. For example, among the Yoruba people, the penalty for theft was referred to the gods for punishment. Such punishments included illness, paralysis, and partial blindness. In many cases the gods revealed the thieves publicly or forced them to confess. The culprits could return the stolen property to avoid further punishment and a propitiatory sacrifice would be offered to cleanse the thief and the society. Witches and wizards were usually stoned to death.

The Muslim community in Yoruba towns advocated for the appointment of a Muslim *Qadi* (judge) in the local courts to promote justice and equity in the political system. The *ulama* (Islamic scholars) argued that it was their right and responsibility to practice their religion, but the traditional leaders rejected the approval of a Muslim judge in the local courts. The reason was that the Yoruba people wished to preserve their traditional laws and customs and they were against any form of religious intrusion. This point shows why disagreement occurred between the Muslim groups and the traditional political authority. Also, in the Yoruba society, the Muslims were often prevented from erecting a central mosque. This affected the relationship that existed between the Muslim groups and the traditional religious worshippers in a negative way.

The Role of Emirs and Priests

Religious leaders occupied conspicuous places of influence in the administration and organization of precolonial Nigerian societies. In northern Nigeria, the Muslim emirs used the Shari'a (Islamic Law) and promoted the spread of Islam. Indeed, the whole of the Sokoto Caliphate adopted a theocratic form of administration. Islam became the official religion of the rulers and their subjects. The position of the emirs was very crucial to the existence and development of Islamic political ideology because they enforced the rules and regulations of Islam with their political power. Alongside the emirs, learned cleric (Imam) were appointed to lead the community in prayers as well as teach and guide the people. Emirs also provided security and protection to the community against the opposition and persecution from the traditionalists. The collaborative efforts of the emirs, imams, and Muslim missionaries accounted for the rapid spread of Islam. Before and during the colonial period, Islam and politics went hand in hand and the concept of separation of religion from politics did not exist.

In Yorubaland, the *ifa* and *babalawo* priests were also very influential in the political system of their communities. Bolaji Idowu contended that the Yoruba believed that the priests served as intermediaries between divinities and their adherents.[40] Priests related very closely to the rulers because they provided spiritual advice to, and performed rituals for, rulers. Like in the Hausa states where Islam and politics intertwined, in Yorubaland, traditional religion was deeply entrenched in politics. For the purposes of maintaining peace and stability, rulers and priests participated in religious rituals, festivals, and officiated in sacrifices in the major shrines of their communities.

Priests in traditional religion performed the swearing in ceremony for rulers and were in charge of oath taking as part of their judicial functions. According to Hugo Huber, the handling of oath taking was treated with discretion and moderation. The priests also offered propitiatory sacrifices to prevent or ward-off calamity. All Nigerian communities placed emphasis on order, authority, justice, and peace. They realized the importance of political stability and they used religion and priests as means of achieving their objectives.

Divine Rights and Political Authority

Political leaders in precolonial Nigerian societies were regarded as the representatives of the ancestors and divinities on earth. The leadership roles were considered sacred and their authority to rule was preordained and could not be questioned. For example, among the Yoruba the alaafin was referred to as *Iku Baba yeye, Alase ikeji orisa* ("Frightful as death, all-powerful, and second in command to the gods"). The Jukun revered the *akuka* (king of the Jukun Empire) and the *mai* (king of the Kanem Borno Empire*)*. Because of the sacredness of the political position the rulers occupied, they lived secluded lives in their palaces, and their subjects were not allowed to see them in public or communicate directly with them.

Rulers participated in offering sacrifices to the gods in order to bless their subjects with good harvest and to prevent drought and famine. Especially in Yorubaland, many rulers participated in the annual yam festival to commemorate the new yam season. It was a commonplace belief that the gods and ancestors endowed rulers with supernatural or mystic powers. They were regarded as owners and distributors of land, and they owned all the resources of the land. Rulers became wealthy because they controlled the economy of their societies. It was a common belief that rulers did not usually sleep because they were communing with the gods and carrying out day-to-day political activities for their societies.[97] In Yoruba belief, rulers do not die like ordinary people, but are believed to join their ancestors. With a special reference to the Alaafin of Oyo, Julius Adekunle pointed out that:

> The death of an Alaafin was often marked with elaborate funeral rites and sacrifices. In Yoruba tradition, it takes some days before the death of a ruler is announced to the public. As a semi-god, the Yoruba people would not say that the Alaafin died. Instead, they claim that he transposed to a new world. Thus, the announcement would be made to the public with the words *oba wa'ja* ("The King has transposed to the ceiling").[41]

As rulers were considered sacred on earth, they were also regarded as sacred in death. Sacrifices and elaborate rituals often accompanied their burial ceremonies.

In the Hausa society, emirs were seen *as* the *warastul- ambiya*, representatives of the prophet of Allah on earth. Islam provided the basic ideology of governance and selection of political leaders. The Shura committee began the process of selection and interviewed nominated candidates for both religious and secular positions. Often the person most learned in Islamic education, having good character, would be appointed as the ruler.[42]

A. E. Alagoa argued that although in the Igboland and Ibibio communities the people did not have recognized heads of government such as kings, they had political institutions that checkmated the excesses of people in the society. The earliest known local authority was the *Eze Nri* (related to the famous *igbo-ukwu* bronze).[43] The influence of the *Eze-Nri* was based solely on control of ritual activity over the title of *Ozo.* The Aro was an oracle that served to solve political problems, which proved intractable for the internal institutions of the town. Institutions such as the *Ekpe* secret society among the Ibibio were used for social control of deviance in the town.

Since the ruler derived his political authority and power from religion, he was bound to promote social justice, harmony, and political stability. The powers and functions attributed to the state no doubt varied from one society to another because of their different sizes and cultural complexities. Some societies had a more elaborate administrative structure, ritual traditions, and social organization than others. Some rulers essentially acted as priests and presided over the community shrine, others derived their power largely from their military prowess, and yet others were ritual rulers whose functions were primarily religious. All categories, however, relied heavily on the need for the support of the gods in order to succeed. For this reason, at the coronation ceremony, a new king was given the *opa ase* ("staff of authority"), and took an oath to promote peace and stability. Thereafter, he was expected to constantly commune with the gods and the spirits of his ancestors, visit the shrines on regular basis, and offer sacrifices at appropriate times. For example, the Ooni of Ile-Ife sacrificed to the gods and ancestors almost every day of the year.

Religion, Politics, and National Development

Religion, politics, and national development were interwoven in precolonial times. The state was seen as the moral agent that performed the important functions of maintaining religious laws and sanctions. Traditional religion and Islam emphasized the cohesiveness of the society as the basis of a strong political organization. It seems that religion rather than politics constituted the fulcrum on which the fabric of the society rested. Religion was interconnected with politics, culture, military, and the social life of the people. Religious belief and practices were injected into almost every activity. The idea of nation building among the various ethnic groups in Nigeria was viewed from a religious perspective in that the maintenance of peace, unity, and stability was the collective responsibility of the people.

Religion was also tied to the security of lives and property. Though consultation with the gods and through political institutions, rulers maintained public order and discipline and pursued policies of national interest for national development. Examples of such religious and political institutions include the *oro* among the Ekiti, *ogboni* among the Egba, *osugbo* in Ijebu-ode, and *Ekpe* in Ibibioland.

Educationally, traditional religion and Islam had different approaches and objectives. They both provided literacy services that helped to promote the growth and welfare of the society. In the north, Islam introduced Arabic literacy, which made it possible to have some recorded history of the early Hausa states. Learned Islamic scholars were appointed as clerks, administrators, and advisors to the king. Qadis (Islamic judges) were appointed to judge various kinds of cases. Islam therefore contributed significantly to the national development of the Hausa states. The jihad of Usman dan Fodio in 1804 further accelerated the spread of Islam, its literacy, and its civilization to many parts of Nigeria. The political leaders of the Islamic states used the religion as a tool of national development.

Economically, the occupation of the people was closely tied to religion. For success in commerce and in a new business, and for good harvest in agriculture, religious rituals were performed and sacrifices were offered to the gods and ancestors. Economic growth through religion made national development possible. Political leaders and wealthy people relied on religion not only for their own interests, but also for national development.

Conclusion

Religion has played a significant role in the political organization of precolonial Nigeria. Religion guided the nature of leadership and the political tradition of the people. Religion had been a factor in politics and national development, and religious leaders used religion to maintain law and order as well as achieve common good for the people. Political leaders were divinely ordained and their subjects could not challenge their authority.

Islam and traditional religion co-existed and influenced one another before the advent of colonialism. The interaction of religions in precolonial Nigeria was mutual and reciprocal. The main religions believed in one

Supreme Being and they preached peace and stability. Islam and Christianity have written scriptures, but traditional religion does not. Also, the religions had days of festivals and special ceremonies. All of these gave meaning and cohesiveness to the community and strength to the political system.

From all indications, religion and politics were totally inseparable in precolonial times. Religion was the basis of authority and power for the political leaders, and religion was used to maintain law and order. Religious sanctions helped to check bad behavior and to promote good and law-abiding citizens. Religion further contributed to the national development of the precolonial states.

Notes

1. J. A. Atanda, "Collision and Coalition in the Politics and Society of Western Nigeria in the Nineteenth Century," in *Evolution of Political Culture in Nigeria, ed.* J. F. A. Ajayi and B. Ikara (Ibadan, Nigeria: University Press Ltd, 1985), 85.
2. A. A. Oladiti, "The Prison System in Southwestern Nigeria: The Example of Agodi Prison in Ibadan 1800-1960," Unpublished M. A. Dissertation, Department of History, University of Ibadan, 2003, 26-27.
3. R. Hallgreen, *The Good Things of Life: A Study of Traditional Religious Culture of the Yoruba People (*Loberod: Hallgren and Bokforlaget, 1988), 3.
4. E. A. Adegboye, "Traditional Religion in West Africa," in *Traditional Religion in West Africa*, ed. E. A. Adegboye (Ibadan, Nigeria: Ibadan University Press, 1983), 4-5.
5. E. E. Osaghea, "Managing Ethnic Conflicts under Democratic Transition in Africa: The Promise, the Failure and the Future," in D*emocratic Transition in Africa,* eds. Canon B, Gboyega A, and Osaghae E. E. (Ibadan, Nigeria: Credit Documents in Social Sciences and Humanities, Series No. 1, 1992), 45.
6. Osaghae, 31.
7. Adegboye, 22.
8. Ibid., 23.
9. T. G. O. Gbadamosi, "The Immate Question among the Yoruba Muslims," *Journal of Historical Society of Nigeria*, Vol. 6, No 2, 1972, 229-232.
10. Ibid.
11. F. Fuglestad, "Hausa History before the Jihad," *Journal of African History*, 19, No 3, 1978, 335.
12. S. Shankar, "Religion, State, and Society in Hausaland: History and the Politics of Incorporation in the Kano Chronicle," in *Preconontal Nigeria Essays*

in Honor of Toyin Falola, ed., Akin Ogundiran (Trenton, NJ: Africa World Press, 2005), 281-283.

13. O. Otite and W. Ogionwo, *An Introduction to Sociological Studies*, (Ibadan: Heineman Educational Books 2006), 102.
14. C. O. Adepegba. "The Essence of Images in the Religous Sculptures of the Yoruba of Nigeria," *Nigerian Magazine*, 1983, 13-22.
15. N. A. Fadipe, *Sociology of the Yorubas* Ibadan, Nigeria: Ibadan University Press: 1970, 261.
16. S. Johnson, *The History of the Yorubas: From the Earliest Times to the Beginning of the British Protectorate* (Lagos, Nigeria: CSS Bookshops, 1921, reprinted 1997), 22.
17. Ibid., 40.
18. E. B. Idowu, *Olodumare: God in Yoruba Belief* (New York: Frederick Praeger, 1963), 4.
19. W. R. Bascom, *Ifa Divination Communication between Gods and Men in West Africa* (Bloomington: Indiana University Press, 1969), 12.
20. J .F. A. Ajayi, "Promoting Religious Tolerance and Cooperation in West African Region: The Example of Religious Pluralism and Tolerance among the Yoruba," *http.geocitiescom/agboleyorubaschool/sacred.*
21. S. O. Biobaku, *The Egba and their Neigbours* (Oxford: Oxford University Press, 1957), 50; E. A. Ayandele, *The Ijebu of Yorubaland 1850-1950: Politics, Economy and Society* (Ibadan, Nigeria: Heinemann Educational Books, 1992), 268; Adewoye, *The Legal Profession in Nigeria 1865-1962* (London: Longman: 1977), 9; A. Fajana, "Age Group in Traditional Yoruba Society," *Nigeria Magazine,* No. 98. 1968. 16-18.
22. Biobaku, 5.
23. S. A. Adewale, "Crime and African Traditional Religion," O*rita* 25, No 1-2, 1994, 54.
24. Adewoye, 9.
25. R. Olaniyan, "Elements of Yoruba Traditional Diplomacy: An Assessment," in *Yoruba Oral Tradition*, ed., Wande Abimbola (Ile Ife: Ife University Press, 1975), 305-306.
26. The women were active in the economic, political, and religious affairs of their communities. The *Iyaloja* represented the leader of the market women, the *Iyalaje* was the political head of the women, and the *Iyalode* served as the military head of the women.
27. P. A. Talbot, *The Peoples of Southern Nigeria: A Sketch of their History, Ethnology and Language,* Vol. 3 (London: Frank Cass, 1926), 754.
28. Ekong E. Ekong, "The Sociology of the Ibibio," A seminar paper presented in the Department of Sociology, University of Ife, Ile-Ife, 1974.

29. J. F. A. Ajayi and B. Ikara, "Introduction: Nigeria's Evolutionary Political Culture: Issues and Processes," in *Evolution of Political Culture in Nigeria*, ed., J. F. A. Ajayi and B. Ikara (Ibadan, Nigeria: Ibadan University Press, 1985), 2-3.
30. Atanda, 87.
31. Ibid.
32. W. Oyemakinde, "The Derivation of Power and Authority in Nigeria," *African Notes.* Vol. viii, No. 2, 1979, 32.
33. Osaghae, 34.
34. Fadipe, 243; Fajana, 16-18.
35. Julius O. Adekunle, "Yoruba Associations: Sources of Empowerment," in *The Yoruba in Transition: History, Values, And Modernity*, ed., Toyin Falola (Durham, NC: Carolina Academic Press, 2006), 377-390.
36. J. R. W. Haffender, *The Red Men in Nigeria* (London: Frank Cass, 1967), 223-225.
37. Adewale, 54.
38. H. Oppenheimer, *The Rationale of Punishment* (London: University Press, 1913). 121.
39. J. H. Driberg, "The African Conception of Law," *Journal of African Society*, 34, Supplement, 1934, 238.
40. Idowu, 56.
41. Julius O. Adekunle, "Landmarks and Cultural Identity in Yoruba History," *The International Journal of the Humanities*, Vol.5, No. 4, 2007, 185-192.
42. Oral interview with Imam Taofeek Yekeen, at his residence in Ibadan on November 13, 2007.
43. A. E. Alagoa, "The Indigenous Political Systems of the Igbo," *Tarikh* Vol. 4, No. 2. 1973,13-21.

Chapter Two

Religion and Politics in Colonial Nigeria: The Life and Career of Sir Walter Miller, 1782-1952

Funso Afolayan

Walter Miller and four other missionaries arrived in Lagos from London in December 1899. They came in the service of the Church Missionary Society (CMS) and their target was the ancient city of Kano in Northern Nigeria. Their goal was to spread Christianity to the Hausa people. Young and idealistic, each of them had pledged a lifetime of commitment to mission work. However, this daring missionary adventure lasted only a very short time. In less than a year: two members of the party died and were buried in Kano; one retraced his steps back to Lagos, where he remained continued his mission work; a fourth returned to London due to illness; while the fifth, Miller, became deathly ill and taken home to England to recuperate. Of the original five, only Walter Miller returned to Hausaland where he served with distinction and with many accomplishments, from 1901 to 1935. Using the life history and career of Sir Walter Miller as a case study, this chapter examines the nature, main features, and the major consequences of the interactions between religion and politics in colonial Northern Nigeria. In Miller's life and career the cause of religion and politics intersected in many ways and with far-reaching ramifications for the cause, mission, and colonialism in Northern Nigeria.

From his headquarter at Lokoja, Captain Frederick Lugard officially proclaimed the formal establishment of the British protectorate over Northern Nigeria on January 1, 1900. This proclamation marked the culmination of decades of British imperial infiltration, which began with the conquest of Lagos in 1861. After approximately three decades, events in Europe, more than developments in Africa, once again impelled Britain to join other European nations to embark on imperial expansion in Africa. This was the scramble for and partition of Africa, a key episode in Euro-African relations in the late nineteenth century. The scramble among the European nations for colonies in Africa was a spill over of the social, economic, and political competitions that dominated European power politics for much of the nineteenth century. The defeat of the Ilorin and Bida emirates by the forces of the Royal Niger Company (RNC) in 1897 sent shock waves throughout the remaining emirates of the Sokoto Caliphate. The arrival of the British was viewed with considerable apprehension by the Caliphate authorities who saw this not just as a political conquest, but as a threat to, and assault on, their Islamic religion. Established in the wake of the most successful and the most far-reaching jihads in precolonial West Africa, the Sokoto Caliphate was not about to submit to this alien and infidel rule without a fight. For the inheritors of the green flag of Usman dan Fodio, this would be a fight to the death. Everything was at stake: their political paramountcy in Northern Nigeria; their religious autonomy and independence; and the very survival of their culture and civilization.

With the establishment of Northern Nigeria into a British protectorate in 1900, the British policy of maintaining cordial and peaceful relations with the Caliphate authorities changed to one of imperial rule and control. Thereafter, between 1900 and 1902, using a series of pretexts and excuses, Lugard began the progressive conquest and subjugation of one emirate state after another: Bida, Kotangora, Yola, Bauchi, and Gombe. Katsina surrendered to save its city from British bombardment; with the arrest and exile by the British of its recalcitrant Emir, Zaria soon followed suit, leaving only Kano and Sokoto, the two most powerful of the Caliphate city-states, still at odds with the invaders. During a lull in the fighting, Lugard had written to the Caliph of Sokoto asking for the Caliphate's peaceful surrender to British protection and rule. The Caliph replied with a rebuff, informing Lugard that the only relation possible between Sokoto, an Islamic state, and Britain, is the one prescribed in the Holy Qur'an between the land of believers (*Dâr al-Islâm*) and the land of infidels (*Dâr al-harb*): war. Lugard therefore quickened his preparation for war.

Kano fell to the British in 1902. A year later, Sokoto also came under the hammer. In a bitterly fought battle outside the Sokoto city wall on March 15, 1903, superior weaponry on the part of the British invaders prevailed over the brave resistance put up by the Sokoto army led personally by Caliph Atahiru I. The death of Atahiru two months later at the second battle of Burmi, and the installation of a new Caliph, dramatically brought formal resistance from the emirates to an end. Pockets of resentment and resistance as in Hadeija and in Satiru in 1906 would continue, but for all practical purposes the era of Caliphate paramountcy had been replaced by the onset of Pax Britannica.[1]

For the Christian missionary societies, the British conquest of Northern Nigeria was a welcome development. Many of the missionaries had advocated for that conquest. Some had provided intelligent information to the colonizing army to facilitate the process of subjugation, while a few had worked assiduously to aid the process. European missionaries viewed colonial conquest as a divinely ordered event that would open up Africans countries to peaceful and effective Christianization. They saw themselves as working in partnership with the conquerors to bring the light of civilization to this morally dark and culturally benighted region of the globe. The "Cross," working hand in hand with the "Sword," would be a mighty force pushing back, if not totally destroying, the walls of heathen darkness and Islamic domination. African rulers who before the conquest had been opposed to the missionary presence, and in some cases persecuted or even expelled or killed the mission agents and converts would no longer be able to do so with impunity under the new dispensation of Pax Britannica. Assured of certain protection by the military and the enhanced social prestige of the new British conquerors, missionaries and their local converts could now go about their proselytizing with freedom and open access. Defeated and cowed native rulers would be wise to welcome and befriend the missionaries or risk unpalatable consequences from British officials.

Against this background of positive expectations, it is therefore not surprising that missionaries were solely disappointed to learn that the successful conquest of Northern Nigeria by the British would not mark the onset of an era of unrestricted access and an open door policy for Christian missions and their agents. These conflicts of expectations and reality created considerable tension, acrimonies, and often crisis between the missionaries and colonial officials, between the indigenous (or native) authorities and the missionaries, as well as between the colonial officials and the indigenous authorities during much of the early colonial period. No other individual appears to have epitomized these paradoxes of clashing expectations and mutual conflicts than Walter Richard Samuel Miller

(1872-1952), who served as a CMS missionary to Northern Nigeria between 1900 and 1935.[2]

Birth, Early Education, and the Call to Mission[3]

Walter Miller was born in Honiton, Devonshire, England in 1872. His father was a man of courage and strong convictions, a poet, and an elected Fellow of the Royal Society of Literature. His poetry, "St. Kilda," was presented to King Edward VII and he forfeited his chance of being ordained a priest of the Church of England, because of his unconventional association with the "heretical" sect known as Plymouth Brethren. Walter's family moved to Clifton, Bristol, where he came under the evangelical ministry of Edwin Arrowsmith, committing his life to Christ in a "conversion" experience that would have profound impact on the course of his life. At seventeen, Walter enrolled at St. Bartholomew's Hospital Medical School.[4] His six years at Barts were memorable not just for the academic rigor and challenges he went through, but by the making of many friends and connections.

His participation as a student camper, counselor, and mentor at the Keswick Convention, the Children Special Service Mission at Ilfracombe, the Student Volunteer Missionary Union of the Student Christian Movement, and at the Universities camps for Public School boys were clearly formative in setting him on a life and career path of charity and mission. At one of the Keswick meetings, he listened to a stirring and passionate message, from Mrs. Bird Bishop, who was not a missionary herself, but the first English woman to have traveled extensively through Tibet. Moved by the speech, Walter pledged to dedicate his life to God as a medical missionary to help the poor and the sick of the many lands beyond the pale of Western civilization.

After graduating from medical school, Walter served briefly as a Traveling Secretary for the Student Volunteer Missionary Union. This position gave him the opportunity to deepen his connections not only with the Church of England, but also with leading individuals and groups in the Church's Missionary Society (CMS), which later became his mission sponsor and employer. In this assignment, which took him on regular speaking tours to many Universities and Colleges all over England, Walter was:

> surprised to find how many men of the best type - athletes, scholars, and men of great ability who when brought face to face with the need of the world, medical, social,

> educational and above all spiritual, were willing to listen to the voice of God in their plans for the future, and make a complete surrender of life and prospects to the claims of Christ and His Kingdom.[5]

In subsequent years, many of these men forsook everything for the cause of Christ's kingdom, distinguishing themselves as missionaries in many parts of the world. A few would pay the ultimate price as matyrs for their faith. Less than a year later, Walter found himself among this group, as he too would abandon country, home, family, kiths and kins, forschewing worldly fame and pleasure, as he embarked on a life of missionary adventure to Africa. This leap of faith into the much-dreaded "dark" continent, apart from occasional breaks or leaves, consumed the remaining years of his life.

Pioneers in Sudanese Africa

In December 1899, the party of five missionary pioneers sailed from Liverpool en route to Lagos. At every port along the West African coast, most notably Freetown, Cape Coast, Accra, and Lagos, they went ashore both to begin to experience as much of real African life as possible, as well as to seize every opportunity to test practice their knowledge of Hausa, especially among Hausa traders and travelers, who were surprisingly quite common in all these ports, emphasizing the extent of the Hausa commercial diaspora and the cosmopolitan nature of their language and culture. At Lagos, the party spent a few days to rest as well as gather supplies for what was then a journey into the unknown and to a land that was decidedly and understandably turning hostile to all European activities in the region. In the last few years, British forces had attacked and reduced to submission virtually the whole of Yorubaland. Two years before the arrival of Miller and his party, the forces of the Royal Niger Company had taken on the powerful emirate states of Ilorin and Bida and soundly defeated their armies, eliminating them as autonomous states in the region.[6] These defeats, most especially of the more powerful state of Bida sent shock waves of terror and fear through the spines of the remaining rulers of the emirates of the Sokoto Caliphate. To the once proud and powerful Fulani rulers of these Sudanese Islamic states, the infidels from across the ocean are nothing but harbingers of doom and destruction. Resisting their infiltration through whatever means necessary, became both a moral and a political obligation.

The missionaries received enthusiastic welcomes in all the major towns where British rule and CMS presence had already been established. This pleasant phase of the journey ended at Jebba. Located on the Niger River, Jebba had recently become the headquarters of Captain Frederick Lugard, the commander and administrator, who would soon become responsible for the eventual conquest, pacification, and governance of Northern Nigeria. At Jebba, they received a most kind welcome and were amply supplied for the three weeks they stayed there and for their subsequent journey northward. At Zaria, the Emir was quite cordial in his reception of the missionaries, but he made it clear to them that because of the tenuous nature of his position, he could not afford to incur the displeasure of either the Emir of Kano or his overlord, the Sultan of Sokoto, by harboring white men in his emirate without their authorization. After staying in Zaria for two days, the party left for Kano.

Rebuff and Rejection in Zaria and Kano

At Kano, the missionaries, who seem to have been prepared for anything, were shocked by the intensity of the hostility expressed and displaced towards them by the Emir Aliyu. The emir refused to grant them an audience in the city. Instead he ordered them to be kept in a dilapidated grass hut several miles from the main city and in a sweltering 104-degree temperature. When eventually he received them at Paniso, the missionaries were roughly handled and shabbily treated. They were ordered to take off their shoes and stockings, and were told not to look directly at his royal highness, but to hold their heads and faces to the ground. Bishop Tugwell's attempt to protest their shameful treatment was hushed up by the emir's officials. The emir turned down everyone of their request. As Miller reported it: "Start a school? No. We have our own and our children are taught the Holy Kur'an." Medical work? No. Our medicine is in the Holy Kur'an and the name of Allah!" "We don't want you; you can go. I give you three days to prepare; -- a hundred donkeys to carry your loads back to Zaria, and we never wish to see you again."[7]

The decidedly hostile reception meted out to the missionaries in Kano though shocking to the missionaries, should not be surprising. The emir had reasons to be worried and suspicious of all European movements in the region. The missionaries could not have come at a worst time. The previously peaceful and cordial relations between Africans and European interlopers had taken a turn in the direction of conflict and conquest. To the north of his emirate, the French were conquering states and kingdoms. The French had seized Zinder, an Islamic state subordinate to Kano, following the murder of two French men. In fact while the missionaries were pleading for an audience with the Emir, the later was meeting with a deputation from Cinder, which had come to brief the emir about events in the northern parts of the emirate. To the south, unbeknown to the missionaries but known to the emir through his intelligence networks, a detachment of the West African Frontier Force (WAFF) commanded by Colonel Lowry Cole, commissioned to begin the conquest of the remaining emirates of the Sokoto Caliphate, was encamped in Girku, in the Zaria emirate. For Aliyu, the presence of these white infidels in his kingdom could portend nothing but trouble and he was determined to have nothing to do with them. Aliyu was almost certain that the four uninvited white visitors were probably an advanced party of the invading army sent ahead to spy. At a hurriedly convened meeting with his principal chiefs and advisers, the majority voted to have the missionaries executed. Aliyu was inclined to support this decision, but for the timely intervention of his Waziri (Prime Minister), who vehemently insisted that no harm be done to these strangers.

The Waziri's position was most probably influenced by the realization that the missionaries were not alone. They were part of a larger onslaught of European intrusions that were making quick work of powerful states in the region. Both the Waziri and the Emir were aware of how the killing of two French men in Zinder had provided the French with the excuse to militarily subjugate the town and bring it under French rule. The Zarian authority would be living in delusion to believe that they could murder these four British visitors with impunity and without incurring both the displeasure and certain punitive attack from the British army, which was already wrecking havoc in the Caliphate's frontier emirates to the south. Every answer the emir gave to the requests of the missionaries shows his understanding of the inextricable link between religion and politics, and between religion and all other spheres of life, whether education or medical works. For this ruler of an Islamic state, there was no separation between the secular and the sacred, between religion and politics. To Aliyu and his brother emirs, the missionaries were not and could not be neutral agents; they were part of the same package being thrust on them by the Europeans sowing everywhere death and defeat and the loss of political and religious autonomy. Hard as Miller and others would try to present themselves and their missions as neutral and harmless agents of civilization, their efforts would prove generally futile in the face of an indigenous perception which refused to recognize any separation between religion and politics, and the attitude of British political officers who continued to regard the fate and mission of the missionaries as intricately entwined with the goals and fate of the colonial enterprise and civilizing mission. Throughout the colonial period, most especially in northern Nigeria, religion and politics would remain locked together in mutual combat, cooperation, and coexistence. At the vortex of this mutual engagement, sometimes peaceful and other times adversarial, no figure would appear to have loomed larger than Sir Walter Miller.

Thus rebuffed, the missionaries left Kano and returned to Zaria. As Miller would write later, throughout his over fifty years sojourn in Nigeria, he was never closer to being killed than during the five days spent in Kano under the fury and hostility shown them by the Emir Aliyu. More importantly their expulsion from Kano, "the object of our hopes, prayers and plans," was a huge disappointment. Rumors spread rapidly that the missionaries had, in fact, been killed at the order of the emir. Thus by the time they returned from their conference with the emir, many of their porters had deserted, in fear for their own lives as well. Heart broken, the missionaries trudged their way back to Zaria, with their "hopes....dashed, answers to prayers deferred, and plans left in abeyance for the finger of God to guide."[8] Back in Zaria, the Emir Kwasau, who previously had welcomed the missionaries, was now no longer receptive, most especially after learning of how the Emir of Kano had received and summarily turned them back. He informed them that like his brother Emir in Kano, he too could not harbor them anywhere in his domain, without the express permission of his overlord, the Sultan of Sokoto. In the meantime, two members of the party, Richardson and Ryder, had fallen sick en route to Kano. Their untoward experience in Kano did not help to improve their health. In their present conditions, additional exertion through further travels would exacerbate their deteriorating conditions and sent them over the edge. This meant that further travel south to Jebba to come under British military protection was precluded for both sick men. Unable to dissuade the emir to alter his position and denial of residency permits to his Christian visitors, the missionaries, after considering and rejecting various alternatives, resolved to make the dangerous journey to Sokoto to meet the Sultan and ask him directly for permission to settle somewhere in any of the Hausa emirates. Miller and Tugwell went on the journey, while Burgin was left in Zaria to take care of the two invalids.

Just as the party was preparing to set out for Sokoto, a message came from Colonel Lowry Cole. Lugard, who had been monitoring the movement of the missionaries and had received reports through his own informants of their treatment in Kano, had directed Colonel Cole to extricate the missionaries from Zaria and bring them under his protection at Girku, forty miles to the south of Zaria, where Cole had under his command a large detachment of the WAFF. At Girku the belenguared missionaries were well received, but their excitement was cut short by the sudden death of Ryder from dysentery. Three days after Ryder's burial, the group agreed to release Richardson, who was only getting worse, to be returned back to England to recoup his health. He was never able to return back to the mission field. Before the missionaries could recover from these two losses, words came requesting Colonel Cole and members of his WAFF and other forces that could be spared to immediately proceed to Jebba and thence to the Gold Coast, where war had broken out among the Asante who were in rebellion against British overlordship. In spite of persistent urging by Colonel Cole, the remaining missionaries refused to march south with their military protectors, considering it an act of cowardice for them to abandon the land of their mission target, and for which one of their members had paid the ultimate price and another was fighting for his life.

While at Girku, Emir Kwasau of Zaria kept the missionaries under constant surveillance. The missionaries' developing friendship with some of the inhabitants of the region, their frequent proselytizing visits to the neighboring villages, and the continuing threat of British invasion remained a source of uneasiness for the Emir. After his many attempts to surreptitiously scare away the missionaries from Girku failed to dislodge them, he resorted to more drastic measures. Early one morning, a few hours before daybreak, the missionaries woke up to find their huts and all their supplies, medical equipment and medicine in flames. Kwasau had had enough. Though nearly prostrated by these adversities, the missionaries recouped and were encouraged by supplies brought in to them by Rev. J. J. Williams, the resident CMS priest at Lokoja, acting on the instruction of Governor Lugard, then based in Zungeru. Soon, Lugard's increasing concern and anxiety over the safety of the missionaries impelled them to move to Loko on the Benue River and within eyeshot of British military protection. Hans Vischer and George Percy Bargery, two newly recruited missionaries from England, joined them at Loko.[9] With the arrival of these two, Bishop Tugwell took his leave of the Hausa Mission Party and returned to his diocese in Lagos. Burgin, on account of ill health, also took his leave and returned to England to recuperate. In the meantime, a fresh attack of dysentery and fever compelled Miller to also return to England. In due course, Vischer also left Loko. He had nine attacks of fever in six months and on Miller's recommendation returned to Europe. A telegraph from Switzerland, informing Vischer of the sudden death, in quick successions, of his father and one of his brothers, and the need for him to return home and put the family affairs in order, would further delay his hope of returning back to Nigeria as a missionary. Thus ended the first daring attempt by the CMS to carry the message of the cross into the heartland of

Hausaland. Miller, however, did not give up hope. As soon as he returned to England and began to recover, he also began to make preparation for his return trip to the "dark" continent. By the end of 1901, Miller was back in Loko.

Loko by its location and circumstances was considered unsuitable as a permanent base for the CMS in northern Nigeria. Located on the Benue it was far from the center of the Hausa country. Besides, its environment was not particularly accomodatious. Miller described it as "a wretched, deserted spot where (man-eating) hyenas, sand flies, mosquitoes, and donkeys alone seemed happy." A more appropriate site, probably located within or close to the heartland of Hausaland had to be sought and settled, but who would grant permission or facilitate the realization of such a desire. The mission now sought assistance of the colonial authority to actualize its intentions. The budding partnership between the cross and the crown had to be called into play. Finding himself now as the leader of the mission party, Miller sought an audience with the Governor, Sir Fredrick Lugard, to discuss what the mission's next line of action should be in its objective of spreading the light of civilization and of faith in Hausaland. The interview with Governor Lugard went well and beyond Miller's expectations. Permission was granted for Miller and his team to return to the north, with very little restriction and with valuable advice to learn to travel light and to always remain a layman. More importantly a form of mutual friendship and trust developed between the young missionary doctor and the seasoned administrator and statesman, which would have major consequences for the cause of religion and of politics in colonial Northern Nigeria.

Religion and Politics in Colonial Zaria

After Miller's surprisingly welcoming conference with Lugard in Lokoja in 1901 and the later's positive disposition to and encouragement of mission work, Miller and his one remaining partner, Bargery, left Loko, and headed for Zaria, the nearest and the most central of the Hausa emirates. On arrival in Zaria, they were surprised by the positive reception given them by the Emir Kwasau, who had made their lives miserable during their last sojourn in his domain. This change in attitude was due to the prevailing political situation at the time. Events were moving rapidly in the ever-changing relations between the British and the Caliphate authorities in northern Nigeria. Having successfully subdued the southern frontier emirates of the Caliphate, Lugard was making preparation for his take over, either by peaceful or by military means, of the remaining emirates to the north. Letters and embassies were being exchanged between Lugard or his representatives and the emirs. Some of the emirs like those of Kano and Sokoto were outrightly hostile, while others like those of Katsina and Zaria were prefabricating. In the meantime, Lugard was amassing his forces together, determined to resolve the problem of conquest and submission one way or the other and as soon as possible. Lugard was also mindful of the French, who were moving in closer to northern Nigeria, in the course of their multi-prong imperial expansion to the east, north, and west of Hausaland. Zaria, which would later be described by Sir Hugh Clifford as the gateway to the Hausa States, was in the mind and strategic plans of Lugard and his associates, the next emirate to be brought under control. British control of Zaria, the most central of the Hausa states, would deal a fatal blow to the unity of the Caliphate and open a direct access to the gradual subjugation of the remaining emirates.

Recognizing the precariousness of his position and that of his state, as being on the next line of attack, the Emir of Zaria was resolved to play it safe with both Kano and Sokoto as well as with the British. In the meantime, for not being too openly resistant to the British, the Emir of Zaria had incurred the displeasure of Sokoto, whose sultan was making plans to remove him. This was to be carried out through the Sultan's son, N'Gwamatse, emir of Kontagora, who had laid siege to Zaria. As a result of its impregnable walls, Zaria could not be easily taken, but the Sultan's son was content to ravage Zaria villages for slaves and supplies, waiting for a good opportunity to assault the city and punish its recalcitrant emir. Within the city itself, Zaria was seething with intrigues, with most people advocating loyalty to Sokoto and resistance to the infidels. With Sokoto and Kano allied against him and with a scion of the Sultanate family laying in wait ready to pounce on his city and its beleaguered inhabitants, Kwasau was sure there was no way he could successfully resist a British attack. Besieged from without and surrounded by hostile brother emirs, Emir Kwasau must have concluded, though without informing his people, that his best guarantee of survival was an alliance with or surrender to the British.

Before Miller arrived in Zaria, Kwasau had already sent some desperate secret messages to Lugard to come to his rescue by helping him raise N'Gwamatse's siege of Zaria. This was the situation when the Miller party arrived. For the Emir, Miller and Bargery's arrival was a kind of God sent; he could enlist their support in pressuring Lugard to come speedily to his aid. Thus, he was very happy to see them. He immediately welcomed them back to his domain, putting them under the care and custody of one of his high-ranking officials, the Sarkin Makera, the chief of the blacksmiths. Miller suddenly found himself an unofficial adviser to the emir, who frequently invited him to the palace for consultation on how best to deal with his ongoing predicaments. Miller for his part counseled his royal highness that his best course for safety and survival was a peaceful submission to the forces of Lord Lugard. He advised him not to give up hope that help will come from the British and that if Lugard had given his word, the emir could rest assured that he would keep his promise of help.[10] Then suddenly one morning, Miller received a note from Captain Abadie, informing him that on instructions from Lugard he had just captured N'Gwamatse's and had dispersed his large army, and was in the outskirt of Zaria with N'Gwamatse's in chains. Before going to meet Captain Abadie, to celebrate this victory, Miller stopped at the palace to inform the emir of the good news. The emir was both elated and relieved, and there was much excitement in the city. Abadie soon moved on to Zungeru with his illustrious captive, but before leaving he secured a promise from the emir to allow Miller and his partner to establish their mission station once again in Girku with the full support of the emir. After staying for a few weeks in Zaria as the emir's special and protected guests, Miller and Bargery moved to Girku.

Girku remained the CMS base until 1905. The people of Girku village were both welcoming and friendly. They were quite receptive to the medical help that the missionaries offered, but the continuing fear of Zaria made them reluctant to embrace the message of a new religion being propagated by the visitors. Soon two new missionaries, both ordained ministers of the Church of England, F. H. Lacy and W. P. Low, joined the work at Girku, but continuing frustration over the failure to see any appreciable progress in conversion from Islam made them leave. Both started a new work in a non-Muslim area, where they were more success, and which they would later turn over to the Sudan Interior Mission (SIM) to continue. Finally in 1905, Miller with the express permission of the British administration and the new Emir of Zaria, Aliyu, relocated from Girku to Zaria city, which then became the base of CMS work in Northern Nigeria, and where Miller would spend the bulk of his many years as a missionary to Hausaland.

The Politics of Mission Education in Colonial Zaria

In the light of his difficult experiences trying to convert Muslims to Christianity or interest them in medical works, Miller came to the conclusion that the best strategy of breaking through the local resistance to missionary efforts would be through the provision of Western education by the missions. In a report written in Girku in 1903 and forwarded to the CMS head office at Salisbury Hall for onward transmission to Lugard who was then on leave in England, Miller proposed that the CMS be mandated by the Colonial Administration to assume responsibility for the program of education for the Northern Protectorate. He proposed the establishment of two kinds of schools.

The first would be a school for Mallams, to which each province would send two mallams well learned in Arabic scholarship. The mallams' school tenure would last for six months and students would reside in a boarding house near Miller's compound in Zaria. The first three months would be dedicated to teaching the students reading and writing the Hausa language using the Roman script. The last three would be spent exposing the students to subjects such as geography, arithmetic, grammar, hygiene, and sanitation. The CMS missionary agents working with West Indians or Christian educated Yoruba from the southern provinces would offer instructions in these subjects. Lessons would last for two hours each, during which no religious instructions would be given. Miller, however, reserved the right to discuss matters of religious truths with the students in their private times and by their own free choice without any force or compulsion from the mission agents. These mallams, after graduation, would be expected to return back to their provinces and become the pioneers of new forms of education among their own people. This proposal indicated how far the mission was prepared to go to subscribe to the cardinal principle of the indirect rule system, in this case educating the people through their own scholarly elite.

The second school would be a boarding school for the sons of chiefs. This school would be located in Zaria, and the boys would live with Miller. Emirs of the various emirates would be encouraged to nominate two of their sons or of other important chiefs to attend this school. Each emir would be charged whatever is considered appropriate to take care of the students while in residence at the school. The emir of Zaria would serve as the chief host and protector of these boys who would be housed in a dormitory run by the CMS. Residents would be expected to assure the emirs that this was a "secular" school and that students were free to practice their religion and that there would be no attempt to force conversion to Christianity. Miller was honest enough to admit that the ultimate objective, besides providing the colonial administration with a class of western educated elite, was the spread of the Christian faith. He was, however, careful to stress that no pressure would be applied to force conversion or do anything that might offend the religious sensibilities of the students or cause trouble for the administration.

In the meantime, the colonial Administration, in 1905, under Lugard, and acting on the invitation of the various residents, gave the CMS permission to start mission works in Kano, Katsina, and Kontangora, in addition to Zaria for which permission had already been granted. The CMS, pleading lack of manpower and a little suspicious of the compromise proposed by Miller, which made the cause of proselytizing secondary to that of education, turned down the offer. Two years later when the CMS renewed the request to be permitted access to these emirates, the offer was no longer on the table. Lugard who made the offer was no longer in charge. Under the new High Commissioner, Sir Girouard, the official position on the ground had changed to one of strict control and even curtailment of missionary activities in the Muslim emirates, rather than one of cooperation, which marked the Lugard years.

Before this, on receiving Miller's proposal, Lugard forwarded it to the Colonial Office with his own recommendations. He spoke highly of Miller and of his value to the colonial administration. He noted that while there might be difficulties in attracting mallams to volunteer themselves for the proposed school, he saw no reason why the school for sons of chiefs should not work as it was already working in the Sudan. He noted that the alternative to a mission-controlled school would be a secular institution, which would be too expensive to undertake in the current state of colonial finance. While admitting that Miller's ultimate aim was the spread of Christianity, he believed Miller could be trusted not to force religious conversion or do anything that might jeopardize his efforts and that of the colonial administration. He recommended that strict supervision by the colonial administration should ensure that the school continued to abide by the guidelines approved for it by the government. Elgin, the colonial secretary, after some consultations with other officials in the colonies and the colonial office, tentatively agreed with Lugard's recommendations to give the proposal a trial.

The CMS General Committee welcome Miller's proposal and the opportunity it offered the mission to carry on the work of education in the region, but they were quite critical of Miller's decision to subvert the more important goal of proselytization out of fear of offending the religious sensibilities of the Muslims. They gave the proposal a conditional approval, demanding that Miller should "secure from the Government full liberty for the teaching of the Bible in school hours in the boarding school, and for presenting Christianity to all pupils on a constructive basis."[11]

The qualified response from Salisbury House while understandable was disturbing to Miller. He was sure that insistence on the part of the mission on unrestricted freedom to teach religious instruction at the school would end up jeopardizing the whole project and thus close this narrow door of opportunity being offered. Lugard, Miller's friend, was no longer in charge in Nigeria. The Acting High Commissioner, Wallace, while favorable to the scheme, was resolved to find out what the views of the various Residents on the ground were towards the proposal. What he discovered was not encouraging: the majority of the Residents were opposed to the plan. Many recommended aborting it or revising it substantially to eliminate any form or semblance of religious instructions. In March 1907, Wallace informed Miller and the CMS that, in the light of the strong opposition from many of the Residents, he could no longer approve the plan, as proposed by Miller and endorsed by Lugard and Elgin, and would leave the matter to Sir Percy Girouard, Lugard's successor as High Commissioner.[12]

This turn of events was particularly devastating to Miller. In anticipation of official approval, he had virtually finished constructing the buildings that would house the school and was planning to open the school on May 1, 1907, in an attempt to present the new High Commissioner with a *fait accompli*. To save the scheme from total collapse, even before its inception, Miller, joined by Bishop Tugwell, who was then in Zaria on a working visit from Lagos, held an urgent meeting with Orr, the Resident of Zaria Province and Festing, the Resident of Kano. Recognizing that the major bone of contention was the mission's insistence on presenting to the sons of Chiefs the basic truths of the Christian faith, Miller and the Bishop agreed to pressure the Mission Executive Committee to grant the Zaria scheme an exception to its general requirements that all mission educational programs must include religious instruction in its curriculum. In addition, it was agreed that the school for the boys would be a day school, thus taking care of one of the fears of the emirs of having sons of prominent families living so closely under the control of a representative of the Christian missions. Very reluctantly and in the face of the desperate appeal and pressure from two of its most trusted and seasoned missionaries in Nigeria, the CMS General Committee relented and gave its approval. The school started as planned by Miller in May 1907.[13]

The story of the new school for boys was rocky from the start. Apart from Zaria, none of the emir nominated or sent any pupil to the school. Since the proposal stipulated that attendance or nomination was voluntary and no pressure was to be applied, there was nothing anyone could do. This failure on the part of the other emirs should not come as a surprise. First, with their history of mutual rivalries and inter-state warfare, it is difficult to expect that the emirs would want to send their sons to go and take up residency or receive education from another rival emir. Second, as some of the residents would point out to Wallace as well as to Girouard later, some of the more powerful Emirates such as Kano, Katsina, and Sokoto, regarded Zaria as a junior emirate, and considered it below their dignity to send their sons to its emir for education. More important would be the general indifference, and in some cases opposition, to the scheme on the part of some of the Residents, who shared with the Emirs suspicion about the CMS' true intention, and whose expressed hostility to the scheme on political grounds was often palpable enough for the emirs to take a cue that the project was not to be given more than nominal support.

In this event, only the Emir of Zaria recruited fifteen boys from prominent families in the emirate to form the foundation class for the school. Getting the boys' school to take off was a real challenge. Many of the boys saw no reason why they were at the school. Since attendance was voluntary, absentee rates remained high, often as high as fifty percent. Besides some of the boys were "boys" only in name and by European definition, and were already married with wives and children to look after. In this situation, discipline was a huge problem, and many of the boys remained quite disruptive. At one point, Miller became so exasperated by the indifference of the students that he planned to shut down the school, but the emir would have none of that. The emir paid a personal visit to the school, ordered the expulsion of the troublemakers, leaving only six pupils who appeared committed to learning, each of whom he presented with a beautiful robe, as an incentive to ensure their continued commitment.[14]

The Mallam's school fared a little better, largely due to the fact that the mallams were older, and as part of the indigenous intellectual class, were already used to learning, and after their initial reluctance to accept Miller as a real scholar, rather than a colonial technocrat, settled down to imbibe and acquire what new knowledge this alien had to impart. One of the early products of the school for Mallams, by the name of Fate, was very useful to Miller in his Bible translation project. Another became memorable for secretly teaching the emir of Zaria to read Hausa in the Roman script. The fact of the emir's new literacy came to light when in the course of a visit to the school he took Miller and everyone by surprise by asking to be tested and demonstrated his Hausa reading competence in the Roman script. So delighted was the colonial administration, that this development was noted in the colonial Annual Report for Northern Nigeria in 1907-08.[15]

While direct religious instructions could not be given at the school, it is important to point out that books selected or available for Hausa readings in the school were the Gospel of St. John, the Gospel of St. Mark, the First Epistle of St. John, and stories in Hausa from the New Testament. This fact, of course, was well known to both the emir and the resident, but they had little or no room to maneuver. These were the only books or readings available anywhere in Hausa in the Roman scripts, and they were all translations by Dr. Miller and his team of students and teaching assistants.

Miller's school struggled on with only very limited success. The Emir showed keen interest, and paid periodic visits to the school, but failed to recruit additional boys for the school, in spite of his promise to do so. The Waziri also showed interest, and like his boss, paid occasional visits to the school, in the course of which he often spoke to the kids encouraging them to remain committed to their studies. The school for mallams also failed to develop as Miller had envisaged it, since no other province ever sent any mallam there. It ended up as a school for any adult interested or curious enough to come under the wing of Miller and the CMS to study. The boarding school for sons of chiefs also failed to come to fruition under Miller: first, because all the emirs, including that of Zaria, declined to send any of their sons to the school; and second, because the overwhelming majority of the Residents, who could have enforced or encouraged such recruitment, remained opposed to the scheme on political grounds.[16] Eventually, a prototype of the school as proposed by Miller, would be established by the colonial administration and put under the superintendence of Hans Vischer, who had changed his citizenship from Swiss to British, resigned from the CMS and had returned back to Nigeria no longer as a missionary, but as a junior Resident in Bornu Province.[17]

The Ombudsman: The Making and Unmaking of Emirs in Northern Nigeria

Miller's advent during the critical years of British conquest, his strong friendship with Lord Lugard, and the later's mutual respect for him, placed him in good stead in the politics of colonial Northern Nigeria. As the only Western missionary permitted to live in and operate relatively freely in an emirate city, his residency gave him considerable advantages. Within Zaria itself, this special guest was probably the most famous individual in the city apart from the Emir and the colonial resident. Miller had open and free access to the emir anytime he so desired to see him, the emir's frequent visit to the CMS compound to greet, sit with and chat with the CMS doctor; while the resident and other European visitors maintaned regular interactions with the veritable CMS missionary. All these must have considerably enhanced Miller's status among the people of Zaria.

Miller's friendship with Lugard and the fact that he was frequently consulted by British political officials on the affairs of the region were open secrets. For the common people of Zaria, this whiteman, whom they called "Likita" (from "Doctor"), must be from a different breed of white men: he was not aloof as the other white officials who visited the emir and had little or no interaction with the ordinary people; nor did he consider it beneath his dignity to visit the home of the common people, befriend some of them, and even keep his doors, and more importantly, his ears open to them any time of the day or night. Unlike other British officials, who would neither listen nor speak directly to the common people, except through the emir or his agents, their Likita was different. He was always welcoming, always inviting, and always attentive. Seeing in him a great friend and ally in their struggle against oppression by the emir and his agents, they began to take their complaints to the Likita, hoping that he would use his great influence with the emir, but more importantly with his brother British officials, to ensure relief from their suffering and justice for their causes.

Miller, on his part, appeared to have seen it as part of his mission and that of any missionary to be a light that is shining in the darkness, whether the darkness of Islam, or that of paganism, or that of the emirate's feudal social and political oppression. His writings, the bulk of which came after his retirement from active mission works in Nigeria, are full of strident diatribes at what he considers to be the failure of British administration in Nigeria. His most severe criticisms were reserved for the Islamic Emirate Authorities of Northern Nigeria, whom he described as short-sighted, blind, irredeemable, anachronistic, and oppressive. Time and again he deprecated the adoption of the Lugardian system of indirect rule, regretted the failure of the British to make a clean sweep of the Fulani administration and the old order they had defeated, and wished for a more direct rule approach that would have permitted a wholesale socio-cultural transformation of Northern Nigeria. Only such an approach, rather than the tolerant and indulgent one developed by Lugard, would have ensured the sweeping away of decades of Fulani feudal oppression, and the restoration of the more "enlightened" Hausa back to leadership. He especially deplored the British administration's protective and even paternalistic attitude towards Islam, their iron-clad restrictions on Christian missionary activities, and their tolerance of many of the abuses of the emirate authorities. To Miller, progress in Northern Nigeria could only be measured by how well the two civilizing forces of education and Christianity are able to percolate into the crevices of northern Nigerian societies. Thus, colonialism can only be legitimately justified on how well it was able to advance these forces. He never ceased to argue that the colonial administration's consistent pursuit of a policy that closed the commanding heights (i.e. the emirates) of Northern Nigeria to the modernizing and civilizing influence of Christianity was a recipe for the continued backwardness of that region and for the unmitigated failure of British rule in Northern Nigeria.[18]

Escounced at the very nerve center of a key Islamic emirate, Miller took his civilizing mission seriously. His medical program remained useful to the few who were curious, daring, or desperate enough to go against the general attitude of skepticism to seek his help. Miller reported on an elderly Muslim who for long remained skeptical and even hostile towards his persistent preaching, but whose "miraculous" rescue from death by the medical intervention of Miller's female nursing assistant, resulted in his whole hearted conversion from Islam to Christianity.[19] Unfortunately, for the doctor, such cases were rare. In spite of the early, though clearly misinformed, optimism of the missionaries, the wall of Islam remained largely impregnable to the multi-pronged assaults of the Christian missions throughout much of the colonial period. The hopes and dreams of a rapid and mass conversion of Muslims, in the wake of the British conquest, soon turned to disillusionment and disappointment. Miller's mission efforts yielded precious few converts. In his writings, Miller spoke with passion and fondness about these few converts, some of who, as pioneer western educated elite, went on to distinguish themselves in various careers in the socio-political affairs of late colonial and post-colonial Nigeria.

It was, however, in his role as the voice of the oppressed and the voice of the voiceless that Miller gained his reputation or, from the perspective of some of the colonial administrators, his notoriety, as the unofficial British ombudsman for lost causes. In this role, politics and religion became inextricably entwined with far-reaching consequences for the cause of mission and administration in northern Nigeria. The British adopted the policy of indirect rule in Nigeria for reasons of administrative exigencies and convenience. Direct rule would have meant the presence of more British nationals for administrative and police duties at a cost too prohibitive for the new and fledgling administration to bear. Even if the money was available, there was not enough manpower or British citizens willing or enthusiastic about serving in Africa. In 1900, the reputation of Africa as the whiteman's grave, remained largely intact, in spite of progress made in the medical treatment of African diseases like malaria and yellow fever. Europeans were still dying or taking ill, as a result of being in Africa, in unacceptable numbers and regularity in the early 1900s. The British adoption and use of local authorities also assured their loyalty and cooperation as dependent co-rulers of their people, while minimizing the possibility of widespread revolt against British rule.[20]

Indirect rule as espoused by Lugard and operated in Northern Nigeria, meant building up and maintaining, by all means possible, the prestige and influence of the emirate authorities, in their governance of their people. That prestige must not be permitted to suffer or the cause of orderly governance would suffer. The emir must be perceived by his people at all times to be in charge. The Resident or other officials must not publicly reprimand him. Care must be taken to maintain a chain of command running down from the Emir to the village head and thence to the common people. This meant that a commoner who felt cheated or abused by the emir or any of his agents could not complain directly to British officials, but had to channel their complaint through that agent or through the emir himself to the colonial authority. The implications of this have been extensively examined in various studies[21]; suffice it to say that this meant complaining was not just futile but potentially dangerous. The majority simply accepted their lot, being wise enough not to add to their problems by speaking against constituted authorities. Those who did not complain but did not accept their oppressed condition and powerlessness migrated to other places. The few who would not or could not migrate nor accept their lots turned to the one alternative left to plead their case: the veritable and reputedly influential Lakita, Dr. Miller.

Dr. Miller took his role as the chief representative of Christ, the friend of the poor and the oppressed, in the emirates, very seriously. His doors were always open and welcoming to anyone in search of medical help, educational training, or religious enlightenment. Miller himself went regularly, contrary to regulations, to itinerate both within Zaria city itself as well as in its surrounding villages. He was welcomed into the houses of peasants as readily as into those of chiefs. Over the years, he established many friendly contacts, though not converts, with various classes of people in the society. His fluency in the Hausa language gave him direct access to the people, while his considerable prestige as a white man and a friend of Lugard and other colonial administrators, ensured his welcome any where he went, while making him a valuable individual to befriend. Beleaguered individuals, most especially among the common people, took their complaints to the Likita, assured from experience of his attentive ears. Depending on his own judgment on the merits of the complaint, Miller would take such cases directly to the Resident or other political officials, drawing their attention to the continuing practices of feudal oppression and urging them to intervene to redress the injustices or reprimand the emir. At other times, depending on the urgency of the case, Miller would go straight to the emir's palace, to remonstrate with him about the abuses of his agents or even of the sovereign himself.

In some cases, when the British officials either failed or refused to intervene in a fashion deemed appropriate by Miller, he had been known to take his case directly to the Lt. Governor of the Northern Provinces in Kaduna or the Governor-General of Nigeria in Lagos and at times directly to the Colonial Office in London. In one case amply documented in his *Reflections of a Pioneer*, a young man had been beaten to death by agents of the emir on a recruitment mission for railway construction. The young man was the youngest of three siblings. The two eldest ones had already been recruited for the railway construction. The British "forced labor" regulation stipulated that an only son with elderly parents should be excluded from conscription, while in cases where there was more than one son in a family; one of the sons should be left to care for the parents. In violation of this ordinance, the emir's agents had mortally assaulted the young man for resisting recruitment. As the young man lay dying, Miller was hurriedly summoned to come and save his life. It was too late; the beating was too brutal for him to recover. Miller brought this case to the attention of the Resident, who promptly directed the emir to investigate.

The next thing Miller heard was that the emir, at the conclusion of his investigation, had the eighty year old father of the murdered young man imprisoned for insubordination to rightfully constituted authority. Certain of the death of the old man in the emir's jail, Miller hurried to the palace. He pleaded with the emir to release the old man, since he had been wrongly imprisoned. The emir refused, telling Miller that he loved and understood his people more than the missionary. He informed Miller that he had already submitted his report finding the old man guilty to the Resident and it was already too late to change it. In desperation, Miller played what he believed was a last card on the sovereign. He informed Emir Aliyu that he was on his way to London for his annual leave, that he would pass through Lagos, and would be calling on his friend the Governor General of Nigeria, and that he had left instructions at the mission station in Zaria that he should be kept informed by telegraph of whatever happened to the old man. With a smile, a handshake, and a twinkle in one eye, Emir Aliyu bade Miller a safe trip to England. By the time Miller arrived in Lagos, a telegraph informed Miller that the old man had been freed by order of the emir.[22]

Needless to say, neither British officials nor the emir were particularly enthused by the unofficial ombudsman's role assumed by this missionary agent. Most British colonial officials held Miller in high regards. Miller was the leading authority on the Hausa language in all of colonial Nigeria. He was their teacher: many of them received their compulsory Hausa lessons and passed their Hausa language competency exam under him. Notable among those examined by Miller were; C. D. Temple, Resident of Sokoto and later Lt. Governor of Northern Nigeria; Sir W. Gowers, later Governor of Uganda; and Sir H. Palmer, later High Commissioner for Cyprus. Miller had many friends in the colonial office in England; where the influence of many political officials could not be easily discountenanced without consequences. Besides, Miller was not necessarily a nuisance. Unlike the political officers, who were usually subject to frequent transfers, Miller, as the long term resident on the spot and with an ear to the ground, knew more than the usually aloof administrators about the true state of affairs in the colony. It was not uncommon for administrators to "secretly" consult with the missionary when seeking to redress grievances, depose recalcitrant rulers, or make important appointments. His recommendations were often followed with positive consequences.[23]

While considering Miller a valuable partner in the promotion of British interests in Nigeria, political officials were often quite wary and unwelcoming about his ombudsman's role, most especially when such meddling was interfering with the smooth running of the administration and threatening the cause of order and stability in the province. For instance, in 1918, Turaki Kerami, District Head of Kudaru, lost his position after taking offence at the emir's removal of a Village Head in his district. Though perfectly loyal to the British administration, Kerami was accused of insubordination to the emir, a behavior, which, according to the colonial administration, "can on no account be tolerated." More important is the comment on the case by the Lt. Governor: "I do not think he would have been so cantankerous (to the emir) had he not felt sure of being backed up by Dr. Miller and the CMS who took up his case warmly."[24]

While continuing to express their regard for Dr. Miller and his valuable services to the colonial administration, colonial officials took the pain of reporting on the negative impact of his ombudsman's role on the administration. They also reported on how tactically they continued to handle the situation while maintaining cordial relationship with him. Writing in his Annual Report for 1907, the Resident of Zaria noted: "I find that Dr. Miller has been in the habit of discussing political matters rather freely. There is a great deal of correspondence from him on various local and other matters." While reporting that he does not intend to continue the practice of discussing political issues with the mission authorities in the future, he stated that he "shall always, however, be glad to receive their reports and communication," but that "these will, of course, be acknowledged with the courtesy to which they are entitled." Noting that the Islamic emirates were hotbeds of intrigues and factionalization, the Resident advised political officials to be both simultaneously welcoming to the missionaries, while remaining skeptical about the tales they told. These tales, while providing precious little information that could help the cause of colonization, were useful mainly as "insight into the native character." He concluded his report with a disclaimer and on a cautionary note: "I do not wish to imply that the missionaries do any real harm by listening to the tales brought to them and so long as their reports are taken by us with a grain of salt they may even serve some good purpose."[25]

Relations between Dr. Miller and the Emirate authority were generally cordial. As noted earlier, Aliyu's predecessor, Emir Kwasau, had welcomed Dr. Miller back to Kano in 1900, determined to use the missionary's influence to secure the military assistance of Lugard in his conflict with his Sokoto sovereign who was then resolved to depose him for his temporizing stand in the Caliphate's resistance to British conquest. The strategy worked. Zaria submitted peacefully to British conquest and was spared from the devastating defeats experienced by the more recalcitrant emirates such as Ilorin, Bida, Kano, and Sokoto. Emir Kwasau retained his throne, but his continued intrigue with Kano, which was yet to be conquered, soon caused him to fall out of favor with the colonial administration. In 1902, Kwasau was relieved of his title and dethroned. Shortly thereafter, a messenger of Aliyu, one of the many princes contesting for the vacant throne, arrived in Girku to see Dr. Miller. He brought with him a letter in Arabic and a turkey as present to the missionary from Prince Aliyu. Puzzled as to the intent of this present, since he did not even know the prince, Miller asked the messenger for an explanation. After being assured that no one was within earshot of their conversation, the messenger whispered in Miller's ear: "Aliyu knows that you are a most important person...the throne of Zaria is vacant ... his father was emir... and he believes that your influence may be used!"[26] Despite this attempted "bribery," which the missionary promptly reported to a higher authority, and which almost landed the ambitious prince in trouble with the Acting Resident, Aliyu, eventually obtained the throne.

Aliyu, of course, knew where his bread was being buttered. Recognizing the influence that Miller had with the colonial administration, the new emir took steps to cultivate his friendship. He permitted the CMS under Miller to relocate from Girku to within Zaria city in 1905; gave them land on which to construct their mission compound, school, and church; and supplied them with whatever materials they needed for their survival. The emir paid Dr. Miller regular visits and permitted him to visit his palace freely and at will. As Dr. Miller noted, the emir "used to ride down from his house to mine very informally with just a few mounted retainers; and here he would sit for hours, chatting most pleasantly and affectionately with me."[27]

The Missionary and the Emir: The Final Show Down

Beneath the surface, there were deep misgivings. While mutually respectful of each other, Dr. Miller and Emir Aliyu remained deeply suspicious of each other. On the part of the emir, there is no evidence to indicate that this suspicion was inspired by the fear that the missionary's proselytizing efforts would overwhelm Islam in the emirate. By 1920, years of dedicated hard work and proselytizing by Dr. Miller and his associates had produced no more than a handful of converts from Islam. Conversion among non-Muslims or followers of indigenous religions, most especially in the southern part of the emirate, could have yielded better results. These missionaries were, however, not enthused about pursuing such missions, in spite of repeated encouragement from British officials. As the CMS authority would point out again and again it was not easy for missionaries who felt called to the land of Islam to suddenly change the direction of their callings and mission. Nor is there any evidence to believe that the emir and his people felt threatened in any serious manner by the missionary's medical and educational works, both of which they seem to genuinely appreciate, though infrequently patronized.[28] As noted earlier, the emir recruited the first set of fifteen students for Miller's experimental school for the sons of chiefs; visited the school regularly; and showed an active interest in its progress. In addition, Emir Aliyu himself became one of the early beneficiaries of the new literacy in Hausa, secretly learning to read and write Hausa in the Roman script from one of the early students of Dr. Miller.

Had Dr. Miller limited his activities solely to these seemingly harmless but beneficial areas there would have been no trouble, but this missionary saw his work as being more than just the saving of souls and the healing of mind and body. As a follower of Christ, he believed it was his duty and prerogative to fight against oppression and for justice whether social, economic, or political. In his campaigns and letters against what he saw as injustice in the emirate, he spared neither the British administrative officers nor the emirate authorities. More worrisome and more galling to the Emir and the colonial administrators, was Dr. Miller's self-appointed role as the ombudsman and spokesperson for the oppressed and defender of anyone who had an axe to grind with the emir or any of his agents. This was what brought him into a running battle with the emirate authorities and periodic but subtle advice from political officials to concentrate on the saving of souls while leaving political affairs to them. On many occasions, in his pursuit of justice and fair play for the aggrieved parties who had sought his intervention, Miller did not hesitate to use his influence with the colonial administrations in Kaduna, Lagos, and in London, to bring about change in colonial policies and practices in the emirate, or to compel the Emir of Zaria to rescind his judgments or those of his associates.[29]

For the emir, matters came to a head in 1919. After enduring the antics and meddlesomeness of this overbearing missionary for nearly two decades, the emir was determined to force a show down: Dr. Miller had to go. To do this, the emir needed the support of the Resident, his immediate boss in the province. This did not appear to have been too difficult to obtain. Without appearing to be the initiator, the Resident was probably delighted to get rid of this clog in the wheel of the colonial administration. After securing the consent of the Resident for his plan, the emir waited for an appropriate time. The first opportunity came with the visit to Zaria Province of the Governor, Sir Hugh Clifford in 1919. At his conference with the governor, the emir requested that the missionary be deported from his province. The governor thanked the emir for his request, but informed him that for him to take such a drastic action against a veteran missionary of Dr. Miller's experience and good standing, the emir would need to provide him with more concrete evidence of wrong doings to justify the need for his deportation.[30]

For an ordinary missionary, such a request from an emir would have been enough to send the missionary packing, but Dr. Miller was no ordinary missionary. To deny the emir's request by retaining Dr. Miller against the wish of his host, amounted to a loss of prestige for the Native Authority, which went against a cardinal principle of the Indirect Rule system. On the other hand, to accede to the emir's request by deporting this influential missionary simply because the former no longer wished to see his face, exposed the colonial administration to ridicule and serious criticisms, while incurring the wrath of the powerful CMS authority in Salisbury Square. It was clear to everyone that the matter would not rest where the governor had left it. Dr. Miller had become *personal non-gratta* to the emir, theoretically his host; either the emir or the missionary would have to go. Matters came rapidly to a show down.

On his part, Dr. Miller had no intention of leaving Zaria, but recognizing the difficulties of his position and the predicament of the colonial administration, Dr. Miller had to walk a very fine line. Informed of the emir's request, he sought and was granted two interviews with the Governor-General of Nigeria in Lagos. Assured of the Colonial Government's backing in his campaign to oust the emir, Miller returned to Zaria to, in his own words, "prepare a full case against the Emir of Zaria."[31] It was a herculean task, made more difficult by the fact that Aliyu kept the missionary under watch. It took the versatile missionary three months to gather all the evidence and prepare a full report on the many failings, atrocities, and wrong doings of the emir. As the missionary himself reported:

> There were twenty major counts, of which murder was one. For three months I hardly slept. My house was surrounded by spies, some of whom I recognized, and it became exceedingly difficult for people known to be bringing information to get near me. I was informed that my cook had been bribed to poison me, and an evil face awaited anyone known to be helping me. And yet taking their lives in their hands, some real patriots brought me all their evidence, supported by witnesses. Strange devices were adopted by these people to get into my compound at all hours of day and night. . . . The case was at last complete. Eighteen sheets of foolscap, in close type, went to Kaduna. Muslims and Christians were praying and longing for some strong action to be taken.[32]

Miller's report on the Emir was damning, not just because of the seriousness of the allegations, but because for the most part they were true.[33] There is no doubt that Miller's attempt to oust the emir of a key Hausa state would not have been successful, if the emir had not himself played into his hands. Over the years, several political officers had commented on Aliyu's loyalty to the colonial administration, his administrative competence, hard work, and commitment to the development of his province, while constantly pointing out the continued existence of various abuses and acts of oppression.[34] In the name of maintaining the prestige of the Native Authority, many of these abuses had either gone unnoticed or generally ignored by the colonial officials. The excuses given by the political officials were that things were still better off than they were before the British advent, and that time and patience were needed before these conquered feudal rulers could be expected to learn and imbibe by more democratic and humane ways of governance.[35] Before the colonial conquest, the emir had ruled with the advice and support of his principal chiefs and district heads. Following the conquest, the emir's position was strengthened vis a vis that of his principal chiefs and advisers, who no longer served as a check on his power, since he was now responsible only to the British. In the absence of a real credible check on the emir's enhanced power, abuse and oppression festered undetected and un-redressed, creating considerable disenchantment among the populace toward the emir and his British protector. Into this vacuum, stepped the missionary doctor. It is thus not surprising that the doctor had many to help among the discontented population, many of who were prepared to risk everything to assist the alien missionary in his quest to rid them of their overbearing master. It is not surprising that when the show down finally came, the emir found himself alone. On trial by his British protectors, who could no longer continue to defend his failings as a ruler, and abandoned by his people, who were tired of the oppression perpetrated under his rule, Aliyu resorted to various stratagems, all of which would prove ultimately futile, to keep his throne. Having managed to alienate so many people in the course of his eighteen-year rule, Aliyu's fall did not evoke more than a whimper from his chiefs and people.

After receiving Miller's report and additional ones by the Resident of Zaria Province and other officials, the Governor dispatched an official from Lagos to Kaduna to investigate the allegations. Preliminary findings established the veracity of most of the cases against the emir. Aliyu was summoned to Kaduna to appear before the Lt. Governor for the Northern Provinces and defend himself against the charges. Unable to mount any serious rebuttal to the allegations, the emir was given two options: accept deposition and exile on a salary of £100 a year; or proceed to Lagos to stand trial for murder and other capital offences. Aliyu chose the former and proceeded to exile. After consultations with Dr. Miller and other colonial officials, a new emir was appointed for Zaria. While remaining grateful and indeed differential to the "untouchable" missionary doctor, the new emir and his younger brother, Madaki Ibrahim, who succeeded him, would work assiduously with the colonial administration to eventually move the CMS Mission station from within Zaria city to the outskirt of the city in 1929. The presence of this missionary and social crusader and his little flock of adherents, at the nerve center of the emirate power, was too close for comfort. Dr. Miller continued his missionary and other works in the Zaria province and later in Kano, undeterred and unmolested until his voluntary retirement from the mission field in 1935. Nevertheless, in this singularly notable contest for supremacy between the emir and the missionary in Northern Nigeria, during the early colonial period, the missionary had triumphed.

Notes

1. On the British conquest of Northern Nigeria and the collapse of the Sokoto Caliphate, see: Obaro Ikime, *The Fall of Nigeria: The British Conquest* (London: Heinemann, 1977); R. A. Adeleye, *Power and Diplomacy in Northern Nigeria, 1804-1906: The Sokoto Caliphate and its Enemies* (London: Longman, 1977),

213-313; and Risata Marjomaa, *War on the Savannah: The Military Collapse of the Sokoto Caliphate under the Invasion of the British Empire, 1897-1908* (The Finish Academy of Sciences and Letters, 1998).

2. For an examination of the role of missionaries as pathfinders of European influence and as precursors of Western imperialism, see E. A. Ayandele, *The Missionary Impact on Modern Nigeria, 1842-1914: A Political and Social Analysis* (New York: Humanities Press, 1967), 29-115; Roland Oliver, *The Missionary Factor in East Africa* (London: Longman, 1952).
3. The brief sketch of Walter Miller's early life and education in England is based on information derived largely from his two memoirs: W. R. S. Miller, *Reflections of A Pioneer* (London: Church Missionary Society, 1936) and *Walter Miller, 1872-1952: An Autobiography* (Zaria, Nigeria: Gaskiya Corporation, 1952), 1-13.
4. As if he needed to reaffirm the comparatively high standard of his medical training, Walter was always in the habit of pointing out that St. Bartholomew "has an older educational foundation than either Oxford or Cambridge," *Reflections of a Pioneer*, 14; *An Autobiography*, 3.
5. Miller, *An Autobiography*, 12-13.
6. Ikime, *The Fall of Nigeria*, 119-129. On the Royal Niger Company, see J. E. Flint, *Sir. George Goldie and the Making of Nigeria* (London: Oxford, 1960).
7. Miller, *An Autobiography*, 35.
8. *Ibid.*, 34.
9. George Bargery later distinguished himself as an accomplished linguist, compiling and publishing, in 1934, the first comprehensive dictionary of the Hausa language that would prove most valuable to missionaries on the ground for many years, at least before the appearance of the much richer dictionary by R. C. Abraham in 1958. See Bargery, *A Hausa-English Dictionary and English-Hausa Vocabulary* (Zaria, Nigeria: Ahmadu Bello University Press, 1943/1993); and R. C. Abraham, *Dictionary of the Hausa Language* (London: Hodder and Stoughton, 1958/1978).
10. C.M.S. G3/A9/01, Miller to Baylis, 18 Feb. 1902.
11. C.M.S Letter-book (N), pp.88-101, S.S to Miller, 16 November 1906
12. C.M.S. 1907 (H) No.50, Miller, Zaria, 19 March 1907.
13. C.M.S. 1907 (N.N.) No.58, Tugwell, Between Onitsha and Forcados, 10 May 1907; No. 64, Executive Committee Minutes, Vida, 30 April – 4 May 1907; and C.M.S. 1909 (N.N.) No. 4, Report on Zaria schools for 1907-08.
14. NAK., SNP. 942/1909, *Annual Report*, CMS (Hausa Section), 1909
15. NAK. *Annual Report*, Zaria Province, 1908; Miller, *An Autobiography*, 57-58, 152-154.

16. For a fuller discussion of the debates and controversies surrounding Miller's proposal and experimental schools, and the major source for the discussion in this section, see Sonia F. Graham, *Government and Mission Education in Northern Nigeria, 1900-1919 with special reference to the work of Hanns Vischer* (Ibadan, Nigeria: Ibadan University Press, 1966), 32-57. See also C.M.S. 1909 (N.N.) No. 4, Report on Zaria schools for 1907-08.
17. Hans Vischer, originally of French Swiss origin, but educated in England, would go on to distinguish himself in various capacities, serving as a linguist and working for the British Government in Berlin during the First World War, and later as Director of Education in Nigeria. He was knighted in 1936. See Graham, *Government and Mission Education in Northern Nigeria*; and Miller, *An Autobiography*, 18.
18. Miller, *Have We Failed in Nigeria?* London: United Society for Christian Literature, 1947; Miller, *Reflections of A Pioneer*, 57-67.
19. Miller, *Reflections of A Pioneer*, 142-143.
20. On the rationale for the adoption by the British of the Indirect Rule system, see Lord Fredrick Lugard, *The Dual Mandate in British Tropical Africa* (New York: Routledge, 1965); A. H. M. Kirk-Green, *The Principles of Native Administration in Nigeria: Selected documents, 1900-1947* (London: Oxford University Press, 1965).
21. See Nicholson, *The Administration of Nigeria, 1900-1960: Men, Methods and Myths* (Oxford: Clarendon Press, 1969); Kirk-Green, *The Principles.* For a case study of the operation of the indirect rule system at the grassroot level in the Ilorin Emirate of colonial Northern Nigeria, see Funso Afolayan, "Colonial Rule and Anti-Fulani Revolts in Igbomina," in *ODU: A Journal of West African Studies*, New Series, 36, July 1989, 24-42.
22. Miller, *Reflections of A Pioneer*, 135-138.
23. Miller, *Reflections of A Pioneer*, 95, 154-156.
24. SNP to Resident, Zaria Province, 17-4-1919 –Annual Report, Zaria Province, 1918.
25. NAK (Nigerian National Archives, Kaduna), *Annual Report*, Zaria Province, 1908.
26. Miller, *Reflections of A Pioneer*, 127.
27. Ibid., 133.
28. In his report for 1908, the Medical Officer in charge of Zaria Province, noted: "Dr. Miller has done some medical works during the past year chiefly of a surgical nature. I gather however, the people do not very readily go to him for medical treatment." NAK., Annual Report, Zaria Province, 1908, 82.

29. NAK, Annual Report, Zaria Province, 1905, 9; Miller, *Reflections of A Pioneer*, 135-138.
30. Miller, *Reflections of A Pioneer*, 138.
31. Miller, *Reflections of A Pioneer*, 138.
32. Miller, *Reflections of A Pioneer*, 138-139.
33. In his speech at the installation of the new emir, the Governor confirmed most of these accusations and stated inter allia, that after full investigation, the ex-emir Aliyu, was "found guilty of unjust, unrighteous and oppressive acts." See full text of Speech of His Excellence, Governor Hugh Clifford, enclosure, *Annual Report*, Zaria Province, 1918. As early as 1910, the Resident of Zaria province had accused the emir of perfidiousness and abuse of office, while in 1914, the charge of nepotism was laid at the emir's feet. See the *Annual Reports*, Zaria Province, 1910 & 1914.
34. NAK, *Annual Report*, Zaria Province, 1910; *Annual Report*, Zaria Province, 1914.
35. NAK, Comment, C. L. Temple, Lt. Governor, Northern Protectorate, *Annual Report*, Zaria Province, 1910.

RELIGION, POLITICS, AND ETHNICITY

Chapter Three

Ethnic and Religious Conflicts: Challenges for Sustainable Democracy

Philip Akpen

Nigeria has experienced many disastrous ethnic and religious conflicts, which have not only undermined and threatened the corporate existence of the pan-Nigerian agenda,[1] but they have also frustrated efforts made towards achieving national development.[2] Issues of national development have been relegated to the background. Instead, ethnic and religious sentiments have become the goal to achieve national unity and sustainable democracy. This chapter focuses on the ethnic and religious conflicts, which have become challenges for the sustainability of democracy in modern Nigeria. The chapter is divided into key sections: the first section attempts to look at ethnic and religious conflicts and situate them in a theoretical perspective.[3] Section two examines Nigerian precolonial situation where arguments are advanced to show that issues of religion and ethnicity were not after all so prominent.[4] The last section considers the contemporary times. In all of these sections, the connecting theme is the implications of ethnic and religious conflicts on sustaining democracy.

Ade Obayemi, in his examination of the early Yoruba and Edo-speaking peoples, categorized the precolonial political structures of sub-Saharan Africa into "mini and mega states"[5] without emphasis on ethnic and religious differences. In Nigeria, however, there has been interaction between religion and politics. The interplay of religion and politics has existed centuries before the European imperialism changed the map and configuration of Nigeria. Thus, the section on the colonial period asserts that the survival of European colonialism, and industrial capitalism, rested greatly on a stable and peaceful environment, enabling Nigeria to be a proper place for economic exploitation.

The British employed the divide and rule tactics for their economic interests and for successful political control on Nigeria. Ethnic and religious identities developed strongly during the colonial period because social and economic projects of the time instigated and exacerbated ethnic and religious consciousness and identity contestations. Ethnicity and religion provided extensive contact points for individuals and groups from Nigeria's diverse cultural and linguistic communities.[6] Thus, a struggle for survival resulted from harsh and difficult intra-ethnic competition. This placed some groups at a disadvantage. It led to constant conflict between ethnic and religious groups.[7]

In the post-colonial period, Nigeria has witnessed unprecedented conflicts of different kinds partly because those at the helm of political affairs did not possess the sense of patriotism that was necessary for building a viable and formidable country. They were interested in pursuing ethnic and religious goals, which in most cases conflicted with the needs of national unity and development. This raises the argument that political leaders put selfish political goals ahead of national interest. Instead, they have been ethno-centric and pursued religious interest to achieve their political goals. In most cases, their interests have conflicted with the issues of national unity and democratic stability.

Precolonial Background

It is important to emphasize that conflicts exist in every human society. While ethnic, religious, and political conflicts are normal, if not quickly resolved, they become dangerous when they turn violent and destructive. In a multi-ethnic and multi-religious country such as Nigeria, there is often the challenge of conflicts. When conflicts arise, how widespread they are may determine the magnitude of property destruction and human loss. Some scholars believe that conflicts bring out the best or worst in human beings, depending on the management skills or style applied towards their resolution.[8]

Although there were conflicts during the precolonial period, ethno-religious conflicts were uncommon. This is because ethnic groups were fused into the various sovereign chiefdoms, states, and village confederations. The Europeans merged together the numerous autonomous political units to constitute what is now known as Nigeria. Thus Nigeria accommodates many ethnic groups that have various cultural backgrounds and that practiced different religions, especially traditional religions and Islam. As mentioned earlier, conflicts between and within states were not ethnically based, but were simply used as tools to foster formidable and viable political authority. In the case of religions, Islam became a mobilizing tool to bring different ethnic groups together, a development that led to the establishment of the Sokoto Caliphate in the nineteenth century in the wake of the Sokoto jihad that Usman dan Fodio led.

The political units such as the Hausa states, the Benin, Igala, and Nupe Kingdoms, and Oyo Empire, disintegrated not because of ethnic or religious conflicts, but because of internal contradictions associated with environmental, political, and economic factors. The consciousness of ethnic and religious differences in Nigeria was a creation of the colonial and post-colonial order. Inter-regional wars among these polities sometimes occurred, but there was also a cooperative and symbiotic relationship between host and migrant communities.[9]

One important issue that merits attention is Y. B. Usman's argument that: "the sovereign kingdoms, chiefdoms, city states and villages confederations which the British conquered to establish the colony and protectorate of Nigeria were not ethnic entities with Yoruba, Edo, Kataf, Fulani, Nupe, Hausa, Ogoni, Kanuri, Ijaw etc."[10] This shows that ethnic or religious issues were not paramount and ethnic or religious conflicts non-existent. What existed in precolonial times was neither "sovereign ethnic political blocs"[11] nor religious ties. Usman argues further that religious conflicts that occurred were largely among the emirates in the Sokoto Caliphate and they were wars among Muslims. He cites examples of the conflicts that occurred in Bauchi in 1881; Bida in 1881-1882; Kano in 1893-1895, and Muri in the 1890s. These conflicts, as Usman observes, "did not pitch one ethnic group against another, but represented political conflicts within the same ethnic group or groups."[12] In the Yoruba kingdoms, Muslim elements including rulers engaged in traditional ritual practices. Among the northern Edo-speaking people as well as the Ekiti village groups, there were small Muslim polities who were more hostile to one another than they were to non-Muslims.[13]

Why do conflicts in the contemporary Nigeria take on a more dangerous dimension despite the level of development? Why is it that Christians or non-Muslims instead of fighting themselves (as it were in the precolonial days) are today killing either non-Muslims or non-Christians? What are the causes of the "ethnic and religious cleansing" that Nigeria has been experiencing in modern times? The changing phase of religious and political relations in Nigeria is working against sustainable democratic system (as represented by several religious conflicts).

Colonialism and Ethno-religious Conflicts

The seeds of ethnic and religious conflicts were sown in Nigeria during the colonial period. The nature of the colonial economy triggered migration of people from rural to urban areas for colonial or industrial jobs.[14] The demographic change negatively affected the economy of the rural areas. The European merchants and companies needed labor and several measures were used to build up a workforce. Also "during the colonial period, Islam and Christianity spread rapidly"[15] and most especially Christianity "produced a new elite, that controls the post colonial economy and bureaucracy."[16] The evolution of colonial Nigeria therefore created an integrative system whereby Muslims and Christians had to live in the same country, in some places,[17] while the numerous ethnic groups from different backgrounds[18] similarly cohabited together, due to the nature of the colonial economy.[19] The British did not care for the ethnic conglomeration, but were more concerned about their gains and the success of their political and economic policies.

The British colonial administration established "a new bureaucracy with some holdover elements from indigenous politics."[20] Although some ethnic groups suffered setbacks, several others were upgraded in status and enjoyed more power than before. In the 1930s and particularly during the economic depression, colonial policies became very harsh, and the reality forced many to migrate from one region to another, or from one urban center to another to survive.[21] This development brought together people from different ethnic and religious backgrounds. Meanwhile, more and more urban centers continued to receive "strangers" in what many urban historians referred to as the "Sabon gari" quarters.[22] Thus, ethnic as well as religious consciousness grew and was taken very seriously; most especially late in the colonial period. The demographic change was partly because of the aggressive drive for taxation.

The British policies continued to foster the consolidation of ethnic and religious identities so that new administrative units, based on cultural and linguistic differences, further promoted these identities, and encouraged inter-group struggles for privileges and resources. This means that the "British continued to enjoy a great deal from their tactics of divide and rule and at the same time continued to promote linguistic and cultural divisions."[23] Also, very significant is that the federal system continued to witness the emergence of three powerful and autonomous regions, namely, the North, the West, and the East as provided for in the 1946 Richard's Constitution.[24] The 1954 Constitution gave the regional governments power over education, agriculture, local government, health, and public works. The regions also shared with the federal government the power of economic development and higher education. The federal government itself retained the control over foreign policy, the police, and the army and some capital-consuming aspects of development like communication and transportation.[25] One major problem with the federal system was that it exacerbated ethnic and religious divisions because it became an outlet for ethnic patronage. This laid the foundation for modern politics where ethnic and religious patronage is wrecking damaging effects on Nigerian democracy.

The fear of marginalization by the various minority groups, which began in the colonial period, continued till independence and after.[26] Going by the role of regionalism in the distribution of power, every political party sought to consolidate and expand by appealing to ethnicity, and in some cases, religion. The British were able to contain most of the ethnic and religious conflicts that took place in the colonial period because of their political and military control of Nigeria. However, they were sowing a seed of division, which now poses a major challenge for sustainable democracy.

Post-colonial Ethnic and Religious Conflicts

With great jubilation and high expectations, Nigeria gained independence from Great Britain on October 1,1960. Nigerians were expecting radical and rapid socio-economic changes following independence. The euphoria, however, soon died down and the immediate complex socio-political experiences made it difficult to have "a unified national identity."[27] With the lack of experience in the parliamentary system and the multi-ethnic composition of Nigeria, it did not take long for the weak foundation of a democratic rule to begin to crack. The pre-existing ethnic and religious divide did not end with independence, and intra- and inter-regional problems persisted. Instead of peace and unity, a divisive civil war broke out in 1967.[28] The question of ethnicity and regionalism played prominent roles in the outbreak of the war. For many years, the Nigerian government had to grapple with uniting the country. After the war in 1970, the government embarked on reconciliation, rehabilitation, and reconstruction programs, but the wound, caused by the Civil War would not heal easily.

Within each region, ethnic minorities complained bitterly that majority ethnic groups dominated and marginalized them. For example, in the northern region the non-Muslim communities complained that the Hausa and Fulani dominated them, and many turned to Christianity as a form of protest against Islam. A series of politically-motivated riots degenerated into conflicts between 1960 and 1965, spurred by the Tiv's rejection of NPC domination.[29] In the East, minorities in the Delta area complained of Igbo's domination and similar complaints were made in the West. Inter-regional relations were characterized by profound hostilities resulting in uneven development.[30]

The inherited problems and institutions from colonialism in addition to the economic and political changes of the period, laid the foundations of the numerous religious conflicts that followed. For example, there were religious conflicts between 1970 and 1975. This was followed by the Shari'a controversy that resulted in crisis in 1976.[31] In 1978, a clash occurred between Muslim and Christian students of Ahmadu Bello University Zaria, killing six students.[32] Every attempt to unite Nigeria has been jeopardized by one crisis or the other. The collapse of the Second Republic in 1983 has been partly blamed on prevalent crises and conflicts, which caused insecurity throughout the country. More ethnic and religious conflicts took place in the 1980s and 1990s during General Ibrahim Babangida's military regime, with all of them having serious and devastating effects not only on the lives and properties of Nigerians. The series of conflicts also undermined attempts towards national development.

In 1980s, devastating riots broke out in Zaria, Kaduna, and Kano in which properties belonging to both Christians and Muslims were destroyed. The most prominent one was the Maitatsine conflict that erupted in December 1980 and which led to the killing of many people and resulted in extensive destruction of property. Between 1980 and 2005 ethnic and religious conflicts also resulted in massive human and material loss.[33] Table 1 shows some ethnic and religious conflicts that took place between 2000 and 2005.

Table 1: Selected Religious Violence between 2000 and 2005

Date	Location	Principal Actors
February 28, 2000	Kaduna (Kaduna State)	Kaduna city exploded in violence as Muslim and Christian extremists and other hoodlums clashed over the proposal to introduce *Sharia.*
February 29, 2000	Aba (Abia State)	The riot which began in Aba as a reprisal to that of Kaduna, which later spread to other Eastern states.
September 8, 2000	Kaltungo (Gombe State)	A religious violence that was sparked off by the presence of the state *Sharia* implementation committee.
December 2, 2000	Hadejia (Jigawa State)	A sectarian disturbance that was caused by a debate between Muslims and Christians. There was wanton destruction of worship places.
September 7, 2001	Jos (Plateau State)	A violent ethnic/religious crisis between Muslims/Hausa-Fulani and Christian/indigenes. The subject of discord between the Jasawa Development Association and Plateau Youth Council was originally over a political appointment in Jos North LGC.
September 15, 2001	Onitsha (Anambra State)	A reprisal killing of Northerners in Onitsha following the Jos crisis in which several Igbos were killed.
October 12, 2001	Kano (Kano State)	A peaceful anti-American protest over the bombing of Afghanistan turned violent, taking ethnic and religious tone. It degenerated into uncontrollable violence which claimed lives and damaged properties and places of worship.
June 2002	Yelwa Shendam Mayhem (Plateau State)	An ethnoreligious fracas between the native people (predominantly Christians) and Hausa settlers (predominantly Muslims).

November 21, 2002	Kaduna (Kaduna State)	A violent protest in Kaduna following a Newspaper editorial on hosting of beauty pageant in Nigeria.
January 2004	Yobe State	Militant Islamic group operating under the name of *Muhajirun* launched a Taliban- like attack on police. Men of the Nigerian Army killed five and arrested several others.
April 3, 2004	Makarfi (Kaduna State)	Religious protest in Makarfi town over alleged desecration of the *Qur'ran* by a Christian teenager.
May 1, 2004	Yelwa Shendam (Plateau State)	An ethnoreligious mayhem that claimed over 500 lives and many women and children were abducted by suspected Taroh militia. This was a revenge killing.
September 27, 2004	Limankara, (Borno State)	A self-styled *Taliban* group hiding on the Goza hills and Mandara mountains on the north-eastern boarder with Cameroon raided police stations killing officers and stealing ammunition.
January 16, 2005	Ipakodo (Lagos State)	A religious mayhem between OPC and Muslims over the erection of Ogun Shrine in a Muslim praying ground. Over 50 lives were feared lost.
August 20, 2005	Isale-Eko area of Lagos Island Local Government; Lagos State	No fewer than 30 Muslim youths feared dead when cultists and members of the out-lawed Odua Peoples Congress (OPC) attacked Muslims.

Source: J. I. Elaigwu *Crises and Conflict Management in Nigeria since 1980, in Crises and Conflict Management in Nigeria since 1980 Volume I: Causes and Dimensions of Conflict, ed.,* A.M Yakubu, *et al* (Kaduna: Nigerian Defence Academy, 2005), 57 – 76.

Challenges and Conclusion

During the colonial period, the British recognized the role a stable and conflict-free environment could play in enhancing economic exploitation and even the survival of the colonial economy. Hence, they established coercive institutions in order to deal with all forms of ethnic or cultural conflict and violence. Today, development is tied to peace and stability and conflicts can hinder achieving these. Lessons should be learned from the experiences of Sudan, Burundi, Rwanda, Liberia, and Sierra Leone. Terrible experiences of all forms of conflicts have made Ethiopia, Angola, and Mozambique backward and less developed democratically.

Poverty is one of the worst forms of violence, and in Nigeria, the gap between the rich and the poor is so wide that people use issues of religion and ethnicity to express their economic grievances. Many Christian preachers emphasize prosperity as a spiritual means of ending poverty. In many situations, those recruited into fighting are the people without any form of creativity and education or whose creative ingenuity is suppressed by poverty. Mostly the youth and unemployed, the perpetrators often use the opportunity of conflicts to loot and enrich themselves. Thus, high rate of unemployment and lack of democratic stability are associated with poverty and conflict. Apparently, a sustainable democratic system cannot be established where there is instability. Nigeria's greatness and its position as the "giant of Africa" have been hindered by the perennial occurrence of violence and concomitant destruction. Political instability has become the vogue and leaders use the poor and ignorant people to achieve their selfish interests. Political leaders have failed to appreciate the significance of a peaceful and violence-free environment.

All of the foregoing, especially religious and ethnic conflicts had serious implications for a sustainable democracy and national development. Ethnic and religious conflicts often jeopardize efforts to build a sustainable and stable democracy. Nigeria is blessed with abundant human and material resources and the channeling of these toward national development can bring about positive economic transformation. There is an organic relationship between democratic stability and socio-economic formation, which determines the nature of democratic stability.

A volatile social formation would produce an unstable democratic process and would lead to bad governance. The energy dispensed on ethnic and religious conflicts can be channeled toward achieving peace, unity, and national development. Issues of national interest should remain a top priority while the pursuit of ethnic or religious agenda should be minimized. Nigeria is blessed with rich historical and cultural heritage, which are a great national asset. These can move the country to achieving great heights. The reality, however, is that ethnic and religious conflicts have continued to suppress national integration and national development.

Religion and ethnicity can play a very major role in the development of Nigeria if they are properly utilized. In many countries of the world, religion has been a very powerful tool of development. This chapter has argued that for Nigeria to attain a stable and sustained democracy and development, ethnic and religious interests should be differentiated from core national issues. Ethnic and religious issues should be put aside in the development and the principles of universal choice, rule of law, accountability and legitimacy should be encouraged. Nigerians must turn away from ethnic and religious sentiments and work out democratic frameworks, devoid of ethnicity and religion but what suit the environment. There should be a balance of the primacy of democratic politics with that of economics for betterment of all in full equality and justice.

Notes

1. The forces that have continued to threaten the Nigerian unity and its survival are exhaustively discussed and analyzed in Y. B. Usman, "History and the Challenges to the Peoples and Polities of Africa in the 21st Century," The 1999 Dike Memorial Lecture delivered at the 44th Annual Congress of the Historical Society of Nigeria, November 22, 1999; Y. B. Usman, "Nigerian unity and Nigerian History: Beyond Fairy Tares (Abuja: An opening contribution to the 1st Annual Dialogue, organized by the Citizen Magazine, at Conference Hall, Sheraton Hotel, Lagos, August 20, 1992; Y. B. Usman, "Nigerian Myths and Nigerian Realities," A lecture delivered at the National Institute for Cultural Orientation course on "Perspectives in Nigeria Cultural Diplomacy," Federal Palace Hotels, Victoria Island, Lagos, 1994; Innocent Jooji, *Mending the Cracked Pot: Perspective on Conflict, Non-Violence, Social Justice and Reconciliation in Nigeria* (Ibadan, Nigeria: Daily Graphics Nigeria Ltd., 2003).
2. For more information on this and other related issues, see: E. M. Uka, "Ethnic, Religious and Communal Conflicts in Nigeria: Implications for Security" in *Security, Social Services, and Sustainable Development in Nigeria*, ed., Chidi Ikonne, I. O. Williams and E. N. Nwagbara (Port Harcourt, Nigeria: Fulbright Alumni Association of Nigeria, 2005), 115-127, Chudi Uwazurike, "Urban Violence as Metaphor: Insecurity, Ethno-Religions Fault Lines and the Crises of Democratic Legitimation," in *Urban Violence, Ethnic Militias and the Challenge of Democratic Consolidation in Nigeria*, ed., Tunde Babalola (Ibadan, Nigeria: Malt House Press Ltd, 2003), 77-89.
3. E. M. Iji, "Theoretical Perspectives on Conflict," in *Crises and Conflict Management in Nigeria since 1980*, ed., A.M Yakubu, *et al* (Kaduna: Nigerian Defence Academy, 2005), 83 -106.

4. Y. K. Gandu, "Blood and Race: Intellectual Schizophrenia and Racial Theory of Ethnic Conflicts in Africa," in JOSUGA, *Jos Journal of Humanities*, Vol.1, No. 3, 2003, 105-119.
5. Ade Obayemi, "The Yoruba and Edo-speaking peoples and their Neighours before 1600" in *History of West Africa*, Vol. 1, eds., J. F. Ade Ajayi and Michael Crowder (London: Longman Group Limited, 1971),196-263.
6. Gandu, 107.
7. Ibid., 107. See also G. W. Skinner, "The Nature of Loyalties in Indonesia" in *Social Change: The Colonial Situation*, ed., J. Wallastein (New York: Wiley, 1966).
8. Iji, 86.
9. O. Nnoli, *Ethnic Politics in Nigeria* (Enugu: Fourth Dimension Publishing Co. Ltd, 1978), 35.
10. Usman, "Nigerian myths and Nigerian Realities," 5.
11. Ibid., 6.
12. Usman, "Nigerian Unity and Nigerian History," 11.
13. Ibid.
14. Nnoli, 51.
15. Falola, 1-2.
16. Ibid., 2.
17. Ibid., 49.
18. The statistics of Nigerians ethnic group are available at the following sources: Falola, 310; Ralph Uwedue, *Reflections on the Nigerian Civil War: Facing the Future* (London: Meier and Homes Ltd, 1971), xxx, especially the information contained in his maps showing the tribal/ethnic distribution in Nigeria.
19. Detailed analysis on the colonial economy could be obtained from M. Y. Mangvwat, 1985 "The Colonial Economy and Society of Nigeria, 1900-1960," paper presented to the seminar on Nigerian Economy and Society since the Berlin Conference: 1884-1985, organized by the Faculty of Arts and Social Sciences, ABU Zaria, 11-15 November, 1985; others are: Nabudare Dan, *The Political Economy of Imperialism* (Dares-Salam: Zed Publishers, 1977); and Bade Onimode, *Imperialism and Underdevelopment in Nigeria* (London: Macmillan, 1983).
20. Falola, 58.
21. Detailed analysis on this and other major issues is available at: M. S. Abdulkadir, *Structuring, Struggling and Surviving Economic Depression in Northern Nigeria: The 1930s as a Preview of the Present.* Inaugural lecture series, Bayero University Kano, Kano, No. 9, 2004; J. A. Ohiare, "The History of Migra-

tions from the Okene Area to Cocoa Belt of Western Nigeria: 1900-1939," B.A. Thesis, Department of History, ABU, Zaria.

22. The population at Sabon-gari in northern Nigeria for instance cut across the different ethnic groups with different religious backgrounds. For more on these and other information, see: E. O. Oyedele, "Colonial Urbanisation in Northern Nigeria: Kaduna 1913-1960," Ph. D. Dissertation, Department of History, ABU, Zaria, 1987; A.V. Dhliwayo, "A History of Sabon-Gari Zaria 1911-1950: A Study of Urban Colonial Administration, " Ph. D. Dissertation, Department of History, ABU, Zaria, 1986; R.O, Olaniyi, "Nationalist Movement in a Multi-Ethnic Community of Sabon-Gari Kano," in *Perspectives on Kano British Relations*, ed., M. O. Hambolu, Kano: Gidan Makama Museum, 2003, 222-231.
23. Nnoli, 51.
24. E. O. Awa, *Federal Government in Nigeria* (Berkeley: University of California Press, 1967).
25. Falola, 53.
26. Ibid.
27. Ibid.
28. Akinwumi, *Crises and Conflicts in Nigeria*; R. Uweche, *Reflections on the Nigeria Civil War.*
29. For a detailed account on this see R. Anifowese, *Violence and Politics in Nigeria: The Tiv and Yoruba Experience* (New York: NOK, 1984); J. I. Tseayo, *Conflict and Incorporation in Nigeria: The Integration of the Tiv* (Zaria: Gaskiya Corporation Ltd, 1975); Apegba Ker, *Tiv Poetry and Politics: A Study of Tarker Golozo* (Abuja: Kia Books, 2002); and T. Makar, *The History of Political Change Among the Tiv in the 19th and 20th Century* (Enugu: Fourth Dimension Publishing Co. Ltd).
30. Falola, 54-55.
31. For More information, see the following: M. H. Kukah, *Religion, Politics and Power in Northern Nigeria* (Ibadan: Spectrum Books, 1994; F. U. Okafor, *et al*, *New Strategies for Curbing Ethnic and Religious Conflicts in Nigeria* (Enugu: Fourth Dimensional, 1997).
32. E. M. Uka, "Ethnic, Religious and Religious and Communal Conflicts in Nigeria: Implications for Security," in *Security, Social Services, and Sustainable Development in Nigeria*, 119.
33. For sources on conflicts, see: J. I. Elaigwu, "Crises and Conflict Management in Nigeria since 1980," in *Crisis and Conflict Management in Nigeria since 1980*, 28-77.

Chapter Four

Beyond Secularism: The Shadow of Religion on Nigerian Democracy

J. Shola Omotola

This chapter is a critical reinterpretation of the problem of secularism in Nigeria, given the continuous ominous shadow of religion on the country's democracy. Nigeria is a plural society with several ethnic and religious groups. While this ethno-religious configuration may not be all that unique, there is an apparent overlap of ethnic and religious boundaries. Each dominant ethnic group in a geographical area is associated with a particular dominant religion and this has added troubling twist and turns to the configuration. This diffusion and attendant woes particularly recurrent ethno-religious conflicts would appear to have informed the constitutional adoption of secularism in Nigeria.[1] By secularism, the Nigerian state seeks not only to maintain some form of a neutral and independent posture on religious matters, but also to allow Nigerians the freedom to associate with any religion of their choice. The essence was to demarcate between the two realms – state and religion – and by so doing reduce the influence of this powerful force of identity on the nation-building system. In reality, Nigeria does not appear to be a complete secular state and the situation led to many challenges, which almost brought about a collapse, the most recent example being the Shari'a debacle under the fledging democracy.[2]

To what extent has Nigeria been able to uphold its secular posture? What have been its accomplishments and failures especially with respect to the democratization process? How can the secular ideology be reinvented to strengthen democracy in Nigeria? These are the core questions, which this chapter addresses, the primary thrust of which is to explore the shadowy nature of religion on Nigerian democracy with a view to charting an alternative way forward. The chapter seeks to contribute to the existing literature on the understanding of the dynamics of secularism vis-à-vis democratization in a plural and complex setting like Nigeria. Drawing insights from state and societal practices in contemporary Nigeria, the chapter argues that religion has continued to cast an ominous shadow on democracy. This is largely due to the poverty of ideology and the weak institutionalization of democratic forces, especially political parties and civil society; the economic softness of the state, both of which create room for the exploitation of forces of identities in popular mobilization; constitutional ambiguities; and the absence of democratic citizenship with democratic mindset, willing and capable of playing politics of issues, instead of politics of identity.

The analysis is underscored by some assumptions. The first is that the presumed positive correlation between secularism and sustainable inter-religious and ethnic relations in a plural state like Nigeria is problematic and may be in the mythical realm. The second is that for secularism to produce the desired results, it must be deeply rooted in political institutionalization capable of generating sustainable social capital, that is, a generalized sense of trust among the citizenry. The third is that in the absence of such institutionalization and social capital, secularism may become a liability, rather than an asset, in the socio-political processes of the state. The rest of the chapter is organized into a number of sections: the first provides an analysis of the concept of secularism; the second explores the politics of secularism in Nigeria; and the third examines the shadow of religion on the democratization process in Nigeria. This is followed by an analysis of the imperatives of political institutionalization. The final section summarizes the central arguments, delineates its conclusions and recommendations.

The Concept of Secularism

The concept of secularism certainly falls into the category of social science concepts regarded as essentially contested. Across different political systems, secularism is "unquestionably the most misused word."[3] This is partly because the concept can be used in several related, but different ways, thus making it difficult to know the exact meaning. It is not surprising that secularism is often equated with an ideology or a philosophy. Secularism is also sometimes used to imply separation of state from religion - a social movement. In some cases, secularism is considered a religion.[4] Against the background of these conceptual problems, a survey of definitions of secularism may not really advance our knowledge of the concept. This is why Hammed Agberemi suggests that it is "more useful to describe a secular society or a secular state, than to define 'secularism.'" Agberemi's position emanates from his perception of secularism "as a historic construct; a worldview, an ideology or philosophy, or a political practice."[5]

Secularism is commonly regarded as "an ideology that holds that religious issues should not be the basis of *Politics,* or (in the extreme) that religion has no place in public life."[6] Essentially, secularism seeks to preserve the religious neutrality of government and cultures. As Andrew Coates put it, secularism connotes "the freedom of the public sphere from religious dogma."[7] All of these conceptions have been hotly contested and largely flawed. For these scholars, reducing secularism to separation of state and religion amounts to conspiracy against religion and a contradiction of the facts of history.. This is because "the secular," according to Antje Jackelen, "is a companion of religion rather than its enemy."[8] For John Hendryx, the pretended neutrality, which secularism presupposes, has placed secularists in a dominant position, thereby handling them exclusive power in public policy processes. This, according to him, has not allowed for the use of secularism against the "intrusive religious tyranny" of the secularists into public policy.[9] Given this array of criticisms, it is better to examine the epistemology of the concept.

George Jacob Holyoake formulated the foundational work connecting secularism to multicultural societies in 1846. He coined the term secularism to describe "a form of opinion which concerns itself only with questions, the issues of which can be tested by the experience of this life."[10] Holyoake, a leader of the English secularist and free thought movement, was concerned with a humanist philosophy, one capable of guaranteeing human needs in life. While secularism, in this sense, generally encompasses a sphere of knowledge, values, and actions, which are independent of religious authority, there seems to be nothing about its original formulation that excludes possible interactions between religion and the state. Indeed, secularism was originally developed within a religious context particularly Christianity for the sake of preserving peace among Christians.[11]

By implication, it seems that the perversion and contradictions that surround the concept in the post-Holyoake era emerged from the neo-Holyoake exponents of the concept. Scholars appear to have substituted secularism with secularization, which emphasizes a kind of total separation of religion and state. It is, perhaps, this secularization of secularism that breeds secular fundamentalism because the more religious groups are alienated from the state, the more such groups become a symbol of resistance and the more the proclivity of such groups to fundamentalism. It does seem that one of the pretensions of neo-secularists is the idea of a completely neutral public sphere in religious matters. Such pretensions find resonance in political realities across nation states, making it difficult for "secular states" to live a truly secular life. The result, as in the Nigerian experience, has been rising ethno-religious conflicts, amidst deepening constitutional crisis over religious affairs. The relative weakness of alternative frameworks of socio-political engineering such as political parties and civil society, has only served to complicate the problem.[12]

Politics of Secularism in Nigeria

The politics of secularism in Nigeria began in the colonial period. Prior to the advent of colonialism, each major group of what later became known as Nigeria had its distinct religion under what is generally referred to as African Traditional Religion (ATR). Many gods and goddesses were revered in different parts of Nigeria. These include Ogun (god of iron), Sango or Amadioha (god of thunder), Oya (goddess of the river), and several others.[13] The coming of Islam and Christianity, however, altered the religious setting of the country. Islam penetrated several parts of the Nigerian society long before the arrival of the Europeans. As part of their "civilizing mission," the Europeans introduced Christianity as an instrument of civilization. While the southern part of Nigeria received Christianity, the northern part was predominantly Muslim. By the early decades of the twentieth century, Islam had dominated the northern region while Christianity had been widespread in the south. For their political expediency, the British prevented European missionaries from operating in the Muslim-dominated North, where their indirect rule system was very efficient. Thus religious tension and dichotomy existed in Nigeria throughout the colonial period.

The religious division of the country played major roles in the political arrangement and set up, which came into existence at independence in October 1960 when Nigeria inherited a parliamentary democracy deeply implicated in ethnic and religious pluralism. The religious dimensions have been very unique, given the fast ascendancy of Islam and Christianity over the ATR, the oldest and only autochthonous form of religion. Given the advantages of education, health, and other social services associated with

Islam and Christianity, and the political support they received from the government, there has been a deliberate marginalization of the ATR.

The flawed religious configuration and attendant inter-religious relations set the tone of the politics of secularism in post-independence Nigeria.[14] The Nigerian state realized a long time ago the deadly impact religious issues could have, following the virulent and vituperative debates it generated in the 1977–1978 constitutional conference, which gave birth to the Second Republic. However, its interventionist strategy particularly by constitutionally making Nigeria a secular state has not been able to yield the desired result. All Nigerian constitutions since 1979 have always provided in Section 10 (1) that, "the government of the federation or of a state shall not adopt any religion as state religion." This provision is further strengthened by section 38 (1-3) of the constitution, which guarantees freedom of thought, conscience and religion. Section 38(1) stipulates:

> Every person shall be entitled to freedom of thought, conscience and religion, including freedom to change his religion or belief, and freedom (either alone or in community with others, and in public or private) to manifest and propagate his religion or belief in worship, teaching, practice and observance.[15]

Despite these provisions, religious issues continue to be problematic in the country. The eventual politicization of religion has limited the effectiveness of the secular clauses. It does seem, as the Nigerian experience illustrates, that religion can hardly be separated from the state and its politics, in so much as people give serious considerations to it when they are confronted with political issues and decisions. A number of issues in Nigerian secular politics certainly lend credence to this claim. For one thing, discourses on secularism in Nigeria have since been reduced to engagement and or confrontation between Muslims and Christians, allowing adherents of ATR little or no space to engage the state. This may not be unconnected with the relative powerlessness that has come to characterize ATR, especially given its limited population vis-à-vis other religions. The exact population of each religion has been controversial, but the most popular estimate puts it at 50:40:10 for Islam, Christianity, and ATR, respectively. This has been challenged as another source, which claimed to be relying on "informed estimates," puts it at 53:45:2 in the same order.[16] Given this configuration, Christianity and Islam have not only asserted their dominance, they have also dominated politics.

Another dominant feature of the secular politics in Nigeria is the upper hand of Islam over Christianity in the public sphere. The merging of ethnic and religious identities along geographical boundaries has made the North predominantly Islamic and the South primarily Christian. At independence, the North had only one region and the South had two (East and West), but the northern region was larger in size and population than the two southern regions combined. Today, the continuous processes of adjustment to the Nigerian federation have altered the balance in favor of the Islamic North. Through state creation exercises (1967, 1976, 1989, 1991, and 1996), the North has gained at the expense of the South, as they now have nineteen and seventeen states respectively. The same thing goes for local government creation, a development that gave the North more access to national wealth since these state and local government structures are the bases of revenue allocation.[17] This development may not be unconnected with the long rule of the military where ethnicity was an issue and northern officers were more prominent than southerners. Of the thirty years of military rule in Nigeria, the northerners have led for twenty-five years, leaving the south with only five years.

The politics of secularism in Nigeria violates what has come to be known as the principle of institutional separation, that is, "the constitutional provision which forbids the making of any law, and therefore the taking of any executive action, that involves the interlocking of the official functions of the state with the official or institutional functions of any [religion]."[18] Some of such contradictions manifest in state patronage and involvement in religious institutions or affairs in various forms. For example, the federal government provided ₦10 million (approximately $10,000.00) each to Muslim and Christian groups to build their places of worship at the Federal Capital Territory, Abuja in 1982.[19] A rehabilitation committee for the National Mosque was set up with President, Olusegun Obasanjo as the Chairman and Vice-president Atiku Abubakar acting as his deputy. This is a contradiction given the country's much-orchestrated secular claims. The government at all levels is known for its huge financial input to sponsoring pilgrims to the "holy land" from both religions. In all these, the ATR has little or no place, calling into question Nigeria's secular posture. The politicization of secularism by all principal actors (the state, Islam, and Christianity) has been a major factor in its ineffectiveness in guaranteeing religious harmony and stability in Nigeria.

The Shadow of Religion on Nigerian Democracy

The politics of secularism has allowed religion to cast its ominous shadow on the politics and policy processes of the country. Nowhere was this better manifested than in the democratization process, where religious identities have been severely and severally manipulated for personal and ethnic ends. Manipulation has been explained as "essentially controlling the action of a person or group without that person or group knowing the goals, purpose and method of that control and without even being aware that a form of control is being exercised upon them at all."[20] In the religious context, manipulation connotes a campaign of systematic utilization of religious sentiments for the sinister and reactionary purpose of diverting attention away from reality. This wears "a cloak of religion in order to confuse and divert the attention of our people from their harsh conditions of existence."[21] One major factor that has aided the easy manipulation of religion is connected with massive poverty, which makes people easily susceptible to different kinds of identity transformation. This became more prominent beginning from the Babangida regime (1985-1993), essentially because of the major dislocations brought to bear upon the political economy by the implementation of the Structural Adjustment Program (SAP) and has since assumed a frightening proportion.[22]

Religious considerations and manipulation have always influenced political debates in the country. Beginning from the 1977-1978 Constitutional Drafting Committee (CDC) to the 2005 National Political Reform Conference (NPRC), religious issues have been very influential. At the CDC, for example, one of the hottest issues that almost tore the committee apart was secularism and the Shari'a question. For the Muslims, secularism was an equivalent of atheism, which must not be allowed or made a constitutional matter. At the same time, Islamic leaders advocated very strongly for the introduction of Shari'a as a binding legal system for the Muslims. The Christians were, however, vehemently opposed to these demands, pointing to their potentially damaging effect on the fundamental human rights of citizens, including Muslims and non-Muslims, and national, peace, unity, and stability.[23] The Muslims eventually gained an upper hand as they succeeded in ensuring that the word "secularism" did not appear anywhere in the constitution, not even in the secular clauses. In addition, the CDC recommended the establishment of a Federal Shari'a Court of Appeal to serve as an intermediate Court of Appeal between the states' Shari'a Courts of Appeal and the Supreme Court of Nigeria. The states' Shari'a Court of Appeal shall be established at the discretion of each state.[24]

One other crucial issue in inter-religious relations in Nigeria was the controversy that surrounded Nigeria's entry into the Organization of the Islamic Conference (OIC) in 1986. This followed the decision of General Ibrahim Babangida to take advantage of Nigeria's observer status into full membership. To this end, Babangida sent a powerful delegation, comprising Rilwan Lukman, Abubakar Alhaji, Abdulkadir Ahmed, Ibrahim Dasuki, and Abubakar Gumi to the 16th OIC in Fez, Morocco. Upon tabling their request for membership, the OIC offered Nigeria full membership. The debate and controversy that followed pushed the country further the brinks of religious violence. This forced the government to withdraw its membership. As Toyin Falola describes the impasse:

> In every way, Nigeria's entry into the OIC turned out to be a costly miscalculation. The resulting controversy polarized the country along the religious divides more than had any other issue in Nigeria's history. Unlike the other major religious-political issues, al-Sharia and secularity, which has been brewing for decades, the OIC crisis erupted overnight, and as it happened, the Nigerian population did not know about the OIC crisis until it was already well underway.[25]

The precarious balance of religion and politics came to the fore again at the National Political Reform Conference (NPRC) in 2005, which the Obasanjo administration convened to address some national questions, including religion.[26] Justice Niki Tobi was made the chairman while Rev. Father Mathew Hassan Kukah was the secretary. Because the two are Christians from southern Nigeria, there was a spontaneous response from the Muslims, who demanded for representation in the high hierarchy of the conference. In reaction to the demand, the government appointed Professor Ishaq Oloyede, then Deputy Vice Chancellor of Administration at the University of Ilorin, as co-secretary with Hassan Kukah. This action shows that the government was sensitive of the pivotal position of religion and the balancing factor in a multi-religious and plural polity such as Nigeria.

From all indications, religion has played and continues to play decisive roles in national politics and national development. Religion has been an important factor underlying electoral politics in Nigeria, except for the 1993 election that not only featured a Muslim-Muslim ticket in the Social Democratic Party (SDP), but the two parties, SDP and National Republican Convention (NRC) featured Muslim presidential candidates.

Subsequent elections in 1999 and 2003 had strong imprints of ethno-religious forces. This was reflected in the winning pattern of the parties and candidates in their ethno-religious strongholds.[27] This may have been so as a result of the strong influences of religious leadership and organizations, which have assumed the role of political mobilization. These organizations include the Christian Association of Nigeria (CAN), the Jama'atu Nasril Islamiyya (JNI), and the Supreme Council of Islamic Affairs (SCIA). Because of the strong influences of these and related bodies, mosques and churches have become the targets of politicians, using clerics to mobilize their adherents primarily for electioneering purposes. Among notable religious leaders who used religion as a mobilizing instrument were the Archbishop Anthony Olubunmi Okogie and the late Sheikh Abubakar Gumi, both of whom have been described as "deeply religious, strongly motivated and controversial leaders. Both are manipulative men, able to make political gains for their religions while claiming to represent the masses."[28]

Muhammed Buhari, (the All Nigerian People's Party's Presidential flag bearer) in the 2003 and 2007 elections called on Muslims to vote for only Muslim candidates. This comment received wide condemnation and became a major issue in the media in the 2007 presidential election. The situation was not so different at state levels where Alhaji Rauf Aregbesola, the Action Congress (AC) gubernatorial candidate in Osun state, reportedly gave Islamic clerics and mosques "gifts," claiming that it was the turn of Muslims to govern the state. This religio-political gimmick failed owning to the opponent's power of incumbency and support from the ruling party. In both the 2003 and 2007 elections, there were people who voted for candidates who belonged to a particular religion. Pastor Chris Okotie of the Household of God Church claimed that God wanted him to become the president of Nigeria therefore he was the presidential candidate of Fresh Democratic Party (FDP) in the 2007 elections. Although he was not successful, he drew his supporters mainly among Christians. In a society that claims to be secular but sharply divided by religion, it is not difficult to detect the shadow of religion in the democratic system.

The most dangerous dimension of the shadow of religion on Nigerian democracy has been the pervasiveness of religious crises, shrouded in ethnic garbs across the country.[29] From the 1980s, there has been a high level of religious intolerance and the country has been engulfed in inter-religious conflicts. All of these have led to violent and disturbing eruptions. For this list of the religious riots that occurred in Nigeria between 2000 and 2005, see Chapter 3. The table below shows the frequency and severity of the religious riots:

Table 1: Selected Religious Violence between 2000 and 2005

Date	Location	Principal Actors
February 28, 2000	Kaduna (Kaduna State)	Kaduna city exploded in violence as Muslim and Christian extremists and other hoodlums clashed over the proposal to introduce *Sharia.*
February 29, 2000	Aba (Abia State)	The riot which began in Aba as a reprisal to that of Kaduna, which later spread to other Eastern states.
September 8, 2000	Kaltungo (Gombe State)	A religious violence that was sparked off by the presence of the state *Sharia* implementation committee.
December 2, 2000	Hadejia (Jigawa State)	A sectarian disturbance that was caused by a debate between Muslims and Christians. There was wanton destruction of worship places.
September 7, 2001	Jos (Plateau State)	A violent ethnic/religious crisis between Muslims/Hausa-Fulani and Christian/indigenes. The subject of discord between the Jasawa Development Association and Plateau Youth Council was originally over a political appointment in Jos North LGC.
September 15, 2001	Onitsha (Anambra State)	A reprisal killing of Northerners in Onitsha following the Jos crisis in which several Igbos were killed.
October 12, 2001	Kano (Kano State)	A peaceful anti-American protest over the bombing of Afghanistan turned violent, taking ethnic and religious tone. It degenerated into uncontrollable violence which claimed lives and damaged properties and places of worship.
June 2002	Yelwa Shendam Mayhem (Plateau State)	An ethnoreligious fracas between the native people (predominantly Christians) and Hausa settlers (predominantly Muslims).

November 21, 2002	Kaduna (Kaduna State)	A violent protest in Kaduna following a Newspaper editorial on hosting of beauty pageant in Nigeria.
January 2004	Yobe State	Militant Islamic group operating under the name of *Muhajirun* launched a Taliban- like attack on police. Men of the Nigerian Army killed five and arrested several others.
April 3, 2004	Makarfi (Kaduna State)	Religious protest in Makarfi town over alleged desecration of the *Qur'ran* by a Christian teenager.
May 1, 2004	Yelwa Shendam (Plateau State)	An ethnoreligious mayhem that claimed over 500 lives and many women and children were abducted by suspected Taroh militia. This was a revenge killing.
September 27, 2004	Limankara, (Borno State)	A self-styled *Taliban* group hiding on the Goza hills and Mandara mountains on the north-eastern boarder with Cameroon raided police stations killing officers and stealing ammunition.
January 16, 2005	Ipakodo (Lagos State)	A religious mayhem between OPC and Muslims over the erection of Ogun Shrine in a Muslim praying ground. Over 50 lives were feared lost.
August 20, 2005	Isale-Eko area of Lagos Island Local Government; Lagos State	No fewer than 30 Muslim youths feared dead when cultists and members of the out-lawed Odua Peoples Congress (OPC) attacked Muslims.

Source: Isawa J. Elaigwu, *The Politics of Federalism in Nigeria* (Jos, Nigeria: Aha Publishing House Ltd, 2005), 213-217.

The numerous conflicts show the extent to which religion especially the politics of Shari'a, has intermixed with politics to cause disturbances, riots, and insecurity in a country that has just begun to enjoy democratic rule. The implications of these religious conflicts have been negative on Nigerian democracy. One negative effect is that instead of unity, religions are dividing the people of Nigeria. Religious conflicts send threats to sustainable national security, integration, and development. Not only do they weaken democratic institutions by overstretching them, they also drain national resources, as substantial amount is spent on conflict management and conflict resolution. As much as they divert the government's attention away from governance and developmental issues (which are most often substituted with conflict management), they also scare potential foreign investors away.[30] Nigerian economy is negatively affected because foreign investors are reluctant to invest in the country due to instability and insecurity.

The Imperative of Political Institutionalization

The foregoing analyses suggest the heavy presence of religion in politics and the monumental failure of secularism as a political practice in Nigeria. The failure is well connected with the politicization of secularism as an ideology of religious balancing, giving rise to the manipulation of religion, especially in the politics and policy processes. However, the failure seems rooted in a higher domain, which allows for the heavy reliance on forces of identity particularly ethnicity and religion as bases of political mobilization. Politicians utilize Christianity and Islam to garner supporters to achieve or promote their political ambitions. This situation relates to the weak institutionalization of political instruments of mobilization such as political parties, civil society organizations, and the mass media. Under these circumstances, it seems preposterous to believe that a nebulous constitutional provision as Nigeria's secular clauses would offer the magic wand to curtail the politicization of religion and religious excesses.[31]

Ideally, entrenching a sustainable regime of religious tolerance and balancing requires a great deal of social capital, defined as the building of a sense of generalized trust among citizens. Building such a trust has limited relationship with the constitution, though not excluded from it, than with the political actors. These actors can also function well provided they operate within institutionalized contexts, where basic political institutions have become mere routine. In such instances, political parties would be founded and organized upon clearly defined ideological stance, which constitutes the core basis of affinity and mobilization.[32] By the same reason of deep-rootedness, civil society can also organize and mobilize around issues, not forces of identity. Unfortunately, these are institutions that are weakly established as a result of prolonged military rule, attendant culture of violence, and strong adherence to religion. Nigerian parties are not only grossly deficient ideologically, but also behave like mini-armies with little or no regard for due process. This has tended to make them more of a liability than asset. The same thing goes for the civil society and mass media that are not only polarized along the line of identity forces, but are also not well-rooted in the society. As such, these organs manifest tendencies toward fragmentation and organizational weakness.[33]

The result is their inability to build social capital that would unite Nigerians across religious divides, capable of generating and sustaining generalized trust among the citizenry. This weak institutional capacity has been complicated by the less than altruistic dispositions of the power elite manifested essentially in their adversarial elite behavior. Such behavior is informed by and rooted in ethno-religious considerations, through which they champion ethno-regional and personal interests. In such a situation, secularism and indeed any other constitutional public policy can work effectively to the extent that the wider political context allows it and in most cases, the political context as one that characterizes the Nigerian setting briefly illustrated above suffocates, rather than strengthen public policies.[34] It is for this reason that the secular posture of the Nigerian state has, for the better part of its declaration and practice, remained largely problematic. The situation may continue for years to come unless something drastic is done about the wider institutional political context to make it serve as formidable bedrock of the true practice of secularism.

Conclusion

This chapter has undertaken a reinterpretation of the problems of secularism in Nigeria vis-à-vis the democratization process. It underscores how the faulty implementation of the secular clause (an offshoot of its misleading theoretical premises), has continued to cast an ominous shadow on democracy in Nigeria. This manifests in the manipulation and transformation of religious identities for political ends, resulting in a threatening sustainable regime of ethno-religious violence across the country, even as crucial national political debates are being influenced and colored by forces of religion. In the ensuring struggle for ascendancy by the two dominant religions, the "secular" state, that is supposed to be neutral and unbiased if it must intervene, has been severely compromised. Not only has the Nigerian state become an active participant in religious affairs, given its "secular practices," it also has been grossly incapacitated in maintaining fairness and equity in its relations with existing religions. In this "secular marginalization and exclusion," traditional religions and other neo-religious movements such as Eckankar that cannot be classified as Islamic or Christian, in the real sense of the terms, have been the worst hit.

The problem, as the analysis suggests, may really not be with secularism as praxis per se. Indeed, there seems to be nothing inherently wrong about secularism, especially in a multicultural state like Nigeria. Much of it seems to be largely dependent on the wider political context, which encompasses the level of political institutionalization of core establishments and their actors in the democratization process. In the Nigerian context, such institutions as political party, civil society, mass media, and so on seem to be fragmented and organizationally weak, thereby limiting their democratic credentials.

If the secular clause would help to engender religious balancing and a truly secular state in Nigeria, there is need to address the problem of weak institutionalization of politics and its institutions. This means that a continuous process of socio-political reengineering at all levels of governance has to take place. This may be a difficult task given the fact that the state is expected to play a leading role in the mobilization process. The state would have to develop a stronger level of political will to divest itself of inherent sentiments and contradictions in its secular practices.

Notes

1. Hameed Agberemi, "Nigeria Beyond Secularism and Islamism: Fashioning a Reconsidered Rights Paradigm for a Democratic Multicultural Society," in M. A. Baderin, et al, eds. *Islam and Human Rights: Advocacy for Social Change in Local Contexts* (New Delhi: Global Rights, 2006), 301-374; Toyin Falola, *Violence in Nigeria: The Crisis of Religious Politics and Secular Ideologies* (Rochester, NY: University of Rochester Press, 1998), 69–102; Simeon O. Ilesanmi, *Religious Pluralism and the Nigerian State* (Athens: Ohio University Centre for International Studies, 1992), 55–207.
2. E. Davies, "Secularity and State Practices in Nigeria," in *Contemporary Issues in Nigerian Affairs,* ed., H. O. Danmole, et al, (Ibadan, Nigeria: Sunad Publishers Ltd., 1995), 98-130; J. Isawa Elaigwu, *The Politics of Federalism in Nigeria* (Jos, Nigeria: Aha Publishing House, 2005), particularly Chapter 8 entitled "The Shadow of Religion on Nigerian Federalism," 203-242.
3. M. V. Kamath, "What is Secularism?" *News Today,* www.newstoday.com/guest/2702gu1.htm.
4. "Secularism and Separation: What is Secularism? Who are Secularists?" http://atheism.about.com/od/secularismseparation/Secularism_Separation_What_is_Secularism_Who_Are_Secularists.htm. Retrieved on 19/03/2007.
5. Agberemi, "Nigeria Beyond Secularism and Islamism," 332.

6. See, "Secularity (Non-religiosity)" http://help.com/tag/663808-secularity-non- religiosity. Retrieved on 19/03/2007.
7. Andrew Coats, "In Defence of Militant Secularism," *What Next?* No. 29; Cited in Ian Birchall, "So What is Secularism?" www.whatnextjournal.co.uk/pages/Back/Wnext30/Secular.html. Retrieved on 19/03/2007.
8. Antje Jackelen, "What is "Secular?" Techno-Secularism and Spirituality," *Zygon: Journal of Religion and Science*, 40, 4, 2005, 863.
9. John Hendryx, "Why is Secularism Exempt from the Separation of Church and State?" http://www.monergism.com/thethreshold/articles/onsite/secularism_exempt.html.
10. Cited in "Secularism and Separation: What is Secularism? Who are Secularists?" http://atheism.about.com/od/secularismseparation/Secularism_Separation_What_is_Secularism_Who_Are_Secularists.htm. See also George Jelliss, "What is Secularism?" Leicester Secular Society, First Draft, 13 June, 2005. http://homepages.stayfree.co.uk/lss/secular.htm. Retrieved on 19/03/2007.
11. Ibid.
12. Samuel G. Egwu, *Ethnic and Religious Violence in Nigeria.* Jos, Nigeria: African Centre for Democratic Governance (AFRIGOV), 2001; Daniel A. Omoweh and Dirk van den Boom, *Blocked Democracy in Africa: Experiment with Democratization in Nigeria, 1999-2003* (Abuja, Nigeria: Konrad Adenauer Foundation, 2005), 60-95.
13. Abdulrasheed A. Muhammad, "The State and Religious Balancing in Nigeria," *Nigerian Forum,* 27, 9-10, 2006, 196-218.
14. A. Akwenife, "Politics and Religious Intolerance: The Nigerian Situation," in Razaq D. Abubakre, et al, eds., *Religion and Politics in Nigeria* (Ilorin, Nigeria: Nigerian Association for the Study of Religion), 1993, 106-123.
15. Section 38(1) of the 1999 Constitution of the Federal Republic of Nigeria.
16. Hameed Agberemi, "Nigeria Beyond Secularism and Islamism, 315, 369.
17. John A. Ayoade, "The Federal Character Principle and the Search for National Integration," in Kunle Amuwo, et al eds. *Federalism and Political Restructuring in Nigeria* (Ibadan, Nigeria: Spectrum Books, 1998), 101-120; Rotimi, T. Suberu, "States Creation and the Political Economy of Nigerian Federalism," in Kunle Amuwo, et al, eds., *Federalism and Political Restructuring in Nigeria,* 276-294.
18. David Hollenbach, "Religion and Public Life," *Theological Studies,* 52, 1 (March 1991), 104; Quoted in Ilesanmi, 187.
19. Mathew H. Kukah, *Religion, Politics and Power in Northern Nigeria* (Ibadan, Nigeria: Spectrum Books, 1993), 62, 65.
20. Cited in Kukah, 229.

21. Bala Usman, *The Manipulation of Religion in Nigeria, 1977-1987* (Kaduna, Nigeria: Vanguard Printers, 1997), 11.
22. Ibrahim Muazzam and Jibrin Ibrahim "Religious Identity in the Context of Structural Adjustment in Nigeria," in *Identity, Transformation and Identity Politics under Structural Adjustment in Nigeria*, Attahiru, M. Jega, ed., (*U*ppsala, SW: Nordiska Afrikainstitulet, 2000), 68-93.
23. Falola, 69-102.
24. Reports of the Constitution Drafting Committee Containing the Draft Constitution (Lagos, Nigeria: Federal Ministry of Information, 1978), 5.
25. Falola, 95-96.
26. Hassan A. Saliu and J. Shola Omotola, "The National Political Reform Conference and the Future of Nigerian Democracy," in *Perspectives on Nation Building and Development in Nigeria,* eds., Hassan A. Saliu, et al, (Lagos, Nigeria: Concept Publications, 2008).
27. J. Shola Omotola, "The 2003 Nigerian Second Election: Some Comments," *Political Science Review*, 3, 2, 2004, 126-137.
28. Falola, 115.
29. Olayemi Akinwumi, *Crisis and Conflicts in Nigeria: A Political History since 1960* (Munster, GER: Lit Verlag, 2004); Emmanuel O. Ojo, "A Survey of Ethno-Religious Crisis in Nigeria and its Implications for Democracy," ed. *Challenges of Sustainable Democracy in Nigeria*. Ibadan, Nigeria: John Archers Publishers, 2006, 365-378.
30. Shola, J. Omotola, "Group Violence and Governmental Response: The Declaration of State of Emergency in Plateau State, Nigeria," in Olayemi Akinwumi, et al, eds, *Inter-Group Relations and Conflicts in Nigeria in the 19th and 20th Century* (Makurdi, Nigeria: Aboki Publishers, 2006), Ojo, "A Survey of Ethno-Religious Crisis in Nigeria," 375-376.
31. For the Institutional weaknesses of these Organizations in Nigeria, sce, Fatai A. Aremu and Shola J. Omotola, "Violence as Threats to Democracy in Nigeria under the Fourth Republic, 1999-2005," *African and Asian Studies*, 6, 1-2, 2007, 53–78.
32. Anthonia T. Simbine, *Political Parties and Democratic Sustenance in Nigeria's Fourth Republic.* Monograph series No.11 Ibadan, Nigeria: Nigerian Institute of Social and Economic Research (NISER), 2002, 14-21.
33. Shola J. Omotola, "The Civil Limitations of Civil Society: Insights from Nigeria," *Unilag Journal of Politics*, 2, 2, 2005, 58-78; see also Abubakar Momoh, "Democracy and Good Governance: The Nigerian Politician as a Patriot," paper presented at NICO Annual Conference, Kwara Hotels, Ilorin, 6-7 June, 2007, 11-14.

34. Fred Onyeoziri, *Alternative Policy Options for Managing the National Question in Nigeria* (Ibadan, Nigeria: Programmes on Ethnic and Federal Studies, PEFS), 2002; Eghosa E. Osahae, *Crippled Giant: Nigeria Since Independence* (London: Hurst and Company, 1998); Daniel A. Omoweh and Dirk van den Boom, *Blocked Democracy in Africa: Experiment with Democratization in Nigeria, 1999-2003* (Abuja, Nigeria: Konrad Adenauer Foundation, 2005).

Chapter Five

The Countervailing Forces: Politics and Religion in Nigeria, 1993-2002

Lateef A. Adeniran

One significant feature about Nigeria relates to its resilience. In spite of a series of challenging events, Nigeria has continued to retain its integrity as an entity. The nature of the elections that ushered in political independence in Nigeria in 1960 was such that none of the three major political parties won substantial votes beyond their respective ethnic regions. The leaders of the Northern Peoples' Congress (NPC), which controlled the Northern Region, jealously guarded their interests in protecting what they regarded as the monolithic North against what they considered as intrusion from southern Christians. To this end, they adopted various methods to prevent the Action Group (AG) from the Western Region (which was predominantly of the Yoruba stock) and the National Council of Nigerian Citizens (NCNC), from the Eastern Region (which was dominated by the Igbo) from gaining any strong political foothold in the North. In the same vein, the NPC did not make any attempt to canvass for votes in either of the two other regions. It relied on its demographic advantage to gain the simple majority in the elections. But then, the NPC had to work out a political arrangement with the NCNC to form the first post independence government.

The foundation of the First Republic was laid on a coalition government. It was an uneasy political arrangement, which stemmed from the unhealthy rivalry among the three major ethnic groups during the early years of independence. The struggle for political power and mutual suspicion constituted major factors that contributed to the *coup d'etat* of January 15, 1966 as well as the retaliatory *coup d'etat* of July 29, 1966. Henceforth political instability set in and tension continued to build up, leading to the outbreak of the Civil War, which took place between July 1967 and January 1970. Political instability was further manifested in the *coup d'etat* of January 29, 1975 as well as the botched *coup d'etat* of February 13, 1976. Under the Obasanjo-led military regime, power was eventually transferred to an elected government on October 1, 1979 and the Second Republic came into being. Political instability continued as civilian rule was once again terminated on December 31, 1983 when Gen. Buhari came to power. A hybrid administration of elected governments at the local and state levels with a military president at the Federal level, between January 1991 and July 27, 1993 has been considered as the Third Republic. On May 29, 1999 the military handed over power to an elected government, by which the Fourth Republic evolved.

The institution of a military regime led to the suspension of the constitution, since the military ruled by decrees. One major feature of the dictatorial tendencies that this development created was the demise of the rule of law. Issues of governance became coterminous with the personality of the Head of State as well as his favored ones. Decrees were arbitrarily issued and sometimes backdated. Jurisdiction of the civil courts was ousted, so also were policies imposed without due consultations. As the military leaders proved unaccountable, corruption became pervasive. In the process, the socio-economic lives of a majority of the people progressively deteriorated. Political repression created a backlash as poverty and hopelessness succeeded in driving many people into seeking recourse in religion. The outbreak of the Maitatsine riot in Kano in 1980 can be traced to this development. A study carried out by Omar F. Ibrahim reveals that the leader of the religious group, Muhammadu Marwa, over the years, "had grown very powerful as a result of the swelling of his followership from a few hundreds in the early 1970s to over ten thousand on the eve of the crisis in December 1980."[1] Approximately 500 lives were lost in the riot.[2] And, since then, violent religious disturbances with ethnic undertones became recurrent issues in Nigeria. This was the basis on which the Federal Military Government promulgated a decree in June 1987, which set up the Advisory Council on Religious Affairs as an instrument 'to mediate and maintain religious harmony in the country.'[3]

Given the tortuous process by which democratic rule was restored, there were high expectations that the harsh realities of having to live under military regimes for so long, would have proved quite instructive to political leaders who took over the reins of government as of May 1999 and in the process instituted a regime of good governance.

The Politico-Religious Linkage

There are some points of disagreement between the values of religion and those of politics. Religious issues border on the metaphysical and normative, while political matters are essentially concerned with the mundane and real. However, studies have shown that in real terms both are closely intertwined. Based on this intertwining relationship, M. Kampuchean argued that unless religion "goes along with non-material values such as democracy, human dignity and honesty, material progress is no progress at all."[4]

It is in the context of the above that this chapter argues that the pursuit of the good life for man represents a fundamental element that can easily be identified in religious beliefs as well as in the philosophical basis of politics. This essence is well captured in the political philosophies of classical Greek thinkers such as Plato and Aristotle. Making reference to this issue, C. L. Wayper pointed out that, "For Aristotle the State is a moral institution, existing not that man might live but that he might live the good life. From that view Plato never wavered. For Aristotle every true State must seek the welfare of all its members, not of a part only-and it was Plato who first taught this."[5]

Plato's and Aristotle's discourses as they relate to religion needs to be seen in the context of their times. Classical political thinkers tended to refer to ethical issues in the sense in which religion is discussed in modern times. To them, the political and the ethical are complimentary. Viewed from this perspective, C. E. M. Joad submits that, "the purpose of ethics, according to Greek philosophers, was to prescribe the nature of good life for the individual, politics, the nature of the good life for communities of individuals."[6] Bertrand Russell buttressed this argument by stating that, "The fundamental problem of ethics and politics is that of finding some way of reconciling the needs of social life with the urgency of individual desires."[7] Based on these propositions, this chapter will examine to what extent Nigerian elite have utilized the instruments of politics and religion to either foster or impede the well being of their people. In drawing from global developments, Christianity in modern times owes largely to the influence of Emperor Constantine, who in 313 A.D.:

> Proclaimed the Edict of Milan, which for the first time recognized the legality of the Christian religion throughout the empire. He ordered restitution for wrongs done to Christians under the recent persecutions...Thus the conversion of Constantine becomes one of the most important events in the history of western civilization.[8]

By this action, it is possible to deduce that political power can be applied to promote the cause of religion, while religion on its own part, when judiciously accommodated within a pluralistic society, has the propensity to secure political stability and in the process, facilitate human civilization.

In the same vein, the relevance of religion as a major element in shaping the political life of a people, becomes manifest when attention is drawn to the reign of Louis XIV, King of France (1643-1715). The Edict of Nantes was enacted to accommodate Protestants among the predominantly Catholic French people. Louis XIV's uncompromising stands that religious differences did not threaten the political set up, led to the enactment of the edict. However, Louis XIV, in his later quest for political unity became convinced that uniform religious practices were essential and non-negotiable. Consequently, in October 1685, he revoked the Edict, and with it began the persecution of the Huguenots, who were, otherwise known as Calvinists. They were adherents of the sixteenth century French protestant, John Calvin (1509-1564) whose doctrines tended to question established Catholic practices. Deriving from the deprivation of their privileges, "Thousands of them [Huguenots], in spite of legal prohibitions, fled the country, which thus lost many of its most illustrious and intelligent inhabitants."[9] This had dire consequences for Louis XIV's reign, and was adjudged to be "the greatest single error,"[10] which he made "in his long and troubled reign."[11] Such is the nexus between politics and religion that at the onset of the modern state system in Western Europe, various rulers ensured that they secured the endorsement of the Pope in Rome to legitimize their accession to the throne of their respective domains.

In the Nigerian context, one logical outcome of the Sokoto Jihad of 1804 was the evolution of a supra-national political entity known as the Sokoto Caliphate, which in turn became a dominant part of the British-created nation-state, Nigeria. Though unwittingly, the activities of missionaries operating from the coast beginning in the 1840s, tended to complement that of the "Jihadists" in the formation of what eventually came to be known as Nigeria. The Sokoto jihad succeeded in bringing together a single political entity from the various Hausa city-states, which had hitherto existed independent of one another. The Sokoto Caliphate also exercised political control over the area, which is today referred to as the Middle Belt of Nigeria. This was the political platform upon which the British colonialist constituted into the Northern Provinces. Under colonial rule, the political foundation of the Sokoto Caliphate significantly determined the mindset of those who governed the territory. There was the sweeping notion that the people who lived north of the River Niger were Muslims, while their compatriots to the south were Christians. In reality, while Muslims were, and are, predominant in the North, this same part of the country had pockets of Christians in the Northeast as well as the Middle Belt. To the southwest is a sizeable mixture of Muslims and Christians, while in the southeast some Muslims live among predominant Christians. During the 1967-1970 Civil War, secessionist propagandists sought the support of certain international bodies by indicating that the secessionist forces (Biafrans) were fighting to liberate themselves from the yoke of the Muslim North. According to H. B. Momoh, "Biafran propagandists had wiped up sentiments among their sympathizers in the international community that 'the battle was between Christian Easterners and the Muslim Northerners."[12]

The foregoing events point to the fact that while both issues could be mutually self-reinforcing, they could as well be applied to promote interests antithetical to one another. In the quest to seek relevance and to assert themselves, the elite resorted to the use of either political power or religious influence. The consequence of this was conflict.

It is germane to state here that religion has been a controversial issue in modern societies, as can be observed in the writings of political philosophers. One of the most cited is Karl Marx who avers that, "Religion is the sigh of the oppressed culture, the heart of the heartless world…It is the opium of the people."[13] Durkheim agrees with Marx that religion is an instrument for maintaining the status quo, but he differs from the latter by arguing that religion serves as a unifying force for "members of a community as a group."[14] Ideas of this nature influenced the thinking among both Western liberal democratic theorists and Marxian scholars to predict that, "scientific progress will push religious people and movements to irrelevance."[15] In spite of these positions, religion has continued to play significant roles in the political developments of many countries. Typical examples are Israel, the Irish Republic, and Pakistan. With a particular reference to Nigeria, Mundt and Aborishade observe that:

> As in many other countries, religious institutions and associations play an important part in Nigerian politics. These groups are especially durable and resilient, because

> when political activity is repressed they remain organized around denominational objectives, and where an ethnic association might have to play a less obvious role, neither Christian nor Muslim religious groups and leaders find it necessary to camouflage their identities.[16]

From this, one can discern the interplay of religion and politics in Nigeria. However, the application of either of these by Nigerian leaders is a matter of expediency.

The June 12 Issue

A defining moment in the political history of Nigeria took place on June 12, 1993, when the final election, which was to usher in a democratic government after a decade of military rule, took place. In addition, June 12 represented the first time in the history of Nigeria, when a southerner, freely elected by Nigerians, was to assume leadership of the country. It would be recalled that General Aguiyi Ironsi (January to July 1966) and General Olusegun Obasanjo (February 1976 to October 1979), assumed office as heads of state through a military *coup d'état,* which neither of them participated in. Therefore it is possible to argue that the annulment of the June 12, 1993 election was an attempt by the northern elite to deny their southern counterparts an opportunity to lead the country. This incident marks a reference point in the development of the country, as it succeeded in throwing up certain elements in the political configuration of Nigeria. Among these elements are the struggles for political power among the leaders of the various ethnic groups in Nigeria to further the interests of their respective ethnic groups. So also is the exploitation of religious sentiments to achieve personal political goals. In addition to that, it revealed that the civilian political class was not united in wresting political power from the military usurpers. In that regard some of them became ready collaborators with the military leaders, if such disposition would ensure for them access to political offices. Apart from that, one can observe the preoccupation of the political leaders with capturing political power rather than the pursuit of the general good of the country. As part of General Ibrahim Babangida's transition program, a nation-wide election was conducted to produce a civilian president and return the country to democratic rule.

As a means of putting the linkage between politics and religion in the Nigerian setting in a proper perspective, it becomes imperative to elaborate on General Babangida's long-drawn transition program from military to civilian rule. The Babangida had allowed the formation of only two political parties – the Social Democratic Party (SDP) and the National Republican Convention (NRC) - to contest the election. In the process, M. K. O. Abiola and Bashir Tofa (both Muslims) emerged as the presidential candidates for SDP and NRC respectively. Abiola picked Babagana Kingibe (a Muslim) as his running mate, while Bashir Tofa picked Sylvester Ugoh (a Christian) as his running mate. Given the dimension which religious consciousness had assumed in Nigerian politics, the SDP candidates (both Muslims) became an issue of attack by the rival NRC whose candidates were balanced (Muslim presidential candidate with a Christian running mate) in the presidential election. In fact, the NRC, as part of its campaign weapon, emphasized the SDP's Muslim-Muslim combination as a deficiency, which the voters should not ignore. It is, however, significant to state that in spite of this challenge, the SDP won the presidential election, but the final result was abruptly annulled. During a nationwide address on June 26, 1993 General Babangida adduced reasons for the annulment as:

(a) tremendous negative use of money during the party primaries and presidential election;
(b) documented and confirmed conflict of interest between the government and both presidential aspirants, which would compromise their position and responsibilities were they to become president;
(c) to proclaim and swear in on the basis of the June 12 election, a president who encouraged a campaign of divide and rule amongst Nigerian ethnic groups would be detrimental to the survival of the Third Republic.[17]

The military leader's justification for the cancellation of the result can be seen as tenuous, given the fact that he had initially pledged to the nation to relinquish political power to an elected government in 1990. Before this date, Babangida subsequently came up with excuses why this was no longer feasible and thus shifted the transition period first to 1992, and later to 1993. His Machiavellian tactics to hold on to political power on flimsy excuses was the major reason why a Nigerian political analyst dubbed him the "Maradona of Nigerian politics."

The abortion of an imminent civilian regime has brought to the forefront, certain features in Nigerian politics. Among these is the preoccupation of Nigeria's political elite (both civilian and military) to acquire political power with a view to entrenching themselves in power, and utilizing same to dispense favors to their clients. However, this chapter focuses on the extent to which the annulment impinges on the avowed religious interests of the people. Although religion is essentially a matter of personal conviction, it assumes a social dimension when political leaders seek to manipulate it as an instrument of acquiring political power, while the less-privileged find in it, a means of self-identity. As a matter of expediency, religion becomes a non-issue when ethnic considerations can be evoked to achieve sectional interests. This became manifest in the aftermath of the political backlash that attended the annulment of the June 12, 1993 election.

Babangida's scheming that peaked with the June 12 political crisis, clearly demonstrated the overriding interest of the Nigeria political elite to control political power, over considerations of political stability or improvements in the living standards of the people, much less the protection of common religious interests. For instance, on the basis of the political clout, which the Sultan of Sokoto (Ibrahim Dasuki)-leader of Muslims in Nigeria - had over political leaders in the northern part of the country, it was assumed that his intervention would bring about the resolution of the crisis. This could have been done by prevailing on Babangida to allow the transition program to run its expected course by relinquishing power to the winner of the presidential election –M. K. O. Abiola.

This argument is anchored on the extent of influence, which Muslim leaders from the northern part of the country (particularly the core sphere of influence of the Sokoto Caliphate) have been exercising in determining the fate of the country. This issue needs to be reiterated given the fact that certain scholars have posited that there are at least two aspects of political influence in Nigeria. As R. J. Mundt and O. Aborisade point out, the first aspect is "the effect of organized interest groups such as unions and religious bodies."[18] Thus, with reference to the June 12 crisis, the Sultan, Ibrahim Dasuki, was not forthcoming in terms of exercising his political leverage to douse the political tension.

While it can be argued that the position of the Sultan can be justified on the basis that his influence on the military leadership was limited, a critical look at the situation tends to belie an outward appeal to divine design. This argument is better appreciated when cognizance is taken of the struggle for political power, primarily among the three major ethnic groups in Nigeria – the Hausa/Fulani, Igbo, and Yoruba. The development tended to underscore the suspicion that the northern political elite would contrive any means to continue to hold on to political control. For instance, one of the prominent northern political figures, Umaru Dikko, was alleged to have "written to all important northern leaders, irrespective of their political parties, to do everything possible so as to prevent Chief M .K .O. Abiola from becoming the next president of Nigeria."[19] His argument was hinged on the impression that "political power belongs to the North while economic power belongs to the South."[20]

From this incident, one can discern that the overriding factor was not the protection of religious interest, but rather that of ethnic considerations. This is underscored by the fact that even before the election, much pressure had been mounted on "Chief Moshood Abiola, to pick a northern Christian as his running mate."[21] The same report indicates that a northern governor, Saleh Michika (civilian governor of Adamawa State) had declared that Abiola was "the best aspirant from the two parties, but that their support may have been contingent on Abiola picking a Muslim running mate from the North."[22] This ethnic and religious divide was manifested further with the annulment of the election. The annulment provoked a groundswell expression of regional and ethnic sentiments, rather than the appeal to religious sentiments among prominent Nigerians. In one of the such instances, the then Bishop of Akure Diocese, Anglican Communion, the Right Reverend Bolanle Gbonigi vehemently condemned the annulment and called for civil disobedience, arguing that:

> The military is advocating dialogue alone because it will enable them to remain in power for a long time. A situation in which our fellow citizens from whose area of our country will derive little resources to our economy cleverly and even forcefully consume large proportion of the proceeds from our resources, turn around to treat the rest of us as inferior citizens has to stop now.[23]

The June 12 crisis succeeded in widening the ethnic divide, particularly between the Yoruba of the southwest and the Hausa/Fulani of the North.[24] It is important to mention that Abiola had won much acceptance among a cross-section of Nigerians through his business interests as well as philanthropic activities. Consequently, denial of the opportunity to assume the highest political office in the land was not so much a deprivation to not only Abiola, but also to the Yoruba who, with the Igbo, had become weary of the domination of the Nigerian political leadership by the Hausa/Fulani. The treatment meted out to Abiola was therefore interpreted to be marginalizing the Yoruba. From that perspective, Abiola was considered the symbol of the Yoruba identity. It stands to reason that General Sanni (a northerner) who ruled Nigeria between November 1993 until his death in June 1998 contended with the stiffest opposition to his government from the National Democratic Coalition (NADECO), which was predominantly led by the Yoruba elite.

It is imperative to state that the northern political elite had been mindful of the implication of losing political control to others - majority or minority ethnic groups. Given the relative weak socio-economic development of the North, its elite created the impression that political power was the veritable means of achieving the desirable leverage for the North in the national scheme. This was particularly appealing with the advantage of population on their side, as well as their domination of the military and security agencies. Therefore, tacit support for the annulment would facilitate the entrenching of the Northern hold on political power, and in the process facilitate the appointment of their people into strategic public offices, as well as allocate greater resources to enhance development in their part of the country, thereby redressing the socio-economic imbalance. The predominant Islamic culture in the North expected to be spared from the undue influence of the more westernized Yoruba, if power was retained in the North. Deriving from the June 12 issue, the agitation for a power shift became strident among the political class of the southern part of the country.

Politico-Religious Crises

At the dawn of independence, as well as during the first two decades of the post-independence era, ethnicism had been the major centrifugal force in the nation-building process in Nigeria. Religious threats were isolated instances. However, beginning in 1980, especially with the Maitatsine religious riot in Kano, this trend changed. From then on, outbreaks of religious violence intensified with the attendant destruction of lives and property.[25] This phenomenon shook the foundations of the peace, stability, and continued existence of Nigeria as a single political entity. A significant feature of the acts of religious violence is that those physically involved are under privileged members of the society, while the political elite are the instigators who capitalize on the poverty and ignorance of the poor people.

By the latter part of the twentieth century, religious sentiments had crept into politics on a global scale. In a study on religious conflicts, W. S. Banjo reveals that "...more than ever before individuals, groups and even states are employing religion to achieve goals and objectives that include socio-economic and political aspects...."[26] In the Sudan Muslims/Arabs are pitched against Christians/Traditionalists who are mostly black people. Similarly, Islamic fundamentalists are pitched against the Egyptian government. In Algeria, the government has been engaged in using the military to suppress Islamic fundamentalism. Also recently, the incumbent Turkish government has had to contend with its' courts and military that are opposed to the new government's interests in reviving certain Islamic practices.

In adducing reasons for this, Banjo argues that, "The seeming failure of development ideologies coupled with increasing hardship has resulted in enhancing the success of religious sentiments and values."[27] This viewpoint is supported by Samuel P. Huntington's study, *The Clash of Civilizations* wherein he posits that:

> The process of economic modernization and social change throughout the world are separating people from long standing local identities...In much of the world religion has moved in to fill this gap, often in the form of movements that are, labeled "fundamentalist". Such movements are found in western Christianity, Judaism, Buddhism and Hinduism, as well as in Islam.[28]

Where religious tension had political undercurrents, the threats or outbursts of violence were not limited to inter-religious rivalries, but were also derived from sectarian/intra-religious differences as well. For example, there was the report of simmering tension in Kaduna in May 1995. The development arose when the Yoruba Muslim Community, in an attempt to carve a sense of self-identity for themselves, sought police permission to hold the Eid-ul-Adha prayers at the Ahmadu Bello Stadium. A section of the indigenous Kaduna Muslim Community could not countenance this move. Consequently, they:

> Threatened to unleash mayhem on the city during the forthcoming Eid-il-Kabir Sallah holiday if the Yoruba Muslim community goes ahead to observe its Sallah prayers at a separate praying field other than the usual Murtala Muhammed Square in Kaduna where all Muslims have been using.[29]

Incidents of this nature indicate the extent to which certain individuals could go in the pursuit of their religious interests.

Given the above background, it is appropriate to identify some instances in which religious fervor has challenged established political authority. Religious zealousness has put to question the ability of political authorities to respond to the challenges of governance by reconciling the series of conflicting interests. One significant event that demonstrated the extent to which people who claim to protect the interest of religion could undermine constituted authority happened in Kano in December 1994. A Christian, Gideon Akaluka, had earlier been remanded to the Goron Dutse Federal

Prisons in Kano on an allegation of desecrating the Quran. In a daring move, some Muslim youths stormed the prison, seized Akaluka and beheaded him as a means of meting out punishment for disparaging Islam.[30]

The political crisis that bedeviled Nigeria in 1993 resulting from the annulment of the election result, assumed more ethnic considerations than religious. However, at the onset of the Fourth Republic on May 29, 1999, religious influence became the primary factor among the destablizing elements in the country. One after the other religious crises broke out in different parts of the country, seriously undermining the new democratic government, led by President Olusegun Obasanjo.

The issue of reading political meanings when implementing a religious injunction or giving a subjective religious interpretation to certain political policies became manifest as soon as Obasanjo was sworn in as the president. Olusegun Obasanjo, as a Christian from the southwest, chose Atiku Abubakr, a Muslim from the northeast, as his deputy. This was a religious and regional balancing strategy, which failed to prevent the outbreak of a national crisis when the governor of Zamfara State, Ahmed Sani Yerima, declared the adoption of the Shari'a Legal System in his state in October 1999. It should be mentioned that Yerima was elected on the platform of the All Peoples Party (APP) now All Nigerian Peoples' Party (ANPP), a rival political party to the Peoples' Democratic Party (PDP) that controlled the federal government. The controversy generated by the above proclamation was widespread across the nation. While some acknowledged it as long overdue, others viewed it as having the tendency to accentuate the differences between the two major religions. Among the opponents were those who questioned its' timing, arguing that it was intended to compound the problems of the president who was a Christian. While this controversy was raging, the Kano State governor, Rabiu Musa Kwankwaso, also proclaimed the adoption of the Shari'a Legal System in his state in June 2000. After this, ten other states from the North followed suit, and the Shari'a became a national issue and a cause for conflict.

The deduction from these developments is that certain political leaders have sought to manipulate religion as a counterpoise to the political leverage of their opponents. Without doubt, a number of events have buttressed the fact that violent disturbances witnessed during the period of study have revealed that the underlying motive of such incidents was not as much as religious, as it was a strategy to secure political leverage. In 1996 a group of eminent Muslims from the southwestern part of the country complained about discrimination against their section of the country. In a press statement titled "A Call For Fair Hajj Administration," the leaders of the various Islamic groups alluded to the ban placed on pilgrims from Nigeria traveling to Saudi Arabia for "Hajj" activities in 1996.[31] In that year, there was an outbreak of Cerebro Spinal Meningitis [CSM] epidemics in northern Nigeria. Consequently upon representation to the Saudi authorities that the southern part of the country was CSM free, the number of pilgrims was limited to 3,000.[32] The approach of the Federal authorities in sourcing this number, turned out to be contentious. In the process, Muslims from the southern states felt marginalized. The group then lamented that:

> In utter disregard of logic and fairness, the airlift operations were hastily resumed elsewhere, precisely in the CSM affected area, while ridiculous quotas, such that none of them was to airlift up to 100 pilgrims. Furthermore, confusion was deliberately contrived to sideline the Nigeria Airways which was to operate from the Lagos Zone to airlift most of the 3,000 pilgrims now allocated to Nigeria.[33]

There are instances whereby veiled religious motives were deployed to cause violence. In April 1994, the Plateau State Government rescinded its earlier decision to appoint Aminu Mato (as Chairman of the Local Government), after he had earlier been sworn in as Chairman, of the Jos Local Government Area. It should be noted that like most parts of the country, Jos area was home to many ethnic groups. Prominent among these were the Berom, Tiv, Angas, and Hausa/Fulani who after a long period of settlement often laid claim to being indigenes of the town.

The withdrawal was based on the protest of the indigenes that Mato was a Fulani and a non-indigene of Jos. The Berom people in contrast to the Fulani were predominantly non-Muslims. In reaction to the government decision, supporters of Mato mobilized an action, which resulted in violence. One significant backlash of this incident was the destruction of the Jos Main Market, which was described as "one of the biggest in West Africa."[34] The incident deserves concern when cognizance is taken of the fact that in most cases in Nigeria such standard public facilities are uncommon. In most cases traders usually make do with ramshackle structures as market stalls, while a large number of such traders display their wares in open spaces at the mercy of natural elements. Incidentally, the government has yet to come up with a program of reconstructing the Jos market. This implies that the adverse effect of that destruction is being felt up till 2008.

The city of Jos in Plateau State was a major scene of religiously instigated violence between 1993 and 2002. In one instance, what started as a minor argument, whereby some Muslim youths accosted a lady wearing a mini-skirt, passing by a mosque during the Friday prayers, got out of control and eventually developed into destruction of lives and property. According to one account, "within a few hours, scores of people were exterminated while properties worth millions of naira were destroyed."[35] Yet it was reported, "the battle raged for days."[36]

Another outbreak of ethno-religious crisis in Jos, in 2002, had a national backlash. One needs to reemphasize the fact that various ethnic groups have established permanent settlements in Jos. The Berom (mostly non-Muslims) are the dominant ethnic group in Jos and have often resented the growing influence of the Fulani who settled in Jos in the aftermath of the Sokoto Jihad of 1804. But the Fulani were mostly herdsmen. A disagreement over the grazing of cattle on the farmland of a Berom in the Riyom district of Jos resulted in armed confrontation. Due to simmering tension among the various religious leaders in Jos, the farm incident was given a religious interpretation leading to further outbreaks of violence between the two religious groups in 2002.

In sympathy with Muslims who lost their lives in the latest crisis in Jos, retaliatory violence broke out in Kaduna leading to the loss of over 1,000 lives and property worth billions in naira.[37] There was a counter reaction in the southeastern part of the country in Owerri and Aba, predominantly Christian, where fatal attacks were launched on the Muslim Hausa-Fulani residents in those areas.

In 2002, Nigeria experienced an unusually large number of incidents involving religious violence, which could not be divorced from the ambition of the various interest groups to achieve political ends. One of such occurred in Enugu in eastern Nigeria. According to an account, a Catholic priest, Rev. Father Ejike Mbaka, was in the habit of using his revival sessions as a platform to attack the government for failing to make any meaningful impact on the lives of the people. On one occasion, a stampede resulted in the death of fourteen people. When the governor of Enugu State, Chimaroke Nnamani, set up a Judicial Commission of Inquiry to probe the incident, both the Anglican Church and the Catholic Church turned down invitations to have their prominent members serve on the Commission.[38]

The trend continued towards the end of 2002 such that the issue of a beauty contest formed the basis of another round of violence in Kaduna and Abuja. The outcome of the staging of the Nigerian phase of the Miss World beauty contest led to a comment in the *ThisDay* newspaper wherein Isioma Daniel made an allusion to the beauty of the contestants and wrote that the Prophet Mohammed himself would probably have chosen a wife from one of them. This comment angered the Muslims who had earlier viewed the involvement of the Federal Government in the pageant as indecorous.[39]

Conclusion

Nigeria has been bedeviled by outbreaks of sectarian violence, and the combatants have been polarized along religious lines. These differences have adversely impacted on political stability. Most of the crises, however, have not originated from religious fervor. Some of the perpetrators of violence are attempting to carve out a religious identity for themselves, others are essentially motivated by the need to engage religion as a platform to advance their political leverage. A number of studies carried out tend to validate this argument. One study carried out by Oguagha (in Vasudev Das) submits that, "Conflicts between Islam and Christianity have quite often revolved on political power sharing."[40] Okolocha (also in Vasudev Das) shares this view by contending that, "Political power is seen as a tool for protecting the religious interest of office holders and advancing the spread of such religions."[41] The nature of these armed confrontations is fluid, such that a study by the Internal Displacement Monitoring Centre observes that at the onset of such incidents:

> Mobilization that followed was often along religious lines, and the conflict was easily stereotyped as a 'religious crisis'. The same dynamic has often been observed with regard to 'ethnic conflicts.' Ethnic identity and mobilization play a prominent role in the political landscape, and impact frequently on political stability, but they are mostly created to access spoils of a different nature.[42]

This situation poses a paradox, bringing to mind the questions: What is the essence of politics? Of what value is religion if the polity is conflict-ridden? The situation shows the burden, which the various political and religious leaders have placed on the Nigerian polity. The role of religion in politics has been a basis for concern among scholars as well as political thinkers and has led them to the conclusion that Nigeria is tending towards a failed state. In an allusion to the political philosophies of Thomas Hobbes and John Locke, Paul Johnson asserts that both thinkers "rightly treated violence as the antithesis of politics."[44] In the same vein, religion aims at promoting peace in human society. Thus, it can be said that both religion and politics have the propensity to promote human civilization.

Conversely, either or both can be exploited to cause political instability. Both civilian and military leaders have used all resources at their disposal to advance their political interests. In the process, religion to them has been a weapon of expediency in terms of wiping up religious sentiments when it suits them or underplay the value of religion if this latter option undermines their political interests. Religious leaders on their part, seek recourse by inciting their followers to public violence as a means of registering their identity as well as winning political influence.

Notes

1. O. F. Ibrahim, "Religion and Politics: A View from the North," in *Transition Without End, ed.,* L. Diamond, A. Kirk-Greene, and O. Oyediran (Ibadan, Nigeria: Vantage Publishers, 1997), 511.
2. Ibid.
3. R. Suberu "Religion and Politics: A View from the South," in Diamond, et al, 482.
4. M. Kampuchean, *Beyond World-Denial* in *Development and Cooperation* Vol. 34, No.10, 2007, 376.
5. C. L. Wayper, *Political Thought* (London, The English University Press, 1974), 38. See also A. Appadorai, *The Substance of Politics* (Oxford, Oxford University Press, 2004), 10.
6. C. E. M. Joad, *Philosophy* (Kent: Hodder and Stoughton, 1977).
7. B. Russell, *Unpopular Essays* (London: George Allen & Unwin, 1976), 13.
8. J. K. Sowards, ed., *Makers of the Western Tradition: Portraits from History* Vol. 1 (New York: St. Martin's Press, 1983), 115.
9. G. Clark, *The Seventeenth Century* (Oxford: Oxford University Press, 1972), 309.
10. G. P. Judd, *A History of Civilization* (New York: The Macmillan Company, 1966), 421.
11. Ibid.
12. H. B. Momoh, ed., *The Nigerian Civil War, 1967-1970: History and Reminiscences* (Ibadan, Nigeria: Sam Bookman Publishers, 2000), 182.
13. W. Kid, G. Czerniawski, and D. Abbott, *Heinemann Sociology As for OCR,* (Oxford: Heinemann Educational Publishers, 2003), 270.
14. O. Soyinbo and P.Ogunlade, "Religion and Cultural Issues," in *Perspectives on Nigeria's Fledgling Fourth Republic*, ed., M. Ade Adejugbe (Lagos, Nigeria: Malthouse Press, 2002), 99.

15. W. S. Banjo, "Religious Conflict Fundamentalism and Terrorism in Africa," *Nigerian Forum: A Journal of Opinion on World Affairs,* Vol.27. Nos. 1-2, Jan/Feb., 2006, 32.
16. R. J. Mundt and O. Aborishade, "Politics in Nigeria," in *Comparative Politics Today: A World View,* ed.s, G. A. Almond, G. B. Powell, K. Strom and R. J. Dalton, (Delhi: Dorling Kindersley, 2004), 720.
17. B. Akinterinwa, "The 1993 Presidential Elections Imbroglio," in Diamond, 296-297.
18. Mundt and Aborishade, 720.
19. T. C. Omogiate, "The Letter from Umaru Dikko," *The Guardian*, May 29, 1993, 12.
20. Ibid.
21. R. Adedoyin, and A. Esajere, "Religion Complicates Abiola's Search for Running Mate," *The Guardian*, April 4, 1993, A1 and A2.
22. Ibid.
23. R. Ajayi, "Clergy wants new approach to June 12," *Vanguard,* September 19, 1994, 3.
24. C. Obi, "Oil and the Politics of Transition in Nigeria," in *Transition Politics in Nigeria, 1970*-1999, eds., B. Onuoha and M. M. Fadakinte (Lagos, Nigeria: Malthouse Press, 2002), 103.
25. For more information on religious violence in Nigeria see Toyin Falola, *Violence in Nigeria: The Crisis of Religious Politics and Secular Ideologies,* (Rochester: University of Rochester Press, 2001).
26. W. S. Banjo, "Religious Conflict, Fundamentalism and Terrorism in Africa," *Nigeria Forum: A Journal of Opinion on World Affairs*, Vol. 27, Nos. 1- 2, January/February, 2006, 33.
27. Ibid. 34.
28. S. P. Huntington, *The Clash of Civilizations*, www.digitalnpg.org./archive/2007.
29. D. Oyewole, "Kaduna Boils Again," *Third Eye*, May 7, 1995, 1-2.
30. Osa Director, "The Kano Time Bomb," *TELL*, July 3, 1995, 16-17.
31. Press Statement, "Concerned Southern Muslim Leaders," *Nigerian Tribune*, May 3, 1996, 6.
32. Ibid.
33. Ibid.
34. Wola Adeyemo, "Fire on the Mountain," *TELL*, April 25, 1994, 21.
35. Vasudev Das, "Resolving Religious Crisis for Sustainable: Democracy in Nigeria," a paper presented at the CESNUR International Conference, San

Diego State University, San Diego, California, July 13-16, 2006, 6. http://www.cesnur.org/2006/sd das.htm.

36. Ibid.
37. O. Soyombo, and Bola Ogunlade, "Religious and Cultural Issues," in *Perspectives on Nigeria's Fledgling Fourth Republic,* ed., M. Ade. Adejugbe, M. Ade (Ikeja, Lagos: Malthouse Press, 2002), 101.
38. Chris Oji, "Religion Threatens Enugu Politics," *The Comet*, April 21, 2002, 36.
39. Project Ploughshares "Armed Conflicts Report: Nigeria (1990–First Combat deaths)," 1-15, www.ploughshares.ca/libraries/ACR-Nigeria.html.
40. Vasudev Das, Resolving Religious Crisis."
41. Ibid.
42. Internal Displacement Monitoring Centre, "Nigeria: Institutional Mechanism Fail to Address recurrent Violence and Displacement," Internal Displacement Monitoring Centre (IDMC), 3–4, www.internal-displacement.org
43. Ibid.
44. Paul Johnson, "Is Terrorism an Effective Political Instrument?" Quoted in H. M. Levine, (New York: McGraw-Hill Book Company, 1983), 250.

Chapter Six

Evangelization and Inter-ethnic Conflicts: The Benin Diocese, 1995-2002

Uyilawa Usuanlele

The evangelization of Africa in the nineteenth and twentieth centuries encountered various problems associated with European missionaries. The situation led to the early training of Africans as missionaries and to the writing of Christian literature in different African languages. These developments were not uniform overtime and place. Initially, the non-uniformity gave some advantages to the ethnic groups, which had earlier contact with Christian missionaries and embraced Christianity. The advantages manifested in access to employment opportunities as well as power and authority in both the state and church. The disparity in advantages affected inter-ethnic relations in the church especially where and when it intersected with political relations in the community. This development had the potential and capability of reinforcing ethnic animosity.

This chapter explores the intersections of political ethnicity and church administration and its development and manifestations in the Benin Diocese of the Anglican Communion of Nigeria, which snowballed into a violent crisis that divided the Diocese for over five years. This crisis has been blamed on the xenophobic ethnicity of the indigenes of Benin City by a section of the Anglican Church who supported the Primate and some of the media reports.[1] This chapter goes beyond the explanation of the

Benin people's xenophobic ethnicity and argues that this crisis can only be understood through an awareness and understanding of the history of the diocese. It further argues that the Church is a major resource and source of power affecting politics, which in turn affects the church. In the case of Benin Diocese, it has continuously been influenced and affected by the struggle for ethnic and sub-ethnic autonomy that has characterized the politics of the area.

This chapter is divided into sections. The first part examines the historical development of the Diocese along with the evolving language and ethnic problems and their resolutions. This is followed by an examination of the struggle for ethnic autonomy of both the people and diocese from Western Region/Yoruba domination. The next section looks at the recent struggle that resulted in crisis and conflicts along with resolution while the last section is the conclusion.

Christianity and Inter-group Relations

Christianity first made its debut in Benin City in the sixteenth century with the arrival of Portuguese explorers and later with traders and missionaries. But the religion did not take root because of its conflict with the Benin indigenous culture and restrictions on Portuguese activities by the Benin ruling aristocracy. The withdrawal of the last missionaries in the eighteenth century led to its extinction. It took the conquest of Benin in 1897 for Christianity to make a comeback as Consul-General Ralph Moor immediately invited Christian Missionaries to move in to play a "civilizing" role. It was not until 1901 that Bishop James Johnson of the Church Missionary Society (CMS) moved into Benin to accomplish his dream of Christianizing Benin, where his parents had sojourned as slaves before they were sold, recaptured and resettled in Sierra Leone.[2] Johnson found accommodation with Queen Arokun (a.k.a. Ayosore and wife of the exiled Oba Ovonramwen) who was already a Christian and had been converted to Christianity in Calabar during her stay with the exiled Oba. Johnson gathered Queen Arokun, her few friends, and the non-Benin African staff of the British administration to start his Benin mission.[3] To this church was attached the St. Matthews School in 1902.

The Benin City of 1902 was virtually a shadow of its former self still struggling to recover from the conquest, destruction and flight of its former inhabitants. The defeated Benin people were still bewildered and skeptical about British intentions and as a result many did not return to their capital city to participate actively in trade and administration. Of the hundreds of titleholders in the previous administration, only a few titleholders were appointed by the British administration while the rest were rendered virtually redundant and had no role in the city in the absence of the Oba. The colonial administration and trade were for a long time in the hands of British officials and few people from Sierra Leone and Gold Coast as well as Yoruba, Itsekiri, Kalabari, Hausa, Igbo, and Urhobo merchants.[4] The administrative position of Benin City as headquarters of the Western division of Central Province and later Benin Province continuously attracted an influx of fortune seekers from within and outside the Province to the city. As a result Benin City quickly developed a multi-ethnic population. Some of the migrants who were already Christians consequently had an upper hand in the affairs of the church and dominated the newly converted indigenous Benin people.

The Church was not without its problems. The slow response of the missions to Benin had forced Moor to establish a Government school in Benin City in 1901 for Benin children. The hope of using St. Matthews CMS School to make converts out of Benin children was not much of a success. According to Bishop Johnson, the Government School was better funded, equipped, and its secular education complemented the indigenous religion of the pupils and their parents, which made it more popular.[5] The church also faced the problem of a hostile local British administration. Apart from the intolerance of some officers like Crewe-Reade, the administration was also not happy with Johnson's legal challenge of the deposition and exile of Oba Ovonramwen.[6]

The main problems of this early church were lack of personnel and language barrier. There were no indigenous Benin priests and the available ones did not speak the local language. A good understanding of the indigenous language was necessary for effective evangelization. Problems were further compounded by the attitude and behavior of colonial officials and non-Benin personnel in charge of the church. The colonial administration had from its beginning adopted English as the language of administration and education. In the 1910s, it claimed that the people were interested in learning English.[7] As a result, the administration was indifferent to the indigenous languages of the area. In 1914, Bishop Tugwell argued that because there is no fund for the translation of literature to satisfy the linguistic heterogeneity of the area, the Yoruba language should be adopted as the language of instruction of the non-Igbo speaking groups, and the District Commissioner concurred with him in 1914.[8] In fact, the District Commissioner reported punishing the son of the village head of Igarra for failing to speak the Yoruba language in court.[9] The church and its Yorubanized leadership under Pastor Oyesile (an Ora man who had adopted Yoruba) continued with the Yoruba language policy in Benin and even taught it in St. Matthews School, Benin City. By the 1920s, Rev. W. J. Payne reported that it was an acceptable policy because the Benin people were unwilling to learn the Yoruba language.[10]

Apart from the language problem, which was hampering evangelization, the non-Benin personnel's attitude and behavior towards the local people were elitist. They felt superior and were intolerant of the non-Christian practices of the Benin people. Bishop Johnson had in 1913 accused the non-Benin members of living in concubinage with local women and setting a bad example to the people.[11] The CMS reports of the 1920s confirmed this practice along with illicit sexual dealings with local women and financial impropriety amongst its Catechists and teachers.[12] These activities and policies alienated the people from the church and engendered inter-ethnic group conflicts within the Church. By 1916, there was an anonymous petition alleging that the Yoruba Church agent neglected his duties, was more involved in his wood trade, inspired disharmony in the congregation by preaching against the Benin people and helped the non-Benin to organize their own service.[13]

The appointment of a European Priest Rev. Kidd in 1918 could not check the conflict over the administration of the church. By 1919, the Resident accused the church of not keeping proper accounts[14]and in 1921, the crisis burst into the open over the failure of the administration to render a proper account of the church's finances.

A section of the Benin people under the leadership of one Iyamu split to establish its own church in 1923. The new church was affiliated with the Southern American Baptist Church. Although the accounting problem was the immediate cause of crisis and conflict, ethno-linguistic and cultural issues were underlying problems propelled the crisis. Rev. W. J. Payne, who took over in 1922, confirmed this underlying cultural problem. Those who broke away were largely polygamist.[15] This was an issue of disagreement between the European clergy and African members of the church.

The ethno-linguistic division of the CMS, which Mr. Oyesile had been accused of initiating in 1916, was consolidated in the 1920s and in May 1924 Rev. Payne reported that he had started an English service section for native clerks. This English section transformed into the St. James's Anglican Church in 1933 with a school, which the local people called "Foreigner" school.[16] With this development, St. Matthews Cathedral and St. Peters Church remained bilingual conducting services in Yoruba and using a Benin interpreter.

Economic developments, especially the expansion of the timber and cash crop economy, created increased commercial opportunities and migrations to Benin City. This also attracted various other Christian denominations. Apart from the invitation of the Southern Baptist Mission who arrived in 1923, the Roman Catholic Mission moved into Benin City in 1924. The RCM was already established among other groups before spreading to Benin where it later also transferred its headquarters. The Salvation Army followed them in 1926, then the Evangelicals Mission Band in Siluko, the United Native African Church (First African Church) in 1930, and the breakaway Benin United Native Baptist Mission. The Apostolic Mission, Presbyterian Church, the Methodist Church, the Cherubim and Seraphim Prayer Band, the Jehovah Witness, and the Seventh Day Adventist also established themselves in Benin City alongside numerous Pentecostal and other so called White-Garment Africanist churches after independence. A major outcome of these developments was the sharing of the Benin Christians among the numerous denominations that proliferated in the city from the 1920s. Although the proliferation of churches created employment opportunities, people preferred secular jobs, which paid better wages.

Conversely, many denominations did not establish themselves in the rural areas where commercial opportunities were limited and where non-Benin ethnic groups inhabited. For instance, the Baptist Mission that had been established in Benin City, Sapele, and Warri in the 1920s did not operate in the Ishan and Kukuruku divisions until the 1960s.[17] The mainstream Christian denominations - CMS and RCM - with financial power operated outside Benin Division and Benin City. This restricted denominational rivalry and enhanced the consolidation of the CMS and RCM denomination in these rural areas where they dominated the lives of the Christian communities. As a result, these denominations attracted a larger following among the non-Benin ethnic groups. The large following in these largely rural divisions necessitated the training of personnel for the administration of the CMS and RCM churches in the non-Benin areas. Given the socio-economic character of these areas, with limited employment opportunities, the church became a major employer of labor as well as a source of political and social influence. This attracted more people in the rural non-Benin ethnic group areas into religious vocations.

Yoruba Domination and the Benin Diocese

As the CMS was consolidating its hold in the rural areas, deemphasizing the use of the Yoruba language and establishing ethnic language based churches and schools in the Benin City area from the 1920s, new developments in colonial Nigerian politics in the 1940s intersected with the interest of members of the church and the mode of its administration. The regionalization of the country in 1948 merged many minority ethnic groups including the Benin-Edo people with the more populous and better-educated Yoruba ethnic group. More than any Nigerian group, the Yoruba had also held a longer association with the Anglican Communion since the early nineteenth century. They had produced the first African Bishop, were responsible for the evangelization of most groups and actually dominated the Anglican Communion in Nigeria. These issues raised the fear and threat of a complete Yoruba majority domination of the region including the church.

Since the beginning of decolonization process after WW II, nationalists started to demand the creation of Midwest Region out of the Western Region because of the perceived threat of Yoruba domination. Although the Willink Commission that the federal government established to inquiry into the fear of minorities in 1956 did not recommend the creation of the Midwest Region, the relative neglect of the minority areas were really felt by the people and a ministerial office was recommended to cater to the minorities. Since this did not meet the aspirations of the people who continued to feel discrimination in terms of distribution of offices and scholarships, minority groups intensified their agitation for the creation of a Midwest region out of the Western Region.

The agitation for a Midwest region gradually permeated the church through the activities of some Nationalist politicians and leaders of the Midwest Movement who were also members of the clergy and laity of the Anglican Church. The agitation of the non-Yoruba minorities in the Western Region was for complete autonomy in all spheres. The CMS churches in the non-Yoruba areas had been grouped with some in the Yoruba and Igbo areas as the Ondo-Benin and Niger Dioceses and had been under the administration of Yoruba and Igbo clergy respectively. The agitation for the creation of a Midwest region created a regional separatist consciousness and emboldened some of the clergy and lay members of the CMS to make the demand for the creation of a Benin Diocese from the Ondo-Benin diocese and Niger Diocese. This development was initiated by Senator Dalton Asemota who was an ardent agitator for the creation of the Midwest region and a member of the National Council for Nigerian Citizens (NCNC). Senator Asemota organized a meeting of leading members of the Archdeaconries of Benin and Warri in 1958 and demanded the creation of a Benin diocese for the non-Yoruba and non-Igbo groups in the Western Region.[18] The memorandum of request was considered and a committee was set up to examine the viability of the diocese. The committee recommended the diocese and this was approved. The diocese of

Benin was constituted in 1962 and comprised the area and people that made up the Midwest Region,[19] which was created through a referendum in the same year. The demand for the creation of Benin Diocese was part of the struggle for ethnic autonomy and can be attested by the rejection of a Yoruba Bishop that was suggested for the Diocese. As a result, Archdeacon Agori Iwe, MBE, an Urhobo from Warri Archdeaconry was installed as its first Bishop. He remained the Bishop until his retirement in 1977.

Administration and Politics in the Benin Diocese

In 1962 the Benin Diocese inherited the problems that had bedeviled the area since the colonial period. The major concern was the ability to accommodate the multi-ethnic character of Benin and Warri Provinces, which also constituted the Midwest Region. The diocese and region had a large number of ethnic groups whose languages and dialects were mutually unintelligible.[20] In the first year of the early diocese, it was reported that no funds were voted for evangelism and this shortcoming was noted for correction in subsequent years.[21] In spite of this plan, there did not seem to have been any funding towards resolving the language problem for evangelical work. This was most noticeable with the Edo area and Benin City. Under Agori Iwe's administration, Erivbo noted that, "In the education sector, Anglicanism flourished in Asaba, Isoko, and Urhobo Archdeaconries."[22] Erhiwho similarly recorded only one agricultural project in the Etsako area of Benin Province.[23] This meant that there were no major developments in the Benin Archdeaconries of the Anglican Mission. Bishop Agori-Iwe's administration was not free of crisis as he admitted that he escaped an assassination attempt.

Given the poor development of evangelism in the areas, the problem of catering for the needs of the indigenes of Benin City in terms of language and evangelism persisted. No new Anglican churches and schools were established and publications in the language received little or no attention. Apart from the translation of a few books of the Bible that was stopped after the exit of Rev. Ohuoba and Edegbe from the CMS Benin in the 1920s,[24] no publications in the Edo language were recorded in the Anglican Church until the publication of the New Testament in Edo in 1981 and the complete Edo Bible in 1996 by the Bible Society of Nigeria.[25] Benin City's indigenes and the numerous rural populaces who spoke the same dialect had a peculiar problem of neglect of their own language. But this was not so for some of the migrant communities that resided in Benin City. For instance, the Igbo migrants in Benin City were able to secure approval for the use of their language in some of the Anglican churches. The Igbo even took over two churches, which conducted their services in the Igbo language; namely St. Paul Church and the Rev. William Payne Memorial Church. Other churches retained English as the language of communication while the Edo language was used only in the rural areas.

The language and evangelism problem was worsened when the government took over the administration of voluntary agency schools in 1972. This stressed the resources of the government, which could not provide adequate inspection and supervision. One outcome of this development was that the Edo language, formerly taught in the mission schools as a means of promoting evangelization, started to be neglected. Since the Edo language was not among the subjects written in the Primary and Secondary School Certificate examinations, it was no longer taken seriously. Worsening the situation was the fact that many of the teachers were migrants of other ethnicities who did not understand the indigenous language of the people of the city. The church also lost its schools that have served as agencies of recruitment and evangelization. It now had to struggle with the new denominations and sects particularly the Pentecostals and Jehovah Witnesses that adopted aggressive strategies of gaining converts.

Based on the language and multi-ethnic problems, some people of the Midwest wanted the government to create additional states, which would serve their unique ethnic needs. The three of the four regions that made up Nigeria had been broken into eleven states in 1967 in response to the secession bid of the Igbo, while the Midwest region remained intact. Some of the people of the Midwest region who were already experiencing inter-ethnic problems demanded for the creation of additional states from the Midwest Region, particularly the former Warri Province. The creation of Asaba and Warri Dioceses from the Benin Diocese in 1977 was not a mere coincidence; it was politically motivated. That the people of the Warri Diocese rejected the appointment of Akintayo, a Yoruba Bishop, and demanded the appointment of an indigene, was an indication of the political motive. The diocese was officially inaugurated when the Anglican Communion acceded to the demands of the members of the diocese and Bishop Dafiewhare, an Urhobo, was installed.[26] This was to set the precedent for the later development in Benin and to contribute to the exacerbation of the crisis.

The rest of Benin Diocese enjoyed relative calm because an indigene, Bishop J.W.I. Idahosa an (Benin-Edo), was installed successor to Agori Iwe. No spectacular achievements were recorded under Idahosa except the publication of the New Testament in Benin-Edo and portions of the Bible in Etsako-Edo. Some of the clergy of Midwest and Edo origin were similarly encouraged to return home to serve. The diocese had in 1977 requested and brought Rev. J. K. George, an (Ora-Edo), to head the Archdeaconry of Benin.[27] The first succession to the Bishopric of the diocese went smoothly as Rev. George succeeded Bishop Idahosa without any crisis when the later died in 1985. Though there was relative peace in the church and diocese, the same could not be said for the political situation in Bendel state where the agitation for the creation of more states out of Bendel continued. Eventually, this was achieved in 1991 with the splitting of Bendel into the states of Delta and Edo.

The Benin Diocese Crisis 1995-2003

Edo state was conterminous with Benin Diocese and was made up of the Akoko-Edo, Benin, Esan, Etsako and Ora. Oba Erediauwa of Benin had mobilized support for the creation of Edo state in the 1980s, but the movement was not revived in the 1990s. The creation of the Edo state in 1991 did not sit well with some of the non-Benin Edo people who were concerned that there would be a revival of old Benin Empire and its "oppressive" character.[28] Hence, linguistic theories were advanced to rationalize the agitation for the creation of a separate state (Afemesan State) to incorporate the non-Benin Edo people.[29]

Some Benin political leaders also established the Benin Forum as an umbrella organization to articulate the interest of the Benin people within the state and correct the injustices and perceived imbalances suffered in the state as result of military rule. The Benin people had their own grievances of imbalances relating to the allocation of local government councils and electoral constituencies relative to their less populous neighbours in the state. The imbalance had been created under the General Ibrahim Babangida regime. Admiral Augustus Aikhomu, the Vice President was believed to have favored his Esan-Edo group in the allocation of local Government councils and electoral constituencies.[30] The Benin politicians had hoped that their grievances would be addressed at the proposed national constitutional conference following the annulment of the 1993 general elections. Subsequently, the Benin Forum became a permanent political organization of the Benin people in the politics of Edo state and Nigeria. Among the executive of the Forum were some Benin influential members of the Anglican Communion such as the late Justice S. O. Ighodaro and Justice Isaac Aluyi, who played a leading role in the crisis of the Anglican Church.

It was against this backdrop of politics that the demand to create Sabongida Ora diocese from Benin Diocese was made. Sabongida Ora diocese was conterminous with the Afenmesan state. The new diocese of

Sabongida Ora was created in 1993 and an indigene Rev. A. A. Agbaje (Ora- Edo), was appointed as Bishop. Rev. J. K. George who remained as the Bishop of Benin Diocese was also from the Sabongida-Ora. But the indigenous population of Benin diocese did not protest the retention of Bishop George who remained Bishop until he retired in March 1995.

Before Bishop George retired, the Rev. Joseph A. Adetiloye, Archbishop of the Church of Nigeria, had requested a recommendation of modalities to fill the vacancy. The Archbishops Advisory Committee (AAC)[31] of Benin Diocese recommended:

> Efforts of past Bishops at evangelization appears limited to cities and towns in the old Diocese leaving the rural areas particularly in what is now Benin Diocese almost completely neglected. There is need therefore for aggressive evangelism in these rural areas of the Diocese which is predominantly of illiterate population. This recommendation is rooted in Article XXIV of the Anglican Book of Common Prayer which says "It is a thing plainly repugnant to the word of God and custom of the Primitive Church, to have public prayer in the Church, or to minister the sacraments in a tongue not understandeth of the people." [32] (their emphasis)

The letter was signed by all (except Rev. Can Okoh who was reported to be absent) and sent to the Archbishop in April. The above recommendation, on which the Chancellor and Chairman Justice Aluyi and his supporters rested their case, did not explicitly state or request for the appointment of an indigene who understood and spoke the indigenous language of the Diocese as Bishop.

Rev. Agbaje, an indigene and Bishop of Sabongida-Ora diocese, claimed that, "In March 1995, the House of Bishops at Agbara-Otor elected The Ven. Peter Onekpe as Bishop to fill the Episcopal vacancy in Benin Diocese."[33] If this claim is true, it means that either the recommendation of the Archbishop Advisory Committee was sent late and could no longer be considered or the request for recommendations of the AAC was just only a formality and political ploy to give the impression that laid down procedures were being followed. This also meant that the recommendation of the AAC was not circulated to guide the college of Bishops decision.

According to Bishop A. A. Agbaje, the result of this decision of the House of Bishops was that:

> For as soon as the announcement was made, some members of the diocese went on the war path. Xenophobia raised up its ugly head: they could not see a non-Bini appointed a bishop for Benin Diocese, when they had barely tolerated Rt. Revd. George, a non-Bini, only so soon. Why not an Ovbi-Edo (a Benin Son or proper Bini) this time around? Now, Peter Onekpe, hails from Etsako, a sub-ethnic group of the Edo tribe, which speaks a dialect of the Edo Language.[34]

Agbaje, it must be noted, was a partisan, one of the electors, a beneficiary of Adetiloye and the "*shon-of-the shoe*l"[35] appointment system and an indigene of the Sabongida Ora diocese, from which both George and Onekpe hailed. His explanation of the Benin people's protest as xenophobia and his claim that Benin "barely tolerated Rt. Revd. George," without providing substantive evidence, was rather an ingenious attempt to demonize the Benins. There is no evidence of Benin indigenes protesting against the appointment or administration of Bishop George. According to the Justice Aluyi-led AAC, it was they, the Benin indigenes, who went to Oyo to bring Rev. George to succeed Bishop Idahosa as Bishop of the Benin Diocese. They could have as well demanded another Benin indigene as Idahosa's replacement.

Within one week of the announcement of the appointment of Ven. Onekpe, nine objections were made in response to the request of the Arch Bishop and in accord with the constitutional requirements for appointment of a Bishop.[36] The objectors argued that Benin Diocese should have an indigene of the diocese appointed as Bishop and not an indigene of another diocese who does not understand and cannot speak the indigenous language of the people. They further demanded that the Benin Diocese indigenes be treated in the same way as other ethnic groups including the predominantly Muslim Hausa people for whom a very young and inexperienced priest was appointed as Bishop of Wusasa. The other grounds of objections to Onekpe's appointment in Benin were not published. But when the same Onekpe was again appointed as Bishop of newly created Esan Diocese in 2000, there were objections on the same grounds that were used to reject him in Benin. The Esan diocese went further to add that "If the signal view of the so-called three member Archbishop Committee were heeded, Bishop Onekpe would not have qualified for reasons of acceptability, commitment (Canon IV, Section 10), sound faith (not interested in evangelism), and good morals (Canon IV, Section 18)."[37]

They substantiated their allegations with instances of converting church property, an ostentatious life style, high handedness and vindictiveness.

The Justice Aluyi-led Benin AAC claimed that Adetiloye brushed their objections aside and in spite of meetings and appeals to him by His Royal Majesty Omo n'Oba Erediauwa, King of Benin, he stuck to his guns by insisting on the Diocese's acceptance and consecration of Rev. Onekpe as Bishop of Benin Diocese. The Aluyi led AAC then got a court injunction and in response Adetiloye consecrated Onekpe as "Bishop in Benin" for which a restraining order was then issued on grounds that the office was foreign to the Church's constitution. In addition to this legal challenge, the Aluyi AAC claimed that after they fasted and prayed, " the Holy Spirit gave utterance and someone said: "Venerable Michael Efe Igbinosa is the Anglican Bishop of Benin Diocese, Proclaim, Present and Enthrone him immediately,"[38] and this was done in 1999 thereby matching Adetiloye's "illegality" with their own illegality.

With these developments the Diocese became divided almost along ethnic lines. The so-called "foreigner" churches, St. James's Akpakpava (predominantly Urhobo, Isoko and Itsekiri), St. Paul's Second East Circular (predominantly Igbo) and Rev. W. J. Payne Memorial Church (Igbo) constituted themselves into "The Non-Benin Laity." Some members of the AAC who had signed the earlier recommendation, like Rev. Anyanwu (Igbo) and Rev. Okoh, threw their weight behind Archbishop Adetiloye and Rev. Onekpe. The Aluyi AAC group claimed that their attempt to hold joint Lenten services in March was rebuffed and that the Non-Benin Laity group carried out propaganda of ethnicity against the Benin people.[39] This propaganda was printed in the newspapers by press reporters from non-Benin groups such as Godwin Ifijeh of *This Day* Newspaper who traced the crisis to "Benins ... demanding for a son of the soil as Bishop..."[40] The accusation of ethnicity or xenophobia against the Aluyi group is not fully supported by evidence as they also had some non-Benin Clergy as signatories to their published petitions.[41] The result of this division of the churches almost along ethnic lines was that it became difficult to hold services in some of the churches because of fear and threats of attack and the use of policemen and thugs to maintain security in the churches on Sundays.

With this crisis further deteriorating, some other Christian denominations including the Catholic Church became worried about the impression this development was creating on the non-Christian community in the state, which they were struggling to convert. They set up a peace committee to meet with the various parties to the dispute. The committee subsequently forwarded a petition to the Primate in May 1999 in which they lamented the scandalous situation, which was affecting evangelism and pleaded for reversal of the Bishop's illegal proclamation, the transfer of Onekpe to another diocese, and the consideration of an appointment of a Benin as Bishop of the Diocese.[42] The Episcopal Synod of the Anglican Church was reported to have considered the petition and accepted all the recommendations except the translation of Onekpe to another Diocese.[43]

This was followed by other delegations and meetings, which yielded no agreement until the retirement of Adetiloye in September 1999. His successor, Archbishop Peter Akinola, also rejected the transfer of Rev. Onekpe to another diocese and appointment of an indigene as Bishop. He went further to suspend "Bishop" Igbinosa and his supporting members of the clergy and directed them to surrender all Church properties in their possession while he directed "The Non-Benin Laity" to disband and renounce the name. This development emboldened the "The Non-Benin laity" and Onekpe to test the resolve of the Aluyi led AAC in 2000 by trying to gain control of St Matthew Anglican Cathedral, Benin City. This attempt met with resistance and the crisis took a further violent turn and degenerated into a "free for all" fight in which dangerous weapons were reportedly used.[44] It was only after this episode that Bishop Akinola and the Aluyi-led AAC reached a compromise. The compromise agreement was for Rev. Onekpe to be consecrated and act as Bishop of Benin Diocese for six months after which he would be transferred and an indigene would be consecrated as Bishop of Benin. This settlement was implemented in 2003 after which peace was restored to the diocese.

Adetiloye's biographer and a partisan, Rev. Agbaje, blamed the crisis on Aluyi and Benin xenophobia. He went ahead to praise Adetiloye's refusal to bow to ethnicity and compromise, which had been tolerated in the Warri Diocesan crisis of 1977 to 1980. He further claimed that they chose and towed the line of the Roman Catholics who refused to bow to such tactics in the same Warri Diocese in the early 1990s.[45] The Aluyi-led AAC saw a "hidden agenda" in Adetiloye's refusal to bow to the will of the indigenes of Benin to have their own son as Bishop.[46]

Conclusion

The paper examined the crisis that engulfed the Benin Diocese of the Church of Nigeria Anglican Communion between 1995 and 2003. It traced the crisis to the linguistic and ethnic cleavages that had been incorporated into the administrative policies and practices of the Church since the 1920s and the intersection of local political struggles for ethnic autonomy with church administration. It showed how the resultant ethnic/language group-based churches in the Diocese consolidated ethnic cleavages. It also noted how the rural/ urban character of non-Benin areas and Benin City respectively affected the indigenes acceptance of clerical vocations and their role in the leadership and administration of the church. These developments led to the predominance of non-Benin indigenes in the administration of the diocese and the relative neglect of evangelization in the Benin- Edo dialect.

Although there has been the continuous struggle of various ethnic groups for ethnic political autonomy and control of the churches in their localities in the region and there is a coincidence of Benin political and religious leadership in the struggle, the support by some non-Benin members of the Clergy for appointment of a Bishop that speaks the language or dialect of the indigenous people of the diocese for purposes of evangelism makes the struggle one for the promotion of evangelism rather than an attempt to impose a Benin agenda. The church only needs to be sensitive to the needs of the indigenous people in its fold, instead of relying solely on the wisdom of the Primate and deciding through analogies as done in the Benin diocese case. The church should also take cognizance of local politics for peaceful administration especially as the church cannot be insulated from local politics.

Notes

1. A. A. Agbaje, *Abiodun Lagos: A Blossomy Tree in the Desert A Biography of Joseph Abiodun Adetiloye* (Lagos, Nigeria: CSS Limited, 2001), 119 and Godwin Ifijeh, "Crisis in Church of Nigeria, Diocese Rejects Bishop," http://www.thisdayonline/archive/2001/02/16/20010216dia01.html
2. Emmanuel Ayandele, *Holy Johnson: Pioneer of African Nationalism, 1836-1917* (London: Frank Cass, 1970), 257.
3. Queen Arokun's (a.k.a. Ayosore) mother was Ijesha-Yoruba just like James Johnson's mother. See Ekhaguosa Aisien, *The Benin City Pilgrimage Stations* (Benin City, Nigeria: Aisien Publishers, 2001) 204-5.
4. National Archives Ibadan, File BP 4/2/8 Annual Report of Benin Province for the year ending 31/12/1921.
5. James Johnson, "A Dark Corner of Nigeria: A Report by Bishop James Johnson on the Work of the Benin Mission presented to the Diocesan Synod of Nigeria" *The Church Missionary Review*, Vol. LXIV, No.775, November 1913, 679.
6. Ayandele *Holy Johnson: Pioneer of African Nationalism, 1836-1917*, 278-9 and 349 and Aisien, *The Benin City Pilgrimage Stations,* 205

7. National Archives, Ibadan, File BP 553/1915 Commissioner, Benin Province to District Officers, Benin Province, 23/03/1916.
8. National Archives, Ibadan File BP884/1914 Bishop Tugwell to Inspector of Schools, Niger Division, 28/10/1914.
9. National Archives, Ibadan, Un-numbered File R. L. V. Wilkes "An Intelligence Report on 34 Independent Villages of Kukuruku Division, Benin Province, 01/04/1940, Rev. W.J. Payne, Report on Benin District, 1922.
10. National Archives, Ibadan File CMS Y 2/2:15, Rev. W. J. Payne, Report on Benin District, 1922.
11. Johnson, "A Dark Corner of Nigeria," *Church Missionary Review*, 680.
12. For details see National Archives, Ibadan File CMS Y 2/2:15 Rev. W. J. Payne Report on Benin District, 1922.
13. National Archives, Ibadan File BP 4/1916 Letter to District Commissioner, 19/04/1916.
14. National Archives, Ibadan File BP 611/1919 Resident to Catechist E.E. Ohuoba.
15. National Archives, Ibadan File CMS Y 2/2:15, Rev. W. J. Payne Report on Benin District, 1922.
16. Personal Communication with Pa Gabriel O. Obazee, Aged 73 years at Benin City, 2008.
17. P. O. Ebhomielen "Expansion of Baptist Mission in Edo North (1)" in Dickson O. Uwagboe *The Baptist Mission in Edo Land 1921-2003: A History of Christianity and the Southern Baptist/Nigerian Baptist Convention Missionary Work in Edo State , Nigeria* (Benin City, Nigeria : Allied Press Services International, 2004), 152-162.
18. Sam U. Erivwo, "The Life and Work of Agori Iwe, First Bishop of Benin Diocese (Anglican Communion) 1988," http:// www.waado.org/Biographies/ Agori Iwe/Chapter Eleven.html
19. Ibid
20. Apart from the multi-ethnic character of Benin City, the area covered by the diocese included numerous dialects of Edo, which were not mutually intelligible to the speakers. The Colonial administration administered these dialect groups as separate and distinct entities. This reinforced ethnic identities and increased animosities especially in their struggle over resources. The state went further to promote development of literature in these dialects, which further kept the people apart and worked against the development of a single Edo identity.
21. Erivwo, "The Life and Work of Agori Iwe."
22. Ibid. Chapter 15.
23. Ibid.

24. Uyilawa Usuanlele and K. A. Agbontaen, "A History of Modern Literary Development among the Edos, 1897-1960" in *Africa Rivista Trinestrale di Studi. Decumentazine dell Istituto per l'Africa el. Oriente*, Anno IV No. 1, March 2000, 110.
25. Publication of the complete Urhobo (Language of the Bishop Agori-Iwe) Bible was completed in 1977 under Agori-Iwe's (Urhobo) while only portions of the Bible were published in Esan-Edo in 1974, Etsako-Edo in 1980 http://www.worldscriptures.org/pages.html Viewed on 01/02/08
26. Erivwo, "The Life and Work of Agori Iwe,"
27. Church of Nigeria Anglican Communion, *Genesis of the events in the crisis in the Anglican Diocese of Benin* (Benin City, Nigeria: Temi and Company Press, n.d., 10.
28. There were newspaper adverts protesting the name Edo State and the constitution of the State. Some of the signatories to these adverts were also in the forefront of agitation for Afemesan State.
29. Joseph Eboreime, "Oral traditions and the Pre-history of Edo speaking People of Benin" Roger Blench and Matthew Spriggs (ed.) *Archaeology and Language 1: Theoretical and Methodological Orientations* (Oxford: Routeledge, 1997), 319.
30. Uyilawa Usuanlele "The Edo Nationality and the National Question in Nigeria: A historical Perspective" in Eghosa Osaghae and Ebere Onwudiwe, *The Management of the National Question in Nigeria* (Ibadan, Nigeria: PEFS, 2001).
31. Members included Justice Isaac O. Aluyi (Benin Edo), Rev. Can. O. I. Anyanwu (Igbo), Mr. E. Ogor (Itsekiri), Mrs E. O. Ighodaro (Benin-Edo), Dr. S. I. Urhoghide Esq. (Benin-Edo), Mrs. E. O. Alufokhai (Ora-Edo), Rev. Can. (Dr) S. O. Z. Omokhua (Owan-Edo) and Rev. Can. O. O. Okoh (Ika-Igbo or Esan-Edo).
32. Church of Nigeria Anglican Communion, *Genesis of the events in the crisis in the Anglican Diocese of Benin*, 3-5.
33. Agbaje, *Abiodun Lagos: A Blossomy Tree in the Desert A Biography of Joseph Abiodun Adetiloye*, 118-9.
34. Ibid., 119.
35. A poor ethnic pronunciation of "son of the soil" - local slang for expressing the insistence of appointing only the indigene of a locality to offices in that locality.
36. Church of Nigeria Anglican Communion, *Genesis of the events in the crisis in the Anglican Diocese of Benin*, 6.

37. Quoted in Godwin Ifijeh, "Crisis in Church of Nigeria, Diocese Rejects Bishop," http://www.thisdayonline/archive/2001/02/16/20010216dia01.html
38. Church of Nigeria Anglican Communion, *Genesis of the events in the crisis in the Anglican Diocese of Benin,* 10.
39. Ibid, 10-11.
40. Godwin Ifijeh, "Crisis in Church of Nigeria, Diocese Rejects Bishop" http://www.thisdayonline/archive/2001/02/16/20010216dia01.html
41. Five of the forty-one members of the Clergy that signed the Aluyi group petition of 1999 were non-Benins. See list in Church of Nigeria Anglican Communion, *Genesis of the events in the crisis in the Anglican Diocese of Benin,*13-14.
42. See copy of Petition in Agbaje, *Abiodun Lagos: A Blossomy Tree in the Desert A Biography of Joseph Abiodun Adetiloye*, 122-9.
43. See reply of Rev. Dr. Peter Adebiyi, Episcopal Secretary, Church of Nigeria, Anglican Communion in Ibid, 129-132.
44. Godwin Ifijeh, "Crisis in Church of Nigeria,"
45. Agbaje, *Abiodun Lagos: A Blossomy Tree*," 119-21.
46. Church of Nigeria Anglican Communion, 9.

THE SHARI'A AND THE POLITICS OF RELIGION

Chapter Seven

Shari'a in the History and Political Development of Nigeria

Mukhtar Umar Bunza

The introduction of Islam in Nigeria characterized a number of changes and transformations. One remarkable transformation was the adoption of the Shari'a legal system to regulate the life and day-to-day affairs of Muslims, especially in social and political spheres. The political change that Islam brought about signified a redirection of the society from traditional religious practices to an Islamic polity. Obaro Ikime noted the role of traditional religion on governance and politics in the various societies of Nigeria before the advent of Islam and its concomitant practices. He observed that religion and government were intertwined in the earliest times. According to him:

> Among Nigerian multifarious peoples, religion was inextricably mixed with government. The rituals performed by the Yoruba and Benin Obas, the Sarakuna of Hausaland, the Okpans, Obi or Eze of the Igbo, the Amokouowei or Amaiyanabo of the Ijaw, the Ivie or Oppako of the Urhobo and Isoko, etc, were an essential ingredients in the maintenance of political order and stability and the promotion of the peoples moral code.[1]

The situation did not change radically with the advent of Islam. The mixture of religious and political practices continued with rulers participating in religious activities. Like the traditional religion, Islam also became highly entrenched into the governance, regulating peoples' private and public behavior. The more rulers accepted and practiced Islam, the more the religion penetrated the political system, especially with the adoption of Islamic principles in governance. That brought the question of the Shari'a to the forefront in the politics of northern Nigeria since the fifteenth century.

Islam made inroads into the northern parts of Nigeria through North Africa by the Muslim evangelists. The trans-Saharan trade that networked the Central Sudan and North Africa had been in existence for centuries before for the exchange of goods, ideas, and cultures to be transported across the regions. Islam benefited from this network of trade routes. This suggests Islam had been introduced to northern Nigeria many centuries before the advent of the Europeans. Although the exact date for the introduction of Islam into northern Nigeria is still contentious, the Kano Chronicle, based on oral tradition, mentions how "Yaji (c.1349-85), a ruler of the Kutumbawa dynasty, was converted by a party of forty scholars from Mali, who became absorbed in the general population of Kano."[2] By the fifteenth century, however, Islam had been consolidated in Hausaland and Borno, and it had begun to wield tremendous influence on the political system. According to Abdullahi Smith, fifteenth-century rulers such as Muhammad Korau in Katsina, Muhammad Rabbo in Zazzau, and Muhammad Rumfa in Kano played prominent roles in spreading Islam in Hausaland.[3]

The Shari'a legal system had been adopted in Borno where Islamic culture had been deeply entrenched before the fifteenth century. Two rulers who implemented the Shari'a were Dunama ibn Umme and Dunama Biri. Because Dunama Biri was weak in his conduct of the government, his mother Fatima, who was versed in the Shari'a became very influential. For failing to adhere to the tenets of the Shari'a, Biri's mother had her son imprisoned because he administered excessive punishment when he executed a thief instead of amputating a hand as the Shari'a demanded.[4] In Hausaland, Muhammad Rumfa (the king of Kano), following the advice of Muhammad Al-Maghili (a North African scholar and revolutionary), established a theocratic system of government in 1492.[5] That legacy and history made S. H. A. Malik conclude that the Shari'a was practiced in northern Nigeria, which comprised virtually the Sokoto Caliphate that was established in 1804. In all the emirates under the influence of the Sokoto Caliphate and the Bornu Empire, Qadi courts were established to dispense justice in accordance with the Shari'a.[6]

Since its adoption, Muslims in the Sokoto Caliphate and the Bornu Empire had considered the Shari'a as an integral part of their religious obligation and daily life, especially as it served as an efficacious legal system in curbing and controlling crimes as well as ensuring probity and accountability. Sulaiman Kumo argued that Muslims have come to recognize the importance of Shari'a law and Shari'a courts in northern Nigeria. He stated further that:

> It is perhaps because of their importance and their antiquity, the institution has been in existence for over one and a half centuries now as well as the high esteem in which they have always been held that they have survived to the present day. Throughout the present century no government of northern Nigeria has ever seriously considered abolishing them (Sharia courts) or even diminishing their power.[7]

Hugh Clapperton, a Scottish explorer to northern Nigeria in 1824, attested to the prevailing peace and security as a result of the application of the Shari'a and wrote:

> The laws of the Qur'an were in his (Bellos) time so strictly put ... that the whole country when not in a state of war, was so well-regulated that it is a common saying that a woman might travel with a casket of gold upon her head from one end of the Fellata dominion to the other (without fear).[8]

Clapperton's attestation shows that the Shari'a was adopted as part of the cultural, religious, and political traditions of the people in the region before the advent of the British imperialists. It is important to mention that since the colonial intervention into the politics and affairs of northern Nigeria in the early 1900s, there have been dramatic changes not only in the legal and judicial spheres, but also in the entire socio-political systems. Western civilization in the form of politics and religion gradually pervaded northern Nigeria but since then, Muslims in northern Nigeria preferred the Shari'a to the colonial legal system. The colonial control of northern Nigeria resulted in the marginalization and suspension of the criminal aspects of the Shari'a, leaving the civil cases for the lower Shari'a Courts, and English laws and courts with supreme and unrestricted jurisdiction. The system remained as part of the colonial legacy of colonized Nigeria, which continued as part of the Nigerian legal system and is upheld in its constitutions to date.

Colonialism and the Shari'a Legal System

The British conquered and governed the southern part of Nigeria with the annexation of Lagos in 1861. The British economic and political interests in the Sokoto Caliphate started to manifest when in 1899 the charter of the Royal Niger Company (RNC) was suspended. The Royal Niger Company had controlled the northern protectorate on behalf of the British government. Frederick Lugard led the expedition to and conquest of the Sokoto Caliphate in 1903. With the British taking direct control of northern Nigeria through military conquest, they were confronted with two main difficulties pertaining to control and administration of the emirates under the Sokoto and Bornu Caliphates. First, they were faced with the problem of the position and role of Islam within the fabric of the new political system, which upholds "religious neutrality" in the society. Second, they were concerned about how to handle the Shari'a legal system, substituting it with the English laws with little or no friction in the society. Eventually, they adopted a "friendly but watchful" religious policy in relation to Islam and its practices.[9]

The British colonial government pledged to respect Islam, but Muslims who resisted and objected to colonial domination in the form of 'Mahdism' through migration or armed struggle, and insisted on retaining the caliphal system, were severely dealt with. Sultan Attahiru I (1902-03) led this group of Muslims and the British forces chased him out of Sokoto and killed him at Bormi in July 1903. The anti-colonial ideology continued in different shades and under different leadership, and became a well-known philosophy of resistance in colonial northern Nigeria.[10] The Mahdist group insisted on not following the British legal system or working under the colonial administration because they doubted the legality of the judicial system. In spite of the stiff resistance against the colonial judicial policies, the Shari'a was tolerated only within the realm of civil cases and the principle of "Natural Justice, Equity and Good Conscience," which the British formulated. Frederick Lugard, who had become the British High Commissioner, declared in March 1903 that through conquest, the political authority of the Caliphate to rule had been transferred to the British, and on the application of the Shari'a, he ruled that:

> You Emirs can go on administering justice (i.e. Shari'ah) as before, but without any suspicion and corruption. I also

> add that you should stop cutting hands of thieves; you must leave every one with his feet and hands (the punishment in Shari'ah for robbery, homicide and continuous habit of theft).[11]

In 1906 Provincial Courts Proclamation Ordinances were passed. The colonial government, among other things, established Magistrate, High and Supreme Courts and gave them powers and superiority of unlimited jurisdiction against the Shari'a, through the Proclamation.[12] In order to fully control the aspects of the Shari'a and its application, the British thoroughly studied and modified it to ensure that it did not conflict with their administration. F. H. Ruxton, a colonial officer in northern Nigeria, wrote:

> The advantage to be gained by knowing something of the law of the people we govern is self evident, especially when, as in the case of Muhammedan countries, it is the law that has molded the people and not the people that mold the law. Again, when as in northern provinces of Nigeria it has been the policy of government to rule indirectly through the native administration, a knowledge of Muhammedan law is more than ever necessary, giving us, as it does, a clue to many acts, and supplying the main spring for many motives, which otherwise we should fail to understand. [13]

The colonial administration thoroughly studied the Shari'a and instituted many commissions and committees to further study the legal system and to advise the government accordingly. At the London Constitutional Conference in 1958 pressure was mounted on the Government of the Northern Region to modify its legal system before independence could be granted.[14] S. S. Richardson, a colonial commissioner for Native Courts in the Northern Region, outlines this inter-alia:

> The most important of the Panel's recommendation was that it was necessary for a self-governing Northern Region to establish a system of criminal law which would gain international acceptance, which would apply uniformly to all persons living within the region, which would not discriminate against any section of the community and which would be general acceptable throughout the Region.

> Since the majority of the people living within the Region are Muslims, it was also considered advisable that the new system should not be in conflict with the injunctions of the Qur'an and Sunnah.[15]

From the above, it was understood that the Shari'a judicial system was deficient on the basis of its lack of international acceptance and its discriminatory application. These were considered unacceptable and it required immediate amendments before Nigeria could be granted independence. However, fashioning the law not to contradict the provisions of the Qur'an and Sunnah (the two main source of law for Muslims) was only "considered advisable." This shows the position and fate of the Shari'a in the process of legal modification to attain the level of "international" acceptance.

The government of northern Nigeria appointed a panel of International Jurists to provide a new code of law for the Region in 1958. The Chief Justice of the Sudan Sayyid Muhammad Abu Rannat chaired the panel.[16] In 1959, the Draft Bill, based on the Codes of Pakistan, India, Malaysia, and Indonesia was submitted for scrutiny to the Wazir of Sokoto, Dr. Junaid ibn Bukhari (Wazir of Sokoto 1906-1997), and Haliru Binji former Grand Qadi of Sokoto State. After serious deliberations at the Northern House of Assembly, the Bill was passed into law effective October 1, 1960.[17]

Subsequently, new laws and policies were promulgated to render the Shari'a weaker and inferior to the English laws in statute and jurisdiction. A section of the Penal Code states that, "After the commencement of this law no person shall be liable to punishment under any native law or custom (Native Law and custom includes Moslem law)."[18]

The former Chief Justice of the federation, Justice Muhammad Bello, noted some key areas of conflict within the criminal justice system of the Northern Provinces and the British legal system. Although the emirates evolved a well-established judicial system, capital punishment such as the death penalty for offences associated with adultery, homicide, apostasy, and armed robbery recommended by the Shari'a were abolished. The colonial government upheld imprisonment instead of amputation for theft. The payment of *Diyya* ("blood money") in lieu of capital punishment was similarly abolished.[19]

Justice Bappa Mahmoud, Grand Qadi of the former Bauchi State, pointed out that in an attempt to marginalize the Shari'a, the colonial government established customary courts to dispense justice in accordance with traditional practices of the non-Muslims in a predominantly Islamic community. However, where Muslims constituted the minority, Shari'a courts were not established. Customary courts decided civil cases such as marriage and inheritance (even where Muslim parties were involved). For example, in southwestern Nigeria, Muslim Yoruba were not allowed to have civil cases determined by the Shari'a courts. No single Shari'a court was established in southwestern Nigeria in spite of the sizeable Muslim population there, and the situation remains the same.[20]

The colonial government systematically reduced the jurisdiction of the Shari'a legal system by pronouncing that: "no person shall be tried for a criminal offence except for an offence which is codified under a written law."[21] Since the Shari'a was categorized as an unwritten and un-codified law, the British argued that only the English laws had jurisdiction to try all offences in Nigeria including the Muslim areas. That colonial practice reflected in the constitutional reforms and reviews after independence.

After independence, Muslims persistently called for the return of their legal system. In order to reduce the pressure, the constitution recognized the establishment of Shari'a Courts of Appeal as appellates of the lower Shari'a Courts in 1977. The support for the Shari'a continued since it filled a void believed by Muslims left opened with the present British judicial system.

Factors for the Persistent Demand of the Shari'a

There are various reasons with regards to the continued demand of the Shari'a legal system among Muslims generally and in Nigeria and northern Nigeria in particular. These include:

Shari'a as part of Islamic Faith

The Shari'a legal system has been an integral part of Islamic faith and practice. The concept of the Shari'a among Muslims has gone beyond the modern concept of law. According to Mustapha:

> The word Shari'ah is defined as the complete universal code of conduct drawn by Allah through His messenger Muhammad (SAW) to mankind, detailing the religious, political, economic, intellectual and legal systems. It is meant for universal application, covering the entire spectrum of life, prescribing what lawful (halal) is and prohibiting that which is unlawful.[22]

For Muslims, Shari'a has supremacy over human laws regulating conduct and action. It covers all aspects of human endeavor: economic, political, social, or theological. First, it is a complete way of life for a Muslim.[23] Second, the significance of the Shari'a to a Muslim cannot be perceived and compared with any form of system, which derived its substance from the Western world where religion is considered to be a private, individual affair. Justice Orire argues that it was a Euro-Christian concept and belief to classify life affairs into spiritual and mundane, religious and secular. This, according to him, is the main source of conflict between the Muslims and others who want Muslims to have the same belief and religious perception like them. Failure to do this causes Muslims to be labeled with of all kinds of names.[24] Third, according to A. A. Gwandu, the Shari'a is as important to Muslims as the Ten Commandments are to Christians.[25] P. A. T. Williams noted, "Christianity was (unlike Islam) nowhere entrenched in the political system as was the case of Islam in the Sokoto Caliphate in the British Northern Nigeria."[26] The historical background of the Shari'a, its entrenchment in the political life of the people, and the way English laws were imposed, partly contributed to the resurfacing of the Shari'a among the Muslims.

The Human Rights Watch project extensively explored the position of the Shari'a and concluded that, "for Muslims, it [Shari'a] is also a philosophy and entire set of rules and guidelines which extends well beyond the Western concept of laws and governs day to day conducts in terms of social relations, private life and ethical codes."[27] This suggests that the Human Rights Watch recognizes the importance of the Shari'a to Muslims. The Qur'an unequivocally condemns any partial application of the Shari'a and declares other judicial systems as laws of the people of ignorance and inconsistent with the provisions of the Shari'a. According to the Qur'an:

> Then we put you (O Muhammad and the followers) on an ordained way concerning the matter [Shari'ah]; so follow it and do not follow the inclinations of those who do not know. Indeed, they will never avail you against Allah at all and indeed, the wrongdoers [the opponent of the Shari'ah] are allies of one another; but Allah is the protector of the righteous [who uphold his ordained laws]. [28]

While the Qur'an charged Muslims to follow the Sahri'a, it similarly called on Christians and Jews to uphold the laws of their scriptures. It states: "O people of scripture (Jews and Christians) you are on nothing until you uphold the law of the Torah, the Gospel, and what has been revealed from your Lord" (Qur'an 6:68). The retribution for not applying the Shari'a by Muslims has been stated in three places in the Qur'an as tantamount to disbelief, wrongdoing, and defiant disobedience to Allah.[29] These phrases and verses are daily rehearsed in what Muslims believed to be an absolute truth-the Qur'an. This could well be one of the strongest reasons for Muslims' unalloyed commitment to their legal system. According to Bernard Lewis, this spirit for respect and supporting the religious tenets in Islam is an incessant struggle, which must be expected in the history of Muslim societies because:

> In the classical Islamic view, to which many Muslims are beginning to return, the world and all mankind are divided into two: the House of Islam, where the Muslim law and faith prevail, and the rest, known as the House of Unbelief or the House of War, which is the duty of Muslims ultimately to bring to Islam.[30]

The demand for the Shari'a ought to be expected among the people who are known to be strict in their loyalty to the provisions of their scripture.

The Caliphal History and Legacy

Another underpinning factor for the clamor for implementation of the Shari'a hinges on the history of the Borno and Sokoto Caliphates and their political and educational impacts for centuries before the British intervention. The traditional institutions from the Sultan to the emirs derived their source of power and influence from the defunct Caliphal system. As mentioned earlier, after the Borno experience, one of the consequences of the jihad, led by the Shehu, Usman dan Fodio, was the establishment of a society based on the Shari'a. Consequently, reference to the political organization and other achievements of the Caliphate would not exclude the popularized and institutionalized religious legal system–the Shari'a, which continuously influenced people's behavior and perception.

For many people in northern Nigeria, the Sokoto legacy was entrenched in the educational pursuit of the Muslims. Founders of the Caliphate wrote and left books, which call for the renewal of the society as a result of corruption, ungodliness, and injustice, as it happened in the pre-jihad Hausa societies. Jonathan Reynolds shows that not only the emirs and traditional rulers, but also politicians too refer to the Caliphate's political experience and achievements with respect and reverence in order to win the support of Muslims in Nigeria.[31] The relevance of the policies of the Sokoto Caliphate in solving most of Nigeria's social and political problems is generally exposed in conferences, seminars, and workshops within and outside the country. In the recent bi-centenary celebration of the Caliphate in June 2004 (1804-2004), President Olusegun Obasanjo, although a Christian and with reservation about its application, was proud of the political structure and good governance exemplified by the century long political experience of the Sokoto Caliphate until the British conquest in 1903.[32]

Shari'a as a means of Crime Control

The Shari'a has been an effective means of controlling crimes as exemplified in the days of the Sokoto Caliphate. During the colonial period, some British officers in northern Nigeria believed that the Shari'a, as adopted in the Sokoto Caliphate, provided a better security than the British legal and political systems. For example, Palmer, a senior colonial officer, commented: "It is lamentably impossible to deny that in Hausaland the incident of crimes, notably theft, murder; robbery and burglary have grown worse instead of better since British occupation."[33]

Since the Shari'a has been undermined, the decline in morality and discipline, especially among the youth, has been a disturbing phenomenon to successive governments in Nigeria. In the late 1970s the situation forced the then government of General Obasanjo to embark on what was called "Ethical Revolution." The idea was to restore dignity and ethical behavior to the Nigerian society. The lack of discipline in the mid-1980s, triggered a new campaign, which the Buhari/Idiagbon military government tagged the "War Against Indiscipline" (WAI). The increasing rate of crime, insecurity, and drug-related offences are major concerns of the present administration. Although people have divergent opinions regarding the root causes of the problems in Nigeria, for most Muslims, the society is not at fault, but its legal system is grossly deficient. Muslims believe that the Shari'a is an alternative to the Western legal law that is adopted in the country.

The Human Rights Watch identified the successive governments' failure to protect the life and property of their citizens against the high rate of robbery, burglary, theft and indecent actions as one of the reasons for the increasing demand for the Shari'a by Muslims. Similarly, Muslims' increasing disappointment with the English legal system was engendered by the state's inability to provide for basic necessities for the people. Instead, there is poverty, increase in taxes, and corruption is rife among political officers. The Human Rights Watch observes:

> There is the widespread poverty across Nigeria, and the North is especially underdeveloped. There was the expectation among the general public that Shari'ah, with its emphasis on welfare and the state responsibility to provide for the basic needs of the population, would go some way towards alleviating their plights. People also felt frustrated with the law enforcement agencies and the judiciary: crime was increasing, yet the police and the courts were paralyzed by inefficiency and corruption. Shari'ah was seen as an alternative to these problems, offering a system which promised to be faster, less cumbersome and less corrupt.[34]

Muhammad Tabiu made a similar observation that the secular Western laws have been ineffective in controlling crimes. He stated that, it is necessary to avert the growing problem of insecurity, failure, and frustration. Security, peace, and discipline, which the Shari'a provided effectively in the past, are eluding Nigeria today. Tabiu emphasized further that nowhere has the war against crime been as successfully waged as in the countries where the Shari'a is in force.[35] Saudi Arabia, where the Shari'a is substantially enforced, has a low crime rate, unlike the United States and Western countries.

Shari'a and Freedom from Colonization

The British occupation of Nigeria was met with stiff resistance. In the Niger Delta, Jaja of Opobo led the resistance against the British for political and economic reasons. Unaware of the implications of the treaty of protection he signed with the British, Jaja continued to maintain his political independence. After a military struggle with the British, Jaja was deported to the West Indies in 1887 where he later died.[36] R. A. Adeleye argued that in the Sokoto Caliphate, the primary reason for resistance was to maintain religious freedom. This argument was more applicable to the struggle and stance of Sultan Attahiru I (1902-1903) who opted for a military response and flight against the British invaders instead of accepting or befriending them. The Waziri Bukhari, after the occupation of Sokoto town in March 1903, opined that Muslims could succumb to a stronger force temporarily pending the time of their strength and ability to resist. According to Adeleye, Waziri Bukhari supported peace with the British instead of armed resistance.[37] Since then, most Muslims opted for other forms of opposition against the Western political systems, and they continue to do so. Similarly, the demand for the Shari'a as a right for Muslims against the European imposed laws continued. M. A. Khan argued in favor of Muslims' freedom to practice Shari'a by indicating that Muslims were totally governed by Islamic law until Nigeria became a British colony. The advent of the British and their political system saw the gradual phasing out of Islamic law. Khan argues further that the present truncated form of Islamic law applied in Nigeria is a product of colonial tyranny. In conformity with their social and legal aspirations, Muslims in Nigeria should advocate gradual enlargement of the scope and extent of the application of Islamic laws to them to actualize their freedom from he British legal system.[38]

Although it may be argued that Shari'a was a foreign and imported law like the English legal system, it has been an integral part of Islamic tenets, which Muslims have accepted to practice. The British, by the use of arms, conquered the peoples of northern Nigeria and imposed their socio-cultural and legal practices on unwilling subjects on terms not negotiated. Whereas Muslims in the Sokoto Caliphate enthusiastically accepted Islam and the Shari'a, the British conquest and imposed colonial rule did not receive such a popular acceptance.

In his address at the inauguration of the expanded Shari'a legal system in 1999, the Zamfara State governor, Sani Ahmad Yerima, raised the question of religion and decolonization. He stated:

> This day and event will be marked in the annals of not only Zamfara state but throughout our beloved country, Nigeria as the culminating point in the actualization of the hopes, ideals and aspiration of many of our citizens- the Muslims. The Muslims have for long yearned for the freedom to exercise their full rights (to apply the Shari'ah) since the period they were invaded and colonized by the British.[39]

Most Muslims in Nigeria do not consider the English legal system and the rites associated with it as truly Nigerian or African. In the spirit of nationalism, Muslims advocated for the Shari'a while Christians chose to establish African Independent Churches as a means of protesting against the colonization of the church by European missionaries.[40] It is not surprising that people resisted the foreigners who vandalized their fatherland, enslaved their forefathers, and exploited their natural resources and wealth.

In his research on the Shari'a in Zamfara State, Ostien identified "Ten Good Things about Shari'ah in Nigeria." Among them was connecting the Nigerian Muslims back to their religious roots and history, which was disrupted by the British imperialists. In his opinion:

> This (Shari'ah) is understandable and healthy reaction by a colonized people whose autonomous development within their own ancient and eminently respectful tradition was arrested, or shall we say hijacked, when the British took them over in 1900. View the effects of British rule in the north how you will: The fact remains that the laws and institutions of the British introduced were alien to the culture and that they ousted the Shari'ah from the place of honor it had held; for many Muslims, British laws and institutions supposed to have 'failed' even in the land that gave them birth... by reclaiming their own legal and cultural heritage and the right to develop it themselves... they see that if they don't like it, they can change it. This is an important step in political maturation.[41]

Murray Last, in his study on the implementation of Shari'a in northern Nigeria, emphasized the intersection of religion and politics by stating that:

> To reinstate the Shari'h, therefore, is not only good religion, it is supremely sound politics: only through the Shari'ah people say, can Nigerian Muslim society realistically escape from the morass of corruption and misgovernment, from the breakdown of justice from the immoralities of conspicuous wealth, drunkenness and whoring, from epidemics of both petty burglary and vicious armed robbery, from the desperate joblessness of the urban young... Every other solution, military or democratic, since independence has clearly failed: the only solution now, say many, is the restoration of the Muslim community through a return to the Shari'ah in its entirety.[42]

In this sense, the feeling of being colonized and deprived of one's freedom of choice and determination has remained an important factor in the Shari'a campaign in recent times. In the opinion of Rotimi Suberu, the question of Shari'a shall continue to persist in Nigeria due to: ethno-religious demographics, the struggle to assert or reassert northern Muslim political primacy, the clash of English and Islamic legal cultures, the inherent intractability of the Shari'a as a simultaneously symbolic and technical subject, the ambiguity of Nigeria's secularity, and the constitutional and political instability of the Nigerian state.[43]

The Post 1999 Shari'a in Nigeria

From 1960 to 1998 civil cases such as marriage and inheritance were mainly the issues determined by the Shari'a courts at various levels in northern Nigeria. The question of total application of the Shari'a beyond civil cases and enactments of the Shari'a codes (codified and passed into laws by the Legislature and the Executive) was not known before 1999. The post-1999 has been one of the remarkable epochs in the religious history of the region since independence. The year 1999 ushered in a democratic experiment with the emergence of the Fourth Republic. The termination of military dictatorship and the return to democracy could be considered as one of the factors for the new dimension in the Shari'a demands and its implementation.[44] The post 1999 Shari'a protagonists consistently invoked the constitutional provisions to justify their demand and application of the Shari'a following the fulfillment of democratic and legislative procedures.

Section 38:1 of the Nigerian Constitution, relating to freedom of religion, deals with the right in private or public, to propagate, teach, practice, and observe one's religious belief without hindrance, and is cited as the main constitutional clause for the Muslims' rights under the Constitution to apply the Shari'a. Similarly, with respect to section 36(12) that requires any conviction under criminal offences to be defined and codified, the 1999 Shari'a satisfies the provision. The Attorney General and Commissioner of Justice, Zamfara State responded thus:

> The law is codified and I have a copy to prove that. It is fundamental that before you go the Shari'ah way that you must satisfy the provisions of section 36(12) of the Constitution which states that you cannot prosecute any body unless the offence is defined and codified by the legislative arm.[45]

The declaration of the full-fledged Shari'a in Zamfara in both civil and criminal aspects in 1999 engendered unprecedented debates. The process was unique in its approach, proceedings, and conduct in the history of Nigeria's legal system. For one, it put forward a constitutional provision and approval to legitimize the Shari'a application. It also adopted the formal and democratic legislative procedure, where the state House of Assembly proposed a bill, which was sent to the Executive Governor and was passed into law. This democratic posture, according to Murray Last, made it different from the "fundamentalist" approach in any radical sense. "The people supporting the Shari'ah," according to Last, "were not radicals, but mainstream Muslims. Democracy is a new beginning for Nigeria, and Shari'ah is what Muslims want as their new beginning."[46] What has to be determined is how the application of the Shari'a would meet the demand and aspirations of the Muslims.

In 1992, John O. Hunwick (an expert on the history of northern Nigeria and the Sudan) predicted that, "It would be no surprise if some states with Muslim majorities eventually seek to arrogate to themselves the right to impose Shari'ah as the only form of law within their territories."[47] That prediction came true in the post-1999 era of Nigerian religious and political history. The new Shari'a system entails some features for the restoration of public confidence and morality. As Ostien indicated the Shari'a basically applies to only the Muslims while Christians and other religious groups could take their case to either the Magistrate or the Customary Courts.

Ostein outlined the feature and characteristics of the post-1999 Shari'a to include: the establishment of Shari'a Courts of first instance for the application of Islamic Law to Muslims; establishment of State Council of *Ulama'* with a wide mandate to formulate, interpret, and monitor the implementation of Islamic Law, imposition of *Zakat* (alms) taxes on Muslims; prohibition for Muslims and non-Muslims alike of the sale and consumption of alcohol; concerted effort to drive out prostitution and gambling; segregation of women in the schools and public transportation, and the establishment of a censorship board to check the spread of immorality packaged as cultural products.[48] These offences were codified by either the States as the Shari'a Code or by Local Government Councils as Bylaws. In either case, a similar judicial proceeding will be followed to the enactment of the law. This is an important landmark in the religious and political history of the legislative proceedings of Nigeria since independence.

The implementation of the Shari'a triggered a lot of questions. These include the constitutionality of the Shari'a, the issue of Human Rights, the concern of the international community, and the treatment of non-Muslims under the Shari'a. Several scholars have addressed these issues.[49] A Human Rights Watch report states: "the provisions for and imposition of sentence amounting to cruel, inhuman and degrading treatment and punishment in particular the death penalty, amputation and flogging are among the main Human Rights concerns arising in the context of Shari'ah in northern Nigeria."[50] To this effect, the Human Rights Watch submitted some recommendations to the Federal Government of Nigeria and the states operating the Shari'a, stating that:

> The Nigerian federal and state governments should carry out a review of Shari'a state legislation introduced since

> 2000 and remove those sections of the laws which violate Fundamental Human Rights and breach Nigeria's obligation under the Constitution and International Human Rights Conventions. In particular, they should eliminate provisions for cruel, inhuman, degrading punishments including death sentences, amputations and flogging and provisions, which discriminate against women. They should also decriminalize consensual sex relation among adults.[51]

By implication, the Human Right Watch was directing a reversal in the legislative structure of northern Nigeria to something that is judicially unattainable in the Penal Code of the region. The Human Rights in this case did not care about the rights, freedom, and democratic privileges to enact laws based on the need of the people following the laid down legal procedures. In response to the recommendations by the Human Rights Organizations, Ishaq Oloyede wrote:

> Muslims are understandably angered by the use of Western prejudices and customs to evaluate and adjudge another legal system (the Shari'a). The repugnancy doctrine of the Western Law which condemn some Shari'a provisions and declare them as universally unacceptable since they are considered by the West as incompatible with 'Western 'natural' justice, equity, fair play and Western promulgations is inhibitive to meaningful dialogue between Muslims and the West on the Shari'a.[52]

The position between Muslims, the West, Human Rights, and other civil organizations of Western origin regarding the Shari'a is varied and raises serious challenges. Muslims cannot review any aspect of the Shari'a legal system because, as mentioned earlier, it is believed to be a sacred law. Scholars such as Yadudu, Mustafa, Sanusi, Ostien, and others see the current opposition to the Shari'a and insistence on the observance of strict English laws without any regard for the feeling and perception of the people concerned, as a continuing political and cultural imperialism in the name of freedom and modernity against developing nations.[53] Hence, the Western world attacks the Shari'a in strong terms. Sanusi Lamido Sanusi commented that:

> The Western response to Shari'ah has been near hysterical, characterized by widespread condemnation in the Human Rights of what the West term 'cruel, dehumanizing, even barbaric' punishments. The West speaks to Islam from the position of arrogance, demanding not a dialogue but capitulation to its values... in general, the West demands from other cultures unconditional acceptance of its concepts and values, showing little respect for their desire to protect their own cultural integrity. This makes dialogue difficult if not impossible.[54]

It is therefore necessary for the West to understand the nature of the demand and implication of the Shari'a in the socio-religious life of Muslims. Dialogue and mutual understanding and respect for each other's particularities would bridge the gap instead of the present perceived master-servant relationship where reason and democracy are less emphasized.

Conclusion

This chapter has argued that the quest for Shari'a in Nigeria has historical and religious background. Its long existence since the establishment of the Sokoto Caliphate explains why Muslims, especially in northern Nigeria, support its continuation and its equal status with the English laws for those willing to be adjudged by it. Also, the chapter observed that, the Shari'a occupied an important place in the history and polities of the Muslim communities of northern Nigeria since the fifteenth century and more importantly in the nineteenth century. As a result of the new political system based on the Shari'a, the Hausa state structure, which flourished for centuries, was substituted with the Caliphate and emirates. In spite of the colonial intervention in early twentieth century, that legacy remained and contributed into making the Shari'a a political case in almost all the constitutional reforms in Nigeria.

The current reimplementation of the Legal system and the incorporation of the criminal aspects against what used to be in Penal Code since October 1, 1960 was the result of that historical experience. The chapter, however, observed that the continued suppression of the demand of the Muslims for the legal system (considered as their constitutional right), strengthened their determination for it and made them more uncompromising. Furthermore, the method through which the re-application of the Shari'a was sought in the present time (through peaceful means) ought to have been supported not only by the Muslims, but also by adherents of other religions.

The unique nature of the implementation needs to be encouraged because it upholds the democratic-party politics and modern legislative procedure. It was also different from Ibrahim el-Zakzaky's (leader of Shiite group in Nigeria) Shiite model, which believes that, "Shari'a can only be realized after a jihad, which they must embark upon for its actualization."[55] The legislative and democratic approach to the implementation of the Shari'a is a middle course, unlike the total ban advocated by the Western world or the Shiite revolutionary alternative. In view of the history and other related factors, it was not surprising that the idea of reinstating the Shari'a will continue to receive popular support in northern Nigeria and may well persist to feature prominently in Nigerian politics and state affairs.

Notes

1. Cited by Williams, P. A. T., "Religion, Violence and Displacement in Nigeria," *Journal of African Asian Studies*, Vol. XXXII, 1-2, 1997, 38-39.
2. C. C. Ifemesia, "States of Central Sudan," in *A Thousand Years of West African History: A Handbook for Teachers and Students*, eds., J. F. Ade. Ajayi and Ian Espie (Ibadan, Nigeria: Ibadan University Press, 1965), 94-95.
3. Abdullahi Smith, "The Early States of the Central Sudan," in *History of West Africa*, Volume One, eds., J. F. A Ajayi and Michael Crowder (London: Longman, 1976), 190.
4. Hogben, J. S., and Kirk-Greene, A.H. M, *The Emirates of Northern Nigeria: A Preliminary Survey of their Historical Tradition* (London: Oxford University Press, 1966), 92. In Yusuf Bala Usman's opinion, Borno had established a long history of Islamic learning and development for centuries before Hausaland. Usman, Y. B., "A Reflection of the History of Relations between Borno and Hausland before 1804," in *Studies in the History of Precolonial Borno*, ed. Usman, B. and Alkali, N. (Zaria, Nigeria: NNPC, 1983), 204.
5. See details on this in Gwandu, A. A., "Shari'ah in northern Nigeria: The Experiences of the Sokoto caliphate and Bornu," in *Understanding Shari'ah in Nigeria*, ed., Yakubu, A. M., Kani, A. M., and Junaid, M. I. (Abuja, Nigeria: Spectrum Publishers, 2001), 83-105. See also Kani A. M., "The Meaning and Application of Shari'ah in the Sokoto Caliphate," in *Shari'ah Social Change and Indiscipline in Nigeria,* ed., Rasheed, K. S. (Sokoto, Nigeria: Sokoto University Press, 1987), 160-171.
6. Malik, S. H. A., "The Implication of Shari'ah as a Legal System in Nigeria," in *Understanding Shari'ah in Nigeria*, 131.

7. Kumo, S., "Organization and Procedure of Shari'ah Courts in Northern Nigeria," Ph.D. Dissertation, University of London, 1972, 14.
8. Clapperton, H., *Journal of a Second Expedition into the Interior of Africa* (London: Frank Cass, 1829), 206.
9. See Bunza, M. U., "Political Islam in the Colonial Northern Nigeria 1905-1960," in *Journal of Islamic Studies*, (Special Issue), No. 22, 2002, 66-81.
10. M. A. Alhajj, "Mahdist Tradition on Northern Nigeria," Ph.D. Dissertation, Abdullahi Bayero College/ ABU Kano, 1973; A. G. Saed, "A Biographical Study of Shaykh Sai'd Bin Hayyat (1887-1978) and the British Policy Towards the Mahdiyya in Northern Nigeria, 1900-1960," Ph.D. Dissertation, Bayero University Kano, 1992 and A. G. Saed, "British Fears over Mahdism in Northern Nigeria: A Look at Bormi 1903, Satiru 1906, and Dumbulwa 1923," *Frankfurter Afrikanistische Blatter* 4, 1992, 35-37.
11. Quoted in Doi, I. A., *Islam in Nigeria*, 210.
12. Mahmud, A. B. *A Brief History of Shari'ah in the Defunct Northern Nigeria* (Jos, Nigeria: Jos University Press, 1988), 11.
13. Quoted in Malik, S. H. A., "The Implementation of Shari'ah as a Legal System in Nigeria," 132.
14. That was the resolution after the famous London Constitutional Conference of 1958. See Mahmud, 23.
15. Richardson, S. S., ed., *Notes on the Penal Code Law, 1959* (Zaria, Nigeria: Gaskiya Corporation, second edition, 1960), 1.
16. Members of the panel included Pakistani Supreme Court Judge Muhammad Sherrif, Professor David Anderson of SOAS, University of London, Sir Kashim Ibrahim, Alkali Musa Bida, and Peter Achimugu, an attorney in northern Nigeria.
17. Richardson, 1.
18. Ibid., 10.
19. Keynote Address of the Justice Muhammad Bello, former Chief Justice of the Federation published in *Understanding Shari'ah in Nigeria*, 8-9.
20. Mahmud, 3. For more information on the issue of the Shari'ah legal system in Yorubaland, see Amidu Olalekan Sanni, "The Shari'ah Conundrum in Nigeria and the Zamfara Model: The Role of the Nigerian Muslim Youth in Historical Context," *Journal of Muslim Minority Affairs*, 27: 1, 2007, 117-132.
21. Cited by Mahmud, 23.
22. Mustapha, A., "Shari'ah: A Conceptual Framework," in *Understanding Shari'ah in Nigeria*, 17.
23. Bello, 7.

24. Orire, A., "Shari'ah: A Legal System and a way of Life," in *Understanding Shari'ah in Nigeria,* 25-26.
25. Gwandu A. A., "Shari'ah in northern Nigeria: The Experiences of the Borno and Sokoto Caliphates," in *Understanding Shari'ah in Nigeria*, 83.
26. Williams, "Religion, Violence and Displacement in Nigeria," 39.
27. Human Rights Watch, *Political Shari'ah? Human Rights and Islamic Laws in Northern Nigeria.* Vol. 16, No. 9A, 2004, 10.
28. Qur'an, 45:18-19.
29. Qur'an, 6: 44-47.
30. Lewis, B., "The Roots of Muslim Rage," in *Inside Islam: The Faith, The People, And The Conflicts Of The World's Fastest-Growing Religion*, ed., Miller, J., and Kenedi, A. (New York: Marlowe and Company, 2002), 194.
31. Reynolds, J. T., "The Politics of History: The Legacy of the Sokoto Caliphate in Nigeria," in *Journal of African and Asian Studies*, Vol. XXXII, 1-2, 1991, 54.
32. The address was delivered at the opening ceremony of the bi-centenary celebration in Sokoto in June 2004.
33. Quoted in Ado-Kurawa, I., *Shari'ah and the Press in Nigeria: Islam Versus Western Christian Civilization* (Kano, Nigeria: Kurawa Holdings, 2000), 281.
34. Human Rights Watch, *Political Shari'ah? Human Rights and Islamic Laws in Northern Nigeria.* Vol. 16, No. 9A, September 2004, 14.
35. Tabiu, M., "Controlling the Crime rate in Nigeria through Shari'ah," in *Shari'ah Social Change and Indiscipline in Nigeria,* ed., Rasheed, K. S. (Sokoto, Nigeria: Sokoto University Press, 1987), 187.
36. Obaro Ikime, *The Fall of Nigeria: The British Conquest* (London: Heinemann, 1977), especially chapter V "The British Conquest of Northern Nigeria;" Episode 12, 76-87; and "The Fall of Sokoto," 198-209.
37. R. A. Adeleye, "The Dilemma of the Waziri: The place of *Risalat al- wazir ila ahlal al-ilm wa al-taddabur,* in the "History of the Conquest of the Sokoto Caliphate," *Journal of Historical Society of Nigeria, (JHSN),* Vol. IV, No. 2, June 1968, 285-298. See details about the British occupation and Muslims' continued resistance in Ikime, O., *The Fall of Nigeria*, 76-87.
38. Cited by Ado-Kurawa, I., *Shari'ah and the Press in Nigeria,* 297-298 from Khan, M.A., *A Course for Teaching Mirath as an Independent course in Nigeri*a, 181.
39. See the full text and discussion on this in detail in Imam, O. Y., "Application of the Shari'ah in Nigeria's Third Republic: Problem and Prospects," in Muhibbudden, M. A., *Shari'ah in a Multi-faith Nigeria*, Proceedings of

National Association of Teachers of Arabic and Islamic Studies, (NATAIS), Conference, 2005, 12.

40. Haylword, O. E., ed., *African Independent Church Movements* (London: Oxford University Press, 1979). See also Gray, R., "Problems of Historical Perspective: The Planting of Christianity in Africa in the 19th and 20th Centuries," in *Christianity in Tropical Africa*, ed., Baeta, C. G. (London: Oxford University Press, 1968). Edward Blyden, in his book *Christianity Islam and Negro Race,* discusses extensively on the decolonization movement and emergence Church continued to be a major imperial force for cultural and spiritual domination in Africa. See Agboola, O. O., "The Place of Religion in Colonial Resistance in some parts of Nigerian Area, C. 1900-1910," *DEGEL: Journal of FAIS*, Vol.4, 2000, 165-174.
41. Ostien, P., "Ten Good things about the Implementation of Shari'ah taking Place in some States in Northern Nigeria," *Newswatch*, July 9, 2001, 61-64.
42. Last, M., "Notes on the Implementation of Shari'ah in northern Nigeria, "mimeo, 1.
43. Suberu, R. T., "Continuity and Change in Nigeria's Shari'ah Debates," in Gomez-Perez, M., *L'islam Politique au sud du Sahara; Identities, discourse et enjeux* (Paris: Karthala, 2005), 209.
44. See some relevant discussions on the matter in Sabo Bako, "Muslim, State and the Struggle for Democratic Transition in Nigeria: From Cooperation to Conflict," presented at the International Conference on the Dilemmas of Nigeria Democracy held at Wisconsin-Madison, November 11-13, 1995, 2-10.
45. Cited in Junju, N. I., "Fundamental Human Rights in Civilian Regimes in Nigeria to date: An Evaluation," in *DEGEL: Journal of FAIS*, Vol. III, 2000, 160.
46. Last, M., "Notes on the Implementation of Shari'ah in northern Nigeria," 6-7. Also relevant reading in this line is Yadudu, H. A., "Shari'ah Implementation in a Democratic Nigeria: Between Deference to Popular will and Libertarian Changes," presented at the 3rd Annual Conference of the Center for the Study of Islam and Democracy, held at the Sheraton Crystal City Hotel, Arlington, Virginia, USA, April 6-7, 2002.
47. J. O. Hunwick, "An African Case Study of Political Islam; Nigeria," in *Annals of the American Academy*, 524, 1992, 149.
48. Ostein, P., "Ten Good things about the Implementation of Shari'ah taking Place in some States in Northern Nigeria,"19. See also his Paper, "Islamic Criminal Law: What it means in Zamfara and Niger States," in *Journal of Public and Private Law*, Vol. 4, No. 4, 2000, 3.

49. On the constitutionality of the Shari'ah legal system in Nigeria, see Yadudu A H., "Shari'ah Implementation in a Democratic Nigeria: Between Deference to Popular will and Libertarian Changes." Ostien P. made an exhaustive and elaborate discussion on the Federalism, its application under a secular state in his, "Ten Good Things about Shari'ah;" see also Ostien, P., and Gamaliel, J. D., "The Law of Separation of Religion and State in the US: A Model for Nigeria," in TCNN Research Bulletin, No 37, 2002, 24-35. On Shari'ah and Minorities see an interesting work by Sulaiman, M. D., "The Sokoto Caliphate, Shari'ah and Minorities in northern Nigeria," in Boboyi, H., and Yakubu, A. M., eds., *The Sokoto Caliphate: History and Legacies,* Vol. 2 (Kaduna, Nigeria: Arewa House, 2006), 221-241. See also McCain, D., "Which Road Leads Beyond the Shari'ah Controversy? A Christian Perspective," in *Comparative Perspective on Shari'ah in Nigeria,* eds., Ostien, P., Nasir, J. M., and Kogelmann, F., (Abuja, Nigeria: Spectrum, 2005), 15-21.
50. Human Rights Watch Report, *Political Shari'ah?* 1.
51. Ibid., 6.
52. Oloyede, I., "Comment," in *Comparative Perspective on Shari'ah,* 298-299.
53. Chief Gani Fawhinmi, a Lagos based legal practitioner and Human Rights activist, had accused some NGO's of insincerity as cited in Junju, N. I., "Fundamental Human Rights," 164, quoting from *Weekly Trust*, Vol. 24, August 20, 1999, 8.
54. Sanusi, L. S., "The West and the Rest: Reflections on the Intercultural Dialogue about Shari'ah," in *Comparative Perspective on Shari'ah in Nigeria*, ed., Ostien, P., Nasir, J. M., and Kogelmann, F., 261-262.
55. Bunza, M. U., "The Iranian Model of Political Islamic Movement in Nigeria," in *L'islam politique au sud du Sahara: Identities, discourse et enjeux,* ed., Gomez-Perez, M. (Paris: Karthala, 2005), 227-242.

CHAPTER EIGHT

SHARI'A AND POLITICS: CRISES, CONFLICTS, AND RESOLUTIONS

SA'ADATU HASSAN LIMAN

Islam was introduced to northern Nigeria many centuries ago, but the Shari'a legal system was not applied in governance until the Sokoto Caliphate was established in 1817. The predominance of Islam in northern Nigeria made the application of the Shari'a in that region plausible. The coming of the British colonial power in the late nineteenth century heralded the destruction of the egalitarian ideals of peace and justice, which the Shari'a instituted. By favoring one religion against the other, the British sowed the seeds of discord between the northerners and southerners of Nigeria in order to consolidate their power by adopting the principle of "divide and rule." As a result of the colonial policies and other reasons, Nigeria was engulfed in a series of crises and conflicts, some of which have been erroneously attributed to the implementation of the Shari'a. The ensuing crises negate the course of the Shari'a, which protects human rights and dignity.

It is imperative to appreciate the multi-faith status of Nigeria, though referred to as a secular state. The presence and practice of many religions and how religion has penetrated politics make it necessary to reconsider Nigeria as a secular state. Although in a multi-ethnic and multi-religious state, crises and conflicts are bound to occur, there is always a process of conflict prevention and conflict resolution. This chapter will examine the connections between the Shari'a and politics, and discuss resolutions to the conflicts that have engulfed the country since the re-introduction of the Shari'a in 2000.

The History of Shari'a in Nigeria

Historically, the first place Islam penetrated in northern Nigeria was Kanem Bornu. It came through Muhammad ibn Mani during the reign of Umme Jilmi (ca. 1085-1097). Jilmi became the first Kanem Bornu ruler to convert to Islam, and he promoted it and even performed the pilgrimage.[1] In the Kano Chronicle, Islam penetrated Kano during the reign of Ali Yaji (1349-1385). It does not appear that the Shari'a was enforced at the same time Islam was introduced. As Ahmad Quadri pointed out, Mai Idris Aloma (1571-1603) was the first ruler of Kanem Bornu to enforce the Shari'a in the sixteenth century. Quadri further claimed that Aloma separated the administration of justice from the executive, taking legal decisions out of the hands of political chiefs, and setting up 'Qadi' courts to dispense justice according to the Shari'a.[2]

The Sokoto Jihad, which began in 1804 under the leadership of Shehu Usman dan Fodio, left a considerable and lasting impact on the politico-religious development of northern Nigeria. One of the immediate consequences was the establishment of the Sokoto Caliphate, which allowed the institutionalization of a strong and dynamic socio-political system, including the adoption of the Shari'a. Ahmad Musa puts it succinctly that, "during the period of the Sokoto caliphate a well functional Shari'a judicial structure was put in place and fully operated throughout the Caliphate."[3] It is noteworthy that the reasons for the jihad were primarily religious, among which were: oppression of Muslims in the form of imposed taxes not sanctioned by the Shari'a, and the abduction of Islamic women and the misappropriation of their possessions. Hence, it was justified to institute the Shari'a in order to ensure justice and equity. Shari'a was therefore considered a revolutionary idea, which had come to displace the status quo and replace the socio-political practices with Islamic tenets. Bala Usman noted that unlike other movements in the world at that time, the changes brought about by the Sokoto jihad were meant to redefine citizenship based on the Islamic faith. In the Caliphate, therefore, one was qualified to enjoy the rights and privileges of citizenship on the grounds of faith without reference to race, ethnicity, or descent.[4]

The British overthrow of the Sokoto Caliphate brought about a changing fortune for the Shari'a. Despite its positive intentions, the British set it aside and adopted the English legal system. As Bala Musa argued, "With colonization came the cunning and systematic transformation of the Shari'a to suit the colonial taste. That was put into effect through enactment of laws that curtailed the application of Shari'a system."[5] After almost a hundred years of peace and justice, un-Islamic practices re-emerged and crises occurred as a result of the curtailment of the Shari'a. The period of silence for the Shari'a should not be mistaken for its complete elimination.

Since independence, the Shari'a had not been a subject for crises and conflicts because political leaders did not interfere with its existence and adoption as it operated during the colonial period. It, however, became an issue of national debate and crisis when it was re-introduced in 2000. There is relative peace in contemporary Nigeria, but demagogues have dominated religions and the economy, and quasi-nationalists or regionalists have reawakened ethnic nationalism.

Meaning of the Shari'a

According to M. A. Ambali, the word Shari'a comes from *At-Tashri'*, which is an abstract form of *Sha-ra'a*. The meanings of the two words can be deduced from two paths. First, the straight path as contained in the Qur'an: "Finally, we set thee (Muhammad) on a way (shari'a) by which the purpose of faith may be fulfilled. So follow this way and not the likes and dislikes of those who do not know the truth."[6] Second, the path that leads to the spring where drinking water is available in the desert. The jurists of Islamic law adopted the word for the ordinances that Allah ordained for his worshippers to be faithful and to strive towards their salvation in this life and hereafter. These ordinances are collectively called Shari'a.[7]

Shari'a denotes the sum total of Islamic law as contained in the teachings of both the Qur'an and the Hadith of the Prophet Muhammad (*Sallalahu Alaihi Wasallam*, S.A.W.). S. S. Okenwa explains further that, it is a comprehensive, all-encompassing set of rules, which regulates the entire life of a Muslim ranging from belief system to worship; interpersonal relationships, including property, transactions, contracts, sales, etc; criminal law; and morality. Also contained in it are injunctions regulating a Muslim's relationship with non-Muslims, and even with plants and animals.[8]

In the Shari'a, there is no dichotomy between religion and the state because as a way of life, Islam affects every aspect of human activities. Hence, every individual is mandated to be conversant with basic Islamic teachings, especially those that concern formal worship and inter-personal relationships. These aspects of a Muslim's life are necessary for molding a person into a self-respecting individual who recognizes and respects the rights of fellow human beings. Such an individual exhibits a strong sense of responsibility - a quality that everyone should possess in order to be a good leader.

The critics of the Shari'a point to its application as 'unconstitutional' as a basis to oppose its implementation. The Shari'a legal system has had to contend with tremendous and extensive antagonism from the Nigerian public. It is argued that the country is a "secular nation" where religion would and should hold no place in governance. This argument is based on what prevails in most western countries where there is separation between Church and State.

Arguments and Misconceptions on the Shari'a

Like the Organization of Islamic Conference (OIC) issue in the 1980s, there have been many arguments for and against the Shari'a. The unending debate has crossed ethnic lines and has sharply pitched Christians against Muslims. As expected, the strong opposition to the Shari'a came from Christians who did not understand the legal value and position of the Shari'a in Islam. To the Muslims, the Shari'a is important because it is central to their religious belief and practice. To Christian, the Shari'a is irrelevant and inappropriate legal system in a "secular" society. These conflicting perspectives of the Shari'a have been part of the causes of conflicts in modern Nigeria.

Shari'a antagonists argue that its implementation would send wrong signals to the legal and political systems and deter foreigners from investing in Nigeria. This argument stems from the attempt to protect the multinational corporations and investors who come from countries that do not adopt the Shari'a. However, investors look for places where there is justice, peace, and security in order to protect their investment. These are some of the things the Shari'a promote and intend to achieve. Hence, with the Shari'a in place, Nigeria provides a good place for foreign investors, as Kuwait and Saudi Arabia are to foreign corporations.

There is the argument that the socio-economic situation in Nigeria makes it un-conducive for the Shari'a to be fully implemented. Nigeria has been experiencing socio-economic difficulties for many years. In spite of its oil wealth, Nigeria has been unable to provide the necessary infrastructure for a good standard of living. Poverty and social inequality are apparent in the country. The Shari'a did not cause all of these problems and it is misleading to associate Nigeria's socio-economic crises to the Shari'a. Indeed, the Shari'a aims at creating a favourable atmosphere for everyone. The Shari'a provides an alternative to solving the problem of social welfare and for gearing Nigeria toward economic growth and national unity.

Other critics claimed the Shari'a was implemented purely on a political basis and purposely to undermine the Obasanjo regime. Because Obasanjo is a Christian, Adide Ohiari declared, "I must say that this effrontery

(Shari'a declaration in Zamfara state) is all an attempt to undermine President Olusegun Obasanjo's administration."[9] In a similar way, Stephen Okorie wrote: "Now within only nine months of a southerner (President Obasanjo) coming into power, the so-called core North has opted to fight by declaring Shari'a Law in their States."[10] These arguments are misplaced because the northerners who voted Obasanjo into power in 1999 knew that he was and will always be a southern Christian. In the midst of the Shari'a debate, Nigeria conducted the presidential election in the 2003 and Obasanjo won convincingly in many of the Shari'a states.[11] This proves that the implementation of Shari'a did not have either a political or ethnic motive, but purely a religious basis.

It is unfair to make the allusion that the Shari'a was introduced to discredit or embarrass Obasanjo's regime. The continuing violence in the Niger Delta has been instigated by a group of people who are agitating for a large share of Nigeria's crude oil revenue. In spite of the volatile situation in that region, the problem has not been associated with discrediting Obasanjo's regime. It would be recalled that the military regime suppressed many human rights, including the right to practice the Shari'a. The termination of the military regime leaves room for democracy and freedom of religion. The Shari'a resurfaced at the appropriate time to express freedom of religion and was not directed towards any political figure.

Another misconception about the Shari'a relates to the retired Chief of Defense, Theophelus Danjuma, who castigated Ibrahim Babangida (former military president) for upgrading the status of Nigeria to full membership in the OIC, in 1986. Actually, it was Yakubu Gowon, a Christian, who admitted the country into the OIC in 1969 as an observer. It was not a unilateral decision, but was supported by a decree promulgated by the then Federal Military Government on Economic Recovery, which authorized the President to take any step that would help the economic recovery of the nation. The move was therefore economic and not religious, and would have qualified the country for interest-free loans, which would have benefited both Muslims and non-Muslims (unlike the disastrous loans of International Financial Institutions (IFIs) such as the Paris Club, International Monetary Fund, and the World Bank). Had Nigeria not been a member, it would have been denied economic benefits enjoyed by member states of the OIC.

Another misconception by non-Muslims was that the implementation of the Shari'a would affect their rights and freedom. The report of the Bureau of Democracy, Human Rights and Labor, established under the Secretary for Democracy and Global Affairs, U.S. reveals that, "although many non-Muslims feared that the implementation of the Shari'a would change their way of life, there has been little or no change in the daily lives of most non-Muslims." The report further states that:

> While some state and local governments have interpreted the new Shari'a laws stringently, the majority have interpreted their laws differently and implemented them with moderation. There also is a trend developing among some sections of the Muslim community to shift focus from the criminal law aspects of Shari'a law to its tenets of social justice and charity for the poor. Islamic scholars and many Muslim lawyers began educating the poor and the less well informed about their procedural rights under Shari'a.[12]

Women's place and rights in the Shari'a have been challenged by some groups of people. An example is a Christian group called the "Women Forum of Sufficient Grace Ministry," that urged women to rise against the Shari'a. The group declared that, "it is unfortunate that a woman will be kept in houses with doors and windows shut while their male counterparts move freely out in the streets. One wonders the kind of religion and its law that imprison women, restrict their movement and deny them of every rights enshrined in our constitution."[13] This declaration from the group is a misunderstanding of the specific Shari'a provisions as they relate to women. The Qur'an makes provision for women's rights by stating: "And women shall have rights similar to the men, and men are a degree above them, according to what is equitable" (Qur'an 2:228). Many societies in the world are male dominated and all religions have different provisions for the roles and rights of women. Islam recognizes women as equal to men and this is what the Shari'a applies.

Nigeria and the Concept of Secularism

Nigeria is a multi-religious country. The argument that Nigeria is a secular nation, and should not accommodate any religion-based laws, misunderstands the purpose of the Shari'a. Among other things, the Shari'a aims at guiding the totality of a Muslim's life pattern. Thus taking secularism to mean, "not connected with spiritual or religious matters," implies that any situation that is described as secular is absolutely devoid of a concept of God or any divine power. This interpretation does not support the provision in the preamble of the 1979 Constitution, which reads:

We the People of the Federal Republic of Nigeria having firmly and solemnly resolved:

> TO LIVE in unity and harmony as one indivisible Sovereign Nation **under God** dedicated to the promotion of inter-African solidarity, world peace, international cooperation and understanding: AND TO PROVIDE for a constitution for the purpose of promoting the good government and welfare of all persons in our country on the principles of Freedom, Equality and Justice, and for the purpose of consolidating the Unity of our people: DO HEREBY MAKE, ENACT AND GIVE TO OURSELVES the following Constitution.[14]

The phrase "under God" contradicts the secular assertion of the constitution, which further states: "In furtherance of the social order, the sanctity of the human person shall be recognized and human dignity shall be maintained and enhanced."[15] The government of Nigeria promotes, financially and otherwise, religious activities. For example, federal and state governments often sponsor religious people on pilgrimage to either Jerusalem or Mecca. If Nigeria were a secular state, the government would not have been so deeply involved in promoting religions or sponsoring religious groups.

The Constitution states that: "There shall be a High Court for each state of the Federation,"[16] that would apply the Common Law, which is basically a Christian Law as confirmed by the Hon. Justice Karibi White:

> The claim of the Holy Bible to Devine revelation is not peculiar to Common Law claims to have been derived partly from the Ten Commandments God gave to Moses on the mountain, the several books of the Holy Bible are said to have been written on inspiration. The Roman Twelve Tablets, the Laws of the Greeks, and the laws operating in civilized countries are founded on Devine revelations." Also, "There shall be for any State that requires it a Shari'a Court of Appeal for that State.[17]

The Shari'a does not restrict itself to civil matters, but covers the entire existence of a human being. Hence, the reference to only 'civil proceedings' is considered a deliberate act to deny Muslims the right to apply the Shari'a in all aspects of their legal system.

Post-colonial Ethno-political Crises and Conflicts

Crises and conflicts constitute part of human behavior and experience. They are concomitant results of human interaction. It should be mentioned that not all crises and conflicts result in violence, and there are always negative and positive sides to conflicts. With particular reference to Nigeria, the relative peaceful atmosphere the country enjoyed in the post-independence period has been intermittently shattered by violent communal crises and conflicts. Without providing details here, the Nigerian Civil War of 1967 to 1970 ushered in a period of crisis and conflict. It shook the foundation of unity and shattered the hope of peace. Following that was a conscious attempt to rebuild the country with the process of reconciliation, reconstruction, and rehabilitation. The military intervention in politics terminated the newly established democratic rule, and witnessed a long period of political instability, characterized by numerous (successful or attempted) coups d'etats.[18]

The post-independence crises and conflicts in Nigeria are complex in nature. Therefore, it is difficult to categorize them as exclusively political, religious, or ethnic; they are interwoven. A crisis with social underpinnings may transform into a religious conflict, while an ethnically motivated one may end up being ignited by political undertones. It is clear that as a plural society with multiple religions and an unstable political system, Nigeria has experienced all kinds of crises and conflicts.

The amalgamation of Nigeria in 1914 by Lord Lugard has been heavily criticized as an undertaking primarily for the administrative expediency of the British. E. E. Osaghae contended that, like most other federations, Nigeria has had to deal with the problem of ethnicity since its inception. There have been crises and conflicts among the majority and minority ethnic groups that make up the country, and the problem emanated from the anomalous structuring of the federation at its beginning.[19] Although the British appreciated the need for peaceful coexistence between the diverse ethnic groups, they also realized that maintaining the ethnic divide would promote their divide and rule policy. This prompted the idea of dividing Nigeria into three regions, which was the main feature of the Richard's Constitution in 1946. The regionalization policy was not geared toward unity but meant for the political expediency of the British and it haunted the peaceful co-existence of the people for many years. Similarly, the McPherson Constitution of 1951 created a convenient process for the British to sow seeds of ethnic discord. The constitution "strengthened regionalism by transforming the regional councils into regional parliaments and governments."[20] The crises and conflicts that accompanied the uneven regional division led to the setting up of the Minorities Commission in 1957, as a mechanism to allay the fears of the minorities. It was an attempt to avoid further ethnic crises and conflicts and lay the foundations for equity and justice.[21]

The policies and constitutional provisions indicate that before independence the British had altered the power system and had planted the seeds of ethnic rivalry. Instead of watering down ethnic differentiation, the British promoted it. For example, in the 1959 elections the three ethnically based political parties, the Action Group (AG), the Northern Peoples Congress (NPC), and the National Council of Nigerian Citizens (NCNC), each won in stronghold regions. Overall, the period of colonial rule in Nigeria accelerated ethnic consciousness and ethnic divide, which has determined ethnic relations since independence. Father Matthew Kukah argues that the politicization of ethnic identities led to the emergence of ethnic and community-based organizations, which were used to articulate the pains and grievances of various communities.[22] Ali A. Mazrui is also of the opinion that, "ethnicity has lived to help diminish the scale of Western globalist pretensions. Islamic militancy may challenge Western supremacy. Tribal identity may challenge the nation state."[23] While ethnic crises and conflicts did not abate, they have been compounded by religious differences, which in recent times have been associated with the Shari'a.

The report of the Bureau for Democracy further reveals that, the Constitution of Nigeria provides that states may elect to use Islamic (Shari'a) laws and courts. Twelve northern states have adopted at least parts of the Shari'a law.[24] Adherence to Shari'a provisions may be compulsory for Muslims or may be optional. Non-Muslims are, however, not required in any state to submit to Shari'a jurisdiction. In some states non-Muslims have an option: they may choose the Shari'a where the penalty is less severe (such as paying a fine rather than a jail sentence under secular law). Defendants have the right to challenge the constitutionality of Shari'a criminal statutes through the secular courts. The Constitution also provides for the federal government to establish a Federal Shari'a Court of Appeal and a Final Shari'a Court of Appeal, but the government has not yet implemented it.[25]

The public life and institutions in Nigeria reveal a dominating religious manifestation. For example, the government adopts the Christian calendar for official use while the Islamic calendar is not recognized. Sunday is a work-free day, but Friday is not. The cross is used as symbols in government hospitals and ambulances, but the Muslim crescent and star is discarded. Furthermore, January 1 is regarded as New Year's Day, but the 1st of al-Muharram as the beginning of a new year in Islam is not observed. It should be noted, however, that the government recognizes some Islamic celebrations and holidays such as the Eid-el-Fitr, which marks the end of the Ramadan, and the annual celebration of Eid-el-Kabir, which commemorates the end of the pilgrimage to Mecca. On those days, the Nigerian government declares public holidays. These indicate that religion is deeply engraved in the Nigerian politics to the extent that Nigeria cannot be called a secular state, as it is referred to in the constitution.

The report of the Bureau of Democracy, Human Rights and Labor further reveals that in the north, there is a long tradition of separating schoolchildren according to their gender. Some form of gender segregation still occurs in many secondary schools in northern states. In December 2005, the Kano State Commissioner of Education announced that public and private school pupils should observe "decent standards of dress," although non-Muslim girls would not be required to wear the hijab headscarf. Additionally, the report states that Christians in the predominantly Muslim northern states alleged that local government officials used zoning regulations on buildings to stop or slow the establishment of new churches, while Muslims complained that they were denied permission to build mosques in predominantly Christian southern states. Officials responded that many of these new churches and mosques were being constructed in residential neighborhoods not permitted for religious purposes. State officials also stated that the certification boards were dealing with a large backlog of cases for all applicants regardless of religious faith. State authorities claimed that students were allowed to not attend classes taught in a religion other than their own and that students may request a teacher of their own religion to provide alternative instruction. However, there were usually no teachers of Christian religious knowledge in many northern schools, or teachers for Islamic religious knowledge in some southern schools.[26]

Due to the sharp ethnic, regional, and religious differences, there have been numerous incidents of crises and conflicts, which threaten the unity and national integration of Nigeria. The post-1999 Shari'a crises, the Kaduna conflict in 2000, the Jos conflict in 2000, the Bauchi conflict in 2001 are testaments to the danger religious conflicts constitute to the unity and political stability of Nigeria.

Impact of the Shari'a in a Multi-faith Nigeria

It is appropriate to consider the impact of the Shari'a on Nigerian leadership in the context of the Dan Fodio jihad. The jihad succeeded in establishing the Sokoto Caliphate as a sovereign government with laws covering all the provisions of the Shari'a as they related to every facet of Muslim life. The implementation of the Shari'a brought about the displacement of the existing traditional laws and practices, which were considered oppressive and unjust.

In his *Islam in Nigeria*, Rahman Doi states that the powers of the Sokoto Caliphate stretched from Sokoto to the land of the Jukun where it replaced the chaos wrought by numerous raids in the region with a peaceful political organization. When the jihadists could not conquer Bornu, they pushed southeastward to the frontiers of Bornu and helped found the Fulani State of Adamawa. The jihadists moved south into northern Yorubaland and established Ilorin as another Fulani-ruled state. Thus, Doi argued that the jihad welded Nigeria into a single administrative system and established its Islamic principles based on the Shari'a.[27] Within this large sphere of influence, the Caliphate instituted forms of leadership, governance, human rights, and polity, all according to the provisions of the Shari'a. It is therefore significant to view those aspects of Islam and the Shari'a as they are now practiced in Zamfara and Kano states.

Political leaders became increasingly corrupt and out of tune with the social and religious realities until revivalists, as in Zamfara, blazed the trail in reasserting the Shari'a and reverting back to the political leadership that is guided by divine injunctions. It is fascinating that political leadership is regarded as the highest office and in many instances, when political leadership is corrupt, other forms of leadership such as traditional and religious are negatively affected.

The Zamfara political leadership, in line with the Holy Qur'an, has put in place structures to oversee the implementation of the Shari'a. One of the most important is the Zakat Commission, which has been set up to plan and coordinate the collection and disbursement of "regular charity" within the state. Prostitution and alcohol production and consumption are banned because they are considered detrimental to the development of the state. Imams and preachers are paid allowances by the state in order to encourage and promote godliness, which creates justice and equity among the people. These measures were taken according to the injunctions of the Shari'a in order to promote peace and equality, and to prevent religious crises and conflicts.

The Shari'a was reintroduced in Kano through a program referred to as "*A Daidaita Sahu*" (Societal Reorientation). *A Daidaita Sahu* symbolizes order, discipline, and sense of belonging to a Muslim community. Under this program, the ideals and values of the Shari'a are promoted. The *Hisbah* (a religious institution under the authority of the state) performs the function of educating people on what is right or wrong. The goal is to protect the doctrines and practice of Islam and to ensure the welfare of the people. Since the Hisbah has been in place, the persistent wonderings of the *almajiris* (pupils) has been considerably curtailed and their *malams* (teachers) have been given the necessary tools to teach the pupils.

This points to the fact that prior to the reintroduction of the Shari'a in those states, general discontent with the existing political leadership prevailed. And, because a religiously-guided political class has replaced the former, a more just society has been created within which the gap between the rich and the poor, the Muslim and the non-Muslims, the leaders and the led, is continuously being closed. Through the Shari'a more people enjoy a better life, which has helped tremendously to reduce political chaos and social injustice. For instance, in Zamfara, Sokoto, Kebbi, and Niger states, Zakat Commission and committees have been set up for the purpose of collecting and disbursing charity to the poor people in the communities. Also, Imams and Mu'adhdhins have been appointed to educate the people. In Zamfara, the government pays preachers for their role in enlightening the people on the Shari'a. While these steps were meant to improve the conditions of the poor people, nothing significant has been done by the political leadership towards achieving equality and accountability, part of the goals of the Shari'a.[28] The political leaders in Nigeria should emphasize not only political education, but also religious understanding among their people. In order to avoid violence among the people, adequate information should be give to the people on why political and religious policies are adopted.

Improving the Christian-Muslim Relationship

Religion should not be used as a dividing instrument. Instead, it should bring the people of the country together. Belonging to the same country, adherents of Christianity, Islam, and other faiths should establish an amicable relationship for the purpose of peace and unity. The crises and conflicts that have occurred are not good for the continued ethnic and religious relations in the country.

Many centuries ago, Prophet Muhammad (S.A.W) respected people of other faiths, especially the Jews and the People of the Book. Islam co-existed with other religions as Muslims lived in peace with other people. When the pagan aristocracy began to persecute Muslims, the Prophet chose the Christian kingdom of Abyssinia (Ethiopia) as a place of refuge for the victims because he "had already known that Ashamah Negus, king of Abyssinia, was a fair ruler who would not wrong any of his subordinates, so he permitted some of his followers to seek asylum there in Abyssinia."[29] Negus provided security for the refugees and told the pagan aristocracy: "I am afraid I cannot give you back these refugees. They are free to live and worship in my realm as they please."[30]

Unfortunately, most of the crises and conflicts in Nigeria today are associated with the uneasy Christian-Muslim relationship. Admittedly, conflicts and strife are inevitable, especially between different ideologies or religions, as indicated by the Crusades, which were religious wars in the eleventh century. However, it is the escalation of crises and conflicts, resulting in death and destruction, which is shocking and constitutes a colossal threat to peace. Peace needs to be understood and practiced not only within the context of a cessation of hostilities, but by deeply identifying the underlying causes of the conflict and finding solutions or preventive measures. Crises, conflicts, and violence undermine national integration and peaceful co-existence among people of different faiths. To avoid further conflicts, both Muslims and Christians should engage in dialogue and should be educated on the aims and objectives of Shari'a. Dialogue and religious education are important elements that help understanding and peaceful coexistence in any society. Both religious groups should be made to understand that, Shari'a does not apply to the Christians. Instead, it accommodates them.

Conclusion

Ethnic and religious conflicts have on many occasions challenged the territorial unity of Nigeria. Northern Nigeria in particular has remained the theatre of armed communal and religious conflicts, which has resulted in widespread destruction, thousands of deaths, and enormous property loss. In spite of the various remedies proposed and tried, ethno-religious conflicts continue to recur in the country's socio-political scenes and in recent times have assumed a frightening dimension. The recurring problems suggest the inadequacies of both the prevailing intellectual analysis and prognosis of the problem as well as the remedies proposed and tried.[31] As Juan Somavia noted, integration did not mean suppressing tensions, but rather finding mechanisms to overcome them.[32]

Economic decline and a high level of corruption create a big gap between the haves and the have-nots. Most of the people that engage in the pogrom, ethno-religious cleansing, and or genocide are the youths that have no jobs. They resort to acts of violence to draw attention and to vent their frustration on the community. These groups are found all over Nigeria and they operate under ethnic loyalty. For example, there are the Movement for the Actualization of the Sovereign State of Biafra (MASSOB) and the Oodua People's Congress (OPC), which are strictly ethnic-based militant groups. There is also the 'Yandaba' (although not a purely ethnic group, sometimes serves that purpose, especially when there is an outbreak of conflict between the Hausa people and other ethnic groups, or when a religious conflict ensues involving the Muslims, as the case in Jos with the Christian-Muslim conflict). These are not religious militant groups, but they are partly to blame for the crises and conflicts that tend to destabilize the country.

The causes behind the crises and conflicts in Nigeria lie not only in the impact of colonialism, but also and most importantly in the social devastation occasioned by the prevailing economic turmoil. Khalid also pointed out that the situation further deteriorated as a result of the shrinking of the democratic process and the prevalence of authoritarian political order by the long military dictatorship in Nigeria. Wole Soyinka aptly captured the dialectical interplay between dictatorship and the revival of ethnic and cultural identities. He stated:

> Under dictatorship, a nation ceases to exist. . . The only weapon of resistance that is left intact is a cultural memory. Make a careful study of people under dictatorship, and invariably you will observe that it marks a period of internal retreat into cultural identities...the essence of nationhood has gone underground and taken refuge in that primary constituency of human association, the cultural bastion. And the longer the dictatorship last, the more tenacious become the hold of that cultural nationalism, attracting to itself all the allegiance, social relevance, and visceral identification that once belonged to the larger nation.[33]

The ultimate solution is for the government to improve the economic situation of the country. Christian-Muslim dialogue should also continue as it strengthens the bonds of relationship.

People should be educated on the aims and goals of the Shari'a. Many people (Muslims and Christians) are ignorant of the provisions of the Shari'a. This lack of understanding has partly created the tension and opposition to the Shari'a. For instance, Emma Omuojire mentioned that:

> One thing is clear for sure, a lot of the tantrums are based on ignorance, half knowledge or grave misconception of what Shari'a is all about, and a deliberate distortion in the interpretation of the constitution by most contributors to the debate. The debaters fall into two categories; those who want to score political point, and others mainly Christians who mostly out of ignorance are scared stiff of Shari'a. I make bold to say that majority of Nigerians, Christians and Muslims alike are under informed about Shari'a or Islamic law.[34]

People from different parts of the country, who realize the values, legal implications, and religious importance of the Shari'a, wanted it implemented in their societies. The Shari'a aims at establishing an egalitarian society on the principles of equality, brotherhood, and friendliness. Its goal is to evolve a society where no individual has unnecessary advantage over others. Shari'a demands love, truth, and moral virtue from everyone. It encourages people to be law abiding. Islam does not recognize the superiority of a Muslim over another person except if the superiority is gained through piety, deeper learning, and contribution for the social and religious welfare of their society.

Shari'a should not cause crises and conflicts, but be understood for its true meaning. It is not a subject for political power-play; it is a religious matter. Through dialogue and religious education, Nigerians would be able to resolve the conflicts that have arisen over the Shari'a in a more peaceful way. Religious tolerance should be seen as a strategy to resolve or at least reduce the crises and conflicts that have occurred or may occur with the implementation of the Shari'a.

Notes

1. Thomas Hodgkin, *Nigerian Perspectives: An Historical Anthology* (London: Oxford University Press, 1975), 90-91.
2. Quadri, Yasir Anjiola Quadri, "The Survival of Shari'a in Multi-Faith Nigeria, in *Shari'a in a Multifaith Nigeria*, ed., Muhibbu-din M. A. (Ijebu-Ode, Nigeria: Shobiotimo Publications, 2004), 2.
3. Ahmad K. Musa, "The Effects of British Colonial Administration on the Shari'a Legal System in Northern Nigeria," in *Shari'a in a Multifaith Nigeria*, 48.
4. An Interview with Bala Usman, *Weekly Trust* Newspaper, June 19-25, 2004. 2.

5. Musa, 48.
6. Qur'an 45:18.
7. M. A. Ambali, *The Practice of Muslim Family Law in Nigeria* (Zaria, Nigeria: Tamaza Publishers, 1998), 1-2.
8. For more details see: S. S. Okenwa, "Implementation of Shari'a in Nigeria: Balancing Christian Muslim Concerns and Aspirations." Paper presented at the International Conference on Christian Muslim Mutual Relations, organized by the Association of Christian Muslim Relations Mutual Relations in Nigeria, with the conjunction of the Nigeria Supreme Council for Islamic Affairs, Gusau, Nigeria, March, 2005.
9. Adide Ohiari, *The Guardian Newspaper*, of February 28, 2000,
10. Stephen Okorie, *The Concord Newspaper*, March 2, 2000.
11. A Report by the Nigerian National Electoral Body - Independent National Electoral Commission (INEC) 2003: The Republic of Nigeria Presidential Election of April, 19, 2003.
12. "Nigeria: International Religious Freedom Report 2005," by Bureau of Democracy, Human Rights and Labor, Under the Secretary for Democracy and Global Affairs, U. S. State Department, released Nov. 8, 2005.
13. Seun Adeoye, "Group Asks Women to Resist Shari'a," *The Guardian* Newspaper, February 14, 2000, 5.
14. Chapter 1 of the Constitution of the Federal Republic of Nigeria (FRN) 1979.
15. Ibid. Section 17(3) b, a.
16. 1999 Constitution of the FRN Section 6(4)e.
17. Quoted in Sambo, Muhammad B. *Shari'a and Justice: Lectures and Speeches* (Zaria, Nigeria: Sankore Educational Publishers, 2003), 187.
18. T. N. Tamuno, "Separatist Agitations in Nigeria Since 1914, *Journal of Modern African Studies*, Vol. 8, No. 4, 1970, 563-584.
19. E. E. Osaghac, "Ethnic Minorities and Federalism in Nigeria," *African Affairs*, Vol. 90, No. 359, 1991, 237-258.
20. Quadri, "The Survival of Shari'a," 2.
21. Kukah, Mathew H. "Crisis, Conflicts and Incorporation: Options for a Democratic Nigeria," a keynote address at the Annual General Conference of the Nigerian Bar Association, August 26-30, 2002, 8.
22. Ibid, 7.
23. Ali A Mazrui, "Ethnicity in Bondage: Is its Liberation Premature?" In *Ethnic Violence, Conflict Resolution and Cultural Pluralism*. Report of the UNRISD/UNDP International Seminar on Ethnic Diversity and Policies, New York, August 17-19, 1994, 30.

24. They include: Sokoto, Kebbi, Niger, Kano, Katsina, Kaduna, Jigawa, Yobe, Bauchi, Borno, Zamfara, and Gombe.
25. Section 6(4)f of the Constitution of the FRN, 1999.
26. "Nigeria: International Religious Freedom Report 2005," by Bureau of Democracy, Human Rights and Labor, Under the Secretary for Democracy and Global Affairs, U. S. State Department, released Nov. 8, 2005.
27. Abdur Rahman Doi, I. *Islam in Nigeria* (Zaria, Nigeria: Gaskiya Corporation, 1984), 44.
28. M. K. Ja'afar and M. S. Muhammad, "Impact of Shariah on Leadership Role: A Case Study of Northwest of Nigeria," in *Shari'a in a Multifaith Nigeria,* 3.
29. Al-Mubarakpuri, Safi-ur- Rahman, *The Sealed Nectar [Ar-raheeq al-Makhtum]* (Riyadh-Saudi Arabia: Al-Furqan Advertising Agency, 1979), 99-100.
30. Ibid. 103.
31. Khalid, Sulaiman, "Ethno-Religious Conflicts in Northwestern Nigeria; Myth and Reality," sulkhalid@yahoo.co.uk.
32. "Ethnic Violence, Conflict Resolution and Cultural Pluralism," Report of the UNRISD/UNDP International Seminar on Ethnic Diversity and Policies, New York, August 17-19, 1994, 23.
33. Wole Soyinka, *The Open Sore of a Continent: A Personal Narrative of the Nigeria Crisis* (London: Oxford University Press, 1997).
34. Emma, Omuojire O. "Shari'a Law; How the Constitution Recognizes It," *The Guardian* Newspaper, February 29, 2000, 64.

Chapter Nine

Religion, Politics, and Violence

Julius O. Adekunle

The interplay of ethnicity, politics, religion, and violence has been prominent in Nigerian history. In the precolonial times, there were acts of warfare with strong communities waging wars against weaker ones and the Sokoto jihad of 1804 was an example of religious and political war. At the inception of colonialism, Frederick (Lord) Lugard amalgamated the Northern and Southern Protectorates for political convenience and subsequent British administrators prevented Christian influence in northern Nigeria. Religious differences continue to determine some aspects of Nigerian social and political life, even after independence. Many books and articles have been published on the issue. While ethnic and political divisions had caused most of the conflicts, the escalation of religious violence occurred after the return of democratic rule in 1999. This was precipitated by the reintroduction of the Shari'a. Focusing mainly on the Tiv and Yoruba ethnic groups, Remi Anifowose examined different acts of political violence that have occurred between the colonial period and the fall of the First Republic in 1966.[1] He argued that there is a prevalent assumption that "violence is an effective means of achieving a desired purpose."[2] This argument emanates from the emphasis that Nigerians place on political power and in their ability to participate in top-level political and economic decisions.

The struggle for political power tends to move towards violence considering the social, political and economic gaps that exist between the majority and minority ethnic groups. Even more focused on religion, politics, and violence is Toyin Falola's *Violence in Nigeria*, which brilliantly communicates the danger of mixing religion with politics. Falola's aim was to provide "a comprehensive analysis of the religious violence and conflicts prevalent in Nigeria since the 1970s,"[3] and he accomplished this objective with relevant examples and brilliant interpretation. He rightly points out that "religious violence and aggression involve more than religious beliefs; they also include the interplay of political, economic, and ethnic forces."[4] He concludes that, "religious communities can coexist and that Nigeria does not have to end up breaking apart."[5]

Religion, Violence, and Human Nature

Religion is an inevitable part of human existence. It results from a human desire to communicate with an ultimate power. To many people, religion is a source of comfort, peace, and power. As Bolaji Idowu put it, "religion is an inescapable involvement of every member of the human race" and he adds that, "there is an inherent urge in man which makes religion a matter of ultimate concern."[6]As a Christian writing on African traditional religion, Bolaji Idowu realizes what it means to exist in a region where many different faiths are practiced. Religious doctrines and expressions may vary, but they all attempt to connect the individual to a superior being.

Violence is a common phenomenon. It occurs in almost every facet of life and has the potential to disrupt and polarize a nation's socio-political system. Violence may be least expected in religion where love, peace, and unity are preached, but because it is a part of human nature, violent acts have taken place throughout history involving religion. One must question, does religion promote or discourage turbulent acts? Because of its prevalence, it also can be asked: Is violence an intrinsic part of human nature?

From an anthropological perspective, it depends on who addresses the issue. Many cultural determinists believe that all human behavior is a result of only cultural influences and other forms of learning. Others see strong evidence that violence is influenced by genetic tendencies inherited from our evolutionary past. This view of innate *tendencies* should not be confused with obsolete ideas about all-powerful drives or instincts. The modern theory is that the probability of violent behavior increases under certain circumstances as a result of behaviors adapted by human ancestors. Behaviors that were learned when they were confronted with similar situations. Some examples: a mother defending her child, a man competing for dominance, either sex defending what they perceive to be a key resource. Innate tendencies toward violence are all subject to various degrees of modification by learning. In Nigeria, people have learned to perceive oil as a key resource, which makes them more likely to fight over it and makes sharing oil wealth more difficult.[7] Struggles for political power and position and ethnic affiliation have also been sources of violence. Particularly since 1999 and the introduction of the Shari'a, religion has become one of the main sources of violence in Nigeria. Even when not the main cause, people have sometimes interjected religion as a reason for physical aggression.

Violence in Christianity and Islam

Religion is often used as an excuse to commit violent acts because perpetrators justify their actions by claiming that they are engaging in spiritual warfare. In the Crusades, which began in 1095, Christian beliefs were utilized to justify their invasion of the Islamic dominated Holy Lands. The Inquisitions in Early Modern Europe were also aggressive means of ridding the church of heresy. In Islam, the jihad ("Struggle" or commonly interpreted "Holy War") is fought against the infidels or non-believers. Both Christianity and Islam are portrayed as peace-seeking religions. Jesus Christ is referred to as the "Prince of Peace" and the Prophet Mohammad encouraged his followers to pursue peace. But both religions exhibit evidence of committing acts of violence. Who are the perpetrators of violence in the two religions? On what basis do they perpetrate the atrocities against believers of other religions? Generally, extremists or fundamentalists provoke those who adhere to other religions, either verbally or by public actions. It should be noted that not all Christians or Muslims endorse aggressive actions to achieve spiritual ends. It takes only a small group of people, irrespective of their religion, to start an act of violence that would have significant and lasting consequences.

In Islam, the notion of jihad is prominent and holds both religious and political implications. Its origins stem from the religious wars fought by the Prophet Mohammed against the polytheistic political authorities of Mecca. Although mentioned frequently in the Qur'an (Koran) as fighting against the unbelievers, "it is not clear whether the Qur'an allows Muslims to fight the unbelievers only as a defense against aggression or under any circumstances."[8] Jihad may not necessarily evoke violence because it is geared toward conversion, but in the Western world, the conception is that jihad is synonymous to violence. Karl Maier's opinion that "holy wars are almost by definition bloody affairs because they spring from the very depths of the human soul,"[9] suggests that there is a relationship between violence and human nature. In the Nigerian case, not every act of religious violence has been inspired by "a defense against aggression:" some have been provoked by trivial causes that are totally unrelated to spiritual matters.

Religion and Secular Politics

Religion and politics are two powerful instruments in the shaping of a society. A complication, however, arises because religious members of the society also constitute the secular political structure with a responsibility to carry out the social and secular obligations of government. In many African states, it has been impossible to separate religion and politics. For example, in North Africa, Islamic influences are prominent in governance and as Paul Gifford shows, Christianity has been playing decisive roles in the politics of countries such as Benin, Togo, Kenya, and Zambia.[10] He further indicates that Frederick Chiluba, the former president of Zambia, not only promoted Christianity, he also declared Zambia a Christian nation.

The interference of religion in politics has often created opportunities for religious groups to accuse the government or other religious adherents of marginalization, resulting in unrest or political disturbances. Religion, as pointed out by John C. Raines, "is most productive and most merciful when securely confined to the domain of personal piety, with political discourse kept self-consciously secular."[11] Even under a secular political dispensation, religion must be used as an integrative rather than a disintegrative tool.

Religion is one of the integrative forces among fragmented but historically and culturally related peoples.[12] A society is brought together not necessarily for religious practices, but essentially for political expediency. Nigeria is a good example, because the amalgamation of the Northern and Southern Protectorates in 1914 by Lord Lugard was not for religious but for the political convenience of the British colonial administration. In the post-colonial period, Nigerian political leaders have been influenced either by the regional or religious affiliation and this has caused divisions on many occasions. Table 1 shows the regional and religious affiliation of Nigeria's past and present political leaders.

Table 1: Nigerian Political Leaders and their Religious Affiliation

Name	Term	Religion	Region
1. Nnamdi Azikiwe	1960-1966	Christian	East
2. Tafawa Balewa	1960-1966	Muslim	North
3. J.T. Aguiyi-Ironsi	1966	Christian	East
4. Yakubu Gowon	1966-1975	Christian	North
5. Murtala Mohammed	1975-1976	Muslim	North

6. Olusegun Obasanjo	1976-1979	Christian	West
7. Shehu Shagari	1979-1983	Muslim	North
8. Muhammadu Buhari	1983-1985	Muslim	North
9. Ibrahim Babangida	1985-1993	Muslim	North
10. Ernest Shonekan	1993	Christian	West
11. Sani Abacha	1993-1998	Muslim	North
12. Abdulsalami Abubakar	1998-1999	Muslim	North
13. Olusegun Obasanjo	1999-2007	Christian	West
14. Shehu Musa Yar'Adua	2007-	Muslim	North

Note: Olusegun Obasanjo's name appears twice because he served in two different times and capacities. He first served as the military Head of State (replacing Murtala Mohammed who was assassinated), and second, as an elected president. The table shows that Christians have led the country 46.1% and Muslims 53.8%.

Irrespective of the religious affiliation, political leaders are saddled with the responsibility of protecting the people, and citizens of Nigeria are to operate on and abide by the institutional frameworks of law, justice, respect for one another, and social relations as laid down by the secular political system and in the constitution. The provision for the freedom of religion in the constitution is not to be abused by any religious group. It is, however, the responsibility of a secular government to wage war on acts of violence that would destabilize the nation.

Religion, Violence, and the Nigerian Experience

Nigeria has experienced several episodes of religious violence: some of them were internal conflicts within a religion while others were between practitioners of different faiths; and many of them occurred in the North. Toyin Falola has characterized the period between 1980 and 1985 as "A Reign of Terror"[13] in order to show the severity of the violence in many northern cities during those years. For example, the uprisings in Kano, one led by Muhammadu Marwa (leader of the Maitatsine group) and the other spearheaded by Ibrahim El-Zakzaky (Shi'a leader), left approximately 4,000 people dead. Another period of religious chaos, caused by the Maitatsine group, broke out in Funtua, Katsina State in 1992 leaving in its wake a significant number of dead and the massive destruction of property.[14] During this period, the Shari'a was not a factor. Most of the conflicts were caused by either petty misunderstandings or rivalries between Muslim groups. The speed with which the riots spread and the ability to get the situation under control were matters of concern to the government.

Intertwined with religion is ethnicity and when conflicts occur, it is often hard to detach the two elements. For example, the series of conflicts between the Hausa-Igbo in Kano; the Hausa-Kataf in Kaduna, the Hausa-Yoruba in Ibadan, Lagos, and Sagamu were all a mixture of ethnicity and religion. Religion, as a personal conviction and practice, should not cause dissension or division. Since Nigeria is culturally, ethnically, and religiously diverse, peaceful inter-religious activities must be promoted and inter-religious violence must be discouraged. Like his Christian counterparts, Dr. Lateef Adegbite, Secretary-General of the Nigerian Supreme Council for Islamic Affairs, supported the idea that Nigerians should abhor violence and "begin to engender a culture of peace, tolerance, and forbearance."[15] Although many people agree that the practice of different religions should not be used as a convenient excuse to violence, this has not been so in Nigeria where trivial religious issues serve as opportunities to kill and destroy.

Introduction of the Shari'a

Understandably, the Shari'a has always been an integral part of Islam and the British recognized it and allowed some parts of it to be practiced. Then, the Shari'a was not an issue. The Shari'a became an issue when Sani Ahmed Yerima, the governor of Zamfara, reintroduce the Shari'a in his state in January 2000. Resistance followed, especially from the Christians. Ignoring the protests and the potential danger of ethnic and religious conflicts that his actions could cause, the governor proceeded to implement it. Niger State and ten other northern states followed Zamfara's lead. Many of the Nigerian Muslims who favor the Shari'a are Sunni. Proponents of Shari'a put forth some arguments to justify their action. First, they believed that because the constitution of Nigeria allows freedom of religion, their action was legal. Second, as Bunza and Limaan pointed out in chapters seven and eight, the Shari'a is an fundamental aspect of Islam, it is about divine justice, and it should be adopted to promote Islam. Third, that the Shari'a would reduce crime, would create a society free of violence, theft, and corruption, and would evolve an atmosphere of peace and progress. Fourth, that the adoption of the Shari'a is a means of connecting with the wider Muslim world. It is argued that Nigeria's Shari'a states could receive development grants from Arab and Muslim nations.

Within the Muslim circle, however, there are those who believe that the Shari'a "could not operate properly in a secular nation-state,"[16] because the difference between Islamic law and the legal law of the land would create religious and political chaos. For example, the Zaria-based Islamic cleric, Sheikh Ibrahim El-Zakzaky, believed that "Islamic law is meant to be applied by an Islamic government in an Islamic environment."[17] Given the situation in Nigeria, there is no totally "Islamic environment" under which the Shari'a could operate. Ethnic and religious intermixture would prevent the effective application of the Shari'a.

The Federal Government, represented by the Justice Minister and Attorney-General, Kanu Agabi, declared the implementation of the Shari'a unconstitutional and an illegal system.[18] The Minister indicated that the action would threaten the stability, unity, and integrity of the nation, but that still did not deter other northern states from following the Zamfara example. In a secular society and in a country that has experienced a lengthy period of military dictatorship, the implementation of the Shari'a was considered a divider and a coup against democracy.

As expected, the strongest opposition came from Christians, represented by the Christian Association of Nigeria (CAN), who planned to take legal action if the Shari'a was implemented. The president of CAN, Dr. Sunday Mbang, believed that the adoption of the Shari'a was ill-timed because Nigeria just returned to democratic rule and this could lead the country in a retrogressive direction. The Cross River State Assembly even threatened to declare Cross River a "Christian State." If that had happened, other southern states would have followed the lead, and the whole country would have been thrown into chaos, polarized along religious lines.

Within a very short time of the Shari'a's implementation, riots, killing, and political disorder engulfed the whole of Nigeria. People began to live in perpetual fear of religious violence. In addition, the magnitude of the carnage and the concomitant insecurity generated criticism from the international community about Nigeria's fragile constitution and religious intolerance.

International criticisms were focused not only on the rationale behind the implementation of the Shari'a in a secular nation, but also on the punishment given to offenders. Offenses include consumption of alcohol, corruption, adultery, and stealing. Women are to be segregated from men in all respects, including schools and taxicabs. The Shari'a punishments include stoning to death for adultery, amputating limbs for theft, and flogging for the possession of alcohol.[19] Critics of the Shari'a pointed out that the law was unevenly enforced since it was mainly and unfairly directed to the *talakawa* (the poor) and was repressive to women as proven in Table

2 below. One of the victims, Safiya Husseini, a 35-year old woman, was sentenced to death by stoning for adultery, but after the intervention of the federal government and international human rights organizations, Safiya was set free. Some Muslim scholars believed that Safiya's case was "a misapplication of the Shari'a."[20]

Amina Lawal was another woman who was sentenced to death for having extra-marital sex. She too was eventually set free. An important question to ask is how true is it that most of the punishments are found in the Qur'an? The Qur'an on which the Shari'a is partly based does not recommend a death sentence. The Qur'an states:

> If any of your women is guilty of unnatural offence, bring four of your witnesses to give evidence; if they testify against them, retain them in the houses until death, or until God provide some other way for them.[21]

As things are, the general opinion was that zealous Muslims in Nigeria are attempting to reinvent the Shari'a to draw political attention to themselves. In this case, the critics of the Shari'a who claim it is being used for political reasons against the Obasanjo's administration are justified. However, opinions from the Muslim circle reflected that the Shari'a was simply and purely a matter of religion, not of politics. It became political because people of other faiths inhabit the states where the Shari'a was adopted. Even though it was difficult to arrive at a definite agreement on its implementation, there were apparent clashes and overlapping of interests among religious and political leaders. The collision of religion and politics resulted in several violent outbreaks.

Table 2: Selected Shari'a Victims, Offense, and Punishment

DATE	VICTIM	OFFENSE	PUNISHMENT	STATE
March 2000	Baba Bello Jangedi	Stealing a cow	Right hand amputation	Zamfara
August 2000	Two motorbike taxi riders	Carrying female passengers	20 lashes	Zamfara
August 2000	Amina Abdullahi	Premarital sex	100 lashes	Zamfara
November 2000	Attine Tanko	Premarital sex	100 lashes (boyfriend – 100 lashes)	Kano
January 2001	Two men (unnamed)	Drinking alcohol	80 lashes	Sokoto

July 2001	An unnamed man	Stealing a goat	Right hand amputation	Kebbi
September 2001	Attahiru Umar	Sodomising a boy	To de stoned to death	Zamfara
September 2001	Bariya Ibrahim Magazu	Premarital sex and false charges against the men who raped her	180 lashes	Katsina
October 2001	Safiya Husseini	Extra-marital sex	To be buried up to the neck in sand and to be stoned to death	Sokoto
March 2002	Amina Lawal	Adultery	Sentenced to death	Jigawa
March 2002	Kurami Sarimu Mohammed	Raping a 9-year old girl	To be stoned to death	Katsina
May 2002	Adamu Unusua	Premarital sex	100 lashes	
May 2002	Yunusa Rafin	Adultery	To be stoned to death	Bauchi
August 2002	Ahmadu Ibrahim	Premarital sex	To be stoned to death	Bauchi

One of the death sentences was carried out: Sani Yakubu, a 27-year old man, was hanged for killing a woman and her two children in January 2002 in Katsina State. Lashes and amputations have also been implemented. Non-Muslims in the twelve Shari'a states are uncomfortable with the Shari'a despite the claim that they will not be subjected to its laws. To the Christians in particular, the implementation of the Shari'a is tantamount to religious terrorism within Nigerian borders. Maier clearly states that:

> Living under Shari'a is believed to be an intrinsic right and duty of the Islamic faithful, and any Muslims who oppose it are deemed to be lacking in true belief. The Muslim argument that Shari'a would not affect non-Muslims, however, was clearly false since its ban on alcohol, cinemas, and integration of the sexes in most spheres of life would affect everyone.[22]

From the Christian perspective, the Shari'a violates the secular constitution and they fear that the Shari'a laws are geared toward the growth of Islam and that there is a conscious attempt to turn Nigeria into a Muslim state. Particularly in the northern states, where many of the religious conflicts have taken place, both Christians and Muslims accused each other of religious intolerance.

It has been argued that the Shari'a is only an instrument that politicians employ to achieve their ambition or to enhance their position. Because religion is capable of being manipulated and exploited, what Nigerians are witnessing is the politics of religion through the Shari'a. Its implementation is one of the dangerous agendas that threaten the corporate existence of Nigeria. The ensuing crisis "is a political weapon [that some northern politicians use] to destabilize the country . . . [and] to register their disenchantment with Obasanjo's government."[23] Lending credence to this argument is El-Zakzaky, who has been quoted as saying that the Shari'a crisis is a "political campaign strategy."[24] The Shari'a became such a strong political issue that in the 2003 elections, Muslims vowed not to vote for a Christian presidential candidate and Christians would not support a Muslim candidate, though some governors in the Shari'a states endorsed Obasanjo for a second term.[25] Obasanjo, a Christian, was re-elected, although he lost a substantial number of votes from the Shari'a states.

Stemming from the argument on intolerance is the point that Muslim politicians support the Shari'a in order to curtail the increasing growth of Christianity in the north. Those who use religion to promote their political ambitions and status are doing so at the expense of the peace and unity of the country. An aspect that cannot be overlooked is the fact that some Christians and Muslims have protected their neighbors, even if of a different religion, during this chaotic period. This exemplifies the true spirit of living together and it indicates that co-existence is possible.[26] Evolving peaceful co-existence is a political process, considering the fact that religion has not only been used as a political propaganda, it has also become an instrument of hatred. Neither Christianity nor Islam encourages violence, but political force sometimes instigates hatred that leads to bloodshed.

Many of the religious riots occurred in Kaduna, but some of them were unrelated to the Shari'a. The first riot in February 2000 was triggered by the CAN's protest against the implementation of the Shari'a. That episode indicated how vulnerable Nigerian cities are to destruction because within a very short time, thousands of people had been killed. Like other main cities such as Ibadan, Kano, and Lagos, Kaduna is a cosmopolitan town that is ethnically and religiously diverse. Unlike other northern cities such as Kano and Zamfara, where Muslims are overwhelmingly in the majority, there is a substantial Christian population in Kaduna. Churches and mosques are found side by side. The population is dense, filled with merchants from different parts of Nigeria who find Kaduna a thriving commercial city. Politically, Kaduna is the home of most of the northern politicians generally known as the "Kaduna Mafia." In the 1990s, Kaduna became the center stage for ethnic and religious violence. The riot that attended the announcement of the Shari'a was therefore not surprising. The Kaduna incidence had a ripple effect in the southeastern states, especially in Aba, where approximately 400 northerners and Muslims were killed.[27]

Tensions rose and Christian-Muslim relations worsened in Kaduna after the state government signed into law a modified version of the Shari'a in December 2001. In response to the riots that accompanied the original introduction of the Shari'a, in which over 2,000 people were killed, the revision was considered a compromise because it exempted Christians from being charged in the Shari'a courts. In spite of the modification, riots still erupted in the Christian town of Gwantu; the Shari'a was seen as a religious dividing instrument. Reacting to the crisis, some people advocated living together in a peaceful and civil manner while others suggested that Kaduna State be split into two. The situation was so bad that a resident declared, "We now live in perpetual fear because of the incidents of terror unleashed by rampaging youths in their battle to ensure Islamic Sharia law is in operation in the city."[28]

The riot in Bauchi in June 2001, which left two people dead and many churches and mosques destroyed, was connected with the implementation of the Shari'a, but the one in Kano in October 2001, was a reaction to the US air strikes in Afghanistan. Muslims attacked the Christians and killed approximately 200 people. Another religious conflict broke out in Plateau State in October 2002 where almost 1,000 people were killed and churches and mosques burned down.

Kaduna was again the arena of violence in November 2002 when Nigeria was to host the Miss World contest. While some Muslims diametrically opposed the competition being held in a Muslim environment because of the contestant's body exposure, the violence was actually triggered by an offensive magazine article, which tried to convey the beauty of the contestants by saying "the Prophet Mohammed would have probably chosen to marry one of the Miss World contestants if he had witnessed the beauty pageant."[29] Using this statement as a springboard, Muslim youths in Kaduna not only attacked the office of *ThisDay* newspaper, but they also destroyed houses, stores, and property and killed anyone who crossed their path.

Following the September 11, 2001 attack on America and the subsequent U.S. declaration of war on terrorism, religious riots broke out in Kano with 200 people reportedly killed. The riot was triggered by anti-American youths who were reacting to the American war on terrorism in Afghanistan. They burned down five churches and two mosques. The riot destabilized the peace of the country and displaced many people. For example, James Enoch, a Christian, left the city saying: "I can't live here any more. These youths are dangerous. They promised to come back and said when they come back nobody will be spared."[30] The fear of a backlash, if and when a conflict occurs, forced people to relocate. Again, another episode of religious violence erupted in Kano in 2004. According to a report, thousands of Christians fled the suburbs of Kano "to seek police protection after coming under attack from Muslim mobs."[31] The violence began when a Christian ethnic militia was accused of attacking a Muslim town and killing 200 people. In reaction, Muslim youths retaliated by killing Christians.

Declaring the second phase of Shari'a implementation in April 2004, Governor Ahmed Sani ordered the demolition of all churches in Zamfara State. In a secular state such as Nigeria, this declaration is certainly unconstitutional. The proclamation was tantamount to religious intimidation or marginalization. Power and fear have often been used in politics, and in this case, the governor has used his political powers to discriminate against Christians. Nigerians have always lived in an environment where the fundamental freedom of religion and association is guaranteed. According to Chapter 4, Section 38 (1) of the 1999 Constitution:

> Every person shall be entitled top freedom of thought, conscience and religion, including freedom to change his religion or belief and freedom (either alone or in community with others, and in public or in private) to manifest and propagate his religion or belief in worship, teaching, practice and observance.[32]

Governor Ahmed Sani, who carried the responsibility of upholding the constitution, defied it and caused further damage to the already fragile Christian-Muslim relationship in the state.

In May 2004, in Plateau State (regarded as a traditionally peaceful state), religious violence erupted between Christians and Muslims in the city of Yelwa. Unlike other incidences, the genesis of the Yelwa conflict was totally unrelated to the Shari'a; it was caused by claims to ancestral land rights. The Christian Tarok ethnic group killed many Muslim Fulani with whom they were competing over farmland. In the wake of the violence, approximately 1,000 people were killed while many churches and mosques were burned down.[33] In a quick and escalating response, Muslims continued to kill more Christians and this ring of bloodshed spread throughout northern Nigeria. Although the conflict assumed a religious connotation, looming in the background was a dispute over access to land and the distribution of political offices in the state. Rightly or wrongly, President Obasanjo declared a state of emergency and suspended the governor, Joshua Dariye.

Table 3: Some of the Religious Riots in Nigeria

Date	State	Appr. Number of Deaths
Feb.-May 2000	Kaduna	2,500
March 2000	Borno	Number not available
October 2000	Lagos	40
June-August 2001	Bauchi	400
September 2001	Kano	200
September 2001	Plateau	500
November 2001	Kaduna	500
November 2002	Kaduna	10
May 2004	Plateau	1000
May 2004	Kano	1,000
October 2004	Kaduna	1,000 (63 churches and mosques burned)
December 2004	Plateau	Number not available

The consequences of the numerous religious conflicts have been devastating on the political and social relationships among Nigerians. Between 1999 and 2003 approximately 10,000 people were killed in various religious conflicts. In 2000 alone, approximately 2,000 deaths were reported. Since 2007 when there have been changes in the political leadership of the states, there has been significant reduction in death cases related to the Shari'a.

Aside from the heavy human loss and wanton destruction of property, survivors of religious violence have been faced with the problem of unplanned and forced relocation. Divisions deepened as many people had to relocate among their ethnic or religious groups. For example, Christians were forced to leave their homes in Muslim dominated areas to seek refugee elsewhere. In the same vein, Muslims moved out from where Christians resided. Many Yoruba or Igbo people were displaced and forced to abandon their homes in the northern cities and to relocate in the south. Hausa Muslims in Ibadan, Lagos, or Sagamu left the south to live among their people in the north. Some Christians left Kaduna to settle in Jos where they expected to escape the prospect of living under Islamic Shari'a law, but there too, met inter-ethnic and inter-religious violence.

Conclusion

The combination of religion, politics, and violence is a deadly mix, given the numerous outbreak of violence since 1999. Because both religion and politics seek to pursue and promote peace, unity, and stability, violence should not be the means of achieving that end. No country prides itself or flaunts its accomplishment through violence. Those who use religion to foment trouble are doing a great disservice to their nation. Nigeria, as once referred to as the "Giant of Africa," faces a challenge of establishing a workable and effective mechanism of forestalling or preventing violence at all levels, and institute strong strategies of sustainable peace and unity. The success of democracy in modern Nigeria depends on the measures the government adopts to prevent the outbreak of sectarian conflicts.

Nigerian political leaders and the constitution are clear on the secularism of the country, and the consciousness to maintain national integration has been a major factor. Since the Nigerian Civil War (1967-1970) was not allowed to divide Nigeria, the Shari'a issue or religion in general should not be permitted to cause unnecessary division. Nigerians should strongly uphold the principle of "unity in diversity" and allow religion to be an anchor for unity rather than an instrument of division.

Notes

1. Remi Anifowose, *Violence and Politics in Nigeria: The Tiv and Yoruba Experience* (New York: Nok Publishers, 1982).
2. Ibid., 273.
3. Toyin Falola, *Violence in Nigeria: The Crisis of Religious Politics and Secular Ideologies* (Rochester, NY: University of Rochester Press, 1998), vii.
4. Ibid., 298.
5. Ibid.
6. E. Bolaji Idowu, *African Traditional Religion: A Definition* (London: SCM Press, 1973), 2-3.
7. Discussion with Dr. Glenn King, Cultural Anthropologist, Monmouth University, West Long Branch, NJ, January 24, 2005.
8. Rudolph Peters, *Jihad in Classical and Modern Islam* (Princeton, NJ: Markus Wiener Publishers, 1996), 1-3.
9. Karl Maier, *This House Has Fallen: Midnight in Nigeria* (New York: Public Affairs, 2000), 143.
10. Paul Gifford, *African Christianity: Its Role* (Bloomington, IN: Indiana University Press, 1998), 21-26; 181-245.

11 John C. Raines, "The Politics of Religious Correctness: Islam and the West." *Cross Currents*, http://www.crosscurrents.org/Raines2.htm

12. Kamari Maxine Clarke, *Mapping Yoruba Networks: Power and Agency in the Making of Transnational Communities* (Durham, NC: Duke University Press, 2004).

13. Falola, 137-162.

14. Abiodun Adeniji, "The Funtua Mayhem," *African Concord*, Vol. 7, No. 38, February 1992, 14-18.

15. Adegbenro Adebanjo, "We should be Careful," *Tell*, No. 42, October 15, 2001, 19.

16. Maier, 178.

17. Ibid.

18. Bode Adewumi, Shari'a; "The Controversy Rages On," *Sunday Tribune*, March 31, 2002, 5.

19. In the Muslim world, the Shari'a is applied in a broad way, some are strict, some are moderate, and others apply it within a secular political setting. David Rohde, "A World of Ways to Say 'Islamic Law,'" *The New York Times*, Sunday, March 13, 2005, 4.

20. Adegbenro Adebanjo, "Saving Safiya from the Hangman," *Tell*, No. 49, December 3, 2001, 30-31.

21. Ahmed Ali, translator, *Al-Qurr'an: A Contemporary Translation* (Princeton, NJ: Princeton University Press, 1984), Chapter 4, verse 15, 75.

22. Maier, 145.

23. Ayodele Akinkuotu, "A Dangerous Agenda," *Tell*, March 2000, 14.

24. Ibid.

25. Kazeem Akintunde, "Shari'a," *The Week*, Vol. 16, No. 19, August 12, 2002, 12-14.

26. Danlami Nmodu, "Guns Now Silent while Unease Booms," *Tell*, March 2000, 21.

27. Maier, 146.

28. "Nigerian's Year of Turmoil," BBC, May 25, 2000, http://news.bbc.co.uk/hi/english/world/Africa/newsid_763000/763818.stm

29. "Nigeria Violence Rages On," BBC, http://news.bbc.co.uk/2/hi/africa/2505729.stm, November 23, 2002.

30. "Nigeria Pledges to Curb Religious Strife," http://news.bbc.co.uk/2/hi/africa/1541901.stm, September 13, 2001.

31. "Thousands of Nigerian Christians Flee Riots," *Mail & Guardian*, http://www.mg.co.za/articlepage.aspx?area=/breaking_news/breaking_news__africa&articleid=79152, May 12, 2004.

32. Constitution of the Federal Republic of Nigeria, 1999, Chapter 4, Section 38 (1).
33. "Religions at war in Nigeria-Christian leader," http://naijanet.com/news/source/2004/may/7/1003.html

RELIGIOUS ASSOCIATIONS AND POLITICS

Chapter Ten

Nigeria and the Organization of the Islamic Conference

Bukola Adeyemi Oyeniyi

The Organization of the Islamic Conference (OIC) is an inter-governmental organization that comprises fifty-seven countries. These countries are mostly Islamic, Arabic, English, and French speaking nations in the Middle East, Africa, Central Asia, Europe, Southeast Asia, the Indian subcontinent, and South America. The Conference began in Rabat, Morocco, on September 25, 1969 in reaction to an arson attack against the Al-Aqsa Mosque on August 21, 1969.[1] Since then, the Organization has developed into a platform for social, economic, and cultural cooperation among Muslims. The OIC has a Permanent Delegation in the United Nations, but its members consider their organization to be the United Nations of Muslim countries. According to the Protocol set up by the organization, the OIC aims at promoting:

> Solidarity among all Islamic member states; to consolidate cooperation among member states in economic, social, cultural, scientific, and other fields of activity; to endeavor to eliminate racial segregation and discrimination and to oppose colonialism in all its forms; and, to support all Muslim people in their struggle to safeguard their dignity, independence and national rights, bridging gaps between different cultures of the world, etc.[2]

The OIC system consists of the Islamic Summit, which serves as the highest policy-making organ, and convenes every three years. It is opened only to the Kings and Heads of member States. Other organs of the Organization include the Islamic Conference of Foreign Ministers, which examines progress reports on the implementation of decisions taken within the framework of the policy defined by the Islamic Summit. With its seat in Jeddah, Saudi Arabia, the Permanent Secretariat, as the executive organ of the Organization, implements the decisions of the two preceding bodies. To attain efficient operations; the Organization works through numerous committees such as the Al-Quds, the Standing Committee on Information and Cultural Affairs (COMIAC), the Standing Committee on Economic and Trade Cooperation (COMCEC), the Standing Committee on Scientific and Technological Cooperation (COMSTECH), the Islamic Committee for Economic, Cultural and Social Affairs, the Permanent Finance Committee, and the Financial Control Organ.[3] To attain its set goals, the OIC has subsidiary organs saddled with different responsibilities. The table below shows subsidiary organs of OIC and where they are located.

Table 1: OIC Organizations and their Location

Subsidiary Organ	**Location**
Statistical Economic, Social Research and Training Center for Islamic Countries	Ankara, Turkey
Research Center for Islamic History, Art and Culture (IRCICA)	Istanbul, Turkey
Islamic University of Technology	Dhaka, Bangladesh
Islamic Center for the Development of Trade	Casablanca, Morocco
Islamic Fiqh Academy	Jeddah, Saudi Arabia
The Executive Bureau of the Islamic Solidarity Fund and its Waqf	Jeddah, Saudi Arabia
Islamic University of Niger	Say, Niger
Islamic University of Uganda	Mbale, Uganda
Islamic Development Bank (IDB)	Jeddah, Saudi Arabia
Islamic Educational, Scientific and Cultural Organization (ISESCO)	Rabat, Morocco
Islamic States Broadcasting Organization (ISBO) and the International Islamic News Agency (IINA)	Jeddah, Saudi Arabia

Islamic Chamber of Commerce and Industry (ICCI)	Karachi, Pakistan
World Islamic Economic Forum (WIEF)	Kuala Lumpur, Malaysia
Organization of Islamic Capitals and Cities (OICC)	Jeddah, Saudi Arabia
Sports Federation of Islamic Solidarity Games	Riyadh, Saudi Arabia
Islamic Committee of the International Crescent (ICIC)	Benghazi, Libya
Islamic Conference Youth Forum for Dialogue and Cooperation, (ICYF-DC)	Istanbul, Turkey
Islamic Ship-owners Association (ISA)	Jeddah, Saudi Arabia
World Federation of International Arab-Islamic Schools	Jeddah, Saudi Arabia
International Association of Islamic Banks (IAIB)	Jeddah, Saudi Arabia

This long list shows that the OIC is a full-fledged organization with clearly defined goals and functional systems.[4] There are two groups of members to the OIC: the full member and the observer. The table below shows member countries and their membership status.

Table 2: Member States and their Status in the OIC

Countries	**Since**	**Status**
Full Member States		
Afghanistan	1969	suspended 1980-1989
Algeria	1969	
Chad	1969	
Egypt	1969	suspended 1979-1984
Guinea	1969	
Indonesia	1969	
Iran	1969	
Jordan	1969	
Kuwait	1969	
Lebanon	1969	
Libya	1969	

Malaysia	1969	
Mali	1969	
Mauritania	1969	
Morocco	1969	
Niger	1969	
Pakistan	1969	
Palestine	1969	
Saudi Arabia	1969	
Yemen	1969	from 1990 as Republic of Yemen
Senegal	1969	
Sudan	1969	
Somalia	1969	
Tunisia	1969	
Turkey	1969	
Bahrain	1969	
Oman	1970	
Qatar	1970	
Syria	1970	
United Arab Republic	1970	
Sierra Leone	1972	
Bangladesh	1974	
Gabon	1974	
Gambia	1974	
Guinea Bissau	1974	
Uganda	1974	
Burkina Faso	1975	
Cameroon	1975	
Comoros	1976	
Iraq	1976	
Maldives	1976	
Djibouti	1978	
Benin	1982	
Brunei	1984	
Nigeria	1986	
Azerbaijan	1991	
Albania	1992	
Kyrgyzstan	1992	
Tajikistan	1992	

Turkmenistan	1992	
Zanzibar	1993	Withdrew August 1993
Mozambique	1994	
Kazakhstan	1995	
Uzbekistan	1995	
Suriname	1996	
Togo	1997	
Guyana	1998	
Cote d'Ivoire	2001	
Observer Muslim Organizations and Communities		
Moro National Liberation Front	1977	
Observer Islamic Institutions		
Parliamentary Union of the OIC Member States	2000	
Islamic Conference Youth Forum for Dialogue and Cooperation	2005	
Observer International Organizations		
League of Arab States	1975	
United Nations	1976	
Non-Aligned Movement	1977	
Organization of African Unity	1977	
Economic Cooperation Organization	1995	

Source: http://www.oic-oci.org/oicnew/member_states.asp

The goal of this chapter is to trace the origin of Nigeria's membership in the OIC, the politics associated with her membership in this Islamic body, and its implication for growth and development in Nigeria over the years. It is also to show that Nigeria's membership in the Islamic body is not an isolated event, but an integral part of an Islamization process that has historical reality. As shall be demonstrated shortly, Nigeria joined the OIC, initially as observer, in 1976 under General Muritala. The Observer status was later converted to full membership in 1986 by General Babangida. Many Christians, other religious groups, and some Muslims within Nigeria and elsewhere reacted to Nigeria's membership in the OIC, especially because it appeared to negate the constitutional secularity of the nation. Radical Islam in Nigeria stemmed from the OIC affairs and culminated in the various religio-political crises that have shaken the growth and development of the country, and blossomed into the re-emergence of the Shari'a legal codes in some states.

Nigeria, International Organizations, and the OIC

Nigeria's participation in international organizations dates back to the colonial times. Immediately after independence in 1960, Nigeria demonstrated her new found freedom by denouncing some of her bilateral relations that connected the nation with Britain. For example, Tafawa Balewa, the first Nigerian Prime Minister, boldly declared on the floor of the Nigerian House of Parliament on August 20, 1958 that:

> We shall, of course, endeavor to remain on friendly terms with every nation which recognizes our sovereignty. Besides, *we shall not blindly follow the lead of anyone*. So far as possible, the policy for each occasion *will be selected with proper independent objectivity. We consider it wrong for the Federal Government to associate itself as a matter of routine with any of the power blocs.* This freedom of action will be an essential feature of our foreign policy, and will ensure that full attention is paid to the opinion expressed by our Representatives (in Parliament)[5] [Emphasis mine].

Nigeria began to align herself with nations that were trying to carve new paths for themselves in the international arena by alligning with any nation that: "recognizes and respects our sovereignty. Besides, we shall not blindly follow the lead of anyone. So far as possible, the policy for each occasion will be selected with proper independent objectivity in Nigeria's national interest."[6] This independence was demonstrated with Nigeria's support for the admission of "Red China" into the United Nations Organization in December 1960. The Prime Minister noted in Parliament on November 24 and 25, 1960:

> We do not believe that the policy to block Red China from admission into the United Nations is the right one. We do not believe it because it is unfair and unwise to leave out 650 million people in the World Assembly. Nigeria is going to see to it that Red China is admitted into the United Nations Organization (UNO).[7]

When confronted with the question as to whether the subject of the admission of Red China be listed on the Agenda for debate at the General Assembly of the UNO, the Nigerian Minister of Foreign Affairs, Hon. Jaja

Wachuku, simply voted in favor of the motion. Later when confronted by Britain and other Western powers, he responded: "Look this tantamounts (sic) to intellectual imperialism if you will not allow us to think and vote the way we like in accordance with our Foreign Policy. What is the use coming here (United Nations)."[8]

This hardline stance over who to align with, when, and under what conditions, resulted in the establishment of diplomatic relations between Nigeria and China, at the ambassadorial level, on February 10, 1971. While China opened its Embassy in Nigeria on April 6, 1971, Nigeria did not open its Embassy in China until October 1 of the same year.[9] The delay was caused by the Nigerian Civil War, 1967-1970.

Procedurally, membership of any international organization remains the constitutional imperative of the president or prime minister or head of state. An integral part of the plenipotentiary power of the head of state, the president or prime minister (as the case may be) is the power to enter into any bilateral relation with any organization or nation with the consent of the National Assembly. The guiding principle is to foster relations with other nations or organizations that respect and recognize the nation's sovereignty.

Except on few occasions, Nigeria's membership in any international organization must be debated and thoroughly analyzed before such bilateral relations are agreed upon and implemented. Exceptional situations occurred largely during the different military regimes, when autocratic leaders maintained relations with any nation or organization that recognized their claim to power, regardless of national interest. They joined organizations that suited their personal philosophies and were responsible only to the tiny group of people that installed them in government. Usually, the military heads of state wielded enormous political power and were able to dictate whatever international organization Nigeria could join. The Foreign Affairs Minister was not even permitted to take unilateral decisions on joining any international organizations, no matter how beneficial such relations might be. The procedure was for such minister to seek the approval of the head of state, and once secured, the nation automatically became a member nation of the organization.

Nigeria's membership in the OIC in 1986 was fostered under military rule and, as such, no constitutional procedure was followed. It was not discussed at any forum. The Armed Forces Ruling Council (AFRC), which acted like the parliament, did not discuss the issue. It was unilaterally promoted by General Ibrahim Babangida and his loyalists. Although the decision to join the OIC was never discussed, Nigeria's membership was heavily and extensively debated by Nigerians when the issue became public knowledge. Some argued that prior to the military rule of General Muritala Mohammed in 1976, efforts were made to declare Nigeria a Muslim nation.[10] Mohammed's attempt had historical background that went back to the colonial times. In 1956, Anthony Enahoro made the famous motion for Nigeria to become independent in 1958. The northern political elite who were in attendance, openly declared that if Nigeria became independent in 1958, they would carry on the Islamization of the nation, which Uthman dan Fodio began in the early nineteenth century.[11]

Yakubu Gowon who became the first military head of state from the North was a Christian and could not follow up on the Islamization process. When General Mohammed became the head of state in 1976, he tried to satisfy the northern oligarchy by nursing the idea of Nigeria as an Islamic state. On this basis, he enrolled Nigeria as an Observer Member in the OIC.[12] After six months in office, Mohammed was assassinated in an aborted military coup. This presumably prevented him from executing the plans to Islamize Nigeria. Although Mohammed died, the plan to Islamize Nigeria did not. What he could not achieve, Shehu Yar'Adua, Ibrahim Babangida, and Mohammed Buhari (members of the Supreme Military Council) were available to accomplish. These were people in the geo-ethno-military-clique who were well aware and committed to the plan for Nigeria to evolve into an Islamic nation like Libya.

Olusegun Obasanjo, a Christian and the successor of Muritala Mohammed, had problems with pushing through the Islamization plan at the upper echelon of the military. Some members of the Supreme Military Council who could have supported the plan did not hold powerful positions to influence the decision, and they were faced with severe opposition from the Service Chiefs - General T. Y. Danjuma (Army), Commodore Isa Doko (Air Force), and Rear Admiral Adelanwa (Navy) - who were more interested in defending secularism than promoting Islamization.[13] Eventually, the plan was pushed to the 1977/78 Constitution Drafting Committee (CDC), which Obasanjo was a member.[14]

At the CDC, efforts were made at pursuing the Islamization cause by advocating for a separate judicial (Shari'a) system for the North. Eminent southern lawyers such as Rotimi Williams, Ben Nwabueze, Richard Akinjide, and Bola Ige were members of the CDC, but they acquiesced to the Shari'a Clause in the draft constitution. Opposition to the Shari'a clause, however, came largely from Paul Unongo and Solomon Lar (representing the Middle Best states) and minority groups from the South.[15] It would appear that the southern eminent lawyers and politicians were unaware of the ploy to remove the article on secularism and substitute it with the Shari'a clause. The clause did not make it to the draft constitution, but it was included in the minority report. In spite of being a Christian, Obasanjo agreed to the Shari'a clause and it was included in the constitution. Hence, the Shari'a became the second step taken in the attempt to turn Nigeria into an Islamic state.

Omo Omoruyi and Most Reverend Olubunmi Okogie were of the opinion that those who sought the Islamization of Nigeria believed that the future presidents and heads of government in Nigeria (either voted into power through election, by military coup, by appointment, or by selection) would or should always be Muslims.[16] This, they argued, led Ibrahim Babangida to convert the Nigerian Observer status in the OIC to that of Full Member in 1986. Even if it was the plan to retain Muslims in power, the appointment Chief Ernest Shonekan as the head of the interim government, and General Olusegun Obasanjo (both Christians) as the president in 1999, has removed and rendered such views unsubstantiated.

In recent times, newspapers have reported that while in power Olusegun Obasanjo paid Nigeria's back dues to the OIC. Hence, many have reasoned that, by so doing, he made Nigeria a full member in the OIC. This view was predominant among Christians, non-Muslims and liberal Muslims alike. This is diametrically opposed to another insinuation among Nigerian Muslims that General Obasanjo actually nursed the ambition of reversing Nigeria's membership in the OIC.[17]

Proponents of this view cited the example of the furor generated, especially in southern Nigeria, over the implementation of the Shari'a in the North and the attack on rioters in Jos. As many have argued, the Jos crisis and others that involved Christians and Muslims in Lagos, Sagamu, and Ibadan were treated with "kid-gloves" and the number of Muslim causalities in the conflict should have been enough for the former president to declare a state of emergency in the affected places. On the basis of Obasanjo not declaring a state of emergency, it was argued that he must be planning a desecration of Islam. It was further argued that Obasanjo's refusal to send representatives to the Tenth Meeting of the OIC in Putrajaya, Malaysia, was an effort to pull Nigeria out of the OIC. Other allegations included the purported plan to sell some of Nigeria Airway's land to a church; the using of the Nigerian Television Authority (NTA) to promote Christianity; and Obasanjo's refusal to attend important Muslim projects such as the Dialogue among Civilizations initiated by the OIC. Generally, the Obasanjo administration was believed to have been hostile to Islam both openly and secretly. The culmination of the allegations was that he planned to downgrade Nigeria's membership in the OIC to an observer status.[18]

Opposed to this view was the position taken by Malam Umar Zaria of the Jama'atu Nasril Islam (JNI) or/and the Supreme Council for Shari'a in Nigeria (SCSN), that Obasanjo did actually register Nigeria as a full member of the OIC.[19] While this is yet to be confirmed, there is evidence that Obasanjo did not make any attempt to remove Nigeria from the OIC. He paid Nigeria's outstanding debts with the organization for reasons that Akinjide Osuntokun claimed may be connected with Obasanjo's attempt to run for the third term as the president.[20]

As Table 2 above suggests, Nigeria's observer status has long been converted to full membership. What Obasanjo did was to make Nigeria a fee-paying member, which invariably converts to full-membership. Obasanjo did not say anything on the OIC, but his making Nigeria a fee-paying member raised two important issues. First, he made Nigeria a fee-paying member when he was promoting his Third Term ambition. Paying the backlog of debts created an avenue for him to gain the support of the Muslims to consolidate his chances for his third term ambition. Second, his action validated the argument that he supported the Islamization agenda, which northern political and religious leaders were promoting.

In Babangida's biography, written by Gabriel Umoden, the view was expressed that he (Babangida) converted Nigeria's membership in the OIC from Observer to Full Membership status in order to expunge the perception being bandied by a "high-level Arab diplomat," and others in the Arab circle, that the Nigerian leader was not a "good Moslem." In response to this supposedly high-level Arab diplomat, it was said that General Babangida "mandated the Ministry of External Affairs to arrange for a Nigerian delegation and give the delegation a diplomatic cover to the Conference of OIC in Fez, Morocco in 1986."[21] The issue of the OIC did not die with Babangida's rule; rather, it continues to trail Babangida out of office.

During the elections in 2003, there was the general perception, especially among Muslims, that Obasanjo was anti-OIC. This was probably a political gimmick to prevent Obasanjo from being reelected. Many have argued that, since his reelection, Obasanjo has been planning to de-link or withdraw Nigeria's membership in the OIC.[22] This suspicion was strengthened by Obasanjo's failure to attend or send representatives to the Tenth Islamic Summit, held in Putrajaya, Malaysia. Supporters of OIC have also asked why Nigeria would withdraw when nations such as Russia, India, South Africa, Liberia, and the Philippines were seeking admission. Although Obasanjo did not send a delegation to the summit, he, however, attended the meeting of the Committee of Eight Developed Muslim Nations (D8), another organ of the OIC. He was the only Christian head of state at this meeting. As expected, this action put him at odds with Christians.

Many people ask why Obasanjo would de-link Nigeria from the OIC when about 60 million Nigerian Muslims were yearning to remain part of an organization, which others countries were interested in joining. It is argued that the organization has numerous developmental programs, which Nigeria can benefit from. For example, The Islamic Development Bank (IDB) grants interest-free loans for development projects to member countries, and this assistance is extended to Muslims in non-member countries. The only condition for becoming a member of the IDB is membership in the OIC. Nigeria, despite fulfilling this qualification, has since refused to benefit from the economic advantages available through the IDB.

Aside from the IDB, many Nigerian students have enjoyed scholarships from the OIC. There are in Nigeria today many medical doctors who were trained through an OIC scholarship program and who now use their knowledge, skills, and expertise to treat Nigerians, irrespective of their religion. To such people, the question is: Why did Obasanjo refuse to tap into the OIC, in view of Nigeria's poor economic situation and take advantage of the enormous benefits Nigeria could derive from richer members of the OIC? If the IDB were to finance the construction of new refineries in Nigeria, the Muslims would not be the only ones to enjoy a steady availability of fuel. Indeed, the IDB have financed special assistance projects such as hostel accommodation for university students from such non-member countries as Cameroon, Togo, and Ghana. Students from IDB member countries, Muslim and non-Muslim, can obtain up to $15,000 from the IDB's Young Researchers Support Programme. The IDB's development objective centers on the pooling of resources from the rich and developed member countries to finance developmental projects in poor and less-developed member countries with a view to empower people and make the world prosperous for all. In this same vein, loans from the IMF or World Bank carry with them interest payable over the period of the loans, whereas with the IDB's loan a country is only charged a service fee with no penalty for default.[23] Can Nigeria afford not to take an interest-free loan with the poor state of its economy?

It should be understood that Babangida's intention in joining the OIC as a Full Member was hinged on an unreasonable factor. He unilaterally made Nigeria a shareholder of the IDB in January 1988 when Nigeria held 0.32 percent of its shares. Nigeria still remains a shareholder with the bank. Juxtaposing the various arguments, one is confronted with the fact that Nigeria's membership in any international organization, whether before, now, or in the future, must have been predicated on some apparent or latent gains. What objective(s) underwrites Nigeria's membership in the OIC? Nigerians can only guess since the military was not accountable to anybody other than its tiny cabal.

Nigerians' Reactions to the OIC

When the media made Nigeria's membership in the OIC known to the public, Christian leaders were enraged, and immediately called on the government to withdraw. Unlike Christians, Muslims were thrilled and hailed the government for taking that step. While Muslims were citing a 60 percent to 35 percent Muslim-Christian population ratio, the Christians were calling attention to the secular nature of the nation and the nation's constitution. A major crisis ensued. In the first few days, the government regarded the Christians' stands as mere bluff that would calm down within a few days. The opposition became stronger and the separation of Christians and Muslims became sharper. Christians were concerned about Nigeria becoming an Islamic state. While the media interpreted the OIC issue as a true religious crisis, others considered it as a matter of government policy. However, everybody wondered why the government failed to consult with the people before joining the OIC.

The Christian Association of Nigeria (CAN) spearheaded the agitation and immediately mobilized against the OIC.[24] Throughout 1986, the CAN used the media, sermons in churches, and church publications to voice their objection to the OIC, which was believed to be a body of Muslims who were bent on promoting the course of Islam. The CAN cited the charter and activities of the OIC and concluded that it was simply an organization of Muslims for the propagation of Islam.

Many people were confused about the status and role of Nigeria in the OIC. Was the OIC saga not part of a grand scheme to install Islam as the country's official religion? Is Nigeria now an Islamic country? As Gabriel Umoden put it, "the situation was terribly aggravated, when Commodore Ebitu Ukiwe, the Chief of General Staff, indicated publicly that the issue of OIC was not discussed at the Armed Forces Ruling Council."[25] Babangida tried to explain away his action by arguing that the decision was borne out of pure national interests and that he would hoist the nation's flag wherever the nation's interest was best served.

For all intents and purposes, the implications of the nation's membership were not lost on the Christians. As indicated in one of the Christian pamphlets, which Falola quoted, "it would mean that the posts of the President and the Foreign Minister will [sic] be reserved for Muslims if they have to attend and meaningfully take part in the OIC meetings."[26] Christians also ask: "Will a Nigerian Christian Head of State support Islamic; sometimes anti-Christian resolutions?"[27] From this perspective to Nigeria's membership in the OIC, it is apparent that religion has been fully integrated into the politics of Nigeria.

Christians maintain that some of the decisions and resolutions of the OIC are not in accordance with the nation's known traditional foreign policy. For example, the OIC in 1978 declared support for Somalia against Ethiopia. Nigeria, with other members of the Organization for African Unity (OAU), took a different view. With the current situation in Sudan, where Muslims and Christians are engaging in war; should the OIC declare its support for the Muslims, Nigerian Christians, by Nigeria's membership in the OIC, would be forced to declare war against fellow Christians. Overall, Christians considered the OIC as another way of continuing the Islamization agenda of Usman dan Fodio, and as such, they drew parallels between Nigeria and Sudan, arguing that the religious divide, which has been the main cause of the protracted civil war in the Sudan, has begun in Nigeria.

It should be emphasized Nigerian membership in any religious organization is a violation of the constitution, and the religious rights of its people, especially non-Muslims. Nevertheless, some liberal Muslims quickly pointed out that even though Christian heads of states, such as the presidents of Rwanda and Senegal attended OIC meetings, they were not compelled to turn their countries into Islamize states. They blamed the OIC crisis on the religious intolerance of Christians and their leaders. They also cited economic benefits that Nigeria could derive from OIC membership. However, they failed to examine the argument in the light of the constitutional arrangement respecting the religious rights of others. Whatever the economic benefits, it must not be at the detriment of the cooperative existence of the nation, and it should not violate the laws of the land.

Nigeria and the OIC: What Went Wrong?

The question of OIC can be viewed from two perspectives: as a matter of state policy and as a religious issue. It is a state policy because the head of government is permitted to enter into any bilateral agreement with any nation or body that promotes the national interest, but the National Assembly has to approve the decision. In the case of a military government, the Armed Forces Ruling Council (AFRC) under General Babangida functioned like the National Assembly. Under this arrangement, both the head and military council were not "accountable" to the people. Hence, decisions were made through decrees, which people could neither influence nor oppose. In the case of the OIC, the decision to join either as an observer (under Muritala) or as a full member (under Babangida) was the prerogative of the head of state, and both of them (Muritala and Babangida) acted within the context of military rule. Babangida buttressed his action by organizing a mission to the OIC meeting at Fez, Morocco in

January 1986, which the Sultan of Sokoto, Alhaji Ibrahim Dansuki, led to formally admit Nigeria into the OIC. When the Chief of General Staff, Commodore Ubitu Ukiwe, declared that he was neither informed nor the matter discussed at the AFRC meeting, he was immediately removed from office.[28]

Babangida acted with the ethos of military rule, but joining the OIC was a religious and political issue. While not validating military rule, the military in politics remains an integral part of Nigeria's historical reality. Nevertheless, acting within the powers of a military head of state is not a sufficient reason to exonerate either Muritala or Babangida from blame over the OIC issue. Clearly, the decision was unilateral, taken without consultation with government functionaries, and without considering the general interests of non-Muslim citizens. Without doubt, the OIC issue is testimony to an unpopular policy decision taken by the military.

All the arguments presented about the benefits to be gained with OIC membership by Nigeria and the reasons advanced for joining the organization were incidental factors. As long as such arguments did not precede and inform the decision to join the OIC, they are immaterial to the fact. They are mere arguments to justify an action that was not supported by the majority of the Nigerian population. Although different military leaders, from Muritala to Obasanjo and Babangida to Abacha, played one role or another in the implementation of the OIC dream, their inability to come out boldly and admit to Nigeria's membership in the OIC was inexcusable.

As far as the argument is concerned, it is fundamental to underscore that Nigeria is constitutionally a secular state. Any attempt to impose a particular religion, or religious tenet, on any part of the nation is therefore divisive and, by the constitution, illegal. Two different arguments have been advanced respecting the constitutional requirement. First, the constitution had been suspended when the question of the OIC came up. While this was true, it can be counter-argued that freedom of religion remains an important component under the provisions of the United Nations; the Charter of which Nigeria (whether ruled by a military or a democratically elected president or even a king) is a signatory. Under international law, citizens of any nation reserve the right to religious freedom and no government, except as empowered by the constitution, has the right to impose any religious belief on its people. According to Article 18 of the Universal declaration of Human Rights:

> Everyone has the right to freedom of thought, conscience and religion; this right includes freedom to change his religion or belief, and freedom, either alone or in com-

> munity with others and in public and private, to manifest his religion or belief in teaching, practice, worship and observance. [29]

Hence, to register Nigeria as a member of the OIC without the consent of the people, was not only a breach of international protocols, but also a fundamental violation of the nation's governing principles, the constitution.

The Constitution of Nigeria stipulates that power to conclude treaties for and on behalf of the nation rests with the executive arm of government, of which the president is the head. In any case such treaty(ies) is subject to the approval of the legislative arm of government, the parliament (in 1960 constitution) or the National Assembly (in 1979, 1999 constitutions). The relevant section of the constitution in question is Part 4 Section 69 (1960 constitution); Part II Section 12 (1-2) (1979 constitution) and Part III Section 12 (1-2) (1999 constitution). General Babangida abrogated the constitution and the Armed Forces Ruling Council (AFRC) performed the functions of the executive and the legislative organs of the state. Nevertheless, power to enter into any treaty with any nation was vested in the Head of Government, this time, General Babangida, and the Foreign Affairs Minister. In the specific case of the OIC, General Babangida neither informed the AFRC nor sought its approval even after enrolling Nigeria in the OIC. Besides, several provisions of the constitution empowered the president to make appointment which is subjected to the National Assembly (senate) confirmation. Senate must confirm the appointment of Ambassador, High Commissioner or other Principal Nigerian representative abroad according to Section 171, subsections 4, the office of chief justice of Nigeria section 231(1) etc.

A second argument relates to Babangida's declaration of February 5, 1986 that:

i. We note that the assurance given by the Federal Military Government that our full membership of the OIC does not in any way imply that Nigeria has become or will become an Islamic state has addressed the undoubted reservations expressed by some sections of the country.
ii. We also note that the peace and stability can only be cleared with time and after consultation.
iii. Furthermore we agreed that the peace and stability of our multi-religious nation and the secular character of Nigeria must be preserved.

iv. In this respect, we also agreed that nothing should be done to infringe on section 10 of the constitution which states "The Government of Federal or of a State shall not adopt any religion as state religion."[30]

While Babangida was assuring Christians and other non-Muslim Nigerians that the nation's membership in the OIC has, in no way, validated the assumption that Nigeria has become an Islamic country or that the secular clause of the constitution has been negated of abrogated, he nevertheless found it hard to reverse this obviously unpopular policy. All the government did was to eulogize the need for peace and to defer decisions relating to Nigeria's membership of the OIC till a future time and "after consultation." One wonders why consultation with the stakeholders did not precede Nigeria's application for membership in the OIC. In any case, rather than reversing the policy, the government was concerned with selling the ideals of peace and tranquility, which suddenly became Babangida's primary interests. Whether then or now, Nigerians supported the four issues raised in Babangida's speech. No consultation has since been made and successive governments in Nigeria have shied-away from making any pronouncement on the issue.

It is pertinent to ask: Does joining the OIC constitute forcing Islam on non-Muslims? The experiences of many non-Muslims in contemporary northern Nigeria would point to that fact, especially with the implementation of the Shari'a. For example, following the introduction of the Shari'a, Niger State adopted a series of educational policies that promoted a discriminatory system of payment in schools. Muslims pay relatively cheaper school fees than non-Muslims who are sometimes forced to withdraw their children. Non-Muslims are also being forced to obey the Shari'a legal codes.[31] There were even cases of non-Muslims being compelled to flee the North on account of the Shari'a.[32] These are clear indications that Nigeria's membership in the OIC is not in any way different from forcing non-Muslims to imbibe Islam and its way of life.

The OIC objectives, its articles and clauses, are diametrically opposed to the concept of secularism in the Nigerian constitution. For instance, two important clauses in the objectives of the OIC are "to promote Islamic solidarity among Member States" and "to back the struggle of all Muslim people with a view to preserving their dignity, independence and national rights."[33] How can these be achieved in a country such as Nigeria without trampling on the fundamental rights of non-Muslims? How do we foster Nigerian Muslim solidarity with countries such as Iran, Iraq, and Afghanistan and at the same time foster relationships with Israel, the

United States, and Britain? What are the national rights of the Muslims? How are these rights different from the rights of others? Can these rights be enforced without stepping on the rights of others? There is nothing in the OIC Charter that explains how this can be achieved. Article VI of the OIC states that:

> In the performance of their duties, the Secretary General, his Assistants, and the staff of the General Secretariat, shall not seek or receive instructions from any government or authority other than the Conference. They shall refrain from taking any action that may be detrimental to their position as international officials responding only to the Conference. Member States undertake to respect this quality and the nature of their responsibilities, and shall not seek to influence them in any way in the discharge of their duties.[34]

It is morally wrong and a flagrant violation of the laws when an international organization empowers its officials to be responsible to it and be less responsible to their respective states. This is the case with the OIC, which places itself above the sovereignty of member states. In a secular state such as Nigeria, joining and obeying such organizations under any guise is illegal and unacceptable.

Article VI of the OIC states that the "headquarters of the Secretariat General shall be in Jeddah pending the liberation of "Baitul Maqdis" (Jerusalem)."[35] This presupposes that Jerusalem is presently under siege or usurpation by Israel and needs to regain its freedom. To Christians, it is unacceptable that Jerusalem is under siege and would be restored back to Muslims. This clause supports the Israel-Palestine conflict and, reflects the position of member states of the OIC on the Israel-Palestine conflict. Nigeria's membership in the OIC is therefore tantamount to asking Nigerian Christians to abandon Israel.

In Article XIV - Ratification - the OIC states that, "this Charter shall be approved and ratified by Member States of the Organization of the Islamic Conference in accordance with the procedure prevailing in their respective countries."[36] One wonders how a state such as Nigeria with its multi-religious nature would ratify the OIC charter in accordance with the secular clause in its constitution. This explains why the whole process of Nigeria's membership was secretly carried out. This further enlightens why Christians argued that the OIC is forcing Nigerians, Muslims and other non-Muslims, to jettison the secular clause in the nation's constitution.

Undoubtedly, to obey this and other articles, charters and protocols of the OIC is equal to an order to discard secularism, as enshrined in Nigeria's constitution. Given the above, it is only appropriate to abandon the OIC rather than the Nigerian constitution.

Conclusion

In spite of its membership in the OIC, Nigeria remains a secular state. This is a contradiction. Between 1999 and 2007, Nigeria paid its annual dues to the OIC on a regular basis, but owed on its annual contributions to the United Nations. Ironically, the federal government keeps denying Nigeria's membership in the OIC. Prior to 2001, Nigeria's membership in the OIC and its various organs was limited to representation in summits and conferences, but in 2001, Olusegun Obasanjo openly participated at the D8 meeting in Cairo. President Shehu Musa Yar'Adua also attended the 2008 OIC conference in Dakar, Senegal. As long as the secular clause in Nigeria's constitution remains, joining the OIC is a direct contravention of the constitution. It is a clear breach as well as a violation of the fundamental rights of non-Muslims.

There is no ambiguity about what a secular state means in a religiously pluralistic nation such as Nigeria or even in places where only one religion predominates. In Nigeria, the adherents of the three prominent religions share the same parents, homes, territory, and nationality sometimes. Religious freedom must not only be guaranteed by law, but also in practice in order to ensure the continued existence of Nigeria as a united nation at peace amongst its citizens.

Today, there is a new Nigeria, where Arab-Islamic and Euro-Christian influences have dominated. It is important to mention that religious tension in Nigeria is more political than religious; religion is only being used as an excuse for conflict or violence. If proponents of religions are as spiritual as they claim and campaign, Nigeria would not have been in moral ruins characterized by corruption and brazen thievery.

If the general trend of Islamization, taking Syria as a case study, is anything to go by, it is not possible for Nigeria to Islamize as the supporters of the OIC intend. As noted in the Covenant of Umar, i.e. a covenant made by Umar-al- Kahatab with the Christians in Syria, Christians were described as "The Tolerated Classes" — Ahd-Adh-Dhimma.[37] The Covenant, although elaborate as it was, mainly discriminated against the Christians. For instance, the Syrian Christians were proscribed from building "in our cities or in the neighborhood any new monastery, church, monk's cell or hermitage." They were also not to restore "any such buildings, which falls into ruins neither by night nor by day, especially when the building is surrounded by Muslim compounds." They were also not to "display our religion or invite anyone to join."[38] These and many other aspects of the covenant would only lead a nation such as Nigeria into catastrophe. There is no doubt that with the way the OIC and Shari'a were being handled, Nigeria is on the road to a religious war.

If the procedure through which Nigeria registered for membership in the OIC is condemnable, so also is the power- politics associated with the process. From the way politics was handled, those in power realized the error in the whole process, but could not withdraw from the organization in fear of a possible backlash from Muslims. Religion should not divide or destabilize Nigeria. Instead it should promote its unity. It is therefore important for Nigeria to keep its unity and not get involved in any international religious organizations such as the OIC. Nigeria's membership of the OIC contradicts the secular clause of the constitution and the divisiveness that it represents is contrary to national integration and democratic political system.

Notes

1. The Mosque of Al-Aqsa, situated in Jerusalem, is regarded as the holiest Islamic mosque anywhere in the world. The mosque was set ablaze by a deranged Australian Christian, Michael Dennis Rohan. Although the Israeli fire fighters speedily extinguished the fire, and Rohan soon after confessed to the crime, Muslims all over the world were of the opinion that the Israeli authorities paid Rohan between $50,000 and $100 million to burn the mosque. The allegation remains unsubstantiated till date.
2. The OIC Chatter, http://www.oicoci.org/oicnew/page_detail.asp?p_id=53
3. Ibid.
4. A comprehensive list of the various organs (Subsidiary, Specialized, Affiliated, and Standing Committees) of the OIC and their respective duties can be obtained at http://www.oic-oci.org/oicnew/page_detail.asp?p_id=64.
5. Selected Foreign Policy Statements, 1960-1964, published by the Ministry of External Affairs, Lagos, Nigeria. 1980.
6. Government of Nigeria, *Selected Foreign Policy Statements 1960-1964* (Lagos, Nigeria: Ministry of External Affairs, 1980). See also; Victor Nwaozichi Chibundu, *Nigeria-China Foreign Relations, 1960-1999* (Lagos, Nigeria: Spectrum Books, 2000) 1-8.
7. Selected Foreign Policy Statements, 1960-1964, published by the Ministry of External Affairs, Lagos, Nigeria. 1980.

8. Ibid.
9. Chibundu Victor Nwaozichi, *Nigeria-China Foreign Relations, 1960-1999* (Lagos, Nigeria: Spectrum Publishers, 2000), 7.
10. Christian Association of Nigeria (CAN), National Youth Department, *The Shari'a: Implications for Christians* (Nigeria: CAN Publicity Department), 4.
11. G. O. Olusanya, "Nationalist Movements," in *Groundwork of Nigerian History,* ed. Obaro Ikime (Lagos, Nigeria: Heinemann Books, 1980), 568.
12. Omo Omoruyi, in "An Appeal To President Olusegun Obasanjo: Nigeria: Neither an Islamic nor a Christian Country" at http://www.biafraland.com/Islamization%20of%20Nigeria.htm.
13. Government of Nigeria, *Proceedings of the General Conference on the Review of the Constitution,* December 1979. See in particular the Minority Report of the Constitution Drafting Committee (CDC). General Muritala established the CDC on October 18, 1975 to review the old and draft a new constitution for Nigeria.
14. Two notable people who have canvassed this view are Professor Omo Omoruyi, formerly of the National Institute for Policy and Strategic Studies, Kuru, and Archbishop Olubunmi Okogie, former president, Christian Associations of Nigeria, CAN.
15. Government of Nigeria, *Minority Report of the Constitution Drafting Committee (CDC),* December 1978, 145.
16. Omo Omoruyi, in "An Appeal To President Olusegun Obasanjo: Nigeria: Neither an Islamic nor a Christian Country" at http://www.biafraland.com/Islamization%20of%20Nigeria.htm.
17. "OIC and the Nigerian Christians," in the *Nigerian Tribune,* June 5, 1987, 1, 3 & 7.
18. Ibrahim Ahmed, "*In Or Out? Revisiting Nigeria's Membership in the Organization of the Islamic Conference (OIC),*" http://www.salaam.co.uk/news/my_news/217004.txt
19. Hassan Ibrahim, "How Obasanjo brought Nigeria into OIC - Sharia Council," *The Nigerian Tribune,* March 31, 2008. http://www.tribune.com.ng/31032008/news/news3.html. See also Abdul-Aziz Jimoh, *The OIC Debate, Etc,*http://www.nigeriavillagesquare.com/articles/guest-articles/the-oic-debate-etc.html. Accessed on Thursday, April 3, 2008.
20. Personal discussion with Professor Akinjide Osuntokun, former Ambassador of Nigeria to Germany, on December 2, 2007. The payment was indeed made penultimate week to the rejection of the Third Term Debate at the National Assembly. Hence, Prof. Osuntokun's was correct.
21. Rilwan Lukman led the Muslim delegation. Other members of the delegation included Abubakar Alhaji (then Permanent Secretary, Ministry

of National Planning), Abdulkadir Ahmed, (Governor of Central Bank), Ibrahim Dansuki (the Secretary-General of the Supreme Council for Islamic Affairs), and Abubakar Guni, a highly respected Islamic scholar. Gabriel Umoden, *The Babangida Years: The First Authoritative Biography of Nigeria's Foremost Visionary Leader* (Lagos, Nigeria: Gabumo Publishing Co., 1992), 218-220.

22. Ibrahim Ahmed, "In Or Out? Revisiting Nigeria's Membership in the Organization of the Islamic Conference (OIC)," http://www.salaam.co.uk/news/my_news/217004.txt; Hassan Ibrahim, "How Obasanjo brought Nigeria into OIC - Sharia Council," *The Nigerian Tribune,* March 31, 2008, 7. http://www.tribune.com.ng /31032008/news/news3.html
23. Ahmed, "In Or Out? Revisiting Nigeria's Membership in the Organization of the Islamic Conference (OIC)."
24. Prior to the period, Christians in Nigeria formed different associations and organizations that were representing their different denominations as well as agitating for different group interests. It was the OIC agitation that made all these associations and organizations to come together under one umbrella to push for issues that bother on the rights of the Christians as well as other national issues.
25. Umoden, 219.
26. Toyin Falola, *Violence in Nigeria: The Crisis of Religious Politics and Secular Ideologies (*Rochester, NY: University of Rochester Press, 1998). For an in-depth analysis of Nigerians reactions to the OIC issue see Victor Olu Taiwo, *Nigeria on Gunpowder: The Climax of Misrule* (Ibadan, Nigeria: Omo-Ade Publications, 2000); R. T. Suberu, *Ethnic Minority Conflicts and Governance in Nigeria (*Lagos, Nigeria: Spectrum Books, 1996); Imobighe T. A. ed., *The Politics of the Second Republic (*Nigeria: National Institute of Policy and Strategic Studies, Kuru, 1992).
27. Falola, 97.
28. Umoden, 218-220.
29. The Universal Declaration of Human Rights, Article 18, adopted and proclaimed by the General Assembly of the United Nations on December 10, 1948.
30. Umoden, 218-220.
31. The Governor of Niger State in 2002, Alhaji Kure, boldly asked that those who were not ready to embrace the new educational policy should either vacate the state or withdraw their children and wards from the schools. Situations of similar nature were reported in Zamfara and Kano, where open conflict between non-Muslims and Christians actually engaged one another. Many non-Hausa-Fulani residents of Kano, Kaduna, and Zamfara fled to

either their home-state or to neighboring states. See "Southerners Flee Kaduna, Kano and Zamfara Ahead of Shari'a," *The Punch,* August 5, 2000, 17.

32. Between August 10 and 30, 2000, a total of 258 Ogbomoso people fled Kano, Kaduna, and Zamfara penultimate week to the introduction of the Shari'a legal code. Majority of these people could not locate their family houses in Ogbomoso and were consequently forced to reside at the Shoun's palace and the Town Hall, both at Oja-Igbo.
33. The OIC Chatter at: http://www.oic-oci.org/oicnew/page_detail.asp?p_id=53
34. Ibid.
35. Ibid.
36. Ibid.
37. In this Covenant, made by Umar-al- Kahatab with the Christians in Syria, the Christians were described as "The Tolerated Classes" – Ahd-Adh-Dhimma. The Covenant was quoted extensively by Uthman Dan Fodio in "Bayern wujubi al hijra alal-biyan nasbal-imam-wa-iqamatal-jihad," Writings of Usman dan Fodio, *The Human Record: Sources of Global History*, Fourth Edition/ Volume II: Since 1500, 1989, 233-236.
38. A comprehensive listing of the over fifty proscriptions placed on the Christians in Syria can be found in the pamphlet, *The Sharia: Implications for Christians.* The pamphlet was published in 1986 by the National youth wing of the Christian Association of Nigeria. The same can also be found in Uthman Dan Fodio's writing: "Bayern wujubi al hijra alal-biyan nasbal-imam-wa-iqamatal-jihad," Writings of Usman dan Fodio, in *The Human Record: Sources of Global History*, Fourth Edition/ Volume II: Since 1500, 1989, 233-236.

Chapter Eleven

Christian Association of Nigeria (CAN) and Politics

Olayemi Akinwumi
and Ibrahim Umaru

To understand the involvement of Christian Association of Nigeria (CAN) in political activism in Nigeria is to appreciate three popular perspectives on the relationship between the state and religion in Nigeria; namely the principle of institutional separation or secularity; the Christian perspective on separation of power and secularism; and the counter position taken by Muslims.

Many people believe that the principle of religion and state separation should determine what kind of state Nigeria should be. It is argued, only through such clarification can the central issue of political legitimacy be resolved, since "for a state to do more to administer privilege and defend itself against its own population, its acts must seem continuous with the selves of those whose state it pretends it is, its citizens."[1] This can be translated to mean that an attempt should be made to reduce the influence of religious factors in the political arena. From this perspective, religion is seen as a private affair, something between individual believers and their God or gods, a relation that should not penetrate the public domain. Gerrieter Haar points out that "Whereas religion is expected to limit itself exclusively to regulating humans' relations between the secular and spiritual worlds, it is politics, on the other hand, which is deemed solely responsible for regulating their relations with the state that they live in."[2] The official separation of the state from religion has been the hallmark of Western democracies for centuries and was also introduced to other parts of the world, including Nigeria, as evidenced in all three post-civil war federal constitutions, especially in sections II, 37, 242, 259-61 and 272 of the 1989 constitution; and section 10 and 38 of the 1999 constitution.

Separation of church and state would seem to be a concept shared by many political thinkers (both liberal and radical) of Western orientation, Christian organizations, and CAN. Simon Ilesanmi argues that "the state [as] described in section 10 of the 1979 constitution and clause II of the 1988 draft constitution is by implication a secular state."[3] Similarly, in a 1986 memorandum sent to the Constitution Review Committee, the Catholic Bishops of Nigeria described Nigeria's secularity as the only viable mode of existence for it to survive as a nation. A secular state, according to this school of thought, is one in which "there is no official religion but in which religion as such may nevertheless be treated with respect; and religious bodies and their activities are seen as purely social agents within the communities."[4]

Rt. Reverend E. B. Gbonigi, the Anglican Bishop of the Akure Diocese, at the second assembly of CAN held in 1988, objected to the definition of secularism as the "doctrine of public morality based on the citizens' well-being and exclusive of religious consideration." He characterized Nigeria's secularity as "a form of separation between religion and the state which allows for a voluntary relationship and co-operation wherever and whenever necessary and possible."[5] This he rationalized on the basis of the social functions of the state as different from those of the church: The state's duty is "to maintain justice, security, peace, relative wellbeing of its citizens," while the church is "primarily concerned with the inward and spiritual life of the people ... ordained and commissioned to preach the gospel of salvation."[6]

Over the years, the dictum that expressed the relevant portions of all the past and existing constitutions, purporting to describe the guiding principles of state-religion relations is inadequate in explaining the true status of Nigeria as a purely secular state. To more clearly define the operational principle of institutional separation, Yusufu Bala Usman suggests: "the Federal Republic of Nigeria is a secular State and the State shall not be associated with any religion but shall actively protect the fundamental rights of all citizens to hold and practice the religious beliefs of their choice."[7]

Segun Gbadegesin supports Usman's position, and added that secularity is a principle that is "morally defensible" for three reasons. One, it suggests the value of freedom of conscience, something lacking in most social societies; two, it promotes the idea that human beings are equal in the sight of God and thus are equally capable of approaching Him for their various needs; and three, it presupposes respect for individual autonomy.[8] In his own opinion, Simeon Ilesanmi contends that, "for Usman and Gbadegesin, religion is a personal and private affair, and any attempt to conflate it with politics is seen as a threat to national stability and integrity, and secularity requires that this devilish force be uprooted."[9]

Some Muslims find the above position totally unacceptable. For example, Justice Mohammed Sambo argues that deriving secularity from the non-adoption of the religion clause invariably means, "both the Federal and State governments will have nothing to do with the divine religions of their people,"[10] thereby creating hostility between religion and the state, a situation that is repugnant for two reasons. First, this position lends support to the logic that reasoning and not revelation or religion is the transcendent source of law. Second, it ignores the fact that secularism is not recognized in the Islamic lexicon.[11] It therefore advocates a country's secularity, especially where "divine religion [referring to both Christianity and Islam] is a complete way of life for 99 percent of its population."[12]

There are Muslims who argue that to divorce religion from politics is un-practicable and is an expression of shirk [the sin of appearing to partner with God].[13] In other words, the principle of secularism is an attempt to make religion subservient to the state rather than making the state an instrument to implement the will of God on earth. In this light, Justice Sambo suggests that:

> The only solution to the chronic vices which have overcome Nigeria is for the nation to take a distinctive governmental stand on religious, moral and spiritual training of her people … It is only divine religious injunctions backed by those who govern that can stabilize discipline, good morals and obedience to God, and constituted authority.[14]

Taken as a contending standpoint, this argument indicates that it is not enough to provide for freedom of thought, conscience, and religion without formally codifying the mores, norms, and theological principles of the country's dominant religions into the constitution. In the wake of this argument, Justice Sambo suggests a constitutional provision that states, "Once a Nigerian declares for a divine religion, it is the duty of the state to see that such a declarant respects and lives in accordance with the teachings of the religion."[15] Lucid as this position may appear, there are other Muslims who object to it. They believe that Justice Sambo's position is practically too unwieldy and theologically too extremist. For example, Malam Mukhtar and some prominent Muslims in northern Nigeria once argued that in the Nigerian context, it is not realistic or possible to establish a religious state, either Christian or Islamic.[16]

On the issue of religion-state relations, there is a mutual suspicion between Christians and Muslims, a suspicion that emanates from the Christian fear that each time the Muslims raise the issue, Islam is being promoted as the official religion. On their own part, Muslims view any argument in favor of secularism as failing to "foster much more hospitable grounds for the setting of the religious agenda in public affairs," and as far as Islam is concerned, the Muslim *Umma* in Nigeria is not politically and ideologically monolithic.[17] Many Nigerian Christians, under the umbrella of CAN, are therefore of the conviction that the only way to counter or check the growing and overbearing influence of Islam in Nigerian public affairs (a situation unacceptable to them) is to increase the political activism of Christians.

CAN and Political Activism

In the post-Independence period, CAN has been the most unified voice and rallying point for the Christian community in Nigeria. CAN is an ecumenical group that emerged in 1976 during the Murtala-Obasanjo military regime. It came into existence as a result of the government's request for a single Christian group to deal with in connection to a proposed national pledge of allegiance in schools. Being an ecumenical group, the constituency of CAN is broader and more effective than the Christian Council of Nigeria (CCN), formed in 1929 to provide a single theological and ethical voice for the mainstream Protestant churches in the country at both the national and international levels. CAN provides also a wider forum than the Northern Christian Association (NCA), which fruitlessly fought to resist the overwhelming influence of Ahmadu Bello during Nigeria's First Republic. Members of the CAN include Catholics, Protestants, and the Pentecostal churches.

CAN has as its objectives, the promotion of a "common understanding among all the Christians in the country" and the creation of "good fellowship of all the Christians on the social level that will help [them] to the better practice of their faith and the good of the country." These two goals are, however, secondary to their more "militant" and "political" resolution, to stand together for the purpose of "projecting Christian ethics and also defending the rights of the Church."[18]

From its inception, CAN has exhibited the capacity to participate in political discourse and sometimes influence the political fortunes of the country. For instance, while drafting the 1999 Constitution, three issues stood out: attempt to define the status of religion; the posture of the state in religious matters; and the status of Islamic Shari'a laws within the Western judiciary system which the nation inherited from the British. The Constitution drafting members recommended that every person shall be entitled to freedom of thought and religion, and particularly the freedom to receive religious instruction in "any place of education maintained wholly by" one's religious community. Incidentally, the aspects on education which banned religious instruction from State schools tallied with the government's new posture; having declared the ideology of the state to be secularist, the constitution utilized an American ideology to affirm that "the State shall not adopt any religion as the State religion" and therefore shall not permit the proselytization of any particular religion in her schools.

The stance aroused much concern for the Muslim members. This is because the Islamic conception of the state was theocratic: Islam is perceived as a way of life which draws no distinction between religion and other aspects of living, including governance and the use of state apparatus to further both individual and collective interests. In fact, Muslims were of the opinion that political power was to be used in the service of religion, hence declaring that Nigeria was to be a secular state, raised a new obstacle to Islamic efforts to utilize state powers in pursuit of politico-religious ends.

A Christian group under the auspices of CAN which met to discuss the implications of the affirmation of secularity found the constitutional provisions rather imprecise as it did not clarify the limits and nature of state neutrality. Would the state, for instance, include aid to pilgrims or donations to religious organizations or the use of state apparatus or functionaries to assist any religion on the observance of religious holidays, the use of religious symbols, and so on? CAN and its Christian members in the Constitution Drafting Committee (CDC) also kicked against the dovetailing of Shari'a laws and judiciary system for the English one. They called for the application of neutrality by providing a Canon Law judicature for Christians. CAN even formed a committee to draft the Canon Law, and called for equal recognition and treatment of all religious groups as well as privileges for Christian pilgrims to Rome and Jerusalem. Matters came to a head as eighty-eight Muslim members withdrew in the heat of the constitution drafting debate. It resumed seating only when a compromise was struck between the Christian and Muslim members of the Constituent Assembly.[19]

The next major religious and political issue that involved CAN was the purported decision by the General Ibrahim Babangida administration to enlist Nigeria as a member of the OIC in 1986 on the pretext that the country stood to benefit from the generous financial assistance given by the organization. CAN pointed out that registering Nigeria, as a member of OIC, would violate the secularity of the state as enshrined in the 1979 constitution. To force the government to retrace its steps, it threatened to forge strong formal ties with Israel and the Vatican.

The 1987 report of the Political Bureau, headed by Professor Sylvanus Cookey, contained the position of both Muslims and Christians on the issue of the intersection of religion in politics. Since Nigerian Muslims did not believe in the separation of religion from politics, they argued that any attempt to deny their country admission into OIC, was tantamount to denying them their constitutional rights. They even advocated the establishment of Shari'a courts at the state level and a Shari'a Court of Appeal at the federal level. They also demanded continuing state involvement in matters relating to pilgrimage and the cessation of Nigeria's diplomatic relations with the Vatican.[20] The Christian position as articulated by CAN was that:

> The State should not be involved in religious matters; Nigeria should not be a member of the OIC and should withdraw from it; missionary schools that have been taken over by the government should be returned to their proprietors so that ethical and moral values could be properly taught to Nigerian children; [and] government should disengage itself from pilgrimage exercise.[21]

These seemingly irreconcilable differences contributed to the growth of mutual suspicion and further fuelled animosity between Christians and Muslims. The differences led to tensions that almost escalated into religious conflicts. It is against this backdrop that the role and position taken by CAN in the Kafanchan riots (1987), and Kaduna riots (1992, 2000, and 2002), can be appreciated.

The Kafanchan riots erupted at the College of Education, Kafachan in Kaduna State following an allegation that Rev. Abubakar Bako, an itinerant Christian preacher, newly converted from Islam, misquoted the Qur'an and blasphemed the Holy name of the Prophet Mohammed (S.A.W.). Muslim students felt offended and went on a rampage (burning houses and destroying property belonging to Christians) on campus and in Kafanchan town.[22] In response, Christian students burned down mosques and property belonging to Muslims. There was massive destruction in the wake of the two-day mayhem. Although the riot in Kafanchan town was brought under control, it later spread to other parts of the state, apparently triggered by a news report on March 9, 1987 by a local radio station dominated by Muslims indicating that Christians were killing Muslims. The report further stated that two mosques had been burned, copies of the Holy Qur'an had been desecrated, and Muslims had fled into hiding.[23]

By March 10, 1987, Kaduna, the state capital, was already on fire; the homes and property of the Christian group, the *Kaje* people (from southern Kaduna, where Kafanchan is located) were attacked by Muslim youth. Later, the riot degenerated to an outright war on Christians, their property and churches decimated not only in Kaduna, but also in other major cities such as Zaria, Katsina, Funtua, and Kankia. Though the riot was brought under control, it would appear the reaction of the State government was slow considering the scale of destruction and death toll.

From all the submissions tendered to the State government's Panel of Inquiry set up to determine the reasons behind the Kafanchan riots, it was clear that the real causes were in deep-seated economic and political antecedents. Kaduna state is multi-ethnic in composition, with Hausa, Fulani, Gbagyi, Kaje, Katab, Jaba, and Gure being the major groups. Hausa and Fulani, who are largely Muslims and found in the northern parts of the state have dominated commerce and monopolized power since its creation. The other ethnic groups, especially Kaje, Katab, Gbagyi and Jaba who are predominantly Christians and mostly found in the southern parts of the state, dominate the technocracy, military personnel, civil servants and the educated elite from the state. The northern parts of the state appear to be more developed and served with industry and modern social amenities than the southern parts. The latter groups therefore have been complaining of political marginalization and neglect in terms of federal and state appointments as well as infrastructure development. The Hausa and Fulani groups who largely controlled political power in the state were suspicious of the other group arguing that should control of power be tilted in favor of the south, the other group would use their advantages mentioned earlier to marginalize the northern groups. It would appear these mutual suspicions have created the perfect setting for the riots that erupted. In defense of Christians in the state, CAN submitted the following:

> An assertive form of Islam has long existed in many parts of the Northern states encouraged by the numerical and political dominant position, which Muslims have had in these areas. What has happened in the recent past is the

> transformation of this assertiveness into aggressiveness and the deliberate promotion of an anti-Christian disposition among the Moslem population by a prominent section of the Moslem elite. To achieve this, instruments of state power, the media and specially organized Moslem organizations have been used. In addition, massive propaganda has been mounted within and outside the country with a view to portraying Nigeria society as overwhelming Islamic and therefore destined to be transformed into an Islamic State...[24]

As far as CAN was concern, the riots were provoked as a result of growing aggressive Islamism and anti-Christianity in the publicly articulated stance of several highly placed individuals and organizations. It argued that taken together this stance involved the deliberately false characterization of the existing Nigerian system as Christian and an attack on it as such as well as an open aggressive demand for greater Islamization of the system. It also argued that although dating back to the Shari'a debate at the Constituent Assembly in 1977 this concerted attempt at polarization along religious lines has received much greater impetus. Since the OIC issue was raised to the level of national debate last year, there have been much less veiled attempts by certain Moslem leaders to generate and sustain a climate of religious animosity between Muslims and Christians. It concludes that:

> ...the objective appears to be not to polarize the Nigerian society along religious lines but also to engulf the government and organs of government in this polarization. The pressure for Nigeria's membership in the OIC is itself an example of this as is the renewed Shari'a debate, which appears now to have resulted in the unannounced amendment of the Nations Constitution. (See Decree No. 26 – Federal Republic of Nigeria Official Gazette No. 59, Vol.73 of 25/11/86)...[25]

Other instances where CAN was involved in politics included: the Zangon Kataf conflict (1992);[26] the Kaduna Shari'a Crisis (2000);[27] the Kaduna "Miss World" riots 2002;[28] and the Jos and other Plateau State crises (2001-2003, and 2004).[29] The Zangon Kataf conflict started in February 1992 when a dispute broke out over the relocation of the market. The Muslim Hausa did not agree with the predominantly Christian Kataf's desire to move to a larger site. A tractor driver was attacked as he worked on the new site. This led to Muslim-Christian violence. After a panel to examine the immediate and root causes of the violence was constituted, a report by the State Government was released. The Muslims felt it was not favorable to them and hostilities broke out again between the two communities on May 15, 1992. The violence spread to two main northern cities of the state, Kaduna and Zaria, as Muslims went in search of the Kataf to attack. Kaduna State Muslims invited Muslims from other neighboring northern states, Sokoto and Katsina, to come and join them in their anti-Christian violence. After four days of violence, a score of churches were burnt, and an estimated 300 people were killed including Rev. Tachio Duniya (formerly vice-president of the Anglican Church of West Africa), some of his elders, his secretary, Musa Bakut and his young child, as well as the secretary-general of the Kaduna State branch of CAN, Bulus Kaneiyock).

The Hausa and Muslim community saw the Zangon Kataf riots as largely the work of 'frustrated' retired army generals and their Kataf elite who were, presumably, jealous of the prosperity of the Hausa community. It was alleged that army generals and Kataf elite armed and instigated their community to perpetrate the rioting; and that the police and the army called in to quell the subsequent rioting in Kaduna, Zaria, and Ikara actually went out of their way to kill innocent Hausa people and Muslims, presumably because many of the security personnel were from the minority ethnic groups of the Middle Belt or were Christians. Muslim groups and the Hausa community's demand for justice was basically that those who killed innocent citizens must be adequately punished by the state, and compensation paid to the victims.[30]

CAN and the Christian community in the state claimed that the Hausa/Moslem community was using their regional and national connections to victimize Christians and particularly Kataf community leaders and prominent sons, most of whom, it was claimed, had been sentenced to long terms of imprisonment on trumped up charges by special tribunals set up by the Federal Government to teach the Kataf and other southern Kaduna groups a lesson. The Christian community in the state under the auspices of CAN (Kaduna Chapter) assiduously worked for the eventual released of Zamani Lekwot, the imprisoned retired army general, and other members of the Kataf community in 1995.

The Kaduna Shari'a Crisis triggered off when, following the Zamfara State Government passage of Shari'a into law, the Kaduna State Government requested the state House of Assembly consider the possibility of doing the same. An eleven (11)-man legislative committee under the Chairmanship of Alhaji Ibrahim Ali was set up to that effect, and formally started work in January, 2000. By the time the committee finished its assignment (February 17, 2000), events and reaction that followed created an atmosphere of tension and suspicion. The suspicion was that the report would be in favor of Shari'a as the composition of that committee was already lopsided in favor of Muslims. Christians under the auspice of CAN initiated a systematically organized anti-Shari'a demonstration. On Monday 21 2000, CAN (Kaduna branch) called out and organized what was suppose to be a peaceful demonstration to express the frustration Christian leaders had faced trying to get the state's leaders to have a change of heart. On their way back from the demonstration, the Christian demonstrators were attacked by Muslim Shari'a apologies, then full-scale violence ensured.

A major feature of this crisis was that the havoc wrecked on both lives and property was not just limited to the immediate vicinity where the first fights broke out; there was spontaneity in terms of reaction to the whole crisis. As a consequence, the entire state capital was engulfed in the bloodiest clashes ever witnessed in northern Nigeria. The aftermath: 1,944 houses including business premises were destroyed; a total of 606 deaths were recorded; a total of 746 vehicles of various descriptions were burnt; about 123 churches and 55 mosques were burnt in various locations; police outposts at Mararaban Jos was razed; and over 100 persons sustained injuries.[31] Though at the expense of great loss of lives and property, the active involvement of CAN in the anti-Shari'a crusade had in no small measure prevented the wholesome passage of Shari'a into law and perhaps reduced the risk of throwing the state and the north in particular into a deeper religious crisis.

The Kaduna "Miss World" riots came on the heels of the decision to hold the 2002 Miss World contest in the northern, and often volatile, Kaduna town in Nigeria. Initially scheduled for the end of November 2002, the contest was eventually postponed to December in order for Muslim to complete their fasting period during the month of Ramadan. There were, however, a number of low-level protests against Nigeria holding the contest in various parts of the country, especially in the North, and negative public comments, mostly by conservative Muslims who opposed the beauty contest on moral grounds. Although much public outrage was made in the print and electronic media on the issue, the protests against the hosting of the "Miss World" contest passed off without violence. However, a newspaper article published in *ThisDay* on Saturday, 16 November 2002 by Miss Isioma Daniel, which suggested that the Prophet Mohammed would have approved of the Miss World contest by probably choosing a wife from among the beauty pageant contestants. This comment triggered the violence and mayhem that was to follow. On Wednesday, November 20, demonstrators took to the streets in Kaduna town.

An initially peaceful public protest against the content of the article was hijacked by a group of people who were primarily intent on causing trouble, and the demonstration quickly turned violent. A group attacked and burned the newspaper's regional office in Kaduna. At no point did the police intervene to stop the violence by the protesters or make any arrest, despite the fact that the office of *ThisDay* was attacked in broad daylight and in full view of many residents and passers-by. The following day, better-organized groups of Muslim youth in different areas of Kaduna town took up arms and began attacking Christians. They sought out Christians' homes, particularly in Christian-Muslim neighborhoods, and targeted people on the basis of their religion. Several scores of Christians were killed and many injured; others ran for their lives, leaving their homes and property behind which was then looted by the rampaging youth. The attackers also destroyed or burnt houses, commercial buildings, schools, hotels, and churches.

The reactions of and the positions taken by CAN after each of these conflicts, have not only been consistent but predictable. CAN has always emphasized that all ethno-religious conflicts were either masterminded or manipulated by powerful individuals either in power or close to the corridors of power for selfish or collective political goals. For an example, the Kaduna State Secretary of CAN stated after the Zangon Kataf crisis:

> Kaduna is believed to be the capital of the northern states' seat of government. Who is who in the north wants to have a place in Kaduna. Kaduna is also a place where everybody wants to feel: 'I am important here and I should be recognized'. Almost all the generals in the north have taken it [to their] big [gest] base, almost all the one-time big politicians feel Kaduna is their base.
>
> Although they may come from other parts of the country, they will rather have Kaduna as their base. And the moment they come in they want to make the local government chairman of Kaduna listen to them, do what they want not what the people of Kaduna want to do. And they also want to force the governor to do what they want, not what the people of Kaduna want. The fact of the problem is that Kaduna has been under pressures from outside. The governor has admitted that even the local government chairmen admit this. It has been pressures

> from outside, someone from outside who has no business with what is happening here just because he is here in town and has gotten a place here during the Sardauna era and the military era he feels now that you must listen to him, you must know that he is in Kaduna or else he must turn Kaduna upside down and make it ungovernable for the man in leadership. So somehow, he knows the easy way he can get sympathy is to say this is Islam and this is Christianity...So you see this is the serious problem we have in Kaduna. And we will always want to let our people know that look, this crisis they are talking about is not really religious crisis; they are just people using us to achieve a particular aim. After they succeed in getting these, they keep quiet.[32]

A similar argument was made when the leadership of CAN issued a strong-worded statement condemning the 2002 Miss World riots in Kaduna and the violence and carnage that engulfed the country in its wake:

> ...From our perspective we know that ...the incessant call for Jihad in this country by misguided fellows is in itself a clear indication that those people do not think that anyone else has a right to be a citizen of this country except they and they alone. They [Moslems] see Nigeria as their exclusive preserve. The Jihad propagandists do not see any justification for our continued co-existence as one people under God...Our concern in CAN today is to work with other stakeholders, to ensure a sustainable democracy, good governance, to bring the monster of corruption to its knees, and to work for even development of our father land in atmosphere of peace and tranquility. While we are praying and working towards these ideals and goals, others seem bent on bringing Nigeria to ruins. Furthermore, as it seems that the Federal Government is trying to correct some of the imbalances in our body-politic of the past, these diabolic elements who want to plunge Nigeria into a religious war have consistently equated government with the Church ...We call on Law enforcement Agents to carry out their Constitutional responsibility without fear or favor. They should arrest promptly and bring to

> justice those who make irresponsible calls for the destruction of our fatherland. However, should the police fail in this regard, the Christian community in Nigeria will have no other option than to do whatever is deems necessary in every possible way to defend herself.[33]

On the controversial decision to impose a state of emergency in Plateau State and suspend Governor Dariye, which was largely for security reasons and constitutional in nature, CAN politicized the issue, arguing that there had been no precedence by the federal government to take such a stand. Many Nigerian Christian organizations felt that the move against Plateau State (an overwhelmingly Christian state) is an indication of a government bias against Christians. To CAN, the imposition of a state of emergency in Plateau State was selective justice, and it called for an equitable dispensation of sanctions on Kano state where many casualties were recorded in a series of violent riots. The National Secretary of CAN, S. L. S. Salifu, in a petition signed and submitted to the Senate President in May 2004, lamented that:

> The selective state of emergency declared in Plateau State surprise us because of the obvious facts on the ground concerning crisis issues all over the country. The mayhem in Kano is almost ten times that of Plateau. There is a need for equality, therefore we demand that a state of emergency be also slammed on Kano State; otherwise our teeming members will see the measures taken against Plateau State as selective and therefore unjust.[34]

CAN's dismay over the decision was so pitched that the Plateau State CAN Chairman, Rev. Yakubu Pam, asked President Olusegun Obasanjo why the Federal Government did not react when Muslims killed Christians in a church during the February riots in Plateau State. An apparently provoked President Obasanjo responded in a harsh manner, calling Rev. Pam and CAN names.[35] The President's expression of his discomfort with members of the Christian community might have been attributed to his displeasure with CAN for getting involved in what he might have considered a purely political issue; after all, it is the same organization that has always been calling for a separation of the state from religion. As a Christian, Obasanjo presumably wanted the CAN to disassociate itself from political activities. The riots were for the government to deal with, not the CAN.

The most brazen display of CAN's political brinkmanship is its supportive role in the 1992 general elections leading to the late Moshood Abiola's landslide victory against his fellow Muslim opponent. Two interlocking and mutually reinforcing factors facilitated the seeming paradox of reconciling the objective of encouraging Christians to secure political power along with supporting a Muslim-Muslim presidential arrangement. The first was the over-sensationalization and politicization of the OIC debate in the late 1980s and the attendant fear that the Muslims desired to "Islamize" the country; and the second, the high level of mistrust, hatred, and animosity that the various sectarian clashes had generated, incidentally heightened by the 1991 Kano religious crisis. Meanwhile within the same period, preparations were underway to usher in the Third Republic (that was not to be) under the two-party presidential arrangement of the Ibrahim Babangida administration. Two candidates were in contention for the presidency, M. K. O. Abiola [a Muslim and the flag-bearer of the Social Democratic Party (SDP) from the southwest who picked a fellow Muslim as his running mate] and Bashir Tofa [representing the Nigerian Republican Convention (NRC), and a Muslim from the North].

Then the issue became: who should the Christian community support considering the fact that they were not given the option of choosing between a fellow Christian and a Muslim. Bashir Tofa tactically picked a Christian as his running mate, presumably to win Christian votes and to receive support from CAN. CAN, however, had a different political agenda. In what most Nigerians and the world community consider as the freest and fairest presidential election ever in the country, Abiola won the elections convincingly against his fellow Muslim opponent. Interestingly, Abiola received massive political support from the Christian community under the skilful orchestration of CAN, on the grounds that Bashir Tofa once wrote a newspaper article that openly advocated holy war (jihad) in thc early 1980s.

As a way of deliberately encouraging Christians to participate in partisan politics, CAN has been educating its members not to be discouraged by the popular belief that politics is a "dirty game"; that even if it is dirty, it is their responsibility to clean it up, and this can only be done if they participate in politics. For instance, in 2000, Roman Catholic Archbishop John Onaiyeka of Abuja announced the creation of the Christian Social Movement (CSM) in Lagos, asserting that there is a desperate need for Christians to be more actively involved in politics in Nigeria.[36]

Religion and Religionization of Politics

Although the Federal Government was partly responsible for its formation, CAN has always been diplomatic in its relations with the state: strategic collaborative when possible to benefit mutual interest, and antagonistic on issues and state policies perceived as detrimental to the peaceful propagation of the Christian faith or injurious to the wellbeing of its members. As for the relations with its Muslim counterparts, the general perception and attitude has always been suspicion. Over the years, it has enmeshed itself in active confrontation with what is perceived by most Christians as the systematic Islamization of Nigeria through the efforts to implement and promote Shari'a law in the country. It would seem this factor, more than any other, has provided the rationale for the continued existence of CAN and largely explains its orientation to political activism and religious ecumenism.[37]

Until the early 1980s, Nigerian Christians had shown little interest in politics. This should not be construed to mean they were necessarily apolitical or indifferent to politics. Instead, the reasoning then was that as the Scriptures emphasize, less importance should be attached to the worldly kingdom in exchange for heavenly rewards or authentic spirituality more so politics in Nigeria is largely about personal enrichment from public funds and self-aggrandizement. After that period, the Christian view and approach to politics changed as a result of the various riots and crises as well as debates of the 1970s and 2000, along with the fear that the legal system at all levels of government might be 'hijacked' by Muslims. Christians now believed that "the Church must not just sit and watch. [It] must nurture the conscience of the nation; invest in the preparation of promising Godly character to man the affairs of our nation."[38]

Not surprisingly, the dominant ideology and goals of CAN have been political in appearance, as it is in inspiration. The political agenda of CAN has been given fresh blood by the conviction and perception of a state-religion relationship, and the idea that Muslims will use political power and the state apparatuses to further their individual and collective interests, which ironically has its counter-appearance in three forms. One, CAN's opposition to what is perceived as progressive Islamization through the introduction of Shari'a; two, that the government should take Nigeria into the OIC; and three, its insistence that the state upholds the constitutional secular principle of neutrality in religion.[39]

In order to translate its anti-Islamic agenda into a real political struggle, CAN has adopted two broad methodological approaches referred to as the "politics of quiet diplomacy," alternatively called the "politics of persuasion," and "militant politics."[40] In the first approach, diplomatic and peaceful avenues of resolution on issues affecting Christians are explored such as the sending of delegations, the writing of letters or memoranda, and the lobbying of influential Christians in the army or government. This strategy has been quite rewarding and helping to secure peace.

The second approach is rather more proactive, or in the true sense of the word, forceful. This methodology became increasingly dominant especially from 1987 during the presidency of Archbishop Anthony Olubunmi Okogie.[41] This approach emphasizes mass mobilization campaigns that range from preaching, effective use of the media, and civil litigations, all in an effort to generate mass awareness and concern for CAN and its members. The most graphic show of the proactive posture is CAN's direct involvement in political debates, protests and its acceptance of offers to sit on panels of inquiry and tribunals as representatives of the Christian community. This method was adopted in 1988 on the new assumption that unless Christians take control of the realm of this earthly kingdom, politics may undo or marginalize the church:

> If Christians distance themselves from politics that lead to leadership, then the demons will have a field day as had been the case with Nigeria up till today. If demons govern and rule us and burn our churches and marginalize us and treat us like second class citizens in our own country of posting, then why should the Christians complain?[42]

Some powerful individual members of the Nigerian Christian community have heavily criticized this approach to issues. One such voice is Reverend Father Mathew Kukah, of the Catholic Secretariat, in Lagos. He disagrees with the adoption of this method on the ground that CAN's often politically charged statements depict a rather poor reading of the dynamics of political engineering in Nigeria. He claimed that CAN's protestations and concerns over the Shari'a and Nigeria's membership in the OIC were founded on erroneous assumptions for "the constitution of Nigeria was as potent a weapon as it seemed on paper." He also believed that to demonize Islam because of the perceived threat of Islamization was over-dramatizing CAN's cause.[43]

Sunday Komolafe, a social commentator, agrees with Reverend Kukah, but contends that CAN's political agenda or its methodology merely reflected the reality of the political climate of the then military regimes. CAN adopted this approach during General Ibrahim Babangida's administration (1985-1993) because the crisis of religious politics and violence became most pronounced.[44] Moreover, CAN did not have the resources to negotiate for fair treatment of the Christians as was glaringly evident with the government's deference to their Muslim counterparts. Perhaps, it is right to say that CAN became "a victim of the scale of political balance it hoped to tilt and stabilize."[45]

Lamin Sanneh observed that, "all religious systems are equally vulnerable to the relentless incursions of temporal compromise and to the vagaries of human instrumentality even, or especially, where human stewardship is claimed in the service of revealed truth."[46] Thus just like any other political player in the system, the ultimate goal of CAN is to widen its notion of fairness in order that the rule of protecting and engendering its own welfare does not become less valid when dealing with other groups or organizations. As a religious association, CAN wants to protect its members' rights and fair treatment and justice in their own country. That conflicting demands, however, should be dealt with without necessarily compromising the basic political principles of continued common existence.[47]

Conclusion

To appreciate the role of CAN in political activism in Nigeria is to recognize its political philosophy and partisan concerns, especially against the backdrop of its perceived victimization within the Nigerian religious and political structures. To many of its members and the Christian followership in general, CAN stands as an epitome of moral ground, the 'catch-all' embodiment of hopes, and a rallying point of what they perceive as a cancerous problem, Islam. To CAN there are many unresolved political and religious issues.

The constitutional debates of 1978 and 1988, and the continuing controversies have set the pace. The recent spasmodic face-off between CAN and the state, coupled with the uncertainty that rents the political space, a progressively dwindling economy, worsening poverty, combined with frustration and an ever-increasing suspicion of Muslims by Christians will, no doubt, influence further in specific and conspicuous ways the politicization of religion and the religionization of politics in Nigeria. Two ways by which religion can enhance politics are: organizing dialogues among religious leaders and de-emphasizing religion in politics. Religious associations (Christian and Muslim), such as CAN may exist, but their political roles should be minimized.

Notes

1. Clifford Geertz, *The Interpretation of Cultures: Selected Essays* (New York: Basic Books, 1973), 311ff.
2. Gerrie ter Haar, "Religion: Source of Conflict or Resource for Peace?" in Philip Ostien, Jamila M. Nasir, and Franz Kogelmann, eds., *Comparative Perspectives on Shari'ah in Nigeria* (Ibadan: Spectrum Books, 2005), 304.
3. Simeon O. Ilesanmi, *Religious Pluralism and the Nigerian State* (Ohio: Centre for International Studies, Ohio University, 1999), 178.
4. Catholic Bishops of Nigeria: "Memorandum from the Catholic Bishops of Nigeria on the Review of the Nigerian 1979 Presidential Constitution", in *Christian/Muslim Relations in Nigeria: The Stand of Catholic Bishops* (Lagos, Nigeria: Catholic Secretariat, 1986), 9.
5. E. B. Gbonigi, "Religion in a Secular Society," paper presented at the Second Assembly of the Christian Association of Nigeria, Kaduna, November16-17, 1988, 2.
6. Gbonigi, 7.
7. Yusuf B. Usman, "National Cohesion, National Planning, and the Constitution," in *Issues in the Nigerian Draft Constitution,* ed., Suleiman Kumo and Abubakar Aliyu (Zaria, Nigeria: Ahmadu Bello University Press, 1977), 49.
8. Ilesanmi, 179.
9. Ibid., 180.
10. Mohammed Sambo, "Draft Constitution Fails to Provide for Morality," The *New Nigerian*, January 5, 1977, 7.
11. Anwal Abdul Nasir, "Religion and Secularism in the Nigerian Context," paper presented at the 25th Annual Religious Studies Conference, Ibadan, September17-20, 1991, 2.
12. Mohammed Sambo, "Morality and the Draft Constitution," in *The Great Debate: Nigerians' Viewpoint on the Draft Constitution 1976-77.*, ed. W. I. Ofonagoro (Lagos, Nigeria: Times Publications, 1978), 74.
13. Lamin Saneh, "Religion, Politics, and National Integration: A Comparative African Perspective," in *Religion and National Integration*, ed. John O. Hunwick (Evanston, IL: Northwestern University Press, 1992), 157.
14. Mohammed Sambo, "Draft Constitution Fails to Provide for Morality," cited in Ilesanmi, 180-81.
15. Ibid.
16. This statement was made in an interview with the *Newswatch*, May 6, 1991, 16. In an interview with *This Week* of 6 April 1989, Alhaji Aliyu argues "the call for an Islamic state is the misguided view of the radical academics," and

that "the government tends to respect [their arguments] ... because they come from university dons who are supposed to be knowledgeable." He therefore calls on the government to create and nurture a civil environment, which will engender religion to serve as a moral catalyst, by expanding public vision and promoting the broader base of human community.

17. Saneh, 181.
18. A. O. Makozi, and O. J. A. Ojo, eds., *History of the Roman Catholic Church in Nigeria* (Ibadan: Macmillan, 1982).
19. Garba Ashiwaju, "Religion and National Integration," in *Nigeria Since Independence: The First 25 Years* Volume IX, ed., J. A. Atanda, Garba Ashiwaju and Yaya Abubakar (Lagos: Federal Government Printers, 1989), 1-10; Toyin Falola, *Violence in Nigeria: The Crisis of Religious Politics and Secular Ideologies* (Rochester: University of Rochester Press, 1998); and Eghosa E. Osaghae, and Rotimi T. Zuberu, *A History of Identities, Violence, and Stability in Nigeria* (Oxford: Centre for Research for Inequality, Human Security and Ethnicity/University of Oxford).
20. Garba, 1-10.
21. Federal Government of Nigeria, *The Report of the Political Bureau* (Abuja: Directorate for Public Enlightenment and Social Mobilization, 1987), 183.
22. Rotgak I. Gofwen, *Religious Conflicts in Northern Nigeria and Nation Building: The Throes of two Decades 1980-2000* (Kaduna: Human Rights Monitor, 2004), 84-92.
23. The *Newswatch*, March 30, 1987, 10.
24. Gofwen, 93-94.
25. Christian Association of Nigeria (Kaduna State Branch), "Memorandum submitted to the Administrative Panel set up by the Military Government of Kaduna State to investigate into the immediate and remote causes of the Sectarian Clashes in the State, the College of Education Kafanchan," in *Kaduna Religious Riot '87, a Catalogue of Events* (Kaduna: CAN), 32-39.
26. *Islamic Watch*, June/July 1992, 2.
27. Gofwen, 110-123.
28. Human Rights Watch, Nigeria: "The 'Miss World Riots' – Continued Impunity for Killings in Kaduna" *Human Rights Report 15(13A)*, July 2003.
29. Since 2001, Plateau State has played host to a succession of bloody intercommunal clashes that *Human Rights Watch* estimates have claimed at least to three thousand lives. The most devastating of them all have seen Jos and Yelwa's Hausa and Jarawa "settlers" against their indigene neighbors. Precisely in Jos sometimes in September 2001, clashes between indigenes and mainly Hausa non-indigenes claimed more than one thousand lives and left several thousand more people displaced. One of the immediate causes of the

violence was the appointment of a controversial Hausa political figure to a key statewide post within a federal poverty eradication program; indigenes felt that the appointment should have gone to one of their own. Within the first six months of 2004, an excess of one thousand people were killed in clashes that took place in and around Yelwa and tens of thousand of people were rendered homeless. The violence around Yelwa reached a climax in May 2004 with attacks by members of various Christian, indigene communities on Yelwa predominantly Jarawa non-indigene population that saw more than seven hundred (700) people killed in just two days. A large part of Yelwa was razed down and hundreds of dead Jarawa were buried in a mass grave near the center of town. It appears that the long-standing tensions between indigenes and non-indigene in Jos and Yelwa intermixed with Plateau State's increasingly tense sectarian divisions. The Hausa and Jarawa non-indigenes in Jos and Yelwa are overwhelmingly Muslim, and their neighbors are predominantly Christian. In the state, these dual sources of tension have reinforced each other to the level that it has become very hard to disentangle them aside from the fact each has made the other more divisive and volatile. What is more, the Joshua Dariye administration has since 1999 been fuelling the indigene-settler tensions in the state. The 2001 violence in Jos and the 2004 massacre in Yelwa both occurred upon the Governor's watch. It was alleged that the governor made several sweeping and often inflammatory statements to his Hausa constituents. In an interview with the Daily *Champion* newspaper in March 2004, Dariye said: "From the on-set, let me say it again, as I have before that Jos, capital of Plateau State, is owned by the natives. Simple. Every Hausa-man in Jos is a settler whether he likes it or not. In the past, we might not have told them the home truth, but now we have…They are here with us, we are in one state but that does not change the landlord/settler equation, no matter how much we cherish peace… Our problem here today is that … the tenants [are] becoming very unruly. But the natural law here is simple: if your tenant is unruly, you serve him a quit notice! …This unruly group must know that we are no longer willing to tolerate the rubbish they give us. The days of "over tolerance" are gone forever. All of us must accept this home truth." Less than two months after this statement was made, the violence in Yelwa assumed a monstrous dimension. As a federal government's response to this, President Olusegun Obasanjo made the controversial decision to temporarily sack Governor Dariye and replace him with an interim administrator. Obasanjo rationalized his decision by accusing Dariye of incompetence and of being "an instigator and a threat to peace" (Human Rights Watch, "They Do Not Own This Place: Government Discrimination against Non-Indigenes." http:/hrw.org/reports/2006/nigeria0406/6/They%20Do%20Not%2…/6.htm).

30. Abdul Raufu Mustapha, "Ethnicity and Democratization in Nigeria: A Case Study of Zangon Kataf," in *Expanding Democratic Space in Nigeria*, ed., Jibrin Ibrahim (CODESRIA, 1997), 206-219.
31. Gofwen, 119.
32. Ibid., 140-141.
33. The Church of Nigeria, "Christian Association of Nigeria Condemns Call for Jihad: Statement from the President-in-Council," http//www.anglican-nig.org/htm.
34. "Christian Association of Nigeria demands Equitable Justice from Senate," *Christian Today* www.christiantoday.com, 1 (Posted: Thursday, May 20, 2004, 1:05 (BST)).
35. Ibid.
36. "Christians Launch Political Organization," *Worthy New* (Christian Magazine), July 5, 2000, 1.
37. Sunday Komolafe, *Between Jihad and Crusade: Muslim-Christian Clashes in Nigeria* (Lagos, Nigeria: Gospel Light Christian Mission, 2005) 7.
38. Wilson Badejo, the General Overseer of the Foursquare Gospel Church of Nigeria, made this statement: "Sustaining Nigeria's Nationhood," *ThisDay*, June 8, 2002, 5.
39. Ashiwaju, 20-22.
40. Iheanyi Enwerem, *A Dangerous Awakening*, 1995, cited in Komolafe, 119-120.
41. He was of the opinion that the first method "has been tried and we saw that it did not work; probably we got about say, between 20-30 per cent success. Komolafe, 7.
42. Christian Association of Nigeria, "Leadership in Nigeria (To Date): An Analysis," *Periodic News Bulletin* (Lagos, Nigeria: Christian Association of Nigeria, 1987), viii.
43. Komolafe, 8-9.
44. Ibid., 9.
45. Ibid.

46 Lamin Sanneh, *Piety and Power: Muslims and Christians in West Africa*, Faith meets Faith Series (Maryknoll, NY: Orbis, 1996), 128, cited in Komolafe, 9.

47. Ilesanmi, 192; and Komolafe, 9.

CHAPTER TWELVE

WOMEN'S RELIGIOUS ASSOCIATIONS AND DEMOCRACY IN NIGERIA

OLUFUNKE ADEBOYE

This chapter examines the viability of religious associations as political platforms in post-independence Nigeria, using the Federation of Muslim Women's Associations of Nigeria (FOMWAN) as its case study. Established in 1985, at the end of the United Nations Decade for Women, FOMWAN has gradually grown stronger with over 700 affiliate groups in 34 states of the Nigerian Federation. Although involved in several other educational, social, cultural, religious, and economic activities, its political activism and advocacy for women have brought it into national and international limelight.

It is the view of this chapter that FOMWAN, as a civil society body, has aided not only the establishment of democracy in Nigeria, but also its maintenance, despite its own internal challenges first as a religious group, and secondly as a women's body. By addressing the political relevance of women, this chapter goes beyond the issue of gender barriers faced by women in the religious, economic, and social realms, and focuses on the suitability of religious associations as veritable tools of political change. The approach in this chapter is to first historically review the position of women in the Nigerian public sphere, then revisit the civil society theory and highlight those aspects that are relevant to this study. This is followed by a discussion of the background history and political activities of FOMWAN. This chapter also examines the challenges Nigeria faces, and concludes that these have not prevented FOMWAN from making meaningful political contributions.

Women in the Nigerian Public Sphere

The political subordination of women within the patriarchal structures of the Nigerian society is historic though it varied in degree from one locality to another. Women in Muslim societies in the northern part of the country were, more affected than their southern counterparts. Although the Islamic ideology of gender gave Muslim women basic legal rights in marriage, divorce, and ownership of property; their political freedom was circumscribed by the practice of *purdah*, while they were also effectively excluded from formal office within the governing structures of the religious community.[1] The imposition on indigenous societies (both Muslim and traditional) of a Western ideology of a male public sphere and a female, private sphere, during the colonial period, further pushed Nigerian (and indeed other African) women into political and economic peripheries.[2] Women thus found themselves confined to a domestic sphere in which they were expected to be silent and subordinate. Even previously viable traditional sources of female power were devalued or altogether eliminated during the colonial period. Christian women did not fare any better as andocentric interpretations of biblical patriarchy also limited their opportunities for political actualization both within and outside the religious sphere.[33] In addition, the female segment within the national political parties did little to promote women's agenda, such 'wings' being administered primarily as appendages of the main parties. There was thus the need for women to find a platform of power for political expression.

It was not until the military regimes of General Ibrahim Badamosi Babangida (1985-1993) and General Sani Abacha (1993-1998) that the issue of women's empowerment entered the national debate. The Better Life Programme (BLP) and Family Support Programme (FSP) initiated by successive First Ladies (Maryam Babangida and Maryam Abacha respectively) did little to bring women into mainstream Nigerian political life despite official rhetoric to the contrary.[4] Statutory governmental structures such as the Commission for Women Affairs and the Ministry of Women Affairs that could have effectively championed the cause of women were stifled and their activities overshadowed by the "Office of the First Lady," which preferred flamboyant, popular and short-term programs to well-thought out institutional overhauls and long term social engineering.[5]

It was clear from these experiments that the political emancipation of women could not be left to governmental structures manipulated by ubiquitous First Ladies. There was thus a shift to non-governmental structures, otherwise known as civil society.[6] Civil society groups came in different shades; both secular and religious. An interesting paradox in this study is how women effectively utilized the religious platform, not just to claim their basic rights, but also as a launching pad into mainstream politics. What type of women spearheaded this revolution? What strategies did they adopt? What was the reaction of the religious establishment to their activities? How have the women been able to deal with such reactions? This chapter assesses the contributions of FOMWAN to the practice of democracy in Nigeria.

The Civil Society Argument

Within the last decade and a half, there has been a vociferous debate over the concept of civil society in African politics. While it has now become widely recognized that civil society is central to African development and politics, there is still no general consensus on its role and characteristics. One point of agreement though appears to be the rejection by various scholars of western tools and models in the analysis of African civil society.

Civil society is generally within the context of a mediating domain or arena between the state and the society.[7] It is a public sphere of formal or informal, collective activity, autonomous from, but recognizing the legitimate existence of the state.[8] Several issues have been raised over the role and character of civil society. How much socio-political reform can be reasonably expected from civil society? Does civil society enhance state capacity or restrain state power? Is it about social institutions or social movements? While all these have some bearing on the issues raised in this chapter, the immediate attention is on the composition of civil society.

Many scholars identify religious groups as a major component of civil society.[9] Of all categories of civil society, it appears that religious organizations are the most effective in terms of delivering social goods because their tentacles extend to the grassroots (based on their existing networks), unlike secular NGOs that are just establishing their roots. In fact, this claim has been confirmed by empirical studies of several civil society groups.[10] An important role of civil society in the political system is the "creation of influence" through the life of democratic associations and "unconstrained discussions in the cultural public sphere."[11] This, it does by the generation of social capital which has been defined as incorporating "features of social organizations such as trust, norms and networks, that can improve efficiency of society by facilitating coordinated actions."[12]

A central expectation from civil society is that component groups should contribute not only to democratic transition, but also to its stability and continuation in society.[13] Meanwhile, it has also been argued that organizations within civil society that are characterized by values of pluralism and where divergent viewpoints are respected and tolerated almost always foster the type of social capital useful for this transition to, and maintenance of democracy.[14] Religious groups such as FOMWAN, where women of diverse ethnicities, background, and socio-economic statuses work together under the same umbrella readily fit into this category. The task in this chapter is, therefore, to find out how FOMWAN, as a civil society group, has contributed not only to the establishment of democratic channels in Nigeria, but also to its maintenance, through the 'creation of influence' and "unconstrained discussion" in the public arena. In addition, it highlights how religion, which was and still is responsible, to a large extent, for the perpetuation of the barriers facing women now came to provide a veritable platform from which the discourse for political liberalization along gender lines is launched.

FOMWAN: History and Activities

FOMWAN was formed in 1985 by a group of elite Muslim women who were concerned about the low level of education among the majority of Muslim women and their consequent 'invisibility and voicelessness' within society.[15] Their primary desire, apart from propagating Islam, was to enhance the status of the Muslim women. They were quick to realize, even at this early stage, that the main avenue of accomplishing this would be through the education of women. This would also promote their economic empowerment and enable them to contribute meaningfully to national development.

The inaugural meeting was held in October 1985 at Minna, at the Islamic Education Trust.[16] Those who attended this maiden meeting were encouraged to establish chapters of FOMWAN in their respective states. The idea was to encourage already existing Muslim women groups to affiliate with the federation for greater efficiency. In doing this, the experience of FOMWAN pioneers in the south differed significantly from those in the northern parts of the country. It was discovered that numerous Muslim women's groups already existed in the South, most of them attached to mosques and engaged in "various charitable and educational activities."[17] The pioneers only needed to persuade the leadership of those groups about the potential benefits of joining FOMWAN and this often yielded a positive result. On the other hand, the northern situation was more challenging. Due to the widespread practice of *purdah*, very few women attended local mosques and most lacked western education.[18] Their opportunities for associational contacts were thus limited. Consequently, women's organizations were scarce. The only ones were the Sisters' wing of the Muslim Students' Society of Nigeria and the Muslim Sisters' Organization; both connected with campus Islam and effectively excluded uneducated, adult Muslim women. Therefore, FOMWAN pioneers needed to do a lot more to mobilize northern women.

It was clear from the beginning that FOMWAN would be an umbrella organization. This gave it a wider reach and easy penetration to the grassroots. A constitution was put in place, which clearly articulated its vision, mission, aims and objectives, and rules of operation. Its main goal was to "educate Muslim women and facilitate (their) economic empowerment and intellectual development through capacity building."[19] The strategy adopted for realizing this rests mainly on seven programs, namely:

- Education of Muslim women at all levels.
- Provision of health services especially in reproductive health.
- Intellectual and economic empowerment of women through capacity building workshops, seminars etc.
- Care of early school leavers (i.e. drop-outs or school-age children not enrolled).
- Rehabilitation of street children, abandoned children, orphans and refugee children.
- Provision of girl-child education and adult literacy for women both in English and Arabic through the establishment of schools: Nursery/Primary, Secondary, Women's Islamiyya Literacy Schools and Vocational Centres.
- Youth development through youth programmes e.g. Youth Camps for girls etc.[20]

All these were to be implemented within the framework of the propagation of Islam. This emphasis on religion is so crucial to the identity of FOMWAN that it explains the initial reluctance of the founding mothers to affiliate with other secular NGOs. In the words of Aisha Lemu, the pioneer *Amirah* (President):

> FOMWAN is an **Islamic Religious Association** for women and not a **women's association** for women who happen to be Muslim. As a religious association our affili-

> ation, if any, is towards the Supreme Council for Islamic Affairs, and not toward the National Council of Women's Societies (NCWS)....NCWS is a secular organization while FOMWAN is established specifically to enable women to develop in compliance with the teachings of Islam and to enable Muslim women to express their views as Muslims, and not to be swallowed up as part of another organization with quite a different orientation[21] (Emphasis in original).

However, this stance appears to have been modified with time as FOMWAN saw the necessity of collaboration with secular NGOs in its campaign for global issues such as women's education and the fight against HIV/AIDS.[22]

In terms of structure, FOMWAN operates on three levels, namely, the national, the zonal, and the state. National organs comprised the Board of Trustees; the Executive Council; and National Boards e.g. Education Board, Health Board, Project Board etc.[23] The Zonal Coordinators are responsible for the five, and later twelve zones into which the states had been grouped. The state level corresponds to the state structure in the Nigerian Federation.[24] National activities include the annual conference rotated among the states, quarterly meetings of the National Executive Council, and the Publication of *The Muslim Woman*, which is the official voice of FOMWAN.[25] The zone is the intermediate authority between the state and the national levels, and the main function of zonal coordinators is supervisory. They move round the states within their respective zones offering necessary guidance, counsel, and coordination. It is, however, at the level of the state that most of FOMWAN's projects and schemes are carried out. The states establish schools, clinics, hospitals, and orphanages, as well as vocational training for women, and Islamic study centers.[26] They also organize annual youth camps during the long (summer) vacation for school children. The first week in June has been designated "FOMWAN Week" and is observed by all states to create more awareness about the group, celebrate its achievements and further promote Islam.

Although FOMWAN is careful to maintain its primary religious identity it also networks with other bodies in order to realize its goals. For example, to fulfill its educational aspirations, it partners with the Federal Government of Nigeria on Universal Basic Education, Nomadic Education Programmes, the Joint Consultative Committee on Education, and the Quranic Education Programme. It works also with other NGOs such as the Civil Society Coalition on Education for All (CSACEFA).[27] Its health programs have brought it into partnership with several national and international NGOs, some of which even fund its activities. At the international level, FOMWAN officials have visited Muslim women's groups in several West African nations, encouraging them to avail themselves of the benefits of federating. This has produced spectacular results as sister Federations have sprung up in Ghana (FOMWAG), Liberia (FOMWAL), Gambia (FOMWAGA), Sierra Leone (FOMWASL), and Mauritius.[28] All these groups have formed a strong network with FOMWAN playing a central coordinating role.[29]

FOMWAN's activities are funded in a number of ways. These include proceeds of membership dues, sales of publications, donations and *zakat* from well wishers. Substantial funds have also flowed in as grants from donor agencies such as international NGOs, embassies of Islamic nations (e.g. Saudi Arabia and Pakistan), Islamic foundations, Islamic banks and several other corporate bodies.[30]

A major factor in the rapid growth of FOMWAN is that of good leadership right from its inception. These were elite women who had proven their mettle in the secular world before assuming the reins of power in FOMWAN. The pioneer *Amirah*, Aisha Lemu is a renowned educationist, who had taught at several schools in northern Nigeria before establishing the Islamic Education Trust in Minna which she was running before she was called upon to head the new federation.[31] A Briton, with postgraduate training in education from the School of Oriental and African Studies (SOAS), England, (and married to a Nigerian Muslim), Aisha was able to lay a solid foundation for the educational schemes of FOMWAN from 1985 to 1989. Lateefa Okunnu, who had an accomplished career in the Nigerian Civil Service, rising to the post of Permanent Secretary before retirement, succeeded Aisha. She was also the Deputy Governor of Lagos State from 1990 to1992. Okunnu was trained at the University of California, Los Angeles, USA and the Royal Institute of Public Administration, London, graduating in 1978.[32] She brought a wealth of skills, administrative experience, and contacts to the leadership of FOMWAN from 1989 to 1993.

Other leaders of FOMWAN include Khairat Olutoyin Sodique, an accountant and Federal Government Auditor of several years,[33] and Hajiya Bilkisu Yusuf, a journalist and political scientist.[34] A very articulate person with a passion for women's rights, politics, youth and media issues, Hajiya Bilkisu, more than any other leader, most forcefully advanced and defended the position of FOMWAN through her numerous media publications. She also brought her wealth of organizational experience from several secular NGOs into the leadership of FOMWAN. It was not surprising that her tenure as *Amirah* saw the introduction of a new strategic plan that clearly articulated FOMWAN's vision, mission, and future strategy, with practical goals for implementation.[35] These and other elite women at the helm of FOMWAN affairs gave the group a solid foundation, which others are still building on. Their administrative and organizational experiences have advanced the lot of the group substantially.

Political Activities of FOMWAN

The idea of the political empowerment of women was never really far from the mind of FOMWAN even though its official aims and objectives articulated more socio-economic and religious concerns. It appears that the strategy of the group was to deal first with impediments in the way of the political empowerment of Muslim women. It was clear to them that poorly educated, sick, and economically feeble women stood no chance in a political arena dominated by male gladiators. This resonates with Lotsmart Fonjong's observations on Cameroon women's participation in development through non-governmental efforts. According to her, the political advancement of women depends on "expanding the legal, institutional and socio-cultural space that they are able to command."[36] Progress in these areas, she continues, "provides women with the means and mobility necessary for political activities." She concludes that political participation does not occur in a vacuum: "space must be conquered for this to be done."[37] FOMWAN's other policies and programs could be interpreted as having been tailored towards the creation and conquest of space for its political aspirations.

A number of reasons were responsible for what could be termed the 'gradual politicization' of FOMWAN. First was the general political climate in the country in the late 1980s. This was the period of Ibrahim Babangida's political transition to democracy. A lot of debate was generated at this time, and much of it was focused on the role of women in the transition, and also in the anticipated democratic dispensation. Several women groups, among other civil society bodies, started getting themselves prepared for the political challenges ahead.[38] In addition to this was the failure of the programs of the erstwhile 'First Ladies' to effectively empower women beyond the claims of official rhetoric. Second, the tenure of Lateefa Okunnu (1989-1993) as the National *Amirah* of FOMWAN also coincided with her tenure as a Deputy Governor of Lagos State (1990-1992). Her appointment as Deputy Governor was seen not just as a general achievement for all Nigerian women, but also as a feather in FOMWAN's cap. Her visibility enhanced FOMWAN's prominence. This helped to advance the fortunes of the group significantly.

Third, as FOMWAN's activities expanded, the group became increasingly recognized as a major stakeholder in civil society. Consequently, governmental bodies at the (Local, State, and Federal levels) as well as other NGOs began to invite its representatives to meetings and conferences on women's issues, education, health, human rights, political participation, HIV/AIDS, and other matters of public interest. This further increased the visibility of FOMWAN and earned it increasing social/political recognition. Finally, there is the issue of the centrality of politics to Islam. While Islamic law is believed to have given women ample rights, these have not always been clearly interpreted in the interest of women by the relevant Islamic authorities. In the words of Usman Bugaje, "while the text (quoted by eminent Islamic jurists)…. is divine, its interpretations, undoubtedly given with the best of intentions are not."[39] This is what FOMWAN aims to redress by educating women on their rights and enlightening them on the roles available for them within the public sphere.

The political activities of FOMWAN could be classified into three: first is in the area of the provision of civic education; second is their contribution to the Shari'a debate; and third is their election monitoring activity. These three areas are closely interrelated. For example, civic education also extends to the Shari'a debate as it touches on the rights of women under Shari'a, while election-monitoring activities went hand in hand with civic education too. The academic distinction made here is for analytical purposes and to demonstrate that specific circumstances gave prominence to certain activities more than others

Civic Education

In providing civic education, FOMWAN first addressed the question of the role of women in politics. This was to sensitize Muslim women to the possibilities available to them within the political arena. The maiden edition of *The Muslim Woman* in 1988 was devoted to this. Again in 1997, during FOMWAN's 12th anniversary, it organized a conference to which leading Islamic scholars were invited to discuss the following issues:

- Should Muslim women canvas for political office?
- Are Muslim women eligible for political office?
- Can Muslim women be elected as heads of state?
- In a multi religious state as Nigeria, what waiver in the political process can be allowed in the interest of the *Ummah* as far as women are concerned?[40]

Several opinions were expressed during the conference, but the ones that eventually made it to the 2000 issue of *The Muslim Woman* (dedicated to the question of whether Muslim women needed empowerment) were those that supported the empowerment of women. According to Usman Bugaje who was one of the speakers in the 1997 conference, "there is no text in the Qur'an that explicitly impedes or prohibits the participation of women in politics."[41] Instead, he cites many Qur'anic texts that "implicitly approve and encourage" the participation of women in politics.[42] He also expresses a similar opinion on whether a woman could be head of state or not. He argues that, "if we should find the qualities we need for leadership in a woman there is nothing to stop us from utilizing these qualities."[43] However, he believes that there is no need to seek special treatment for women in the political process. If women are not asking for economic and social favors, there is therefore no need to treat them separately in politics. In addition, the editorial opinion of *The Muslim Woman* for the 2000 issue entitled, "Democracy and Political Participation," encouraged Muslims to participate in politics. It stated that, "It is wrong for Muslims to be indifferent to such an issue (politics). Islam has not prescribed a particular form of government but it has made very clear certain principles which should be observed in political leadership."[44] A discussion of those principles ensues after which the editorial concludes:

> Therefore, unless we have a better alternative system to propose, we ought to care about having a democratic system, and about justice, accountability, the rule of law, consultation of the ruled, and about commanding what is right and forbidding what is wrong.[45]

By expressing views such as these, FOMWAN thus encourages and educates Muslim women to step into the political arena not just as passive voters and supporters of male candidates, but also as qualified candidates in their own right, ready to contribute to their country's democracy.

In 2000, FOMWAN published a small book on *The Rights and Responsibilities of Muslim Women*. A summary of the book was part of a larger write-up published in the year 2003 issue of *The Muslim Woman* entitled, "The Rights of Women and their Empowerment Under Shariah," by Hajiya Bilkisu (national *Amirah* 2001-2005). Apart from general rights such as the right to life, right to worship and spiritual development, and twelve other such rights, women's rights were classified as economic rights, political rights, and rights of Muslim women in difficult circumstances.[46] The article also reiterated the civic responsibilities of Muslim women as follows: responsibilities to God, to self, to family, and to society. These guidelines were provided to tackle the issue of women's ignorance about their rights under the law.

With approaching national elections in 2003, FOMWAN continued its civic educational activities for its members in collaboration with secular NGOs such as the Transition Monitoring Group (TMG) with funding from the Department for International Development (DFID) (administered by the British Council).[47] FOMWAN also collaborated with the Independent National Electoral Commission (INEC) in its pre-election zonal workshops, where the people were enlightened on their civic responsibilities before, during, and after elections.[48]

The Shari'a Debate

The Shari'a legal system had been in operation in northern Nigeria since the days of the Sokoto Caliphate in the nineteenth century. It was retained during the colonial period, although then it had no jurisdiction over criminal cases. After independence, Shari'a courts retained jurisdiction over civil matters only. But this was to change after the country returned to democratic governance in 1999.[49] The civilian governor of Zamfara state, Ahmad Sani Yerima, reintroduced the Shari'a to his state, extending its jurisdiction to criminal cases. Eleven other northern states also declared the Shari'a rule in quick succession. This produced a very heated debate in the country.[50] Southern Christians accused the Muslim North of trying to impose a Muslim identity on an otherwise secular nation. Other observers simply saw the Shari'a issue as a political ploy devised by the northern politicians to destabilize the Olusegun Obasanjo regime, while Muslims insisted that the motivation for reintroducing the Shari'a was purely religious. Meanwhile, the Federal Government considered the Shari'a issue as nothing but a political problem that would soon lose steam.

Immediately the Shari'a went into operation in the northern states, several *hudud* (punishment for sexual crimes) sentences were imposed, which aroused international concern. The most popular of such cases involved women who had been accused of *zina* (adultery). The first case was that of Safiyyatu Hussani of Tundar Tudu, Sokoto state sentenced to death by stoning by an Upper Shari'a Court, Gwadabawa Sokoto in 2001.[51] Another case involved Amina Lawal of Katsina state. The local press, especially from southern Nigeria, protested the judgments while several women's groups and NGOs also lent their voices to the debate.[52] Eventually, the Shari'a Court of Appeal both in Sokoto and Katsina states reversed the two judgments on technical grounds. What was the role of FOMWAN in all these?

Fatima Adamu, in discussing the response of Muslim women to the expansion of the Shari'a in northern Nigeria identifies two major groups and emphasizes the fact that it was difficult for the two groups to come together.[53] There was the group she describes as "Islamist Women," which "believe that women's liberation could only be attained within Islam" and they strongly supported and protected the Shari'a, apparently 'blind' to the male biases inherent in the Shari'a document and in its application. The second group she calls "secularist women," made up mostly of Muslim women academics and activists who attacked and condemned the Shari'a wholesale and were equally 'blind' to the rights and protection the Shari'a provided women. The cleavages between those two groups were so strong that they could not objectively monitor Shari'a implementation as it affected women to enable them to strategize how to make a joint case on behalf of Muslim women.[54]

There appears to be a third group represented by organizations like FOMWAN that believe the Shari'a could be used strategically to fight certain cultural practices, which militate against women, and to promote the rights of Muslim women since many agree that the problem was not the Shari'a per se but with its interpretation by male religious leaders. In a summary of the two trials by Aliyu Musa Yawuri, one of the defense counsels to the two accused women notes that:

> The main difficulty encountered in such trials is that most of the judges are not quite conversant with the provisions of the constitution on fundamental rights and with the Islamic criminal trial system be it in terms of procedure, evidence or even the substantive Islamic criminal law. There is need for continuing training of these judges.[55]

In April 2001, six months before a death sentence was passed on Saffiyatu in October 2001 FOMWAN had organized a National Conference on the Shari'a in Gusau, Zamfara state on the theme "Priorities in the Establishment of the Shari'a System."The choice of Zamfara was symbolic because that was where the Shari'a controversies began. By organizing the conference, FOMWAN sought to "contribute its quota to the intellectual debates on how the implementation of Shari'a could advance the status of the *ummah*."[56] At the end of the conference, it issued a communiqué affirming that the Shari'a is divine, goes beyond criminal offences and punishments, and incorporates several social benefits. It also "reaffirm(s) that Shari'a is not oppressive to women" and denounces other women's groups attempting to speak for Muslim women on the Shari'a issue.[57] The communiqué makes an interesting point, which indirectly indicts Shari'a implementing states for their lack of adequate preparation:

> .... That successful implementation of Shariah depends on a fully enlightened, educated, socio-economically enhanced society with exemplary leadership. We call on all states to pay attention to the basic needs of their people as a necessary prerequisite for implementation of Shariah.[58]

Making this call after several northern states had started implementing the Shari'a is a way of drawing their attention to a fundamental 'prerequisite' that had been over looked.

After death sentences had been passed on Saffiyatu Hussani and Amina Lawal in October 2001 and 2002 respectively, FOMWAN became more critical of the implementation of the Shari'a, especially as it applied to women. In a contribution by Hajiya Bilkisu Yusuf, at the Second National Conference of the Supreme Council on Shari'a in Damaturu, Yobe State in 2002, she notes:

> The Shariah as it is currently implemented has done nothing but filled them (the masses) with despair. Nothing has changed and the old order is not about to give way to the new one that is Shariah compliant. Shariah has been reduced to a body of laws in the hands of poorly trained and incompetent judges who abuse procedure. Shariah has also provided jobs for ill-equipped supervisors whose only preoccupation is to fish out women who commit adultery . . . In spite of their pretensions about promoting education, the flawed interpretation and motives of the authorities is underscored through their poor handling of court cases. Equally disturbing is the pervasive ignorance and lack of legal education among the *hisba* members who are supposed to police Shariah compliant communities. Add to this the naivity and ignorance of the majority of Muslims in whose interest Shariah is being implemented, and the picture of despair is complete. Currently only poor women and men seem to be the convicts of the Shariah courts. The elites and rich appear to have some inbuilt immunity

> from Shariah law. This is a clear case of injustice which cannot be rationalized in a Muslim community.[59]

She concludes by calling for massive education and human resources development especially among those saddled with the responsibility of implementing the Shari'a.

Furthermore, in continuation of FOMWAN's civic education programs, a new project on Shari'a and women's rights was launched in all the twelve Shari'a-implementing states. This program involved working with women's rights groups to educate Muslims and non-Muslims about the Shari'a. The project was funded by the Dakar based Open Society Initiative for West Africa (OSIWA).[60] The project took the form of training workshops for women on how to utilize their rights. The idea is to create awareness among women about their rights under the Shari'a. This will further prove that Islam gave ample rights to women, but which have not been appreciated due to excessive reliance on male-biased interpretations and second hand materials on Islam instead of a direct study of the Qur'an.

From the above, it could be seen that FOMWAN's strategy was to work from within to reinforce positive aspects of the Shari'a while enlightening women on their rights and calling on relevant Islamic authorities to reform the implementation structure of the Shari'a. It is therefore not surprising that after the heat of the Shari'a controversy had calmed down and the death sentences reversed, the 2006 edition of *The Muslim Woman* revisited the issue of Islam and Human Rights and even featured an article culled from the *Guardian* (a daily newspaper) of March 15, 2002 where death by stoning as penalty for adultery was questioned. The article concludes:

> The divine orders are a dear indication that apart from flogging, stoning to death was never contemplated in the Holy Quran as penalty for adultery. Let us, therefore, take note that a victim stoned to death cannot according to the Holy Qu'ran 4:16-17 and 24:4 be confined, repent, amend or married to anybody, after his or her death for adultery [sic].[61]

FOMWAN thus participated fully in the Shari'a debate and throughout the period of the controversy. It regularly published in *The Muslim Woman* opinions from other forums where women's rights under Shari'a were discussed both within and outside Nigeria.[62]

Election Monitoring

The idea of observing the management of the various phases in the electoral process and reporting its inherent strengths and shortcomings is meant to enhance the optimum performance of the electoral system. Election monitoring has been defined as "the continuous observation and scrutiny of the electoral process from the moment the election date is announced to the voting day activities, including the counting of votes and the announcement of results, to ensure that nothing is done at any stage in the process to change the verdict of the voters."[63] This definition effectively classifies the observation process into three: pre-voting, voting, and post-voting activities. The overall aim is to ensure free and fair elections. While systematic election monitoring in Nigeria has been dated to the June 1993 elections, monitored by the Nigerian Election Monitoring Group (NEMG) and the Election Monitoring Programme (EPG) of the Civil Liberties Organization (CLO), FOMWAN did not join until the 1999 elections. It appears FOMWAN only participated under the auspices of the Transition Monitoring Group (TMG), which was a coalition of Human Rights, non-Governmental and Civil Society Organizations.[64]

In 2003 FOMWAN 'independently' participated in election monitoring with the collaboration of the Muslim League for Accountability (MULAC).[65] MULAC is also an umbrella body with about 20 affiliate Islamic groups whose objectives are to fight corruption, promote transparency, accountability and good governance.[66] With financial support from the Centre for Development and Population Activities (CEDPA) and technical expertise and training materials from the National Democratic Institute (NDI), FOMWAN and MULAC were able to train and deploy 2000 election observers to fifteen northern states (Sokoto, Borno, Jigawa, Kaduna, Kebbi, Kwara, Katsina, Kano, Kogi, Nassarawa, Plateau, Bauchi, Yobe, and Zamfara) for the national assembly elections of April 12 and the presidential and gubernatorial elections of April 19, 2003.[67]

Some of the electoral anomalies reported by the FOMWAN/MULAC network included:

- Lack of secrecy in voting
- Undue interference from Governors and officials of the Independent Electoral Commission (INEC)
- Inadequate security arrangements during the election of April 12, 2003
- Large number of under-aged voters.[68]

Despite its purported 'independent' participation, FOMWAN also interacted with other local and international monitors. In fact, on May 1, 2003, FOMWAN co-signed a Nigerian Civil Society statement on the general elections of April 12 and 19, 2003 with other groups such as the Election Reform Network (ERN), Transition Monitoring Group (TMG), Justice, Development and Peace Commission (JDPC) of the Catholic Secretariat, and the Labour Election Monitoring Team (LEMT). This statement further recommended:

- Election Tribunals should be just in determining cases brought before them.
- The Electoral Act should be reviewed to make INEC truly independent of government.
- Government-controlled media should stop misrepresenting issues.[69]

On the whole the immediate impact of these monitoring activities could not be easily ascertained since it could not forestall the perpetration of electoral 'frauds.' One might argue, however, that it helped to expose such irregularities, providing alternative information to the propaganda of government-controlled media. For FOMWAN, the election monitoring exercise also had a personal resonance for individual observers. In the words of Rekiya Momoh-Abaji, the coordinator of FOMWAN Election Activities, "... many FOMWAN/MULAC personnel got training for the monitoring as well as ... a chance (for most people the first time) to participate, in some small way in contributing to [the] election of our political leaders."[70]

Again in 2007, under the umbrella of Domestic Election Observation Groups, FOMWAN joined other civil society organizations to monitor the Gubernatorial and State Assemblies elections held on April 14. Altogether these groups claimed to have deployed 50,000 trained observers throughout the country.[71] Aside from reporting that the preparations for the elections were characterized by a general lack of civic education, the Election Observation Groups also noted what they termed "serious malpractices" during the elections. These included: the hoarding of result sheets by INEC, a lack of secrecy in balloting, under-age voting, and the omission of some candidate names and/or pictures on ballot papers, partisanship of INEC, as well as violence and intimidation. They therefore implored aggrieved candidates to protest according to the law, and that Election Tribunals should deliver justice in deserving cases. They also called on the national security agencies to give adequate protection to voters, officials, and electoral materials in subsequent elections.[72]

Challenges Facing FOMWAN

A major challenge faced by FOMWAN in promoting the cause of Muslim women within the political arena is the hostility of conservative Muslim men. Such men employ religion to bar women from positions of leadership. It is paradoxical that while women are trying to use Islam as a platform to make themselves politically relevant, some men are also using the same religion as their own weapon to deny women of any meaningful political role. In fact, the whole idea of having an organization for Muslim women was not even acceptable to some Muslim men. According to Aisha Lemu, the pioneer national *Amirah*:

> In the North, some husbands and local mallams would oppose the whole idea of women having an Islamic Association .... In their own Islamic organizations they have no role for women. Yet they would still resist women forming their own Islamic organizations ... many would equally oppose their women folk attending women's Islamiyyah schools in order to gain Islamic knowledge. In the case of some "mallams" and "sheikhs" this probably has much to do with their desire to retain a monopoly on Islamic knowledge for commercial purposes ... women who know the true teachings of Islam might also come to know their rights as Muslim women and start asking for those rights, and thereby cause a nuisance.[73]

She was quick to add that this type of opposition to FOMWAN's activities was not widespread in Nigeria. She acknowledged the support given to the federation by many of the truly learned Islamic authorities that appreciated the value of Islamic learning among women.[74]

In September 2001, Bilikisu Yusuf published an article in the *Weekly Trust* that attracted a number of reactions from several quarters within the Muslim community. One was an Imam, Abubakar Ahmad Gada, who condemned the liberal views of Bilikisu, claiming that it was unIslamic for women to contest for leadership positions. This provoked a counter-rejoinder from one Sanusi Lamido Sanusi who criticized Abubakar Ahmad Gada.[75]

The exchange did not end there. In 2002, Abdullahi Doki wrote in the *Weekly Trust*, an article accusing educated Muslim women of using Islam as a cover for "feminism and Western European concepts of women's rights," and Bilikisu responded by defending the activities of educated Muslim women, fighting for the rights of other Muslim women, based on the correct application of the Qur'an. She is particularly concerned about "the level of ignorance displayed by some of the Muslim preachers... and about their intolerance of other views and contempt for scholarship."[76] Attacks like these, coming from within Islam, represent a great challenge to FOMWAN. Happily, not all Islamic authorities in Nigeria are conservative. Many appreciate the work of FOMWAN and encourage them spiritually and materially from time to time.

It is pertinent to note here that this challenge of Islamic patriarchy is not peculiar to the Nigerian Muslim community; it is indeed a common occurrence in the Muslim world. Women in several Islamic societies have had to contend with this barrier. Moreover, apart from religious patriarchy, traditional patriarchy still lingers in the Nigerian society. That is why women generally (Muslim, Christian, traditional) have not achieved as much as men politically. Again, the activism of FOMWAN leaders made them a target of official suspicion, thus earning them the hostility of the Sanni's military regime. This could be illustrated with an episode in 1995 when FOMWAN was sending some delegates to attend the NGO forum at the International Women's Conference, Beijing, China. Bilikisu Yusuf, a prominent and articulate member of the group was not allowed to travel and the security operatives of the military junta confiscated her travel documents.[77] Fortunately, other members of the team had gone ahead of her and were able to participate in the NGO forum.

Other minor challenges such as a shortage of funds, the demands of the home front, and a lack of basic education among Muslim women, are gradually being surmounted. The most intractable challenges, however, are two. One is the ideological conflation of FOMWAN demands for women's rights with Western European ideas of feminism by conservative Islamic authorities who consider such to be incompatible with Islam. Meanwhile, FOMWAN's advocacy for women's rights is rooted in the provisions of the Qur'an and Shari'a, as they try to avoid the feminist tag.

What the women desire therefore are female-friendly interpretations of the Qur'an and other sacred texts that would eliminate male biases. But the question is who would produce these interpretations? Elsewhere in the Islamic world, educated Muslim women have started calling on one another to embark on *iJtihad* (the exertion of intellectual efforts in the interpretation of texts), because for several generations, Islam has been presented to women through the lens of male interpretation.[78] The low level of education in Muslim women in Nigeria, however, makes this a lofty goal. Only a minute fraction of Muslim women have the necessary education and theological requirement to challenge existing traditions. This is the second major challenge facing FOMWAN.

Conclusion

From the foregoing analysis, it is clear that religion offers women a slippery platform for political expression and actualization due to its internal contractions and the biases of the patriarchal gate-keeping authorities. The strategy of the women is, however, remarkable. They employ the same tenets of the faith to support their position and expose the bias in androcentric interpretations, while avoiding the 'feminist' label, even though their concerns are essentially 'feminist.' How much reform did FOMWAN effect through its political activities? In its civic education programs and contributions to the Shari'a debate, FOMWAN not only added its voice to the others protesting injustices to women, it also enlightened Muslim women about their legal rights and helped them to be more assertive. It, therefore, enhances the nation's productive capacity by educating women and releasing them in large numbers to contribute their quota to national development. Its election monitoring activities could not be said to have produced immediate results, but taken together with the inputs of their civil society organizations, it has created continuous awareness of the need to reform the electoral process.

FOMWAN has gradually emerged as a major stakeholder in the Nigerian civil society and its role in generating discussion in the public sphere and in the creation of influence cannot be overemphasized. Its major constraints as highlighted above are from within its religious constituency. Moreover, through its numerous activities FOMWAN has also demonstrated the central role of education even in achieving political ends. An illiterate populace cannot nurture democracy. In all, FOMWAN, despite, its challenges has been able to contribute meaningfully not only to democratic inroads in Nigeria, but also to its strengthening and acceptance in Nigerian society.

Notes

1. Margaret Strobel, "Women in Religion and Secular Ideology" in *African Women South of the Sahara*, ed. Margaret Jean Hay and Shawn Sticher (Essex: Longman, 1995), 109; Fatima L. Adamu, "Politicisation of Gender and the Election of Muslim Women into Political Leadership in Hausa Society, Northern Nigeria," http://www/gwsafrica.org/african%20feminist%20thinkers/adamu/adamu%20publication4.htm.
2. Jean O'Barr and Kathryn Firmin-Sellers, "African Women in Politics" in ed. Hay and Sticher, 211-212.

3. Olufunke Adeboye, "Breaking Through Gender Barriers: Religion and Female Leadership in Nigeria," *Journal of History and Diplomatic Studies*, 2, 2005, 145-168.
4. O. I. Aina, "Mobilizing Nigerian Women for National Development: The Role of Female Elites," *African Economic History,* 21, 1993, 16.
5. Wale Are Olaitan, "Women in Politics in Nigeria" in *Nigerian Women in Society and Development*, ed., Amadu Sesay and Adetanwa Odebiyi (Ibadan, Nigeria: Dokun Publishing House, 1998), 79.
6. Ibid.
7. M. Karlstrom, "Civil Society and Its Presuppositions: Lessons from Uganda" in *Civil Society and the Social Imagination in Africa*, ed., J. L. Comaroff and J. Comaroff (Chicago: University of Chicago Press, 1999), 105; N. Kasfir, "Introduction" in *Civil Society and Democracy in Africa: Critical Perspectives, ed.,* N. Kasfir (London: Frank Cass, 1998), 4; E. Nwokedi, *Politics of Democratization: Changing Authoritarian Regimes in Sub-Saharan Africa* (Minster, Hamburg: LIT Verlag, 1995), 68.
8. Stephen Orvis, "Civil Society in Africa or African Civil Society?" *Journal of Asian and African Studies,* 36, 1, 2001, 17.
9. C. Monga, *The Anthropology of Anger: Civil Society and Democracy in Africa* (Boulder, CO: Lynne Rienner Publishers, 1996), 149: Kevin Warr, "The Normative Promise of Religions Organisations in Global Civil Society," *Journal of Church and State*, 41, 3, 1999, 499; Tracy Kuperns, "Building Democracy: An Examination of Religious, Associations in South Africa and Zimbabwe," *Journal of Modern African Studies*, 37, 4, 1999, 644.
10. James Pfeiffer, "Civil Society, NGOs, and the Holy Spirit in Zimbabwe," *Human Organisation*, 63, 3, 2004, 359. See also Kupenis, "Building Democracy," 643-668.
11. Jean Cohen and Andrew Arato, *Civil Society and Political Theory* (Cambridge, MA: MIT Press, 1992), x.
12. Robert Putnam, *Making Democracy Work: Civic Traditions in Modern Italy* (Princeton, NJ: Princeton University Press, 1993), 167.
13. Warr, 450.
14. Ibid.
15. "Twenty Years of FOMWAN," Editorial, *The Muslim Woman Magazine of the Federation of Muslim Women's Association of Nigeria,* No. 9, 2005, 7.
16. B. Aisha Lemu, "FOMWAN History and Experience: A Case Study," *The Muslim Woman*, No. 6, 1997, 23. This article was originally presented at the FOMWAN 10th Anniversary International Conference, Abuja, August 16-20, 1995.
17. Ibid.

18. Ibid., 24.
19. FOMWAN, *Twenty Years of Service to Islam 1985-2005*, Special Anniversary Publication, 2005, 2.
20. The aims and objectives of FOMWAN were not as elaborate as this at inception. It was in 2001 that it "reviewed and adopted a new strategic plan redefining its vision, mission, value statements, goals and strategic objectives." FOMWAN, *Twenty Years of Service to Islam*, 8; and the FOMWAN website on http://www.fomwan.org
21. Lemu, "FOMWAN History and Experience," 24.
22. For instance, FOMWAN representatives sit on the board of the interfaith council of Nigeria and on the International Advisory Board of the Balm in Gilead Inc. (an International Christian NGO fighting against HIV/AIDs in Africa.
23. FOMWAN, *Twenty Years of Service to Islam*, 2.
24. Ibid.
25. *The Muslim Woman* is supposed to be an annual magazine, but it has not been quite regular. Only about 10 issues have been published since it made its debut in 1988.
26. FOMWAN *Twenty Years of Service to Islam*, 18-58. Summaries of the activities of FOMWAN state chapters could also be found in various issues of *The Muslim Woman.*
27. FOMWAN, Twenty Years of Service to Islam, 10-15.
28. B. Aisha Lemu, "Reflections on a FOMWAN Journey Round West Africa", *The Muslim Woman*, No. 5, 1995, 10-13; Katumi Mahama, "A Case Study of Women's Islamic Organisations in Ghana," *The Muslim Woman*, No. 6, 1997, 25-27.
29. In August 1995, FOMWAN organized an International Conference in Abuja, Nigeria, on the theme "Towards a Global Women's Islamic Movement" to mark its 10th anniversary. Apart from delegates from the sister federations in West Africa, Speakers also came from the U.K., Sudan, Austria and Kenya. One of the goals of the conference was to "discuss further steps towards establishment of a West Africa Confederation of Women's Islamic Associations" "FOMWAN Goes Global," editorial, *The Muslim Woman*, No. 6, 1997, 5. It is, however, not clear if this good has been realized up till date.
30. FOMWAN, *Twenty Years of Service to Islam*, 2. See also acknowledgement of grants received by state chapters in the summary of their activities published in various issues of *The Muslim Woman.*
31. "Biodata of Aisha Bridget Lemu," http://www.islamwomen.org/EngIw/HomePage/HPDetails5.aspx?id+464. Accessed on March 27, 2008.

32. Profile of Lafeefa Mopelola Okunnu, http://odili.net/news/source/2006/feb/11/605.html
33. Profile of Kudirat Olutoyin Sodique, http://theummahfoundationtuf.wordpress.com/about-2/
34. Profile of Hajiya Bilkisu Yusuf, http://www.abantu-rowa.org/boardandstaff.html
35. FOMWAN, Twenty Years of Service to Islam, 8.
36. Lotsmart Fonjong, "Fostering Women's Participation in Development through Non-Governmental Efforts in Cameroon," *The Geographical Journal*, 167, 3, 2001, 223-234.
37. Ibid., 231.
38. Rotimi T. Suberu, Sam B. Mala and Deji I. Aiyegboyin, "Religious Organisations," in *Nigeria: Politics of Transition and Governance 1986-1996, ed.,* Oyeleye Oyediran and Adigun A. B. Agbaje (Dakar: CODESTRIA, 1999), 29.
39. Usman Bugaje, "Muslim Women and the Question of Politics: Some Elucidation," *The Muslim Woman*, No. 7, 2000, 35.
40. Selected papers from this Conference were published in *The Muslim Women*, No. 7, 2000, which was devoted to the issue of women's empowerment.
41. Bugaje, 35.
42. Ibid.
43. Ibid., 38.
44. "Democracy and Political Participation," editorial, *The Muslim Woman*, No. 7, 2000, 5.
45. Ibid.
46. Hajiya Bilikisu, "The Rights of Women and their Empowerment Under Shariah," *The Muslim Woman*, No. 8, 2003.
47. "FOMWAN Projects and Activities Around the States," *The Muslim Woman*, No. 9, 2005, 18.
48. Ibid., 21.
49. M. Owolabi Junaid, "The Shariah Legal System in Nigeria: A Historical Survey" in *Nigerian Integrative Discourses: Vol. 1, Shariah*, ed., C. S. Momoh and Segun Awonusi (Lagos, Nigeria: University of Lagos, 2005), 233-245.
50. For a discussion of some of the issues involved in the Shariah debate see Hakeem B. Harunah, *Shari'ah Under Western Democracy in Contemporary Nigeria: Contradictions, Crises and the Way Forward* (Lagos, Nigeria: Perfect Printers Limited, 2002).

51. See Ogbu U. Kalu, "Saffiya and Adamah: Punishing Adultery with Sharia Stones in Twenty-First-Century Nigeria," *African Affairs*, 102, 2003, 389-408.
52. Even groups of Christian women joined in the demonstration against the Shariah death sentences. See Kenneth Ehgiator, "Women Storm Lagos Governor's office, plead for Safiya's Life" *The Vanguard*, December 4, 2001.
53. Fatima Adamu, "Women's Struggles and the Politics of Difference in Nigeria. http://www.grosafrica.org./african%20feminist%20thinkers/adamu/adamu%20publication5.httm Accessed on March 12, 2008.
54. Ibid.
55. Aliyu Musa Yawuri, "Issues in Defending Saffiyatu Husseini and Amina Lawal," *The Muslim Woman*, No. 10, 2006, 22.
56. "Shariah, Education and the Citizenry," editorial, *The Muslim Woman*, No. 8, 2003, 6.
57. "Shariah in Nigeria: Our Stand." Communique Issued at the End of the National Conference on Priorities in the Establishment of Shariah System," held in Gusau, Zamfara State by FOMWAN from 11th-14th Muharrain 1422 A. H. (5th – 8th April, 2001), *The Muslim Woman*, No. 8, 2003, 25.
58. Ibid.
59. Bilikisu, "The Rights of Women," 21.
60. "FOMWAN Projects and Activities Around the States", *The Muslim Woman*, No. 9, 2005, 18. See also "Women's Human Rights Under Sharia: Update on Recent Debates and Publications." http://www.boellnigeria.org/shariaade-batesupdates.html
61. "Is Stoning to Death Penalty for Adultery? *The Muslim Woman*, No. 10, 2006, 24-25.
62. Such include: 1. "Overcoming Obstacles in Achieving the Rights of Muslim Women" by Laila Al-marayati, presented at the Canadian Council of Muslim Women's Conference on "Muslim Women and the Politics of Participation" in October 1998. This was published in No. 7, 2000 of *The Muslim Woman*. 2. "Do Muslim Women Need Empowerment?" by Usman Bugaje, presented at the Symposium on Islam and Contemporary Issues organized by the Movement for Islamic Culture and Awareness (MICA) on Oct. 26, 1997, *The Muslim Woman*, No. 7, 2000. 3. A Two-day Conference on "Promoting Women's Rights through Shariah in Northern Nigeria" organized by the Centre for Islamic Legal Studies, ABU Zaira, March 29-30, 2005 (Summary of Proceedings, *The Muslim Woman*, N. 9, 2005.
63. Nigerian Election Monitoring Group, "A Manual for Election Monitors," 1993, 2, quoted in *Nigeria: Politics of Transition and Governance*, ed., Cyril

I. Obi; Musa Abutudu, "Election Observers," in Oyediran and Agbaje, eds., 292.

64. Rekiya Momoh–Abaji, "FOMWAN Election Monitoring Experience," *The Muslim Woman*, No. 9, 2005, 22.
65. Ibid.
66. Hajiya Bilikisu, "The Veil and Male Chaurinists." http://www.africaresource.com/content/view/42/68/
67. Momoh-Abaji, "FOMWAN Election Monitoring Experience," 22. The 15 Northern States were Sokoto, Borno, Jigawa, Kaduna, Kebbi, Kwara, Katsina, Kano, Kogi, Nassarawa, Plateau, Bauchi, Yobe and Zamfara.
68. Momoh-Abaji, "FOMWAN Election Monitoring Experience," 22.
69. "Nigerian Civil Society Statement on the General Elections of April 12th and 19th 2003," available on http://www.africaaction.org/docs03/nig0305.htm
70. Momoh-Abaji, "FOMWAN Election Monitoring Experience," 22.
71. "Preliminary Report on the Gubernatorial and State Assemblies Elections held on Saturday, April 14, 2007 http://www.tmnigeria.org/pressreleases/prereptguberstateelects160407.pdf
72. Ibid.
73. Lemu, "FOMWAN History and Experience," 24.
74. Ibid.
75. Fatima Adamu's account of this exchange in her "The Politicisation of Gender."
76. Yusuf, http://www.abantu-rowa.org/boardandstaff.html
77. Another way of interpreting this episode is in terms of Bilikisu Yusuf's identity and activities as a very vocal journalist if we recall the zero tolerance of the Abacha regime for media practitioners.

Chapter Thirteen

The Pentecostal Churches: The Politics of Spiritual Deregulation since the 1980s

Adoyi Onoja

There is a strong connection between the nature, form, and transformation of the State and the growth of religion among people all over the world. This has been the case in Nigeria since the 1980s due to declining economic performance as a result of heavy reliance on oil, deepening corruption among the political elite, misrule leading to the non-performance of the State, which has resulted in the proliferation of a wide range of social problems. A connection can be drawn between declining economic performance and rising religiosity. This development has produced a major growth sector in the rise of the Pentecostal movement whose ways of worship (like the economic liberalization that followed economic collapse), is a remarkable departure from that of the traditional orthodox methods of worship.

Economic decline in Nigeria reached its lowest point in the 1980s, coinciding with the fall of the Berlin Wall in 1989. This heightened the universalization and implementation of economic reforms with the Structural Adjustment Program (SAP) as its linchpin. America and Britain, who simultaneously interpreted the end of the Soviet system as the triumph of the free market system and the supremacy of God, encouraged the implementation of the SAP. On the local scene, the proliferation of social crises (in the wake of economic reforms) corresponded with the rise of the Pentecostal movement.

Adebayo Olukoshi and Felicia Oyekanmi noted that this shift in economic and political orientation produced a dramatic result most evident in the systematic attack on the State and its interventionist role in the development process. The battle cry of the 1980s and 1990s was rolling back the frontier of the State and declaring the unfettered dictatorship of the market, which was defined as the "central goal of policy and the direction in which all countries must move."[1] Their observation was based on the changes inaugurated in the United States and Britain in the 1980s, which later translated into the maxim of the Bretton Wood institutions.[2]

The world had inexorably moved in this direction as evidenced by the implementation of economic reforms and political pluralism along the prescribed version, which appears to have become the rule of engagement in international affairs. In Nigeria, State withdrawal from economic affairs commenced on a large scale under the presidency of General Ibrahim Babangida (1985-1993). It was during this period that the Structural Adjustment Program (SAP) was adopted and implemented. The period was tumultuous in terms of social consequences as the reforms were not only painful but the planned democratic transition was protracted and did not establish the promised civilian rule.[3]

The process generated considerable uncertainty, economic disruptions, and social unrest as the government could no longer cater to the majority of citizens. The result was lawlessness, armed robbery, drug trafficking, retrenchment, inflation, and general apathy in the society. Such a situation encouraged the expansion and influence of religious organizations and cultivated a genre that specialized in managing this fallout from the government's shortcomings. Attempting to explain this recourse to religion for solace in times of crisis, John Tusa, former managing director of the BBC, noted that if "religion – the search for something bigger and better than ourselves - is so widespread it may well be because the solutions of rationality and science look less like answers and more like new problems."[4] Karen Armstrong also noted that Christianity's staying capacity was its constant transformation and its ability to "speak to the peculiarity of each new modernity."[5] What are the aspects of this new modernity that are associated with the evolution of churches? How have churches applied themselves in solving the problems of the present age? How have churches transformed the economy and political arena in Nigeria? These are some of the issues that will be examined in this chapter. In order to accomplish this it is necessary to conceptualize the State and Pentecostal movement to understand how both compliment one another.

The State and the Pentecostal Movement in Nigeria

The crisis bedevilling the Nigerian State emanated from the changes unleashed by economic reforms following decades of mismanagement and corruption. The State in Nigeria reflects both left and right wing ideologies. The Marxist viewed the State as an executive committee of the dominant class and the new right saw it as a regulator of conflicting interests in the society.[6] The latter view presents the State within the context of the development of capitalism in which the dominating and wealthier class takes the authority to rule. The former explains the attempt to arbitrate in an ever-changing situation in order to promote the "public good."[7]

A State is defined from the organizational and functional perspectives. The organizational perspective distinguishes the State as a very specialized type of government characterized by five interrelated features. The functional perspective views the State in two ways. The *ex ante* perspective defines the State as a set of institutions which carry out particular goals and objectives that result in any organization whose function overlaps with that of the State automatically becoming part of the State. The *ex post* perspective defines the State by its consequences such as the maintenance of law and order, the development and upkeep of infrastructures, jobs, and social welfare. The State in this context is identified with those institutions or patterns of behavior that have stabilizing effects.[8]

The State in the Nigerian context, which was equated as the government, has not lived up to expectation in its function to serve as a stabilizing factor. Since the 1980s, the State has not been able to energize its citizens with patriotic or nationalistic ideologies[9] nor has it been able to serve as a factor of cohesion in a social formation and as an authoritative distributor of values.

An explanation for the State crisis can be located in the thesis of contemporary dependency and world systems theories which argue that the State structure, form, autonomy and probability of facing a revolutionary crisis can be traced to its position within the capitalist system.[10] Malori Pompamayer asserted that the variation in the evolution of State was the function of the changes involved with, and reorganization of, the world economy.[11] Fitzgerald Edmund located the responses of countries as being conditioned by a specific combination of factors such as late industrialization, infiltration of international capital, dependent development, along with social and political crisis.[12] As scholars of political economy, Pompamayer and Edmund explain the conditions of State grappling with externally-induced changes. While Pompamayer related the world economy and the changes that occur to the evolution of the State, Edmund associated the response of the States to industrialization, the role of international capital operating within the economy, and the dependent development nature of the country, all exacerbating political and social crisis.

All of these variables explained the situation of the State in Nigeria. These factors condition the capacity of the diversely situated classes to affect the State structure and policy.[13] Specific combination of internal and external factors determine State strategy for economic development, the generation of new classes, the distribution of income, wealth, and new forms and intensity of social and political conflict. The changes and reorganization of the Nigerian economy was determined by its location within the hierarchically organized zones of the world capitalist system where its peripheral position consigned it to producing primary products in a fluctuating market place, with a corrupt and inefficient ruling class fending for themselves by perpetually borrowing and squandering the resources. It is within this context that the emergence of the Pentecostal movement as a "new class" in the management of this fallout can be appreciated.

The emergence of the Pentecostal movement in Nigeria can be set in the context of economic reforms that dominated the 1980s and 1990s. By far the whole idea of economic deregulation introduced a lot of changes including the spiritual side of deregulation,[14] which complimented the economic one. It was within the crises generated by economic deregulation that the churches stepped in not only to restructure themselves along the prevailing line, and in line with the now generally accepted view of the failure of the orthodox churches in the face of colossal deprivations, but also to take advantage of the situation and engineer into being an orientation that feeds on the discontent pervading the society. This fit into the frameworks canvassed by Marxists and sociologists alike that excessive religiosity, or the mass embrace of religion, was due to a failure of rationality. Religion appears to have become much more poignant in the social setting of Nigeria from the 1980s to the present. A statement by Archbishop George Carey, the former head of the Anglican Church in England, established the connection between social upheavals and excessive religiosity. According to Archbishop Carey, "Life is not as dramatic in Britain as it is in Latin America or Central Africa and it does not require a Christian revelation to interpret it."[15] The Archbishop was decrying Britain in a post-Christian era. This is because European religions mirrored their social and economic life - a life of seeming conquest devoid of deprivation - when compared to Nigeria. This situation explained the disparity in church growth between the two countries.

Pentecostalism emerged from Protestantism. The origin of Protestantism and within it Pentecostalism can be traced to the Reformation of the sixteenth century that Martin Luther led. The Reformation was an open expression of dissatisfaction with the abuses within the Roman Catholic Church, the role of the priesthood and the ecclesiastical hierarchy itself. At the same time, it adapted to particular regions and was connected with the process of secularization. Radical movements and the expression of dissent were not unique to the sixteenth century. The church had a long record of corruption and there had been attempt at reform long before Luther.[16] Names such as Hus and Wycliffe represent the attempt to call into order the crisis within the church.

Within Protestantism multiple variations of religious practice and dogma can be found. Almost in spite of itself it fostered both political and economic individualism. It allowed greater freedom of interpretation of the faith and, perhaps because of this, it helped the slow drift from religious to secular individualism.[17] Part of its dynamism today is derived from this "freedom of interpretation of the faith" and within it the elevation of the ills of indulgence, in the name of economic individualism, supported by relevant sections of the Holy Book, to provide a fortification for a reinterpretation. The present geography of Protestantism elevates to a wide acceptance the very principles that Luther himself loathed in his 95 theses.

In its dynamism, a strand has emerged, further separating the broader movement called Protestant. This is the Pentecostal movement. As a movement it began in America in the early twentieth century. Pentecostal is a designation for a Christian sect, often fundamentalist, that emphasizes baptism in the Holy Spirit evidenced by speaking in tongues, and faith healing.[18] Pentecostalism can be regarded in the tradition of open expression of dissatisfaction with the conduct of the affairs of the orthodox churches in the management of its followers, especially in the face of the State failure. Borrowing from Karen Armstrong's argument that any major faith has had to undergo constant transformation in order to speak to the peculiarities of modernity, the emergence of the movement can be regarded as a response to the difficult social condition in which people lived.

There is a sense in which the emergence of the Pentecostal movement is directly connected with the emergence of a new economic orientation. Until the 1970s and the early 1980s the Christian scene in the country was dominated by the orthodox churches – Catholic, Methodist, Apostolic, Evangelical Churches of West Africa (ECWA), Church of Christ in Central Nigeria (COCIN) and the indigenous national churches who were identified with the old order of the failing State. Economic collapse opened up the creative energy of Nigerian evangelists who commenced the process of spiritual reorientation as much as economic deregulation revealed the creative ingenuity of the people to learn to physically survive outside the State.

The face of the Nigerian Pentecostal movement reflected two approaches that represented the new and old schools, with the old school remaking itself. However, both approaches reflected what an analyst described as "interpreting religious doctrine far more flexible… these modern-day pastors and so-called prophets practice faith healing and sometimes magic to pry upon the gullibility of their wealthier adherents and the desperation of the poor."[19] Representing these two viewpoints in the Nigeria situation are Bishop Oyedepo, on the one hand, and Pastor T. B. Joshua on the other. Whereas Pastor Joshua ministered to society's losers – the ill and the downtrodden, Bishop Oyedepo geared his sermons to Nigerians' Christian elite. The Pentecostal movement in Nigeria has developed unique features that set it apart from its orthodox counterparts in whose apparent inability to move with the times they came to correct.

The Pentecostal Churches on Economic Matters

The deregulated state and economy caused the deep social crises that defied all the palliatives put in place by the government. This resulted in conflicts in Nigeria since the late 1980s. Of importance here was the inadequacy and suspicion that characterized the government palliative. This triggered the carnage witnessed in Jos in September 2001. The mayhem in Jos was the combination of residual build up from past conflicts, an accumulation of grievances, and the new face of the State in economic and political development. Nigeria's social structure, argued one analyst, is hierarchically prone to generating conflicts from diverse ethnic-cultural interests and goals as well as from the political and economic necessities of survival, as individuals and as identifiable autonomous social groups struggle for advantages.[20]

Jos in Central Nigeria represented this struggle for survival by different groups. The town has been home to numerous groups who came in the wake of the exploitation of tin and columbite during the colonial period. These diversities of population have been the hallmark of its identity until the crisis of the late 1980s began to weigh heavily on the town. The creation of two local governments in Jos in the 1990s and the representation of strong elements of either Christians or Muslims in each government created a situation identifiable along religious lines. Jos Northern Local Government was viewed as belonging to the Hausa who are Muslim and Jos Southern Local Government was largely Christian. However, the situation differs as the different religions intermingle in both local governments. The appointment of a Muslim Hausa as the coordinator of the Poverty Alleviation Programme was seen as an attempt to benefit one group against the other. This triggered the accumulated emotions simmering between the groups with devastating consequences for the whole town.[21]

The above demonstrated the inadequacy of the State and since 1999 the federal government has not been able to solve the problems associated with economic reforms. This partly engendered the growth of the "consolation industry" (whereby people go to church to receive consolation to their problem),[22] the church, with the Pentecostal wing leading, as it became the go between in order to restrain the decay in the society.

An expert on the movement traced its proliferation as being linked to widening poverty while another described modern pastors as doorkeepers of hell controlling the hopes of desperate sinners.[23] The proliferation of these brands of sinners was not the making of the sinners themselves. The whole scenario seemed like a conspiracy between the State and the Pentecostal churches. As the power of the State to provide welfare relief dwindled, the church stepped in to manage the situation.

The most fundamental impact of the Pentecostal churches is the attitudinal change they initiated in the whole society mainly in economic matters. While constantly harping on wealth creation, prosperity, and issues that featured in the social settings, they not only organized workshops, symposiums, talks, and seminars on economic matters, they also led the way in opening businesses and investing in different organizations. As Jide Gbadegesin argues in the next chapter, the lifestyle of the Pentecostal church members is a departure from the orthodox manual of modesty and fastidiousness. Some Pentecostals have even ventured into the political arena.[24] In a replay of the concept of liberation theology in Latin America where priests abandoned the pulpit for politics, Nigeria has instances of the clergy going into politics and contesting offices. In Benue, Taraba, and Ondo States clergymen have been governors. In the current democratic dispensation a Pentecostal pastor established a political party and has contested the presidential elections of 2003 and 2007.

The first area that saw the impact of the Pentecostal churches was in their representation in economic matters and their interest in tackling man's material existence. The Pentecostals jettisoned the view that business was the affair of businessmen and questioned the antiquated morality that had restrained businesses from developing in the past. They promoted moneymaking as a virtue and not as a vice and argued that it could reflect God's glory. Pentecostals argued that the conscientious discharge of the duties of business people is among the loftiest of religious and moral virtues. Through sermons, business luncheons, symposiums and workshops, they encouraged members to believe that it was now time for them to move towards divine abundance. The church had known salvation, divine healing, deliverance, along with signs and wonders, for a long time, they argued. It was now time for the church to embrace wealth.[25]

The Pentecostal churches led the way in establishing various commercial ventures such as business schools,[26] recording companies, publishing outfits, land investment, and development firms, as well as in investment in new generation banks whose members were Pentecostal church attendants.[27] Because of their interests in material matters, the emphasis of most sermons was on prosperity and this consolidated the link between the church and the pursuit of wealth. The lifestyles of the pastors[28] and the kind of sermons[29] they delivered shattered the concept of modesty in all ramifications. These pastors owned businesses, drove customized cars, lived in state-of-the-art mansions and wore designer outfits while constantly encouraging their members to express themselves in these ways.

Apart from the pursuit of wealth and prosperity, the church is also associated with providing solutions to all problems, the performance of miracles and speaking in tongues. As a result of the proliferation of discontents in the society, the approach the churches adopted tended to target vulnerable people. It used the media to advertise how desperate conditions had been remedied through attending their services and other engagements. Thus it had solutions to problems prevailing in the society such as poverty, poor health, barrenness, unemployment, witchcraft, and women and men looking for husbands and wives. The decline in men and women wishing to marry is a product of the insecurity created by unemployment and has little to do with spiritual concerns. The churches have been able to provide some remedies to this problem but at a cost to the beneficiary. In providing jobs, contracts, cures and remedies to problems, the beneficiaries are expected to contribute to the church depending on the nature of the solution. Those who got jobs and contracts courtesy of the intervention of the churches are expected to pay tithes or a percentage of their monthly or annual remunerations.

The Pentecostal churches are mostly city-based institutions. This perhaps is because their kind of audience and business–inclined orientation can only find solace in the cities. Thus they can be found in state capitals, as well as in big and commercially viable towns. Members of the audience inclined toward these churches stay in the urban centers and include the intellectually minded, the middle class, and the nouveau riche. These areas also house a large population of unemployed, which make up the different cadres who regularly attend the programs of these churches.

Part of their reorientation, in line with their economic bent, is the management style and structure the churches adopted. This is because they are not only places of worship, but they also serve as organizations for other business ventures. The founder of the church often monopolizes power and is in control of the finances of the group. The organizational structure and the pattern of investments borrow a lot from the secular world while the church founder is also the president and chief operating officer. Unlike in orthodox churches, where disagreements and break ups were often the result of doctrinal differences, among the Pentecostal churches break ups are caused by financial mismanagement or managerial disagreements. The death of the founder usually creates a power vacuum and a power struggle among intending church leaders.

The Pentecostal churches have worked alongside the changing State in the reorientation of the economic attitude of the people. It has succeeded in removing whatever moral or spiritual hindrance standing in the way of people actively engaging in economic activities. Some of the conduct of these Pentecostal churches has been shocking,[30] but while their impact may not be evident immediately, they have worked to transform the mindset of their members towards accepting a more materialistic minded perspective.

CONCLUSION

The failure of the State in Nigeria initiated a process that consolidated the Pentecostal movement. The view that the movement is profiting from the incapacity of the State has been widely canvassed to discredit the changes the Pentecostals have brought to the Nigerian social scene. What is evident in Nigeria is the reworking of the old State and the orthodox churches whose orientations have been associated with the failures of the past. The new era is characterized by a deregulated State and spiritual sector with the former restricting its role to provide the enabling environment for economic activities initiated by owners of capital, while the latter in the form of the Pentecostal movement is removing the moral and spiritual constraints to the successful operation of the new economics.

The Pentecostals not only encourage, but also lead the way in business and in politics, in some cases directly, while in most cases indirectly through preaching to their members on the appropriate choice of political leaders. The Pentecostal churches have also redefined the passivity associated with

Christians of old who literally took the injunction when hit on the left cheek you should offer your right cheek. They have taken fundamentalism to new heights and have sought to involve themselves in whatever provocation arises within the context of modern Nigerian economics and politics.

Notes

1. Adebayo Olukoshi and Felicia Oyekanmi, "Editorial," *CODESRIA Bulletin* Numbers 1 & 2, Dakar, 2002.
2. The World Bank and the International Monetary Fund were created at Bretton Woods, New Hampshire in 1944. Hence, they are referred to as the Bretton Woods Institutions.
3. Rose Umoren *Economic Reforms and Nigeria's Political Crisis* (Ibadan, Nigeria: Spectrum, 2001), *World Bank Annual Report* (Washington D.C: World Bank, 1994), 82.
4. Quoted in Adoyi Onoja "Deregulating Salvation," *Nigeria Standard,* Jos, June, 6, 9, and 10, 1997.
5. Karen Armstrong, "Where Has God Gone," *Newsweek*, New York: July 12, 1999, 56-57.
6. Patrick Dunleavy and Brendan O' Leary *Theories of the State: The Politics of Liberal Democracy* (London: Macmillan, 1987), 72-204.
7. Ibid., 2.
8. Ibid.,
9. P. B. Evans, D. Rueshmayer and Theda Spokpcol, eds., *Bringing the State Back In* (Cambridge: University Press 1985); Lenin V.I. "The State and Revolution," *Collected Works* 25:293. Moscow: Progress 1980.
10. Immanuel Wallerstein *The Capitalist Economy* (Cambridge: Cambridge University Press, 1979).
11. Malori J. Pompermayer "The State and Dependent Development." *Kapitalistate State*, 1, 1973, 25-27.
12. Fitzgerald Edmund, Valpy Knox, Edgardo Floto and David Lehmann, eds., *The State and Economic Development in Latin America* (Cambridge: Cambridge University, 1977).
13. James F. Petras and Marris H. Morley "Development and Revolution: Contradictions in the Advanced Third World Countries – Brazil South Africa and Iran," *Studies in Comparative International Development* 4, Spring, 1981.
14. Adoyi Onoja "Deregulating Salvation," *Nigeria Standard.* Jos, June, 6, 9, and 10, 1997.

15. Carla Power, "Lost in Silent Prayer," *Newsweek "Is God Dead?"* 1999, 52.
16. Stephen J. Lee, *Aspects of European History 1494 – 1789* (London: Routledge, 1994), 10.
17. V. H. H. Green, *Renaissance and Reformation: A Survey of European History between 1450 and 1660* (London: Edward Arnold, 1962), 124.
18. D. K. Illustrated Oxford Dictionary (Oxford: New Press 1998), 605.
19. Karl Maier, *This House has Fallen, Nigeria in Crisis* (London: Penguin, 2000), 252.
20. Onigu Otite and Isaac Olawale Albert, *Community Conflicts in Nigeria: Management, Resolution and Transformation* (Ibadan: Spectrum, 1999), 19.
21. See Ezekiel Chollom, "Invasion of Beromland: Another Jihad?" in *The Berom News*, Vol. 1, No. 1, 2003, 23.
22. Interview with Mrs. Iberi Odoh 75 years. The term "Consolation Industry" is a direct translation from the Idoma Language.
23. "Postmark Africa," *BBC World Service*, February 9, 2003.
24. Reverend Chris Okotie is a Prominent Pentecostal Pastor and Church Owner. He founded the Fresh Democratic Party F.D.P and contested the 2003 and 2007 Presidential election.
25. "Raising Godly Billionnaires," *Newswatch*, August25, 2003, 9-10.
26. Pelu Awofeso "A Circle of Winners," Af*rica Today,* Volume 10, January 2004, 5.
27. "Highest Paid Pastor, Their Money, Their Life Styles and Their Wives," *Newswatch,* December 23, 2002, 24.
28. Ibid., 25.
29. Ibid., 25; Temitope Oguntokun, "How Pastors Charm Their Followers," *The News*, Lagos, Vol. 20, No. 23, June 9, 2003, 24.
30. "Pastors of Thieves. How Oyakhilome Received Stolen Money," *The News*, Vol. 20, No. 23, June 9, 2003.

Chapter Fourteen

New Religious Movements and the Politics of Nation Building

Olujide Gbadegesin

The emergence, growth, and impact of New Religious Movements (NRMs) have had a profound influence on Nigerian society, especially in relation to their contributions towards nation building.[1] Nigeria had never experienced such a vast and dynamic religious phenomenon until the emergence of the NRMs. If attitudes towards religion and spirituality are declining in Europe as a result of secularism, the reverse is the case in Nigeria where people are deeply or incurably religious.[2] Even though Nigerian leaders have been fascinated by the "secular ideology" of the West, to the extent that a secular clause has been incorporated into the Nigerian constitution, religious plurality and cultural diversity within Nigerian society have not served to support such an ideology. Religion permeates the fabric of Nigerian society, which makes the separation of religion from politics very difficult.

Religion, in general, and the NRMs in particular have contributed considerably to nation building in terms of establishing schools, colleges, and universities. The NRMs in Nigeria have become agents of social and political change. The schools, which they founded, provide moral and religious instructions that are no longer part of the public school curriculum. Through this educational approach, the NRMs have helped to reduce the rate of violence often perpetrated by the youth. Apart from the new dimension of religious experience and expression that the NRMs have created, the great influence exerted on the political discourse of Nigeria has brought about a new awareness in scholarship. This chapter examines the roles the NRMs play in Nigerian socio-economic and political spheres and explores the areas where the NRMs have impacted the nation, especially in the process of nation building.

Defining "NRMs" and "Nation Building"

The term New Religious Movements came into being by the middle of the twentieth century when it was first used in Italy.[3] As congeries of spiritual organizations designated by sociologists, the NRMs have become a part of the global religious landscape.[4] Scholars from different disciplines have produced a vast amount of literature on this new form of religious ideology, but because of its influences on the lives of individuals and what it has exerted on the political life of many nations, there is a need for more research on NRMs. Like any other ideology, the public has received NRMs with mixed feelings. The followers of the NRMs have received them with a positive response, while to others they are simply "deviant" Christians or Muslims.

NRMs are newly formed groups of Christians (and recently those groups have grown to include followers of the Islamic faith, along with followers of various other religions, especially Asian religions) that have adopted practices that radically differ from the old liturgical, doctrinal, and theological ways of looking at reality. According to Eileen Barker:

> An NRM is new in so far as it has become visible in its present form since the Second World War, and that it is religious in so far as it offers not merely narrow theological statements about the existence and nature of supernatural beings, but that it proposes answers to at least some of the other kinds of ultimate questions that have traditionally been addressed by mainstream religions, questions such as: Is there a God? Who am I? How might I find direction, meaning and purpose in life? Is there life after death? Is there more to human beings than their physical bodies and their immediate interactions with others?[5]

Barker described the NRMs in a broad perspective by referring to the common denominators by which the religious groups are recognized globally, but she failed to address their cultural and political impact. Rosalind Hackett refers to the NRM in Nigeria as "an indigenously created religious organization stemming from social and religious encounter, and selecting and combining local and exogenous religious elements in diverse and dynamic ways."[6] She claims that the word "new" is applied because they "do not form an integral part of, or identify wholly with, the major religious traditions…and they emerged after the arrival of the main missionary bodies."[7] While Hackett is right on the time of their emergence, it is also important to analyze their major contributions to the socio-political development of Nigeria.

Nation building is the process of constructing or structuring a society using the power of the state. As Meredith McQuire indicates, "nation building refers to a sense of solidarity and identity as a people."[8] The process aims at unifying the people within the state in order to remain politically stable and viable. Nation building is a conscious process, which may be well planned, but which may also involve the use of propaganda to foster social harmony and economic growth. Politicians are not alone in building a nation. Hence, the NRMs have made their impact felt in that direction.

In Africa, nation building originally referred to the efforts of newly independent nations to mould what they inherited from the colonial authorities, especially territories, which the Europeans carved out without regard to preexisting ethnic or cultural boundaries. The expression of nation building is found in the creation of superficial national paraphernalia such as flags, anthems, national days, national stadiums, national airlines, national languages, and national myths. At a deeper level, national identity is deliberately constructed by moulding different groups into a nation, especially since colonialism used divide and rule tactics to maintain its domination. Religion became part of the identity with European Christian missionaries working hand in hand with colonial officials. The NRMs of Pentecostals/Evangelicals added a new dimension to the relationship between religion and politics by directly getting involved in the process of nation building.

Emergence of NRMs in Nigeria

The emergence of NRMs in Nigeria, with particular reference to the African Independent Churches (AICs), dated back to around the early part of twentieth century. The Aladura movements developed in Nigeria in response to the epidemic influenza, which killed thousands of people, especially in southern Nigeria.[9] During the epidemic, African traditional treatment failed, Western medicine was ineffective, while people's hope and faith began to diminish. Hence, the epidemic spread fast and wide. The worldwide economic depression added more to the hardship of the people and the colonial administration was paralyzed. As a result of the magnitude of the influenza, people gathered together for prayers. It was during one such prayer meeting that a member of the group, Sophia Odunlami (a school teacher), claimed to have seen a vision which communicated the idea that prayer should be said into rainwater and given to the people to drink, to bathe in, and to sprinkle around their premises.[10] Those who believed in the vision and followed the instructions became healed. The positive effect of that prayer led to the formation of a Christian organization, named Precious Stone Society (PSS), which eventually became Christ Apostolic Church (CAC). The church grew rapidly because its' practices and rituals provided a new experience which excited individuals and was acceptable to many people.

It is possible to trace the role of the British colonial power to the popularity of religion in Nigerian politics. The divide and rule system that the British introduced did not favor Nigerians. The British manipulated politics of domination for their own advantage and ended up complicating the fragile nature of the country's multi-ethnic composition. Similarly, the use of ethnic politics on the part of Nigerians to gain political control was characterized by acrimony, intrigue, and treachery. The ethnic and religious rivalry that dominated the colonial period persisted after Nigeria became independent. That socio-ethnic divide was partly responsible for the outbreak of the Nigerian Civil War, 1967-1970, which became one of the bloodiest civil wars in African history. Attempts to use political means to solve peoples' problems failed. Hence, people resorted to religion as a source of empowerment. Tunde Lawuyi asserts that:

> The failure of the state to provide essential services, led to the belief in the civil society that personal and collective problems can be solved religiously by prayers rather than reason, by ritual sacrifices rather than by hard work, or by material means, that is by the creation of tools and 'connections' to serve specific purposes of self preservation.'[11]

Aside from Lawuyi's opinion, religion had become a very important weapon through which people constructed their personal and political identities. This reflects the direct connection of religion and politics in Nigerian socio-political spheres.

Socio-economic changes that characterized the late 1970s and 1980s with the oil boom helped the rapid growth of this charismatic form of Christianity. By the late 1980s when there was a negative economic shift, the result was joblessness, poverty, and a low standard of living. People began to lose hope due to the harsh social conditions and the lack of political stability needed to revamp the economy. Their expectation that politics could solve their economic problems had been crushed. In desperation for solutions, they turned to religions. And, with the charismatic churches flourishing, many people trooped to them, abandoning the mission churches. Focusing primarily on the "Gospel of Prosperity," the Pentecostal/ Evangelical groups raised the hope of the people. What politics could not give, religion offered.

The argument is that the NRMs of the Pentecostal-Evangelical movements emerged within a milieu of political instability, economic recession, and social tension. In their expression of love and loyalty to their country, people sought personal and collective "salvation" through the NRMs. Collective salvation refers to the desire of the Nigerian people to have better political and economic conditions, with religion felt to be the means towards that end. Religion was seen as a practical means of salvaging Nigeria from its political, economic, and social degradation. Leaders of the Pentecostal/Evangelical Christians drew their inspiration from the Bible where Israel was asked to seek the face of God in prayers in humility, and there would be deliverance (salvation) for the land.[12] Hence, in the midst of uncertainties and deteriorating living conditions, many Nigerians embraced religions to solve their economic, spiritual, physical, and psychological problems. Political leaders failed the people due to corruption and bad governance, and religion offered a positive way out.

As in Christianity, religious movements in Islam also emerged in response to Nigeria's poor socio-economic conditions. Muslim leaders such as Sheik Abubakar Gumi and Sheik Ibrahim al-Zakzaky from northern Nigeria accused political leaders of embezzling public funds and mismanaging the country's economy. This economic reason was founded in the marginalization of the *gardawa*, the Qur'anic students, in the Kano labor market, and the growing corruption, consumerism, and inequality produced by the Nigerian oil boom of the 1970s.[13] This poor economic situation overlapped with religious and political protests, which Muhammad Marwa, a learned leader of the Maitatsine group, led. The Maitatsine group attracted a substantial number of urban Muslims because Marwa preached fiercely and fearlessly against the rich, political leaders, and societal moral decadence. Marwa's role was paradoxical. On the one hand, it was that of protest against oppression, the same reasoning for the emergence of new forms of religious expression in Christianity. On the other hand, Marwa was manifesting a "world-rejecting" form of NRMs,[14] a belief in millennium that would usher in the kingdom of God. This meant the triumph of Islam, where human rule would be irrelevant and where there would be an egalitarian society. In spite of his viewpoints, the Islamic NRMs began to gain a stronghold in northern Nigeria.

Demography of NRMs

NRMs are a huge part of the religious groups in Nigeria and their members are distributed all over the country. As it happened in other parts of the world, NRMs in Nigeria were first identified with Christianity. Islam followed in the 1980s with the emergence of the Mai Tat Sine (Maitatsine) group led by Muhammadu Marwa in Kano State.[15] In 1995, the Nasrul-Lahi-il-Faithi (NASFAT) emerged as an Islamic religious movement, with the mission statement: "to develop an enlightened Muslim society nurtured by a true understanding of Islam for the spiritual uplifting and welfare of mankind."[16] Part of the goal of the organization was to promote Islamic education and religious tolerance. The majority of Christian NRMs are in the southern part of Nigeria while the Islamic NRMs are found largely in the north. Since the 1990s, the population of the followers of the NRMs has growing fast. According to statistics, the Pentecostal/ Evangelical movements are 14% of the Christian population, aside from African Initiated Churches (AICs) such as Cherubim and Seraphim, Celestial Church of Christ, and Brotherhood of Cross and Stars.[17] NASFAT, a new Islamic movement, has approximately 1.2 million members within and outside Nigeria.[18]

Since their appearance in the 1980s, the NRMs have acquired approximately four million adherents. Most of these religious movements are Christian-related and documented, but Islamic-related movements are "less common and under-researched."[19] NRM membership consists of more youths and women than men. Qur'anic students of the Maitatsine Islamic group, which perpetrated the religious crisis of 1980, were youths.[20] Amba Oduyoye accounts for why there are more women than men:

> Women spirituality is qualitatively different from that of men because women's experience of socio-economic realities differs from that of men. Similarly, women's dependence on God tends to be expressed more overtly; hence, their dependence on religious beliefs, practices, and ritual is more intensely demonstrated.[21]

It is a universal phenomenon to have more women in religion than men because they have been described as "the primary 'consumers' of religion."[22] Ronke Olajugbu, however, notes a significant shift in this attitude towards women in Nigeria. She observes that "women are allowed with regard to Pentecostal churches in Nigeria, to perform such major functions as preaching, teaching, leading prayers and in most cases, they are allowed to lead churches as Pastors and Evangelists."[23] It is therefore not surprising that women play important roles in the NRMs.

The Relevance of NRMs to Nation Building

The NRMs have contributed immensely to nation building in Nigeria by changing the culture and climate of religious expressions and by altering positively the lifestyles of the majority of people. The NRMs claim to possess the means to unlock people's physical, mental, and spiritual potential without withdrawing from the world.[24] They have effective ways of proffering solutions to the existential needs of their followers, what orthodox churches have been unable to achieve. Francis Cardinal Arinze aptly observes that, there are people in Africa, "who seek in religion an answer to, and a protection against, witchcraft, failure, suffering, sickness, and death. The NRMs seem to them to confront these existential problems openly and to promise instant remedies, especially physical and psychological healing."[25] This shows that people are searching for spiritual answers to their numerous problems.

The NRMs of the Pentecostal Charismatic movements especially manifest the paradox of life as they move from the particular to the universal. The majority of them reject the culture and traditions from which they evolved, but try to contextualize their faith to resonate with the contemporary situation. They lay emphasis on deliverance from evil forces, failures, sicknesses, set backs in social and economic life, and from bad luck as they have come to terms with such cultural mystical powers as witches and ancestral curses that had earlier been denied or ignored by the protestant churches.[26]

People joined these movements for various reasons such as to secure protection from attacks by evil spirits, to seek solutions to problems such as unemployment, barrenness, sickness, loneliness, or spiritual warfare. Indeed, protection against witchcraft and healing from sicknesses appear to be the two strongest motives for most Nigerians joining the new religious movements. Olumba Olumba Obu, the founder and leader of the Brotherhood of the Cross and Star in Nigeria, asserts: "many people are rushing into the Brotherhood of the Cross and Star with the intentions of being healed of their sicknesses or to have an improved condition of life."[27]

Another important area through which the NRMs have impacted the nation is in the area of Africanizing Christianity. The NRMs tried to make liturgy, doctrine, and ritual practices relevant to the people's ways of life. For example, many of the NRMs (Christianity) incorporated into their worship systems elements of African culture. Their services of worship are usually very lively with music, songs, and dance. To minister to all members, many of them use African languages to preach.

Cardinal Arinze describes this situation as "cultural identity search." He elaborates that, "the NRMs can arise or attract because people are searching for meaning when they are feeling lost in a period of cultural change."[28] The search for cultural identity is beneficial to the society because Christianity is being Africanized and people are able to practice their religion based upon their culture without deviating from the original doctrines. In the process, there is also the cultural borrowing from other traditional societies.[29] It is very important to mention that every religion tend to lose its purity as it spreads and encounters other religious ideas and cultures of the world. Each culture practices religion the way it appeals to its socio-cultural settings. For example, all attempts of the jihadists in northern Nigeria to purify Islam were met with stiff opposition from the Yoruba people who held very strong in their traditional religion.

Nigerians' resentment of white domination became manifest after a white bishop was appointed to replace Bishop Samuel Ajayi Crowder, the first African bishop. In response to this non-recognition of African leadership, Nigerian Christians advocated for the establishment of a native pastorate in order to prove to the colonial officials and European missionaries that Africans were capable of running church affairs on their own. Consequently, the Native Baptist Church was founded in 1888, the United Native African Church in 1891, and the African Church Incorporated in 1901. The challenge to the white domination of the church led to the proliferation of African-led churches. The cultural identity search became strengthened in the colonial era when African Christians became more forceful in practicing Christianity in the African way. The establishment of the African Indigenous Religion was therefore a deliberate attempt to deviate from Western culture in order to Africanize Christianity.

It is important to mention that religion played an essential role in the process of politically decolonizing Nigeria. The political decolonization of the country and the religious decolonization of the church went hand in hand. Religion, especially Christianity helped in creating a class of educated elite who became nationalists and the first core of post-independence political leaders. Thus, religion made a significant socio-political impact and transformation, especially after World War II.[30] Religion continues to have influence on political configuration and policy making. NRMs leaders such as the late Archbishop Benson Idahosa, the founder of Church of God Mission International, Pastor Enoch Adejare Adeboye of the Redeemed Christian Church of God, and a host of other Pentecostal and Charismatic Christian leaders are making significant contributions towards nation building. These leaders participate in political debates, they advise politicians, and they encourage their followers to take part in politics. For example, Pastor S. K. Abiara and Pastor Prophet Obadare have, on different and numerous occasions, asked Nigerians to fast and pray for the nation. Pastor Enoch Adejare Adeboye, the General Overseer of the Redeemed Christian Church of God, led his congregation in prayers for the nation several times. The former president Olusegun Obasanjo, many governors, and traditional rulers attended the monthly prayer meetings at Pastor Adeboye's church. The present President Shehu Musa Yar'Adua, although a Muslim, has also visited Pastor Adeboye's church for prayers.[31] This is an indication that there is collaboration between religion and politics in an effort to find peace and stability in the country.

Another contribution of the NRMs to nation building is in the area of health services. It has become increasingly difficult to successive Nigerian governments to provide adequate and quality healthcare for the people. Hospitals are ill equipped, medicines are expensive and scarce, and medical workers are not well paid. As a result, many Nigerian trained doctors and nurses have left the country to find better jobs elsewhere. It was reported in the *British Medical Journal* (BMJ) in 2002, that the government was concerned about the alarming rate at which Nigerian doctors, nurses, and paramedical staff were migrating to overseas countries. They left because of poor salaries, lack of motivation on the part of the government, and poor facilities.[32] Successive governments have failed to invest heavily on health care and the common people are left to suffer from these problems. In the 2007 alone, a startling figure of 37,000 Nigerian medical doctors reportedly left Nigeria for overseas countries.[33]

One of the claims of the NRMs is their ability to provide healing and deliverance for their followers through spiritual power. In open-air services or on television programs, adherents of the NRMs give testimonies of the genuine, complete, and effective cure and deliverance they received. Many people claim that they have been healed of deadly diseases such as cancer and HIV/AIDS through the healing power of the NRMs and survivors have been able to go back to work and to contribute to nation building.

It is commonly said that health is wealth and in a physiologically, psychologically, and sociologically healthy environment, there would be harmony, peace, progress, a vibrant economy, and a stable government.

A large number of NRMs have begun to provide social services such as job opportunities and education to Nigerians. In this respect, the NRMs complement the government's efforts on social services, which are essential to national development. The NRMs have established many schools in order to accommodate and educate many young people who are qualified for university education, but who have not been admitted because of limited admission. For example, Covenant University (1999), Joseph Ayo Babalola University (2006), and Fountain University (2007) founded by the Nasrul-Lahi-il-Faithi Society (NASFAT) are schools providing education to students who would have otherwise been without university educations. Many jobless youth have been taken off the streets and turned away from lives of crime by receiving educations and becoming meaningful members of the society; some even having the potential to carry out leadership roles in the future. Those who graduate have ample opportunities for employment, as they become a major part of the country's workforce. The schools have also provided employment opportunities for many people thus helping the government to reduce the unemployment rate and improve the living standard of the people. However, good as the efforts of the NRMs seem to be, it gives room for the capitalist economy where the 'haves' continue to have more and the 'have- nots' become poorer; the Nigerian government has failed to provide sound and quality education to its citizens because of the little financial allocation it gives towards education.

NASFAT also established a soft-drink company called Nasmalt, whose profits are used to support the poor. The organization has an entrepreneurship program, a clinic, a prison-outreach program, a task force on HIV/AIDS, and a travel agency. Although some conservative Muslims believe that the activities of NASFAT are secular, un-Islamic, and are *haram* (forbidden), NASFAT argues that these are some of the ways by which Islam could attract the people, especially in this world of social and economic competition.[34]

The NRMs strengthen the concept of communal relationship or peaceful co-existence. Living as a community with common aspirations and goals is in agreement with the Yoruba traditional worldview of a*jogbe* (co-residency) and *ajobi* (co-sanguinity).[35] This practice helps to forestall violence, encourage national integration, and promote collective responsibility and security. Through the NRMs, people from different ethnic and cultural backgrounds come under the same religious umbrella. For example, the northern Muslims who used to dissociate themselves from the southern Muslims now work together within the same religious organizations. This is in a way promoting national integration.[36] As part of their ideologies, members of the NRMs adopt the practice of calling each other 'brother' or 'sister.' This concept of brotherhood and sisterhood is a hallmark of identity that promotes a sense of belonging. This practice did not exist in older, traditional Christian or Islamic gatherings. The Pentecostal and Charismatic movements in particular are noted for the way members address themselves as brothers and sisters.

The NRMs of Pentecostal Christians and Muslim NASFAT are making conscious efforts to bring about unity, peace, and political stability. Bishop Oyedepo's Winners' Chapel thrives very well in northern Nigeria, an Islamic stronghold. The Redeemed Christian Church of God, Deeper Life Bible Church, Christ Apostolic Church, Cherubim and Seraphim Church, Celestial Church of Christ, all founded by the Yoruba people, receive followers from other Nigerian ethnic groups. The NASFAT, which started in Ibadan, has gained followers from not only Nigeria, but also from about twenty-five nations of the world.

The NRMs have been able to reach the outside world through media technologies. Nigerian newspapers and magazines constantly focus on the NRMs' activities. Some of the preachers have columns where they write religious articles on a regular basis. Matthews Ojo points out that, "in modern Africa, never before has the role of the media been more central to the formation of religious consciousness and identity than as it is at present."[37] Ojo believes that the media not only acts as a channel of information, but it is also increasingly becoming the purveyor of ideology, taste, and consciousness of other cultures of the world. He further claims that, the mass media is bringing about a complex re-ordering of patterns of human interaction across space and time. Hence, global communication has greatly aided the internationalization of charismatic renewal all over the world. Ojo also indicated that the patronage the NRMs pay to the media give the latter the opportunity to survive economically, especially since the Nigerian government no longer subsidizes many of the media houses.

Legitimizing Political Hegemony through Religious Identity

Hans Mol, in his pioneering work on religion and social identities asserts that, "not only religion sacralizes identity by myths, rituals and the processes of objectification and commitment, but that, indeed, a religious symbol system can be the main fabric of identity itself."[38] The crisis of ethnic and religious identity has created polarity in Nigeria given the multi-ethnic and multi-religious composition. Religious groups define themselves in terms of 'we' versus 'them.' Christians and Muslims identify very strongly with their religions, they develop a sense of brotherhood, and they distinguish themselves from others on religious lines. They have used religion, whether directly or indirectly, to not only polarize the country, but to also cause conflicts and crises. While the government cannot promulgate a law prohibiting religion, it is imperative to de-emphasize the use of religion in political matters. Continuing emphasis on religious differences does not promote unity and it does not facilitate the process of nation building. People often use religion as the basis of their identity, but it should not becloud their political obligations and it should not preclude them from participating in political matters.

Jacob K. Olupona shows that different religious groups, especially Christians and Muslims, preach a new politico-religious order based on the tenets of their faith alone. He buttressed his point by showing an example of a crisis that followed identity creation in Nigeria:

> The central committee of Jamatul Nasril Islam set up a committee to study the nature of relations among the various Muslim bodies in the country. The committee was mandated to look into the causes of conflict and misunderstanding among Muslim preachers of different sects. In a communiqué issued at the conclusion of its consultations, it condemned such practices as "the mixing of sexes in the schools and particularly the universities. Most importantly, the council called on the Federal Government to establish "a national radio station for the propagation of Islam."[39]

The events in some African nations, particularly in the Nigerian Third Republic, show that religion is a big factor in the crafting of self-identity. Religion, both organized and implicit, played an active role in the 1983 elections.[40] In his campaigns in Ilorin and Sokoto, Shehu Shagari of the National Party of Nigeria (NPN), urged the people not to vote for infidels, apparently referring to the Christian presidential candidate, Chief Obafemi Awolowo, the presidential candidate for the Unity Party of Nigeria (UPN). At the end of the elections, religion became a symbol of expressing conflicting political ideas. In his acceptance speech Shehu Shagari thanked God for "a peaceful presidential election." He, however, remarked that "it was only in 1983 that God made Nigerians to see the light and made them follow the path of grace and unity in diversity within our great nation, and it was the first time we cut across ethnic boundaries and hero-worshipping."[41]

To further show his bias for Islam and to legitimize his rule, Shagari set up a department of Islamic Affairs in the president's office. The aims and objectives of the department were not clearly defined, but as soon as Shehu Shagari was sworn-in, he made every attempt to keep his promises to the religious lobbyists and pressure groups who had contributed to his political success. In some northern states where the NPN had a landslide victory, Islamic principles and practices dominated their government structures. The federal government did not oppose or criticize that mixture of religion and politics since the president himself was a Muslim. There was an attempt by a Muslim group to stop the recital of the national pledge of allegiance and the singing of the national anthem because they were composed in a Christian language.[42] The Shagari era widened the existing religious divide because more Nigerian Muslims now performed the pilgrimage to Mecca on government sponsorship than in any other administration.[43]

Nigeria is not the only African country where religion and politics interface. Many African leaders manipulated religion, and especially the Christian NRMs, to achieve political gains in the 1990s. For example, Frederick Chiluba, the president of Zambia, declared Zambia a Christian nation in 1996. As Elias K. Bongmba indicated:

> Zambia presents an unusual situation because President Chiluba is an avowed "born again" Christian who uses his office to promote Christianity - he has even declared Zambia to be a Christian nation. The churches of Zambia, in fact, played a key role in the defeat of Kenneth Kaunda. Chiluba proclaims Christian Zionism, testifies about his faith at crusades, and in the past entertained ministers and evangelists at the presidential Palace.[44]

Although Chiluba tried to use Christianity to consolidate and legitimize his position in power, many people felt he went too far to declare Zambia a Christian nation. In Ghana, the Pentecostal churches moved close to Jerry Rawlings and provided his regime with religious and moral legitimacy. By 2000, however, there was no substantial socio-economic improvement. In fact, the churches challenged Rawlings' abuse of power and his unconstitutional acts. The outcome was that Rawlings developed an antipathy towards them.[45] In Togo, the civilian government of President Eyadema of Togo exploited the Christian churches to legitimize his rule for almost forty years.[46] Many Pentecostal and Evangelical churches aligned themselves with certain political leaders to gain popularity, thereby enhancing their charismatic leadership, promoting their church as well as their own brand of Christianity. Similarly, the presidents who have used Pentecostal and Evangelical machineries were determined to gain political power. Zimbabwean President Robert Mugabe, despite being a Roman Catholic, has sought closer ties with some Pentecostal and Evangelical leaders through his second wife and his sister who are members of the Zimbabwe Assemblies of God Africa (ZAOGA). On June 26, 2006, Mugabe presided at a Zimbabwe National Day of Prayer in Harare.[47] Although prominent Catholic and Anglican leaders boycotted the event, it featured members of the Evangelical Fellowship of Zimbabwe and the Zimbabwe Council of Churches, which both include Pentecostal and Evangelical members.

In Nigeria, General Ibrahim Banagida's regime had been characterized by chaos, corruption, assassination, disregard for the rule of law, and promotion of the Islamic religion. By using dictatorial military power, Babangida "adopted several measures that were considered to favor Muslims and to threaten the secular nature of the Nigerian state."[48] A good example was the issue over Nigerian membership in the OIC in 1986. The OIC issue generated heated politico-religious debates and almost threatened the unity and peaceful co-existence of Nigerians. To explain his action, Babangida declared that Nigeria's membership of the OIC was beneficial because it would allow for bilateral trade relations between Nigeria and Arab nations. This would enhance and promote the socio-economic situation of Nigeria. He also argued that it would place Nigeria into a position to borrow money without interest.

Christians and people who followed the political debate interpreted Babangida's action (a Muslim) as an attempt to subvert the political situation of Nigeria. Given his actions, people believed that Babangida was only reinforcing the Islamic hidden agenda to Islamize the whole country. They believed also that he used Islam and the OIC to curry the favor of the Muslim world and to legitimize and consolidate his position in power. In addition, people believed the attempt was to strengthen the Shari'a debate and legacy and by so doing gain outside support from Islamic organizations all over the world.

There was a great hope when Ibrahim Babangida stepped aside as the president in 1993, but the authoritarian rule of his successor, Sani Abacha (1993-1998), caused much pain, oppression, and anxiety for the people of Nigeria.[49] In his desperate ambition to rule, Abacha tried to eliminate all who opposed him, including Olusegun Obasanjo. On the basis of an acclaimed coup, Abacha imprisoned his Chief of Staff of Armed Force Ruling Council, General Oladipo Diya, Olusegun Obasanjo, Dr. Beko

Ransome Kuti, and M. K. O. Abiola, the winner of the annulled June 12, 1993 election results.

Obasanjo declared that he had become a "born again" Christian while in the prison. After he was released, Obasanjo became not only a presidential candidate but also the president of Nigeria. As soon as Obasanjo was sworn-in on May 29 1999, he called all the leaders of the Pentecostal/Evangelical movements and the Mission-Oriented churches for prayer vigil at the Presidential Villa at Aso Rock in Abuja, the capital city of Nigeria. The NRMs of Pentecostal and Evangelical groups who saw Obasanjo as a symbol of Christian control on political power strongly supported him. There was the high expectation that a Christian leader would bring an end to all forms of oppression, misrule, and end the Muslim monopoly on political power. However, nothing significantly improved on the political and economic fronts during Obasanjo's rule.

In the 2003 elections, Obasanjo of the People's Democratic Party (PDP) and Chris Okotie of the Justice Party (JP) claimed a divine mandate to become the president of Nigeria. In December 2003 when Obasanjo attended the yearly Holy Ghost Congress, the elated Pastor Enoch Adejare Adeboye (the General Overseer of the Redeemed Christian Church of God) declared the visit of the president as the fulfillment of God's prophecy on the church.[50] According to the This Day newspaper reporter, Chikas Ohadoma who witnessed the occasion, "for the first time the President, Chief Olusegun Obasanjo openly led his people to seek the face of God and thanked God for a number of things He has done for him and the nation as a whole."[51] Obasanjo not only used Christianity to legitimize himself in power, but he also raised money to build an interdenominational (ecumenical) church at Abuja, where there already existed a mosque.[52]

While a presidential candidate in the 2007 elections, Shehu Yar'Adua, although a devout Muslim from northern Nigeria, attended the Redemption Camp of the Redeemed Christian Church of God on March 18, 2007. Most newspapers' headlines, especially the *Daily Sun,* declared the presence of Yar'Adua at the Redemption Camp as one who was "seeking for prayer support."[53]

Conclusion

This chapter has addressed the relevance of NRMs, especially in Christianity and Islam to nation building. The chapter has shown some reasons why NRMs are gaining popularity in Nigeria today. In spite of negative conceptions of scholars and certain people about them, these religious groups have contributed meaningfully to the political and economic development of the country. The NRMs, especially the Pentecostal/ Evangelical movements are acceptable to Nigerians because they appeal to the spiritual, physical, and emotional needs of the people. Their practice allows people to express themselves in worship and attempts to proffer solutions to the existential needs of their members by putting emphasis on the message of healing and deliverance.

It is important for both Christian and Islamic groups of NRMs to find practical ways of securing peace, promoting unity, and supporting a stable political dispensation. By preventing violence, the NRMs are making a profound contribution towards peaceful religious co-existence and nation building. Nigeria, as a developing country, needs the unity and cooperative efforts of all Nigerians irrespective of their religious orientation. The NRMs have all the chances to influence their followers against corruption, which is eating deep into the fabric of Nigerian society. To a large extent, morality needs to be addressed and more attention must be paid to justice. The NRMs can assist the government in promoting justice.

Notes

1. Some scholars believe that the incidence of NRMs coincided with the decline in the economic situation of Nigeria, which turned Oil boom era to Oil doom, while scholar like I. J. Hackett argued for the earlier appearance of the NRMs and put the date at late nineteenth century. See Rosalind I. J. Hackett, "New Religious Movement in Nigeria," in *Religion and Society in Nigeria: Historical and Sociological Perspectives*, eds., Jacob K. Olupona and Toyin Falola (Ibadan, Nigeria: Spectrum Books Limited, 1991), 282.
2. John S. Mbiti and Bolaji Idowu agree that African people are incurable religious. John S. Mbiti, *African Religions and Philosophy* (London: Heinemann, 1969), 36-38 and Bolaji Idowu, *Olodumare: God in Yoruba Belief* (London: Longman Publishers, 1962), 5.
3. The term, "New Religious Movements" was first coined in Italy before it found its way into religious language and discourse. See Eileen Barker "'NRMs': Their Incidence and Significance" in *New Religious Movements: Challenge and Response*, eds., Bryan Wilson and Jamie Creswell (London: Rutledge, 1999), 16.
4. Wilson, 1.
5. Eileen Barker "NRMs": Their Incidence and Significance" in, *New Religious Movements: Challenge and Response*, eds., Bryan Wilson and Jamie Creswell (London: Rutledge, 1999), 16.
6. Hackett, 283.

7. Ibid.
8. Meredith McQuire, *Religion: The Social Context* (Belmont, CA: Wadsworth Publishing Co., 1987), 164.
9. Ogbu Kalu ed., *Christianity in West Africa: The Nigerian Story* (Ibadan, Nigeria: Day Star Press, 1978), i-x; and Joseph Omoyajowo ed., *Makers of the Church in Nigeria*, ed., Joseph Omoyajowo (Lagos, Nigeria: CSS Bookshops Limited 1995).
10. David Oláyíwolá, "Joseph Ayo Babalola (1904-1959)," in *Makers of the Church in Nigeria*, ed., Joseph Omoyajowo (Lagos, Nigeria: CSS Bookshops Limited, 1995), 137-150.
11. Tunde Lawuyi, "Nigeria in the 1980s: Religion and National Integration," in Olupona and Falola, 232.
12. The Holy Bible, II Chronicles 7: 14.
13. Lawuyi, "Nigeria in the 1980s," in Olupona and Falola, 256; and Jacob Olupona, "Religion and Politics in the Second Republic," in *Nigeria's Second Republic: Presidentialism, Politics and Administration in a Developing State*, eds., Victor Ayeni and Kayode Soremekun (Lagos, Nigeria: Daily Times Publications, 1988), 124-125.
14. Roy Wallis, "Three Types of New Religious Movements," in *Cults and New Religious Movements: A* Reader, ed., Lorne L. Dawson (Cambridge, MA: Blackwell Publishing, 2003), 36-44.
15. For more information on Maitatsine and Marwa the leader, see Toyin Falola, *Violence in Nigeria: The Crisis of Religious Politics and Secular Ideologies* (Rochester, NY: University of Rochester Press, 1998), 137-149.
16. "About NASFAT," http://www.nasfat.org/about.php
17. "Religion by Location," http://www.adherents.com/adhloc/Wh_245html
18. Eliza Griswold, "God's Country," *The Atlantic*, March 2008, 4.
19. Hackett, "New Religious Movement in Nigeria," 282-283.
20. Falola, 141-146.
21. Mercy Amba Oduyoye, "Feminist Theology in an African Perspective," in *Paths of African Theology*, eds., Rosino Gibellini (New York: Orbis Books, 1994), 167.
22. Elizabeth Puttick, Women in New Religious movements, ibid. p. 45.
23. Olajugbu Oyeronke, Women in the Yoruba Religious Sphere. (New York: University of New York Press. 2003), 45-52.
24. Roy Wallis, Three Types of New Religious Movements, ed. By Lorne L. Dawson, Cults and New Religious Movements: A Reader. 2003, 45

25. Cardinal Arinze, The Challenge of New Religious Movements a paper presented at the Cardinals Meeting, April 5, 1991 in an address to the April 4-7 consistory at the Vatican. pp. 4-5.
26. Matthews Ojo, "Pentecostalism, Public Accountability and Governance in Nigeria," paper presented at the workshop on Pentecostal-Civil Society Dialogue on Public Accountability and Governance on Monday October 18, 2004 at the Agip Recital Hall, MUSON Center, Onikan, Lagos, 2004: 7.
27. Olumba Olumba Obu, Those Who Will Go to Hell (Calabar: Brotherhood Press, n.d.), p. 19. This information was collected from Friday M. Mbon's contribution to NRMs. His title is: "A New Typology for African New Religious Movements," December 15, 1984, http://www.dci.dk/index.php?view=article&catid=157&id=551%3Aa-new-typology-for-africaas-new-religious-movements&option=com_content&Itemid=36.
28. Cardinal Arinze, "The Challenge of New Religious Movements," a paper presented at the Cardinals Meeting, April 5, 1991 in an address to the April 4-7 consistory at the Vatican. 5.
29. Jacob Olupona, ed. , *African Spirituality: Forms , Meanings and Expressions*, 2000: xv-xvii
30. Ojo Matthews "Pentecostalism, Public Accountability and Governance in Nigeria," 1.
31. Uche Usim, "Aso Rock: Yar'adua, Jonathan visit Adeboye, seek prayer support," in *Daily Sun*, March 18, 2007. http://www.sunnewsonline.com/webpages/news/national/2007/mar/18/national-18-03-2007-04.htm accessed on March 18 2007
32. Abíódún Raufu, "Nigeria Concerned over Exodus of Doctors and Nurses," *British Medical Journal* (BMJ), 2002, 325: 65 (6 July). http://www.bmj.com/cgi/content/abridged/325/7355/65/a
33. "Some Stats on Nigerian Doctors," *Grandiose Parlor*, http://grandioseparlor.com/2008/07/some-stats-on-nigerian-doctors
34. Eliza Griswold, "In God's Country," in http://naijablog.blogspot.com/2008/03/in-gods-country.html, March 4, 2008. Accessed today 06/30/2008.
35. A. Akiwowo, "Ajobi and Ajogbe: Variations on the Theme of Sociation" (Inaugural Lecture Series 46, Ile-Ife: University Of Ife Press, 1983).
36. Muslims in the Northern part of the Nigerian nation were said to be discriminatory as far as the issue of their Islamic faith is concerned when they relate with Muslims from the South West especially the Yorùbá Muslims. Frank A. Salamone shows why this is so in the article tilted, "Ethnic Identities and Religion," in Olupona and Falola," 45–65 where he quoted Forde and Kabbery who stressed that, "a nineteen century king of Oyo, Atiba, may

have acted like a Muslim at Ilorin, but after his coronation, he reinstated the annual cycle of ancient rites and also built temples to the Òrìsà. This syncretistic attitude to life that is mostly found among Yoruba people in dealing with religion has not changed significantly, which might account for the reaction of the Muslims in the North to treat their Muslim brothers and sisters from the southwest so."

37. Ojo, "Pentecostalism, Public Accountability and Governance in Nigeria," 5.
38. Hans Mol, *Identity and the Sacred: A Sketch for a New Social-Scientific Theory of Religion* (New York: The Free Press, 1977), 25-27.
39. Olupona, J. K. Olupona, "Religion and Politics in the Second Republic," in *Nigeria's Second Republic: Presidentialism, Politics and Administration in a Developing State*, eds., Victor Ayeni and Kayode Soremekun (Lagos: Daily Times Publications, 1988), 130
40. Ibid., 131.
41. Ibid. See also, Chief Adebo on Constitution Drafting Committee he headed, *West Africa,* No. 3453, October 17, 1983, 2424.
42. Olupona, "Religion and Politics in the Second Republic,"123.
43. Jude C. Aguwa, Religious Conflict in Nigeria: Impact on Nation Building," *Dialectic Anthropology*, 22: 1997, 335-351.
44. Elias K. Bongmba, "Spiritual Development: Its Thought and Public Praxis," *Review Essays in African Studies Review*, 43, 2, 2000, 122.
45. Paul Gifford, *African Christianity: Its Public Role* (Bloomington, IN: Indiana University Press, 1998), 111.
46. Matthews Ojo, "Pentecostalism, Public Accountability and Governance in Nigeria," a paper presented for discussion at the workshop on Pentecostal-Civil Society Dialogue on Public Accountability and Governance on Monday October 18, 2004 at the Agip Recital Hall, MUSON Center, Onikan, Lagos, 1.
47. "Pew Forum on Religion and Public Life," July 3, 2008, http://pewforum.org/surveys/pentecostal/africa. The essay focuses on three important nations: Nigeria, Kenya, and South Africa.
48. Helen Chapin Metz, ed., *Nigeria: Country Study* (Washington DC: CPO, 1991), 224.
49. Karl Maier, *This House has Fallen: Nigeria in Crisis* (Cambridge, MA: Westview Press, 2000), 39-74.
50. Chikas Ohadoma, "Ushering in 2003 with Showers of Blessings," *This Day*, January 1, 2003, http://www.thisdayonline.com/archive/2003/01/01/20030101fea01.htm
51. Chikas Ohadoma, "Ushering in 2003 with Showers of Blessings," *ThisDay*, January 1, 2003.

52. A. K. Karka, "National Ecumenical Center: Story of the Fund Raising," in *The Rochas Foundation*, http://www.rochasfoundation.org/pdf/National%20 Ecumenical%20Centre.pdf
53. Uche Usim "Aso Rock: Yar'adua, Jonathan visit Adeboye, seek prayer support," in *Daily Sun*, March 18, 2007, http://www.sunnewsonline.com/ webpages/news/national/2007/mar/18/national-18-03-2007-04.htm.

RELIGION AND THE JUSTICE SYSTEM

CHAPTER FIFTEEN

THE JUDICIARY AND RELIGIOUS FREEDOM: CONSTITUTIONAL GUARANTEE OF THE SECULARITY OF THE STATE

AKIN ALAO

An examination of a constitutional provision for the secularity of the Nigerian State reveals the gross inability of the various instruments of government to grapple with, and accommodate two differing views on the essence, nature, and character of political authority. As Peter Clarke rightly observed, Christianity and Islam are religions that seek to make politics serve a higher truth, reality, or divine kingdom, but in very different ways.[1] In Christianity, the "Kingdom of God" is not of this world and political authority is something secular and transient. Among the Pentecostal faithful, Christianity does not even allow for full time participation in elective and competitive politics because of its tendency to distract believers' attention from the kingdom of God. However, the Christian position accommodates the separation of Church and State, a secular state and pluralistic forms of constitutional government.[2] According to Bishop John Onaiyekan, Nigerian Christians have:

> Taken for granted that the State was ruled according to God's will, and that religious authorities were the authentic interpreters of this will, which the temporal ruler had to obey. When the idea of a secular state emerged, it referred to State in which the temporal, secular ruler enjoyed full autonomy as a ruler with no control from religious or spiritual authorities.[3]

As a result of the changing character, nature, and dynamics of the Nigerian State, secularism has come to mean, at least to the Christians, making religious faith a strictly personal affair. According to Elisabeth Zoller, the basic teachings of both Voltaire and Thomas Jefferson on the relationship between church and state are that religion is a private affair and must remain so.[4] The Catholic Archbishop of Lagos, Anthony Cardinal Olubunmi Okogie, believes that secularism means, "when you are in a position of trust, forget about your religion because it's a private affair between you and your God. If you want to bring religion in, let it be after office hours."[5] This position does not take into consideration the fact that religion imposes the greatest influence on an individual either in private or official capacities. There is no way that a person's religious belief and confessions would not affect their worldview and therefore their understanding and interpretation of social reality. Religion has what Emile Durkheim describes as a dynamogenic quality in that; it has the capacity to not only dominate individuals, but also to elevate them above their ordinary abilities and capacities.[6]

Most, if not all, of the various collective representations of modern society have their origins in religion. Max Webber asserted that a religious idea system influences individual thoughts and actions completely and in totality.[7] Leading Islamic scholars, clerics, and opinion leaders in northern Nigeria, including Ibraheem El-Zakyzaky [8] and Sheik Abubakar Gumi[9] believed that a secular state is a negation of the Shari'a and therefore harmful to the development and expansionist aspirations of Islam. For instance, Sheikh Gumi believed that secularism is another word for atheism.[10] Yet another scholar, Ibrahim Suleman, submitted that secularism is hostile to Islam and seeks to undermine Islamic values, supplant the Islamic laws with those of its own and deface the sanctity of the Muslim society.[11] The Jamaat Nasr-al-Islam[12] founded in 1962 by the Sardauna of Sokoto, Sir Ahmadu Bello, as an umbrella organization for major Islamic movements in Nigeria, defined "secularism as a system of social teachings or organization, which allows no part for religion."[13]

In contrast with Christianity, Islam regards the caliphate or the Islamic empire, as the direct determinant of political authority that must be employed to serve the greater interest of religion. This position best explains the establishment and role of the Sokoto Caliphate in northern Nigeria between 1804 and 1900.[14] The gross inability of constitutional provisions to guarantee the secularity of the state should be seen as a major contradiction of the state and its obvious helplessness to remain neutral. Some members of the political class (in both religions), exploit this condition to promote personal political interests that are thinly disguised as religious interests. The partisan debate on the exact meaning of the term secular brought to the fore, the limited possibility of the constitution to guarantee its protection by the State. According to the Christian members of the 1979 Constitution Drafting Committee (CDC), the term "secular" meant that the constitution should not favor any religion at the expense of the other, and that the government must be neutral in religious matters.

Secularism believes that morality should be based on the well being of mankind in life, to the exclusion of all considerations drawn from a belief in God or any spiritual existence. Muslims in the CDC opposed the use of the term "secular" in the proposed constitution.[15] In their opinion, this would have meant giving constitutional weight to the belief that Nigeria is a godless state. To arrest the drift toward anarchy or possibly an extension of military rule, a compromise was reached, which subsequently became the section providing for the non-involvement of any religion in the exercise of political authority by the state. As such, section 17 of the 1979 constitution provided that "The state shall not adopt any religion as the state religion no more no less."[16] This meant that the State, not its functionaries (in their personal capacities), shall not practice one religion in preference for or at the expense of another. Section 31(1) specifically provided that:

> Every person shall be entitled to freedom of thought, conscience and religion, including freedom to change his religion or belief and freedom, either alone or in community with others and in public or in private, to manifest and propagate his religion or belief in worship, teaching, practice and observance.[17]

It seems that the addition of this particular constitutional provision, in a supposedly religiously neutral state, was beyond the knowledge and comprehension of the drafters of the constitution. It is even possible that they preferred to provide enough playing grounds for all and sundry, not minding what religious fanatics and bigots could make of the provision, which gave such large latitude for the negative use of religion in politics.

The creators of the 1979 Constitution also believed that one of the practical and most functional means of promoting national integration in a multi-ethnic and multi-confessional society was the prohibition of all forms of discrimination on the grounds of origin, sex, religion, status, ethnic, or linguistic association. The spirit of the constitution found expression in the preamble, where it was stated that Nigerians must live in unity and harmony as one indivisible and indissoluble sovereign nation under God. Despite the attempt to separate religion from the state, the framers of the constitution still wanted religion to legitimize existing moral, social, cultural, and economic arrangements. They were not prepared to see religion as an alternative system of authority and values that could potentially be in conflict with politics. In hindsight, the framers of the 1979 Constitution seemed to be oblivious that the two global religions of Christianity and Islam could come into conflict at certain points with political authority in the context of the State. Sheikh Gumi presumably referred to this when he prophesied the ultimate emergence of two religious parties to contest future elections in Nigeria.[18] As founder and spiritual leader of Jamat-Nasr-al Islam, Gumi believed that there were two ways of being political in the Nigerian way, one, which espoused the idea of a secular society, and the other, which looks to Islam to provide the blueprint of the new social order.[19]

The establishment of a Federal Shari'a Court of Appeal under the 1979 Constitution would have given immediate legitimacy to Sheikh Gumi's prophecy. Christian members of the Constituent Assembly who were called to read thoroughly and debate the draft constitution strongly condemned the attempt to smuggle into the constitution, what would have undermined the secularity of the political authority of the Nigerian State. It was further argued that the creation of a Federal Shari'a Court of Appeal would introduce into the structure of the federal judiciary what would amount to an unhealthy mixture and undue legal and institutional advantage to Muslims. After protracted debates, a compromise was arrived at by the creation of State Shari'a courts in those states where people wanted them. The compromise also permitted the Federal Court of Appeal to empanel three of its judges, knowledgeable in Islamic law, to hear all cases formerly decided by a Shari'a Court of Appeal of a state.

The debates of the Constituent Assembly were not only self-serving, but also petty.[20] The most controversial issue, which generated the greatest emotion and national tension, was the debate over the possible introduction of the Islamic legal system of Shari'a at the federal level. The Christian Association of Nigeria (CAN) had alleged that the state Shari'a courts had gone beyond their mandate and had been involved in matters concerning the interests of Christians in the northern states. It therefore demanded that the federal government redress the discrimination by restoring relations with the state of Israel, set up a welfare board for Christian pilgrims, pay Church leaders who settle matters between Christians and concerning Christians, allow Christians to build their places of worship in any place of their choice, establish ecclesiastical courts fully funded by the federal government and in matters relating to law and political administration Christians should be treated separately from Muslims.[21] The Shari'a issue exposed the extent to which the political class could use religion to manipulate, hoodwink, and rouse sentimental reactions of the unsuspecting masses of the people.

In spite of the furor in the debate over the role of the state and religion on the eve of the Second Republic, Alhaji Shehu Shagari's administration was relatively free of Christian- Muslim religious and political tension. The nature, character, and profligacy of the political class that wielded political authority during this period, remarkable, did not provoke any antagonistic religious claims. Politicians, irrespective of their religious affiliation or confession, acquired enormous national wealth through the award of generous and pre-paid government contracts and by means of the machinery of the party. Bala Usman was right when he observed that the Second Republic was remarkable for the several attempts to manipulate religious sentiments for selfish ends by the National Party of Nigeria (NPN), the Unity Party of Nigeria (UPN), and the so called Kaduna Mafia.[22] Alhaji Dahiru Bauchi declared that Sheikh Gumi was given to making his fortune by fanning the embers of differences, capitalizing on that to attract government recognition and patronage, and "his sickness is looking for power or else, how can someone who is sincere claim that politics is better than prayer, that to vote is more important than to go on pilgrimage."[23]

Between 1979 and 1983, the Shagari administration was unable to grapple with the problems associated with governing a multi religious state because of the inherent contradictions. The administration, being a subset of the dominant power elite, could not mediate class contradictions and impose a viable hegemony on the Nigerian society. According to the Italian Marxist, Antonio Gramsci, "the essential ingredient of the most modern philosophy of praxis (the linking of thought and action), is the historical-philosophical concept of hegemony."[24] He defined hegemony as cultural leadership, which the ruling class uses in contrast to coercion that is exercised by legislative or executive powers, or expressed through police intervention.[25] It became obvious that the Second Republic was doomed because the contradictions assumed catastrophic dimensions at a time of a high level of public indignation against the state. It was generally believed that the coup of December 31, 1983 that removed Shagari from power was an attempt by the elite in the military to redeem the sagging image of the political class and to act as a stopgap measure against any possible revolutionary reaction by the impoverished and diseased Nigerian masses.

By condemning all representative government institutions at the state and federal levels, the Buhari/Idiagbon administration became generally estranged from the people. In an attempt to learn about public opinion, the government turned to traditional institutions and religious organizations. This approach encouraged the further involvement of religion in essentially political matters, disregarding the professed neutrality of the government towards religion. The arrogance of Buhari and Idiagbon, the intransigence and insensitivity of the administration they led, and the double standard noticed in their style of governance, were enough to erode the basis of their leadership of the Nigerian State. Within a short time, the Buhari/Idiagbon regime was removed from power.

Ibrahim Babangida became the head of state at a time when Nigerian society was showing signs of doubt in the ability of their military to deliver. Within a short time, Babangida was able to convince the people that he had a vision and perhaps a mission in government. As rightly suggested by Omar Farouk, Babangida's decision to endorse the upgrading of Nigeria's observer status in the OIC to full membership, was motivated by his personal desire to allay the fears among Muslims in the North.[26] It was speculated that Babangida was under the intense influence of Christian military officers of Middle Belt extraction in taking decisions of grave national consequence.[27] Babangida's decision was, however, unilateral, as the issue of the OIC was not discussed in either the Armed Forces Revolutionary Council or the cabinet. This again confirms how religion could influence the State through the preference of an important state actor.

Nigeria's membership in the OIC, through what the critical press called the "back door," was considered damaging to the assumed commitment of the government to the separation of state from religion. Christians in Nigeria condemned the government and described the decision as an "unprecedented and dangerous effort to elevate Islam to the status of a state religion."[28] Accordingly, the Catholic Laity Council of Nigeria once declared:

> It is clear that in no circumstance can the Nigerian government be a member of the OIC without flagrantly breaching and desecrating the constitution of Nigeria. Undoubt-

> edly, the secularity of Nigeria and ... membership of OIC are mutually exclusive and permanently incompatible.[29]

Again, the Babangida administration promulgated Decree No. 26 of 1986 to expand the jurisdiction of the Shari'a Court of Appeal to embrace all civil proceedings involving questions of Islamic law.[30] The Decree was intended to ease the process of the Shari'a Court system and facilitate prompt dispensation of justice. The 1989 Constitution endorsed the provisions of the 1986 Decree and upheld the expansion of jurisdiction of Shari'a Courts to all non-personal civil proceedings involving questions of Islamic law.[31]

It is remarkable that under the 1989 Constitution non-Muslims were no longer subject to Shari'a law. This provision supplanted section 242(2)(e) of the 1979 Constitution.[32] The clause empowered the Shari'a Court of Appeal in a state to decide questions of Islamic personal law, if all parties to the proceedings (whether or not they were Muslim) had requested to be tried under such a law. Indeed, southern Christians had accepted the establishment of Sharia Courts as a lawful exception to the ideal of official abstention from essentially religious affairs, provided the courts were limited to Muslims or any other person who preferred to be tried under Shari'a law.

Babangida's thinly disguised efforts to re-appraise the relationship between the State and religion, especially Islam, were spuriously attacked when it became obvious that Islam was fast becoming the religion of the ruling power elite and therefore the State. The most articulate reaction to Babangida's mixing of religion with politics was the *Guardian* editorial of March 20, 1987 where the editor stated:

> Where there are many contending faiths, as in Nigeria, secularism is the most prudent policy of the state. Our constitution recognizes this fundamental truth. It guarantees freedom of worship, and states categorically that there shall be no state religion. What this means is not that the state should treat all religions equally but that it should be indifferent to all religions. The more assistance government grants religious organization, the more it tends to assume the state of official state religions, and the more militant its disciples become.[33]

The government's reaction to criticisms of its involvement in essentially religions affairs could be conceptualized in two ways. First, while formally upholding secularity as a concept, the government rejected any restricted interpretation of the concept that opposed official involvement in religious affairs. Second, the administration condemned what Babangida described as an unwholesome and treacherous interpretation of secularity, which either neglected the existence of religion in the country or treated it with disdain.[34] What seemed paramount in Babangida's thinking was how to use religion as a strong influence to rebuild the Nigerian State. In his words:

> Government will consequently continue to discharge all its current obligations to the present major religions. It is our belief that religion as a normative tool, if correctly handled, can play a significant role in our continuing efforts to solve our numerous problems and combat the social ills that plague the country.[35]

It would seem that the continuing patronage of religions by the Babangida administration was a deliberate effort to divert people's attention from the inadequacies of government and from its hidden religio-political agenda. From all indications, the administration showed excessive preference for Islam and all it stood for. The government became involved in the manipulation of religion to keep the masses under control. The promulgation of Decree No.6 of 1989 that replaced the Nigerian Pilgrims' Board with a Nigerian Pilgrims' Commission was an attempt to hit back at Christians who believed that the State should not be involved in religious matters such as pilgrimages to the holy lands of the two major religions. The new commission was set up to cater exclusively to Muslims.

Although attempts by the CAN to challenge the decree in a court of law were unsuccessful on technical grounds, the presiding judge, however, averred:

> I am not in any doubt that Decree No. 6 of 1989 is discriminatory and ... capable of causing disaffection among the generality of Nigerians particularly Christians, thus, generating a situation where the very desirable aim of peace, order and good governments may be in jeopardy.[36]

A flurry of criticisms against the federal government's promulgation of Decree No. 6 of 1989 led to the dissolution of the Nigeria Pilgrims' Commission in 1991. Since then, each state has been coordinating pilgrimages to the holy lands, though the federal government has continued to provide medical and consular services. The endorsement of, and preference for one religion by the Babangida administration adversely affected inter-religious relations in Nigeria. The secularity of the state by any definition was clearly violated and the guarantee of legal protection was circumscribed by decrees that removed the jurisdiction of the courts.

At the risk of over emphasis, the June 12, 1993 presidential election, the annulment of its results, and the aftermath of the government's decision to do so, marked a turning point in the politics of religion in Nigeria. Despite the strained relations between Christians and Muslims during the Babangida era, a Muslim-Muslim ticket won the presidential election. Both candidates were Muslims and Christians voted for them. The resounding victory of M. K. O. Abiola over Alhaji Tofa in all the six geographical zones and across religious boundaries was an eloquent testimony to the failure of the military to polarize the country along religious lines. The annulment caused tension and the country became sharply divided not on religious, but primarily on an ethnic basis. The immediate reaction of the people was the restoration of democracy by allowing the winner of the election to rule. The struggle for the actualization of the mandate of June 12, 1993 was also championed by many Christian organizations, even better than the efforts of the Supreme Council for Islamic Affairs - an organization in which Abiola was the vice-chairman.

It is necessary to critically examine why a Muslim-Muslim ticket was so popular among Christians who had just been brutalized by the arrogant disposition of Babangida towards the concept of secularity. Section 10 of the 1999 Constitution states that the "Government of the federation or of a state shall not adopt any religion as state religion."[37] In addition, section 38 (1-3) guaranteed the right to freedom of thought, conscience, and religion. Section 38 (1) was the exact reproduction of section 31 (1) of the 1979 Constitution as cited above. Section 260 (1-2) provided for the establishment of the Sharia Court of Appeal, as well as the establishment of the Federal Capital Territory of Abuja. The Sharia Court of Appeal shall, in addition to such other jurisdiction as may be conferred upon it by an Act of the National Assembly, exercise such appellate and supervisory jurisdiction in civil proceedings involving questions of Islamic personal law. It shall therefore be competent to determine any question of Islamic personal law regarding marriage, will, custody, and where all the parties to the proceedings are Muslims.[38]

Section 275 established the Sharia Court of Appeal in a state to have jurisdiction on similar matters as the Sharia Court of Appeal for the Federal Capital Territory Abuja.[39] It would seem that the decision to give constitutional support for the Sharia Court of Appeal was based on the need to provide enough access to justice, bearing in mind the level of education in the country. At both the federal and state levels, the Sharia Courts of Appeal were to have jurisdiction over civil cases. However, on January 27, 2000, the governor of Zamfara State, Sanni Ahmed, picked a hole in the constitution to introduce Shari'a Law in all its ramifications (civil and criminal). A strict construction of the law and constitution would suggest that the governor, by so doing, breached a provision of the constitution to fulfill an electoral promise.

Many other northern governors have followed Ahmed's lead to highlight the limited possibility of the constitution to guarantee the secularity of the Nigerian State. In theory, the Shari'a guarantees the exclusion of non-Muslims from its' laws and sentences, but in practice, there are indications that overzealous Islamic vigilante groups do not recognize the fundamental rights of individuals. The case of Livinus Obi, an Igbo Christian based in the commercial city of Kano, who was given fifty strokes of the cane by a group of miscreants who were enforcing the Shari'a law, is an example of how the Shari'a has been misapplied.[40]

The argument is that while no clause of any of the Nigerian constitutions provide for the secularity of the state, there are adequate provisions for the protection of a citizen's basic freedom to profess and practice any religion of his choice. As a fundamental right, freedom of religion is deemed most essential and according to Justice Kayode Eso (JSC), it is considered a primary condition to a civilized existence. The specific clause of successive constitutions provided that every citizen shall be entitled to freedom of thought, conscience, and religion, including the freedom to change their religion or belief and freedom (either alone or in community with others, and in public or in private) to manifest and propagate their religion or belief in worship, teaching, practice, and observance.

The constitution further provided that no person attending any place of education shall be required to receive religious instruction or take part in or attend any religious ceremony or observance, if such instruction, ceremony or observance relates to a religion other than his own, or religion not approved by his parent or guardian. It would seem that the constitution was attempting to democratize the system of education when it provided that no religious community or denomination shall be prevented from providing religious instruction for pupils of that community or denomination in any place of education maintained wholly by the community or denomination.

These constitutional provisions reflect an awareness of the complications of governance in multi-cultural societies, where a balance has to be held between freedom to practice one's own belief and the interests affected by those practices. As Justice Walker in the Williamson case submitted, every one has the right to choose and practice any religion. No one can be forced to adopt any form of religion. However, the corollary is also provided for, that freedom to manifest one's religion or belief shall be subject only to such limitations as are prescribed by law and are necessary in a democratic society in the interest of public order, health, or morals or for the protection of the rights and freedoms of others. The constitution succeeded in making clear and unambiguous provisions for the protection of both an absolute right to hold a belief and a qualified right to manifest a belief. The courts, as arbiters of the law, are saddled with the constitutional responsibility of mediating between these interests and in so doing ascertain if there have been any violations to an individual's right to manifest a belief.

The low level of educational sophistication and the naivety of the civil society have both contributed to the scandalously low percentage of social-welfare cases in the Nigerian courts. In spite of the activities and encouragement of Human Rights Organizations and other positively motivated non-governmental groups, the majority of Nigerians are still not persuaded to use the courts as a shield to protect themselves against the violations of their fundamental rights by the state. There are but very few judicial interventions in cases bordering on denial of religious freedom. The locus classicus was the *Medical and Dental Practitioners' Disciplinary Tribunal v. Okonkwo*, in 2001, which gave the Supreme Court of Nigeria a rare opportunity to pronounce on religious freedom when it was called upon to determine the constitutionality of the refusal of a patient to have a blood transfusion because of his religious profession as a Jehovah's Witness. Justice Emmanuel Ayoola (JSC) in the lead judgment averred that:

> The right to freedom of thought, conscience or religion implies a right not to be prevented, without lawful justification, from choosing the course of one's life, fashioned on what one believes in, and a right not to be prevented, without lawful justification. The sum total of the rights to privacy and of freedom of thought, conscience or religion which an individual has, put in a nutshell, is that an individual should be left alone to choose a course for his life, unless a clear and compelling overriding state interest justifies the contrary. (The) law's role is to ensure the fullness of liberty when there is no danger to public interest. Ensuring liberty of conscience and freedom of religion is an important component of that fullness.[41]

The implication of the judgment was that it asserted the right of the patient to refuse any medical prescription that is contrary to their religious profession or belief.

In the Ojonye case of 1983 which was a clear violation of freedom to profess and hold on to a particular religious belief, the presiding judge affirmed that it would be a violation of Section 35 of the 1979 Constitution to compel anyone to perform a custom, which was contrary to their professed religion or belief. Everyone is entitled to manifest and propagate their religion or belief in worship, and to teach, practice, and observe the tenets of the religion. This ruling was all that was needed at that time to establish the abhorrence of compulsion in religion by the state.

The Nigerian courts and constitutions frowned upon membership in associations that were considered secret in profession and activities. Sections 39 and 35 of the 1993 and 1979 constitutions respectively guaranteed the right to freedom of thought, conscience, and religion, but with provisions against the formation of or membership in secret societies. The 1979 constitution defined a secret society in section 35(4) as:

> A society or association not being solely cultural or religious body that uses secret signs, oaths, rites or symbols, whose meeting or activities are held in secret and whose members are under oath, obligation or other threats to promote the interest of its members, or to aid one another under all circumstances without due regard to merit, fair play or justice.[42]

This definition was, later, transferred to the interpretation of section (s.349) of the 1995 Constitution.

In *The Registered Trustees of the Rosicrucian Order (AMORC) Nigeria* v. *Henry Awoniyi, Gabriel Abikoye, ECWA Productions Limited and Caxton Press (W.A.) Limited,*[43] the Supreme Court of Nigeria held that AMORC was a secret society closely associated with mysticism, astrology, knowledge, or use of the supernatural through scientific studies and experiment and the use of astral projection from what is written in their various publications. There are many other similar organizations that practice mysticism and which would fit into this definition of secret society contained in section 35 (4) of the 1979 Constitution. The Murtala/Obasanjo military administration began the war against secret societies when it was realized that government business was being conducted in a isolated fashion to the extent that merit and fair play had little or no relevance. Many federal and state officials, judges and judicial officers, military officers and male administrators as well as business magnates were professed members of secret societies. This took a heavy toll on the performance of government businesses, which became intolerable to the new military leaders.

CONCLUSION

This chapter has examined the issue of secularism in Nigeria as it is provided for in the constitution. It has been argued that successive governments have struggled with the concept of secularism and religion. From all indications, it is difficult for the state to separate itself from religion because those people who adhere to religion are also members of the political society and taxpayers' money is being expended on religious matters. From time to time, the government involves itself in religious activities. It has often manipulated religion as a tool to control the people.

In spite of the belief and optimism of successive generations of Nigerian leaders, it is unhistorical for religion to promote national unity and integration in a post colonial, multi ethnic and multi-confessional society. The courts are, however, adequately equipped in terms of the preparedness of their officers on the bench and in the bar to use the provisions of the constitution in protecting the fundamental rights of every citizen in the practice and profession of their faith or belief. Maintaining the secular status in the constitution does not preclude the people from practicing a religion of their choice, but the justice system is in place to deal with any religious or constitutional issues or crises as they arise. Although Nigeria has experienced several religious riots, the judiciary has maintained religious freedom as contained in the constitution.

Notes

1. Peter B. Clarke, "Religion and Political Attitude since Independence," in *Religion and Society in Nigeria: Historical and Sociological Perspectives*, ed., J. K.Olupona and Toyin Falola (Ibadan, Nigeria: Spectrum Books, 1991), 217.
2. Ibid. 218.
3. Matthew Hassan Kukah, *Religion, Politics and Power in Northern Nigeria* (Ibadan, Nigeria: Spectrum Books, 1993), 228.
4. Elisabeth Zoller, "Laicite in the United States or the Separation of Church and State in a Pluralist Society," *Indiana Journal of Global Legal Studies*, Vol. 1, Issue 2, Summer 2006, 561-594.
5. Kukah, 228.

6. George Ritzer, *Sociological Theory* (New York: McGraw-Hill Companies, 1996), 93-95.
7. Ibid.
8. Zakzaky led the Nigerian Muslim Brothers (Shiites), which eventually became a radical Islamic brotherhood inspired by the teachings of Yatollah Khoemeni of Iran and Hasa al banna of Egypt. For details see, Joseph Kenny, "Sharia and Christianity in Nigeria: Islam and a "Secular" State," *Journal of Religion in Africa*, Vol. 26, Fase 4, November 1996, 338-364.
9. Sheik Abubakar Gumi was once the Grand Qadi of the Northern Region. For details on the life and career of this renowned Islamic scholar, see Toyin Falola, *Violence in Nigeria: The Crisis of Religious Politics and Secular Ideologies* (Rochester, NY: University of Rochester Press, 1998), 117-129. On his role in the emergence of radical Islamic sects and organizations especially during the military regime, see Kukah, 214-225.
10. Clarke, *Attitude,"* 227.
11. Kukah, 228.
12. The Jama'atu Nasril Islamiyya was a mega Islamic organization founded by the late Ahmadu Bello, Sardauna of Sokoto and first premier of the Northern region, to extend the frontiers of Islamic influence in Nigeria and educate Muslims about the tenets of their faith in a plural and federal state. For details see Falola, 105-107.
13. Ibid., 229.
14. Sa'ad Abubakar, "The Established Caliphate: Sokoto, the Emirates and their Neighbours," in *Groundwork of Nigerian History*, ed., Obaro Ikime (Ibadan, Nigeria: Heinemann, 1980), 303-326.
15. Clarke, 227.
16. Constitution of the Federal Republic of Nigeria, 1979, Section 17.
17. Ibid., Section 31 (1).
18. Kukah, 218.
19. Ibid., 220.
20. Toyin Falola and Julius Ihonvbere, *The Rise and Fall of Nigeria's Second Republic 1979-84* (London: Zed Books, 1985), 26.
21 "Christian Association's Views," *New Nigeria*, January 16, 1986, 7.
22. Y. B. Usman, *The Manipulation of Religion in Nigeria, 1977-1987* (Kaduna, Nigeria: Vantage Publishers, 1987), 12.
23. Kukah, 220.
24 Lynne Lawner, ed., *Antonio Gramsci: Letters from Prison* (New York: Harper Collophon, 1975), 55, cited in Ritzer, *Sociological Theory*.
25 Ibid.

26. Omar Farouk, "Religion and Politics: A View from the North," in *Transition without End*, ed., Larry Diamond, Anthony Kirk-Greene and Oyeleye Oyediran (Ibadan, Nigeria: Vantage Publishers, 1997), 509-534.
27. They are better known as Babangida boys for the roles played in the coup de'tat that ushered in the regime in August 1985.
28. Chief Bola Ige was quoted as saying that the duality could not have been contemplated by the framers of the constitution who bent backward over to accommodate the religious sensibilities of the North during the debates.
29. "Resolutions Passed by the Catholic laity Council of Nigeria on the Issue of Nigeria's Unconstitutional Membership of the Organization of the Islamic Conference," *Nigerian Tribune February 28,* 1986, 15.
30. Federal Republic of Nigeria, "Constitution Suspension and Modification (Amendment) Decree No 26, 1986 in Supplement to Official Gazette, 73 No. 59 of 25th November 1986, 309-313.
31. The Constitution of the Federal Republic of Nigeria, 1979 (Lagos: Federal Government Press 1979), Section 24 (2).
32. For details, see the Constitution of the Federal Republic of Nigeria 1989
33. "Babangida's Agenda for the Crisis," *The Guardian,* March 20 1987, 8.
34. "Religion-Weapon of Social Mobilization- Babangida," *New Nigerian,* January 23, 1986, 1.
35. "Babangida on Religion," *New Nigerian,* October 23, 1988, 2.
36. Commentaries of Justice Olaseinde Silva of the Lagos High Court as cited in the *Nigerian Tribune,* May 11, 1989, 3.
37 Federal Republic of Nigeria Constitution of the Federal Republic of Nigeria 1999 (Lagos: Federal Government Press, 1999).
38. Ibid.
39. Ibid.
40. For details of many other instances of religious intolerance in the Shari'a states, see the Annual Report on International Religious Freedom 2001 as submitted to the committee on International Relations US House of Representatives and the Committee on Foreign Relations, US Senate by the State Department. This is available at http://www.house.gov/international_relations/
41. *Medical and dental Practitioners' Disciplinary Tribunal v. Okonkwo [2201] 19 WRN 1.*
42 Federal Republic of Nigeria, The Constitution of the Federal Republic of Nigeria, 1979 (Lagos: Federal Ministry of Information, 1979), section 35 sub section 4.
43. Here the appellant as plaintiff sued the respondent and cross appellant for libel, which allegedly arose from three published issues of a news maga-

zine called *Today's Challenge*. The offending articles were published in the March/April, May/June and July/August editions of the magazine. In the first edition under reference, the Rosicrucian Order (AMORC) was variously described as secret and sinister. The May/June edition called it satanic in teaching and doctrine, while the July/August edition described H Spencer Lewis as a liar, hypocrite, swindler egoistic charlatan and a man without any modicum of honor or integrity. AMORC sued the publishers of the magazine and claimed ₦10 million as special and general damages.

CHAPTER SIXTEEN

PEACE, SPIRITUALITY, AND JUSTICE: NIGERIAN STYLE

TERESA A. BOOKER

Christians and Muslims in Nigeria have clashed over the presence and implementation of a modified version of Shari'a since 1999. With twelve states implementing the Shari'a, it is difficult to suggest when the religious-based violence will subside. For Muslims, Shari'a not only provides order, but it is a sign of obedience to God as well. For Christians, it is cruel and excessive, particularly when decisions can (and often do), result in painful floggings, amputations, or death. Revenge and retaliation, carried out by both parties and spawned from differing viewpoints, exacerbates long-standing animosities and keeps these wounds raw, precluding all chances for healing. Succinctly put, the followers of the Prophet Muhammad and the People of the Book do not see eye to eye on all matters. Moreover, the seeds for the "next Rwanda" are as good as sown in Nigeria unless communities make an effort to incorporate their traditional, ethnic, and spiritual ways of achieving peace and justice into their daily lives.

The purpose of this chapter is to describe how various groups in Nigeria perceive right and wrong. Using examples from ethnic groups (such as the Yoruba, Anang, Ibibio, Igbo, and the Tiv), as well as religious groups (Muslims and Christians), this chapter seeks to demonstrate how a group's concept of a god affects how it perceives justice and, consequently, treats victims and offenders. A brief background concerning the history of Nigeria and its court system will precede examples of how spirituality shapes the lives of various groups.

In 2002, a 31-year old Muslim called Amina Lawal Kurami (hereafter known as, simply, Amina Lawal) became pregnant. Instead of celebrating her new status as a new mother, she was forced to defend her life in a Nigerian court of law. Lawal was convicted under Shari'a justice as an adulteress because she became pregnant out of wedlock. During her defense, she implicated Mohammed, her boyfriend of 11 months, as a more than willing participant. She added that, although they indeed had intercourse, the two had planned to marry until his family learned that she had been twice divorced and forbade the marriage to take place.[1]

Despite Mohammed's indictment as a co-conspirator in the very same crime of "unlawful intercourse" as Lawal, the court did not make so much as a gesture of considering testing his DNA to verify paternity: Mohammed had only to deny that he ever had intercourse with Lawal to have his side of the case dropped, under Islamic law.[2] According to the law, "if a man denies under oath that he has had sexual intercourse with a woman, [it] is often considered sufficient proof of his innocence." Lawal was unable to disprove his testimony because she could not "provide four independent and reputable eye-witnesses to declare that she did not consent to sexual intercourse."[3]

For her punishment, Lawal was sentenced to having her body "buried up to the neck and stoned" until dead.[4] The ruling brought a storm of responses. Olufunmilayo Para-Mallam asserted, "Anybody who commits a crime against our religion should be judged according to the Koran" while the prosecutor who helped to convict her said, "She deserves to be stoned to death...because pregnancy in a woman who is not known to be married is clear evidence of extramarital sex."[5] To many Nigerians, especially Christians, the punishment was outrageous; it was a violation of the legal system of the country. Therefore an outcry followed the pronouncement of the punishment. The people and government of Nigeria responded in a strong way to oppose the carrying out the punishment. The responses by the international community were equally forceful. Christian organizations and officials from various countries voiced their categorical opposition to the sentence.[6] Amnesty International indicated, "We have continually asked the Nigerian authorities not to introduce punishments which amount to ill-treatment and torture under new laws based on Shari'a."[7]

As Peter Paris shows, scholars have always agreed that religion permeates every dimension of African life:

> Where ever the African is, there is his religion: he carries it to the fields where he is sowing seeds or harvesting a new crop; he takes it with him to the beer party or to attend a funeral ceremony; and if he is educated, he takes religion with him to the examination at school or in the university; if he is a politician he takes it to the house of parliament. Although many African languages do not have a word for religion as such, it nevertheless accompanies the individual from long before his birth to long after his physical death.[8]

Nigeria is a prime example of where religion is carried into politics, and it has become difficult to separate them. Muslims are approximately half of the Nigerian population, found especially among the Hausa and Fulani ethnic groups who dominate the northern part of the country. Christians dominate the southern states. According to Human Rights Watch, "Muslims and Christians are distributed more evenly in the central parts of Nigeria known as the Middle Belt, as well as in parts of the southwest, where the dominant ethnic group, the Yoruba, is made up of both Muslims and Christians."[9] This religious division came into being with the effective introduction of Christianity at the end of the nineteenth century when European missionaries penetrated the southern part of Nigeria. During the colonial period, the British allowed evangelization to take place in the south, but did not permit the penetration of Christianity to the North in order to prevent religious conflict and to ensure a smooth and successful colonial administration.

Brief History

The initial decision of the creation of the Islamic court caused a schism between Muslims and non-Muslims within Nigeria. According to Bolanle Awe, before the British colonized the country, Nigeria was populated by at least three hundred different ethnic groups that formed their own social entities. She is of the opinion that "each was organized to mediate conflicting interests, to ensure that different groups within the polity had an input into how it was organized, and to reflect their views and interests."[10] With the help of the Royal Niger Company, Britain began exploring Nigeria and staking its claim to her. After twenty years of surveying, Britain took over the company's territorial holdings in 1900 and made Nigeria an official colony by 1914 when Frederick Lugard, the governor, amalgamated the Northern and Southern Protectorates.[11]

Nigerian went through several constitutional changes in the process of moving toward self-government. For example, in the Richard's Constitution of 1946, Nigeria was divided into three distinct regions: North, East, and West. The regionalization was for political reasons, but the North was bigger in size and population than the two southern regions. The regionalization also turned out to be a convenient religious divide for Nigeria. The British made a clear distinction between the northern Muslim half of the country and the southern half (a practice which, incidentally, continued until the 1950s). In fact, the British were so impressed with how the "emirs and viziers collected revenue and dispensed justice" and by the "architecture, durbars and horses, the speed of the cavalry, and tone of skin color of the Fulani" that they "concluded that [those were] a non-African people with a culture worthy of protection and preservation."[12] As a result, they enacted a protectionist policy, which barred Christian missionaries from operating in Muslim dominated areas of northern Nigeria.

The British also supported a division in the justice system. Under British rule, separate courts were established for Muslims and non-Muslims. Muslims were allowed to have their cases heard before Shari'a courts while customary courts addressed the needs of everyone else. With regard to the former, Shari'a courts "had jurisdiction only over matters of personal status law, such as divorce, inheritance, and domestic disputes."[13] Repulsed by practices they considered savagely harsh and "repugnant to natural justice, equity and good conscience," the British did allow the practice of Shari'a to continue only when "certain aspects of it [such as amputations] were modified or restricted."[14]

The clash between Christians and Muslims between 1999 and 2000 mostly stemmed from the governor of Zamfara, Sani Ahmed Yerima, promulgating a law to expand the jurisdiction of Shari'a to include cases of criminal law as well as those of personal status. The enactment of this law took placc a year after President Olusegun Obasanjo (a Christian) was elected to office. Devout Muslims greeted the act with exuberance. However, it not only had the unfortunate timing of occurring as the country was just returning to a democratic rule, but was also replicated by other eleven governors in northern Nigeria. Although Human Rights Watch reports that "state governments have not attempted to coerce non-Muslims into being tried by Shari'a courts," in general, when Shari'a is administered to non-Muslims elsewhere, it is viewed as an inappropriate and unjust behavior on the part of the state and its administrating officials.[15] Furthermore, not only is the implementation of Shari'a offensive to indigenous people, it is also repugnant to Christians who were among those acknowledged by the Prophet Mohammed as the People of the Book and completely exempted from the *hudad* [punishment].[16]

In chapters 7 and 8, Mukhtar Bunza and Saadatu Liman both argued that because the Shari'a is an integral part of Islam, its implementation should not cause any conflict. However, in chapter 9, Julius Adekunle elaborated on the series of violence that erupted and the magnitude of the casualties as result of the implementation of the Shari'a. The conflicts only demonstrated how divided Nigeria was on the Shari'a issue. The eight-year rule of President Obasanjo was plagued with conflicts, violence, and insecurity, raising the issue of peace and justice. It is important, however, to examine the implications of the Shari'a to the justice system in Nigeria.

How Spirituality Shapes the Lives of Muslims

Amina Lawal was not the only one brought before the Shari'a court, but her case made tremendous news within and outside Nigeria. Christians, civil rights activists, and liberal minded Nigerians in addition to the international community were involved in denouncing the death sentence. Lawal's sentence was eventually overturned after twenty-four months. Prior to the reversal of the verdict, a court official outlined for Western reporters the nature of the sentence, explaining that Muslim men would be chanting "God is great," while stoning the woman to death.[17] While this may seem incongruous, the motivation behind the behavior is somewhat more apparent in light of a Nigerian spokesman's comment: "We don't care what International organizations say [because we are] only accountable to God."[18]

To show the monotheistic nature of Islam, Muslims say, "There is no god but Allah and Mohammed is his prophet."[19] This doctrine is one of what is commonly referred to as the five pillars of Islam. Those who abide by the word of Allah consider the Qur'an holy and the contents within it to be Allah's will for man's actions as revealed to the Prophet Muhammad. In fact, Muslims believe that the Qur'an commands them to seek upright behavior and to prohibit any act that is offensive to Islam; in short, they are to avoid all practices and behaviors considered to be unjust.[20]

With regard to the judicial process, Islam requires prior notice before incriminating and punishing any behavior. As a Muslim woman, Lawal and her boyfriend were well aware of the crime of adultery and how their community defined it. Under Islam, the burden of proof rests with the accuser rather than the accused, and the existence of the child (and the absence of any marriage license) was the proof.

According to Ogbu Kalu, Shari'a "does not permit the relativist, liberal theology of Christians..."[21] Hence:

> it is not allowed for a person to beg for another who has been brought before a court for the offence of theft or zina punishment. It is compulsory to punish them with Hadd punishment if they are found guilty. Even if they swear not to do it again; and they change to good people. Because the issue of *Hadd*, if it is before an Imam and the suspect is found guilty, this is *Allah's right*; it is not proper for a person to save another from *Hadd* punishment.[22]

This also explains the equally exuberant responses from Christians regarding the final outcome of Lawal's case. While Christians know that their God hates a lying tongue, hands that shed innocent blood, a heart that devises wicked plans, feet that are quick to run to evil,[23] and are instructed to "not spread false reports,"[24] give pervert testimony,[25] or accept bribes,[26] they take comfort in knowing that the wicked will not go unpunished because what a man sows, he will also reap.[27]

Spirituality, Justice, and the Indigenous Peoples

The Yoruba

Since precolonial times, the Yoruba in southwestern Nigeria had established a mechanism of conflict resolution and moral dispensation of justice in which they sometimes employed the services of the ancestors and gods. An approach for resolving conflict was to send emblematic messages to sue for peace. Kings, chiefs, lineage and family heads, as well as elder members of the society, carried out judicial functions. In cases of divorce or misunderstanding, the two parties were expected to state their case and trust that fair and impartial justice would take place. The Yoruba people still believe that it is not appropriate to settle a matter in the absence of the person that is most connected with the case. And, in the Yoruba culture, it is wrong to pronounce judgment by listening to only one side of the case. According to a Yoruba proverb, *A gb'ejo apa kan da, agba osika ni* ("A person who makes a judgment after hearing only one side of a case is a most wicked judge"). This shows that they believed in a legal system comprising both a fair hearing and fair justice. Each party in the dispute was given equally opportunities to defend themselves and judgment is rendered based upon the case presented. At the same time, there were specific punishments for all categories of offenders.

The Yoruba believe in a Supreme Being whom they call Olodumare, the creator. There is no one like him. Olodumare is considered king and just; hence he is known as *oba a dake dajo* ("King who dispenses judgment in silence"). According to the Yoruba, Olodumare knows everything and "there is nothing hidden from him."[28] However, he "is neither so remote nor unconnected that He does not intervene in affairs on earth."[29] According to Awe, under the traditional Yoruba system, the ruler "was never a dictator" but had to share his powers with a "council of chiefs who represented the interest of the community in its different modes.... There were also provisions for other segments of the society. Women chiefs were appointed to sit in council with the other chiefs to represent women's interests, or they had their own separate council."[30] Also, the Ogboni or Osugbo society performed judicial, political, and religious functions. They often acted as the intermediary between the ruler and the council of chiefs. The Yoruba judicial system did not recognize a lawyer, but a witness and the right judgment would be pronounced if witnesses made clear and truthful statements.

The Anang

The Anang people of Calabar constitute the second largest Ibibio-speaking ethnic group in southeastern Nigeria. Religion permeates the social and political structure of the Anang. They say that their god, Abassi, is "omniscient and omnipresent" and rules over mankind, the universe, and the souls of the dead with the help of "more than thirty spirits." However, Abassi "lacks ultimate omnipotence," because evil spirits such as witches are able to usurp his power.[31] Perhaps it is no coincidence, that there is no central authority figure among the Anang. Unlike in other societies, justice among the Anang was the entire community's responsibility.[32] A group of individuals, called the *esop,* meets weekly and is composed of elderly men and women.[33] Although women are present, they may only participate when they testify as witnesses or if they are called upon to advise the court on a proper verdict in the case of another woman. Children are also barred from participation unless they have a specific role to play as witnesses. The plaintiff and defendant address the court following the payment of a "small utterance fee," which the judges use to purchase palm wine. The drinking of palm wine is a common practice, especially after the adjournment of the court.

Like the Yoruba, the Anang have legal proverbs, which they use to speckle their testimony. In his extensive research of proverbs among the

Anang, John Messenger indicated that litigants could persuade judges by using proverbs to support their testimony.[34] All audience members listen carefully to the proverbs that are used to make one's case.[35] An example of a legal proverb states: "If a dog plucks palm fruits from a cluster, he does not fear a porcupine." This proverb is can indicate that the defendant had a previous experience with a particular activity beforehand. Specifically, in Messenger's example, the proverb was used in the case of a thief who was presumed to be the "logical suspect" in a robbery. The thief was exonerated when he defended himself with a counter proverb, which stated that, "a single partridge flying through the bush leaves no path." This two-fold defense served to not only imply that the robbery had no witnesses but that (in a context that seems to make sense only to the Anang) the accused thief had no one present in the court to sympathize with him.

The interpretation of any legal proverb is, however, crucial to its judicial application. According to Messenger, when the *esop* itself initiates a case, the chief justice speaks as the plaintiff:

> The *ekpe ikpe* and those in the audience pay rapt attention to the litigants... Outbursts of applause mark the course of a well-presented accusation or defense. Listeners are especially appreciative of an original or little known proverb that captures their imagination and is cleverly introduced at a crucial moment.[36]

The interplay of religion and proverbs was apparent in the Anang traditional judicial system and it worked very efficiently until the coming of the Europeans. The British introduced the English judicial system, but they were not able to completely eliminate some of the religious beliefs and practices as far as justice and peace were concerned in the Anang society.

The Igbo

Like other Nigerian communities, the Igbo evolved and applied an indigenous justice system, which was intermixed with spirituality. The early Christian missionaries and colonial officers realized that the Igbo were closely attached to religion and the justice system. For example, Arthur G. Leonard remarked that, "among the Ibo [Igbo], religion and law are so closely interwoven that many of the most powerful legal sanctions are derived directly from the gods."[37] Although the British studied the Igbo religion *vis a vis* their legal system, it did not stop them from introducing the English-style justice system to the people. In *Things Fall Apart*, Chinua

Achebe demonstrated that the Igbo evolved a unique and complex society, in which oracles and elders played significant roles in the justice system long before the arrival of the Europeans. For example, he mentioned how the oracle dictated the banishment of Okonkwo and how those who violated the Week of Peace were punished. In his comments on *Things Fall Apart*, Dave Vautin argued that, "the European viewpoint on the governmental and legal system was formed on the basis of a class system superimposed over the traditional Ibo approach of the seniority system within the tribe."[38] The traditional legal system was effectively used to regulate people's behavior, to secure peace, and to promote unity in the community.

The Igbo say that Chineke is goodness and that "everyone is a spark of God's spirit," and as a result, "no one sins against the gods alone [and] punishment for the sin of one man is visited on all."[39] Chineke (or Chukwu), as creator and god of justice, rewards those individuals who are good and punishes those who are not. While he "rarely intervenes in the affairs of men on earth," the Igbo's ancestors sometimes act on the morals that they exhibited when alive with the permission of "the High God."[40] Acting with Chineke's permission, ancestors as well as living elders, expect good conduct and service from the people. When the ancestors are angry or ignored, they cause misfortune to happen. Since an Igbo elder knows that it is necessary to prevent one person's sin from becoming attached to all, he can even ask his ancestors to punish his kinsman so long as "he is impartial" and "his moral point of view [shows] personal detachment, and close alignment to moral objectivity on behalf of his lineage or community."[41] Failure to do otherwise would result in misfortune or ruin to himself, his community, or both. In short, "the principle of moral rectitude by an elder has a vital role in ensuring social justice."[42]

The Ibibio

The Ibibio, found mainly in the Cross River area of southeastern Nigeria, are neighbors to the Igbo. Like the Igbo, the Ibibio's indigenous political system, was based on a group of elders. Revering and appeasing the *ekpo* (ancestors) through sacrifices was central to the religion of the people. The word *ekpo* also referred to the masking society who organized dances to commemorate the deceased. Members of the ekpo society were important because they played political, judiciary, and religious roles. Daniel A. Offiong, in his article on conflict resolution among the Ibibio, points out that religion, law, and politics are interwoven among the Ibibio. He argues that "belief in ancestor spirits, the political importance of the elders and their crucial role as the intermediaries between the ancestors and the living, along with the Ibibio belief in the supernatural powers of *mbiam* (oath), promote conflict resolution and social control in general."[43]

The Ibibio believe in the god Abasi or Aba-nsi-nsi, who "does all things by his knowledge and wisdom."[44] Like the Igbo and the Yoruba, ancestors are considered to be "active living dead" because they prayed to Abasi.[45] According to Offiong, the Ibibio engaged in a practice called *esop ison* in which the elders convened in a village counsel.[46] Their purpose was not actually to condemn or pass judgment, it was to purge disharmony from members of the community.[47] Everyone was considered to be a friend of the court and was free to ask questions of the plaintiff or the defendant as they would like and as the case progressed. Audience members could also express their dissatisfaction with whatever evidence was provided by booing! [48]

For their part, the elders weighed both sides of the arguments and were able to administer an oath or present a Bible on which to swear. Once a verdict was rendered, a guilty party may show remorse for his or her deeds in order to receive leniency from the court. Elders did not simply give the verdict, but they also sought to ensure that it was palatable to both parties. The elders could even administer an oath to both sides prohibiting either of them from seeking their own additional justice via witchcraft.[49] In other words, to prevent the likelihood of this happening, both sides agreed to swear on a Bible (or other sacred object) that they would neither attempt to supernaturally harm (or physically poison) the other side nor his family members. If an oath taker's word was broken after having sworn on a Bible, it was believed that he would be stricken with insanity. If an oath-breaker used a sacred item, it was believed that he or she would either become bloated and die or dry up and die.

By the end of the nineteenth century a rapid change began to take place in Ibibioland. First, European missionaries arrived and condemned the people's religion. Second, the British imposed their colonial authority, partly characterized by the imposition of the English laws and court system. The Ibibio were displeased because the British political and legal systems significantly limited the traditional judicial roles of the elders. In spite of the political change, the religious and traditional judicial systems somewhat exist in a limited form.

The Tiv

The Tiv are not Muslims although they live in the North of the country where the majority of Muslims reside. They believe in *Aondo u Abaverjua*, or the Supreme God. Because God is everywhere, there is no need for an intercessor and man is able to have a personal relationship with him, one-on-one. So close is man's relationship to his god (in theory, at least) that special requests to the Supreme God are made only after taking an oath promising that the special request will not hurt anyone.[50] This practice might explain why arbitration is so important among the Tiv. According to Paul Bohannan, "When an elder or a group of elders settle a quarrel among disputants, both the plaintiff and the dependent are instructed to fill their mouths and "blow it out in a spray to show that they have no suppressed anger in their hearts."[51]

There seems to be qualitative difference between the type of oath that a Tiv takes and the type of "evidence" that a Muslim must provide. The spirituality of the Tiv appears to impose internal obligations to tell the truth, requires the external assertion that the oath is true and not falsely harmful to others and implies assessment of veracity on the part of the elders/community. In contrast, oaths administered by Muslims under Shari'a law appear to lack a corresponding requirement for the oath taker to assert the truth of their statements and the court to assess the veracity of the statement. That is, Muslim oath takers appear to enjoy a type of automatic assumption of veracity when making statements regarding women.

Discussion

Two years after the initial verdict, charges against Amina Lawal were dropped on the grounds that she was pregnant before the judgment was made.[52] Considering the magnitude of her "crime," it is almost certain that various members of the international community - particularly those who were Muslim - succeeded in applying pressure on the Nigerian government. Although it is highly unlikely that the international pressure was interpreted as a type of arbitration on behalf of Lawal, it amounted to that nonetheless. It could very well be that arbitration proved to be the key for improved relations between Muslims and Christians.

According to Said, Funk, and Kadayifci, Islamic societies have engaged in traditional ways to solve their interpersonal, community-based, and inter-religious issues for "hundreds of years" using mediation, arbitration and negotiation.[53] They contend:

> Mediation, arbitration, and negotiation processes resolve, for instance, disputes that involve husband and wife with the "Kadi" (a judge who operates according to [Shari'a] as a mediator and arbitrator; clan disputes with politicians and religious leaders as arbitrators; inter-religious disputes [with] regional leaders, politicians, and military

> officers as mediators. In general, the approach to social conflicts (and in many cases to political strife) is derived from such traditional practices and cultural norms.[54]

Just as the African carries his religion into the fields and wherever else he ventures, in Islamic-based cultures, "negotiation is a skill which is practiced not only by a traditional mediator or arbitrator but is also an integral part of the individual's life such as the interactions in the "*souk*" (market), at work, or during social events."[55]

There are some basic reasons why negotiations between Christians, Muslims, and indigenous groups in Nigeria would give rise to little or no opposition. On the one hand, each group holds (or tends to hold), men in high esteem as decision-makers and the keeper of justice, and the elderly who either sit or serve as judges or jurors are regarded as the keepers of historical wisdom and knowledge. On the other hand, the main barrier to any type of biased weighting of testimony/oaths would be sentencing systems that completely disallow intercession on the part of others to gain leniency or reconsideration.

Ironically, missionaries who converted Africans to Christianity occasionally looked the other way when the newly converted retained some of their old traditions. For example, Skinner says of the Manga (a group within the Mossi province in Sudan):

> The conversion of the Manga chief to Catholicism has not engendered many problems for his pagan subjects. The chief's primary duty---to begin the yearly ceremonial cycle of sacrifices to the ancestors---has been taken over by his father's brother, who is now considered the ritual head of the chiefly lineage. Nevertheless, to the chief still accrue the gains of this ceremony because his followers pay him homage and bring him gifts on his birthday, which comes at this period. Moslems in the community also pay their respects at this time, and they prefer his Catholic birthday celebration to the bloody sacrifices of chickens to the ancestors. On the other hand, the chief shows little of the common Catholic disapproval of Moslems and sends gifts to their leaders on the Moslem feast days. He also entertains the district Moslems when they come to pay him homage.[56]

Skinner says of the Mossi, an ethnic group in Sudan, as well:

> The chief [who is only a nominal Moslem] himself became partially converted to Islam in gratitude to a Moslem Hausa trader who cured his illness. He recites the five daily prayers and observes most of the prescriptions of Islam, but he drinks European beer, subscribes to many pagan rites and beliefs, and supervises the annual Péléga or sacrifice to the ancestors. This dual allegiance is politically expedient because the chief can function as the head of the Moslem community as well as the traditional head of all the people. He does have occasional difficulty with intolerant Moslems who wish him to become a devout Moslem, and with the traditionalists who claim that today the crops are smaller, the people sicker, and the women barren because of the neglect of the ancestors. However, with the approach of holy days, these differences are resolved in the interest of community harmony.[57]

From the above quotes, Skinner has indicated that both Christian and Islamic principles influenced the Mossi rulers and their people, but the practice of some traditions continued. The same thing happened in Nigerian societies where traditionalism continues to exist in spite of the British imposition of the English judicial system. This shows that the indigenous people were proud of the effectiveness of their judicial system. While Nigerians have benefited from Christianity and Islam, they have demonstrated that foreign ideas cannot completely expunge indigenous cultural lifestyle and traditions. The application of the English law and the Shari'a legal code creates confusion, especially where Christians and Muslims live side by side. The Lawal case therefore demonstrates how some political leaders have attempted to prove the superiority of the Shari'a over the constitutional judicial system.

Conclusion

A variety of judicial options in Nigeria have been examined, many of which are exercised on a daily basis in place of Shari'a. The seeds of further violence in Nigeria do not rest on differing views of spirituality or religion. Instead, it is a struggle to determine which system will form the base of settling personal status and criminal cases. While spirituality strongly affects all the religious groups in Nigeria, the Amina case highlights the disadvantages of the Shari'a-only system. While the universal application of one legal system may simplify matters on a superficial level, the Shari'a system imposes an uneven playing field for non-Muslims (male or female) and Muslim women in terms of legal representation, presumption of innocence, and attributes a weighted value to the testimony of Muslim men in certain circumstances.

The abolition of other options that reflect, albeit in differing forms, the underlying values of harmony, community and justice that also form the basis of Islamic law is clearly a source of discontent. Non-Muslim Nigerians seem to be reacting to the fact that abolishing the broader range of judicial outcomes affected by intercession, equal treatment and the concepts of community shared by all segments of Nigerian society causes non-Muslim Nigerians to fear their demise into becoming second-class citizens legally while placing their human rights and property at risk under the Shari'a system. This situation does not just concern those who are denied their religious rights by being Christian but also concerns those Muslims who may see their human rights abused, as in Lawal's case.

Notes

1. Richard Jerome, Silvia Sansoni and Eileen Finan, "Will She Be Stoned To Death?" *People*, Vol. 60, Sept. 15, 2003 Issue 11. http://www.people.com/people/archive/article/0,,20141055,00.html
2. "Saving Amina Lawal: Human Rights Symbolism and the Dangers of Colonialism," *Harvard Law Review*, Vol. 117, May 2004 Issue 7, 2366.
3. Oluwafunmilayo Josephine Para-Mallam, "Faith, Gender and Development Agendas in Nigeria: Conflicts, Challenges, and Opportunities," *Gender & Development*, Vol. 14, Nov. 2006 Issue 3, 411.
4. Jerome et al, "Will She Be Stoned?"
5. Ibid.
6. Human Rights Watch, "International Reactions to Shari'a in Nigeria," http://www.hrw.org/reports/2004/nigeria0904/12.htm
7. Amnesty, "Nigeria: Amina Lawal Must Not Face Death By Stoning," http://www.amnesty.org.uk/news_details.asp?NewsID=13692.
8. Peter J. Paris, *The Spirituality of African Peoples: The Search for a Common Moral Discourse* (Minneapolis: Fortress Press, 1995), 28.
9. Human Rights Watch. "Background," http://www.hrw.org/reports/2004/nigeria0904/3.htm#_Toc82565158. Accessed December12, 2007.
10. Bolanle Awe, "Conflict and Divergence: Government and Society in Nigeria," *African Studies Review*, Vol. 42, Dec. 1999, No. 3, 5.
11. U.S. Department of State, "Background Note on Nigeria," http://www.state.gov/r/pa/ei/bgn/2836.htm.

12. Ogbu U Kalu, "Shari'a and Islam in Nigerian Pentecostal Rhetoric, 1970-2003," *Pneuma: The Journal of the Society for Pentecostal Studies*, Vol. 26, Fall 2004, Issue 2, 245.
13. Human Rights Watch. "Background," http://www.hrw.org/reports/2004/nigeria0904/3.htm#_Toc82565158.
14. Ibid.
15. Human Rights Watch. "The Extension of Shari'a to Criminal Law in Nigeria," http://www.hrw.org/reports/2004/nigeria0904/4.htm.
16. Harun Yahya, "People of the Book" & The Muslims: The Natural Alliance Between Christianity, Judaism and Islam," http://www.islamdenouncesterrorism.com/people_of_the_book_the_muslims.html.
17. "Nigeria: Muslim Justice--More Stoning Sentences Of Women", *Women's International Network News,* Vol. 29, Winter 2003 Issue, 1.
18. Ibid.
19. "Religion Online. Islam: Early History of Islam," http://library.thinkquest.org/26756/islam/index.htm.
20. Khalid Baig, "What Does Islam Teach About Justice: Neither Love Nor Hatred Can be Allowed to Compromise Justice," http://www.soundvision.com/info/peace/justice.asp
21. Kalu, 243.
22. Ibid, 244.
23. *The Holy Bible*, Proverbs 6:16-19, King James Version.
24. *The Holy Bible,* Exodus 23:1, New International Version.
25. *The Holy Bible,* Proverbs 19:9, New International Version.
26. *The Holy Bible,* Amos 5:12, King James Version.
27. *The Holy Bible,* Galatians 6:7, New International Version.
28. Kofi Johnson and Raphael Tunde Oyinade, "Monotheism in Traditional Yoruba Religion," http://organizations.uncfsu.edu/ncrsa/journal/v03/johnsonoyinade_yoruba.htm
29. Ibid.
30. Awe, "Conflict and Divergence," 6.
31. John C. Messenger, Jr., "Reinterpretations of Christian and Indigenous Belief in a Nigerian Nativist Church," American Anthropologist, New Series, Vol. 62, No. 2, April 1960, 270.
32. John C. Messenger Jr., "The Role of Proverbs in a Nigerian Judicial System," Southwestern Journal of Anthropology, Vol. 15, No. 1, Spring, 1959, 66.
33. Ibid.
34. John C. Messenger, Jr., "Anang Proverb-Riddles and Efik Tone Riddles," *The Journal of American Folklore*." Vol. 74, No. 293, 1961, 245-246.

35. Messenger Jr., "The Role of Proverbs," 69.
36. Ibid., 66.
37 Arthur G. Leonard, *The Lower Niger and Its Tribes* (London: Frank Cass, 1906), 30.
38. Dave Vautin, "Things Fall Apart: A Response," *Africa Notes*, http://www.einaudi.cornell.edu/africa/publications/africa_notes/2005/septoct05.pdf, September/October 2005, 2.
39. Steve Nwosu, "Morality in African Traditional Society," *New Political Science*, Vol. 26, No. 2, 2004, 214.
40. Ibid, 224.
41. Ibid, 226.
42. Ibid.
43. Daniel A. Offiong, "Conflict Resolution among the Ibibio of Nigeria," *Journal of Anthropological Research*, Vol. 53, No. 4, 1997, 423-441.
44. Emma S. Etuk, "The Efik/Ibibio," in *Ethnic and Cultural Diversity in Nigeria*, ed. Marcelina Ulunma Okehie-Offuha and Matthew N. O. Sadiku (Trenton: Africa World Press, 2006), 21.
45. Offiong, "Conflict Resolution among the Ibibio of Nigeria," 425.
46. Ibid, 423.
47. Ibid, 425.
48. Ibid, 430.
49. Ibid, 435.
50. Okehie-Offuha and Sadiku, 103.
51. Paul Bohannan, "A Tiv Political and Religious Idea," *Southwestern Journal of Anthropology*, Vol.11, No. 2, Summer 1955, 146.
52. Amnesty International UK "Nigeria: Amina Lawal's victory welcomed, but others threatened" http://www.amnesty.org.uk/news_details.asp?NewsID=14904 Accessed December12, 2007.
53. Abdul Said, Aziz, Nathan C. Funk and Ayse S. Kadayifci, eds., *Peace and Conflict Resolution in Islam:Precept and Practice* (New York: University Press of America, 2001), 128.
54. Ibid.
55. Ibid.
56. Elliott P. Skinner, "Christianity and Islam among the Mossi," *American Anthropologist, New Series*, 60, No. 6, Dec. 1 958, Part 1, 1112.
57. Ibid. 1106.

Chapter Seventeen

Government Reaction to Religious Violence

Julius O. Adekunle

The prominence of religions in Nigerian politics, the role of religious organizations, and the renewed emphasis on the Shari'a have not only heightened tensions between Christians and Muslims, but have also created a climate of fear. Political and religious leaders, as well as the adherents of both Christianity and Islam admit that there is a decline in inter-religious relations and religious tolerance. In modern times differences of opinion between the two religious groups easily find expression in killing, the burning of churches and mosques, and the destruction and looting of property. Such conflicts and concomitant acts of looting or violence often gather momentum and spread quickly. The rapid spread of violence and looting has been associated with the level of poverty, a consequence of joblessness causing disenfranchised youth to take advantage of the situation by stealing other people's property. Usually before the government takes any action, significant damage must have occurred. The Nigerian government recognizes freedom of religion as stipulated in the Constitution, but it has not devised the appropriate means to respect and preserve the clause and it has often failed to find and bring culprits to justice.

It was mentioned in chapter nine that conflicts are a natural development in any society. Between 1999 and 2007, religious violence became prevalent and deadly. It was used as the most acceptable means of expressing response, even to trivial issues. The seemingly unstoppable acts of violence have continuously shaken the foundation of the country on national integration and peaceful co-existence. Understandably, Nigeria is a particularly complex society (in terms of ethic and religious plurality) giving rise to frequent outbreak of violence. Rosalind Hackett pointed out that, "The characterization of modern Nigeria as a nation with three religious traditions – Christian, Islamic and the traditional religions, is to simplify a highly complex and pluralistic religious situation."[1] However, the facts of history do not indicate that Nigerians are especially violent in nature, but several incidents have often triggered negative reactions. When conflicts arise, it is the responsibility of the government to provide a lasting solution and security for its citizens, and failure to do that may result in a further break down of law and order. In a situation where the government is unable to prevent the outbreak of violence, a process of resolution often follows conflicts. During the military regimes, the government made efforts to convene peace and security conferences, particularly in regards to the religious conflicts between the Sunni and Shia Muslims. Outcomes of such conferences resulted in open-air preaching and processions being banned, "provocative and defamatory" religious songs being prohibited, and defiant religious chauvinists and militants bring arrested.[2]

The many incidents of ethnic and religious conflicts raise the question: What does the government do to prevent or to deal with acts of conflict or violence? In a civilized, modernized, and secular society as Nigeria, religious differences are inevitable, but that does not provide any justification for violent acts. Both the federal and state governments, however, have an obligation to deal with violence in a timely fashion, to provide peace and security for their citizens, and to ensure political stability. The improper handling of acts of violence does not give any government credibility. As frequently happens in Nigeria, political leaders sometimes hesitate to take drastic steps against the perpetrators of violence because they belong to the same ethnic, political, or religious group as the instigators. This is why people believe that the Nigerian government sometimes plays politics of double standards when it comes to its reaction to a religious crisis. Reacting to the religious riot that occurred in 1987, President Ibrahim Babangida addressed the nation and indicated that:

> We as a people are very tolerant. The major faiths of Christianity and Islam have co-existed in our society for centuries without bitterness and without violence. I will, therefore, appeal to all our people, especially the young, who were the main tools and victims of the recent riots, not to allow themselves to be used by selfish and faceless manipulators, who lack the courage to come out into the open and fight their own wars, but would rather instigate

> trusting youths to riots and premature deaths. In view of the multi-ethnic and multi-religious nature of our society, we have no choice but to live in peace and concord as we have done throughout the ages.[3]

Babangida followed the rhetoric of peaceful co-existence and tolerance, but his government did not take concrete and effective actions or strategies to prevent conflicts and acts of violence. Religion will always be part of the Nigerian society, but religious conflicts should not be allowed to continue.

Government Actions

The immediate government reaction is to condemn violence and to give stern warning to perpetrators. Depending on the magnitude of the riot, the state or federal government may deplore combined security operatives of the anti-riot police and soldiers to such places to restore peace. The government, federal or state, holds the responsibility of respecting the sanctity of human life, and is expected to protect its citizens. Hence, immediate action has to be taken. In some cases, as happened in Yelwa, Plateau State in May 2004 when there was a massacre between Christians and Muslims, the federal government declared a dusk-to-dawn curfew and a state of emergency. The state governor, Joshua Dariye, the deputy governor, and the state house of assembly were suspended, and an interim administrator was appointed for six months. President Obasanjo met with the Council of Ulamas and promised to end the Plateau crisis. The Yelwa incident had a ripple effect in Kano where Christians were killed and churches burned down. As in Yelwa, the Kano state government also issued several curfew orders. Although the federal government's action in Yelwa was heavily criticized as being too excessive and infringing on the freedom of the people, the step produced the desired result of calm, beginning a process of reconciliation.

Another step the government takes is to set up a commission of inquiry. While this is another strategy of curbing violence, the public has not seen it as an effective or lasting solution. Presumably because of the political and religious tension and the virulent reaction that it could generate, no one has been publicly held accountable for the massive destruction. As mentioned in Chapter nine, President Obasanjo, a Christian and a southerner, showed his distaste for the implementation of the Shari'a and for violence, but he was careful not to offend the northerners and the Muslims. Because of his approach, he was criticized as weak and incapable of dealing with difficult national issues. Obasanjo, however, publicly condemned the actions of the perpetrators of violence by declaring in 2001, "I wonder what sort of Muslims and Christians start burning churches and mosques - places where God is worshipped? True believers in God cannot start killing other human beings."[4]

Since Obasanjo left office in May 2007, there have not been many religious riots. Does this justify the claim that religious violence, especially the Shari'a was meant to undermine Obasnajo's administration? Although tension has drastically died down, a religious riot occurred in Bauchi State in February 2008 where a woman, believed to be a Christian, was accused of blaspheming against the prophet Mohammad. To prevent being assaulted, the woman took refugee in a police station, but some young Muslims attacked Christians, destroyed their homes, and burned their churches. The CAN condemned the action and the Bauchi State government acted promptly by assisting the victims.[5]

The disquieting rate of recurrence of violence would necessitate legislation against religious riots by the government. As things are, the government needs to take a strong step in order to secure peace and protect the unity of the country. Granted, there is freedom of religion and Nigeria is a secular state, but that is not a license to engage in violent actions that can threaten the peace and stability of the nation. The government should not permit anything to undermine the quest for peace and national integration.

Religion, Peace, and Unity

In his book, *African Christianity*, Paul Gifford stated that one of the public roles of religion, especially Christianity, is to "foster democratic virtues like tolerance, respect, moderation, cooperation and compromise."[6] In a democratic state, religion is a strong instrument or institution that promotes public interest and peaceful co-existence. A huge vacuum is created when religion fails to perform that function. Evidence of constant and continuing conflicts suggest that religions in Nigeria are not effectively performing these functions. However, when Nigeria was going through a turbulent period of political dictatorship in the 1990s, Christians, through the CAN, condemned acts of corruption and decried the violations of human rights. Dr. Mbang, the CAN president even declared that, "the interest of Nigeria must be paramount in our minds now and we must all be involved in building it."[7]

The practical roles of religion in public affairs become very paramount given the proliferation of new churches and denominations, especially by Pentecostal or Evangelical groups in the South and the rapid growth of Islam in the North. In a dialogue panel organized in Lagos in 2004, Matthews Ojo, professor of religious studies at OAU reiterated the role of religion in politics by indicating that churches should stay in the struggle for democracy, denounce intolerable regimes, and establish democratic order within their constituencies.[8] Christians and Muslims should maintain a "working together" attitude in the interest of the nation.

Wole Soyinka, Noble Laureate and social activist in Nigeria recently identified religion as one of the potential enemies to Nigeria's progress towards unity and nationhood. Because of the many religious conflicts and the extent to which religion has penetrated politics, he believes that religion hinders peaceful co-existence. He declared: "We cannot continue pretending that, as long as any one religion aspires to dictatorship in secular matters, we can call ourselves a nation. A theocratic order is anathema to nation-being since it implicates exclusion, not inclusion."[9] He further stated:

> Religion is one enemy of potential nationhood . . . The intervention of religion in nation ... has been of the most savage, unconscionable, and increasingly intolerant kind. No other word for it but butchery, waste and devastation. Only the secular order embraces all . . . . Any religious following can evoke parallel but opposing sets of protocols, citing the authority of some unseen and unknowable god in realms that have no perceptible contact with the actual. Religion must therefore submit to community, to nation, otherwise co-existence becomes impossible and the human entity reverts to a state of brutishness.[10]

Like many others, Soyinka embraces and advocates the upholding of the secular nature because Nigeria should not be ruled as a theocratic state. The problem, however, is not religion, but the practitioners of religion and politicians who misuse their religion to satisfy their political ambitions. While maintaining the secular nature, religion can still be practiced and be utilized effectively for the good of the nation.

In a swift reaction, religious groups do not believe that religion itself is a threat to nation building. They believe that the abuse and misuse of religion is the problem and the government needs to put in more efforts in securing life and property, in providing means of free and fair elections, eradicating corruption, avoiding political assassinations, and fostering ethnic and religious peaceful co-existence. The Nigerian Inter-Religious Council (NIREC) and other religious groups are working with the government to achieve peaceful relationship.

Strategies for Peace

Peace is an essential ingredient for a successful and progressive society. It allows the smooth running of a democratic process, and it is indispensable to good governance. Religion should foster peace and believers must be tolerant. Intolerance divides but tolerance unites. Tolerance is indeed a virtue of democracy and it should be allowed to penetrate the hearts of Nigerians. While celebrating the Eid-El Kabir (Eid-Ul-Adha) in 2005, the Emir of Minna, Umar Farouk Bahago, advised Muslims to use religion as a tool for peaceful co-existence among all believers. He emphasized the pertinence of tolerance, especially in a heterogeneous society. Bahago indicated that because Islam preaches peace, "adherents of the faith should emulate the tenets, which include tolerance of other religious bodies."[11] Three recommendations are brought forth as strategies for achieving peace.

Dialogue

History has often dealt with the issue of religious toleration. For example, freedom, secularism, and religious toleration were some of the highlights of the Enlightenment period, and as a secular state, it is imperative for Nigeria to pay critical attention to and engage in religious dialogue in order to address the frequent occurrences of religious conflicts. Dialogue is two-dimensional: speaking and listening; giving and receiving. The goal of both approaches is to achieve peace, mutual growth, and understanding. A dialogue can be between two or more faiths or it may be ecumenical. It is a useful and effective tool to combat fundamentalism and divisive ideologies. This is why dialogue should be all-inclusive and all-embracing to meet the desired goals.

Dialogue among religious leaders and their followers as well as religious organizations foster peaceful inter-religious relations. When conflicts arise, interfaith dialogue serves a useful strategy for reconciliation and it is the responsibility of the government and spiritual leaders to create an environment for peace and understanding in their societies. The road to peaceful co-existence is easier when people of all religions are willing "to meet, explore their differences, and appreciate and find enrichment in each other's ways to the divine."[12] Historically, organizing a successful interfaith dialogue has been difficult, but according to Johan Galtung, "Every religion contains, in varying degrees, elements of the soft and the hard. For the sake of world peace, dialogue within religions and among them must strengthen the softer aspects."[13] Meaningful interfaith dialogues and ecumenical conferences would help in recognizing and respecting the values in other religions since it is impossible to create a single world religion.

Two Nigerians have been promoting reconciliation and peaceful co-existence among Christians and Muslims. Formerly involved in inter-religious riots, Imam Muhammad Nurayn Ashafa, the Imam of Kaduna, and the Rev. James Movel Wuye (Joint Directors of the Inter-Faith Mediation Center in Kaduna), indicated that:

We were two militant religious activists but now we are working to create space, not just for peace, but also for the transformation of society. We were programmed to hate one another, to Islamize or evangelize at all costs. This threatens the very existence of Nigeria. We were both victims of the situation that we had both had a part in creating. What motivated us to transform hate into love, vengeance into reconciliation? In our hearts, we were weeping, but we were still full of hate.[14]

Through dialogue and reconciliation, Ashafa no longer saw Wuye as an enemy but as a friend,[15] both working side by side to promote the unity of Nigeria in spite of their religious differences. This is the spirit of unity in diversity in action. Christians and Muslims should follow this example, seeing each other not merely as fellow Nigerians, but as friends who embrace the doctrines of peace and unity as preached in both Christianity and Islam. Leaders and practitioners of the traditional religions should be included in the dialogue process.

With specific reference to the Palestinian Christians, but applicable to any society, Saliba Sarsar rightly pointed out that activists of social movements are "transforming leaders."[16] As transforming leaders, the onus rests on them to teach their followers, through the ethics of their religions, the ethos of dialogue as a means to achieving peace and unity. Nigerian society has to be transformed from a violent to a peaceful one.

Religious/Social Organizations

The primary objective of these organizations is to create a climate of peace by adopting a nonviolent approach. The climate of fear and intimidation should transform into a culture of peace.[17] As mentioned in chapters 10 and 11, the Christian Association of Nigeria (CAN), established in 1976 in the wake of the growth of Islam and the increasing Muslim influence in political matters, took an active part in the debates against the Nigerian government's decision to register Nigeria as a member of the Organization of Islamic Conference (OIC) in 1986. Clearly, it was wrong for the government to take that step since Nigeria is not an Islamic state. Because there is no separation between politics and religion, the politicization of religion has wrought substantial damage to Nigerian unity. In 1990 Abubakar Gumi publicly declared that Muslims would not accept a Christian president.[18] In 1999, the Nigerian Inter-Religious Council (comprising the Christian Association of Nigeria and the Jama'atu Nasril Islam) was inaugurated in order to foster Christian-Muslim relations, but the arrangement has not had any significant effect.

The chairman of CAN, Lagos State Chapter, Monsignor Bernard Ayodele Okodua, once declared that the idea of a national conference would be a good forum to strengthen dialogue among ethnic and political leaders. He suggested that the conference "should not be such as would break up the country, but rather to consolidate on national unity where no constituent part will feel more superior to the other."[19] Another Christian leader, Bishop Francis Wale Oke of the Sword of the Spirit Ministries, declared:

> We are not politicians. Our stand is that politicians should do whatever they want but they should leave the country in peace. Nigeria is bigger than anybody, any political party or all the political parties put together. All of us met the country here and after our work, we will leave it. Let us have a peaceful, united Nigeria that our children can enjoy.[20]

The point is that instead of allowing religious doctrines and practices to replace the constitution and determine the course of Nigeria's political history, they should be utilized to transform and steer the nation in a positive direction. Religious leaders and their followers all have a significant role to play because to maintain a strong united nation is a task for every Nigerian, whether religious or not.

The Arewa Consultative Forum (ACF) is a socio-political organization with its base in Kaduna. One of its objectives is "to set up machinery for regular dialogue to ensure that issues likely to cause breach of the peace are settled amicably and promptly." While this is a creditable idea, the Forum is a regional organization that strictly restricts membership to northerners over the age of twenty nine. Similarly, there are several ethno-nationalist and political movements in the south, whose aim is to promote ethnic nationality and ethnic politics. Such movements include the Oodua People's Congress (OPC) in the southwest, the Bakassi Boys of Africa (BBA) and the Movement for the Actualization of the Sovereign State of Biafra (MASSOB) in the southeast, the Middle Belt Forum (MBF) in central Nigeria, and the Ijaw Youth Council (IYC) and Egbesu Boys in the Niger

Delta. Social movements should be open to all Nigerians for the effective promotion of socio-political and religious relations, and their grass root efforts and activities should be in line with the national interest.

Peace Education

The government should embark on peace education as a means of liberating people from the shackles of brutality and unwarranted conflicts. Development, in all its ramifications, thrives under a peaceful environment; that is why the government has to pay attention in the development of ways to foster an environment of peaceful co-existence. Political and religious education is paramount to development and nation building. The youth are mostly involved in violence and they constitute the group most likely to benefit from political and religious educational programs. Peace education should begin at the grassroots level, such as in the homes, churches, mosques, and local communities. Parents have the responsibility of instructing their children on the essence of peace and tolerance. It is essential for the government to initiate state or national activities that would promote inter-religious relations. In schools, emphasis should be placed on peaceful relations and the consequences of violent actions, as well as in respecting one another's religious beliefs. Technologically, the Internet is a useful medium in which to provide information on religious tolerance and harmonious living. The government (federal or state) should not promote one religion at the expense of another. If the youth are well-educated in ways to develop peaceful relationships, they would not turn to hoodlumism and vigilantism. The government must invest in its youth in order to produce good and decent future leaders.

In promoting peace and orderly conduct, the government can proscribe social movements whose activities are nefarious and inimical to the peace and stability of the country. Disrupting national peace and unity through organized or spontaneous violence in the name of religion is unacceptable and should be outlawed. In churches and mosques, the youth should be taught the values and virtues of peace. For example, All-Nigeria United Nations Youth and Students Association (ANUNSA), founded in 1958, has organized different peace education programs for the youth. The description of a workshop held in April 2003 states:

> The main purpose of the Nigerian National Youth Training Workshop Against Violence is to reduce the desire, and incidence of violence in Nigeria and to actively campaign for the use of creative and constructive approach to

> conflict resolution in Nigeria thereby building a climate of peaceful co-existence and reconciliation among Nigerians. This will be achieved through the peace education programme armed at sensitizing and educating the youths on the issues relating to peace building and conflict resolution.[21]

Similarly in 2004, the International Center for Reconciliation organized a three-day Youth Empowerment workshop in Plateau State. To empower the youth, they must be educated in religious tolerance, accountability, responsibility to the nation, and ability to cope with challenges. They must be taught on how to live peacefully and avoid conflict. They must learn to put their country first. These are steps to engage the youth in positive thinking and action and to prepare them to assume leadership roles in the future.

The Role of the International Community

The outbreak of religious conflicts and concomitant acts of violence are domestic problems for Nigeria and although the government is trying to curb such phenomena, it is possible to seek assistance from the international community. Unlike other African countries where several international humanitarian organizations often assist the government when religious or communal violence breaks out, Nigeria has not enjoyed this type of support. More often than not, the United Nations agencies, Red Cross, and NGOs believe that Nigeria is well equipped with human and financial resources to curb or to deal with the numerous violent occurrences. There have been demographic movements and refugees, but these are not in the magnitude of what happens in the Sudan or other African countries.

The lack of international assistance poses a challenge to the Nigerian government. Because of the frequency of religious riots, the international community should support government's efforts to guarantee security by providing technical and technological assistance that can help capture culprits. The international community can also assist in training political and religious leaders on conflict resolution. Since September 11, 2001, the war on terrorism has become a global fight and because of the global connections, the government and people of Nigeria can benefit from assistance from other countries in order to forestall violence.

Conclusion

It is important for the government of Nigeria to focus on the root causes of ethnic and religious violence. One of the causes is the inequitable distribution of resources. The ongoing acts of violence and hostage taking in the Niger Delta are intricately interwoven with this factor. Although religion does not play any role in the distribution of economic resources, the widespread poverty among followers of different religions leaves room for violent actions, especially among the young and unemployed. The militants in the Niger Delta take hostages and ask for a significant amount of money for ransom. Many of them have turned into professional hostage takers because it has become a major source of their livelihood.

To be able to effectively curtail or prevent any act of violence, the government needs to invest more in the use of advanced forms of technology, which would provide adequate security for the people. Nigeria can borrow technological ideas or collaborate with other countries on how to promptly respond to emergency cases. Federal and state governments should provide adequate compensation to victims to rebuild their houses, churches, or mosques. This is necessary because of the non-existent or non-effective insurance system.

All six geo-political blocks in Nigeria have experienced one form of violence or another. Although state governments always attempted to stop the acts of violence, the huge responsibility of providing security for the people rests on the federal government. In an attempt to foster and strengthen national unity, and to encourage a national dialogue, some prominent Nigerians called on the federal government to convene a national conference.[22] In 2005 Chief Anthony Enahoro, Chief Abraham Adesanya, and Prof. Wole Soyinka also supported the national conference of all ethnic groups for dialogue. As Chief Adesanya puts it, "dialogue is necessary for peace."[23] The National Conference was meant to meet multiple needs: ethnic, political, religious, and social. Since ethnic and political affiliation often intersects with religious divide, the national conference was envisioned to provide the opportunity for finding a common ground for reconciliation and for understanding each other. It was seen as a move toward securing peace and political stability in Nigeria's homeland.

There was a religious controversy in some states regarding the representatives to the National Conference. For example, Reverend Niven Mshelia, Secretary of CAN, Borno State Chapter, indicated that his association was displeased with the list of representatives because Christians were excluded. But reacting to this accusation, the Secretary to the State Government (SSG) Alhaji Abba Gana Terab, accentuated the point of this paper by declaring, "Religious bodies should please not allow themselves to be used by sentimental individuals or greedy politicians. All religions should be seen to unite the people of the state rather than divide them."[24]

When the National Conference convened, among the 391 delegates were many Christians including Catholic representatives: Rev. Monsignor John Aniagwu, Pastor of St. Leo Catholic Church, Ikeja, Lagos and Rev. Father Matthew Kukah, Vicar General, Kaduna Archdiocese. The Arewa Consultative Forum (ACF) expressed its opposition to the lopsided composition of the conference, indicating that President Obasanjo chose more Christians than Muslims, which was capable of sparking religious hostilities in the country.

In his inauguration speech, President Obasanjo declared that one of the things to be focused on was the sustenance of Nigeria's democracy. He emphasized:

> We want a united, stable, secure, equitable, progressive, prosperous and great country and we should all be irretrievably committed to it. The National Political Reform Conference is not designed to dismember or disintegrate Nigeria. It is not established to encourage mudslinging; not to organise protest or subterranean political activities that would be detrimental to effective discussion. Rather, the conference is about designing the most appropriate and relevant institutional mechanisms for managing our diversity and difference. This conference is not about opposition politics but it is about Nigeria today and tomorrow, for Nigerians of today and tomorrow."[25]

The Chairman of the Conference, Justice Niki Toki introduced a religious dimension by declaring a day of fast and prayer for him and members of the conference, irrespective of their religions. He noted that, "the conference will not deliberate on the possibility of dividing Nigeria," and added, "I will never be party to balkanization of Nigeria."[26] The conference was not organized to promote one religion at the expense of the other or to fan the embers of religious antagonism. Its purpose was to set in motion a process of peace and unity.

Peace and stability cannot be achieved in modern Nigeria if ethnic and religious politics continue to prevail. The federal and state governments must be determined to pursue peaceful and meaningful strategies for peace and unity. Political leaders in various official capacities have the responsibility of providing strong leadership and promoting good governance. The process of nation building is painfully slow often requiring the attention and cooperation of all the citizens of the country. Instead of the deep-rooted ethnic and religious animosity, there should be trust and respect for human life. Violence does not help in nation building, especially when the country is trying to strengthen its democratic system. For Nigeria to be peaceful, to sustain its young democracy, and to maintain political stability and national unity, every Nigerian has a role to play and religion must not be used as a divisive tool. The government should respect and protect the secular clause of the constitution by not diminishing its role in religion and politicians should not use religion as a vehicle of gaining position and power. Nigerians should strongly uphold the principle of "unity in diversity" and allow religion to be an anchor for unity rather than an instrument of division.

Notes

1. Rosalind I. J. Hackett, "Variations on a Theme," in *New Religious Movements in Nigeria*, ed., Rosalind I.J. Hackett (Lewiston, The Edwin Mellen Press, 1987), 1.
2. Elise Aymer, "Nigeria: Clash of Religions," *The Yale International Forum*, Winter 1996, www.yale.edu/iforum/Winter1996/nigeriaWin96.htm
3. *Newswatch*, March 30, 1987, 14-15.
4. "Nigerian Troops Curb Religious Violence," http://news.bbc.co.uk/2/hi/africa/1532639.stm, BBC Report, September 8, 2001.
5. "Churches Destroyed in Wave of Religious Violence in Nigeria," *Christian Today*, February 9, 2008, www.christiantoday.com/article/churches.destroyed.in.wave.of.religious.violence.in.nigeria/16769.htm
6. Gifford, *African Christianity*, 347.
7. "Corrupt Public Officials in Nigeria Face Expulsion from Churches," http://lists.essentials.org/shell-nigeria-action/msg00128.html
8. "Pentecostal-Civil Society Dialogue," Professor Paul Gifford of the Department of Oriental and African Studies, University of London, and Professor Matthews Ojo were the Keynote speakers.
9. Dapo Akinrefon and Charles Kumolu, "Nigeria: Religion Threatens Country's Nationhood – Soyinka," *The Vanguard*, March 4, 2009, http://allafrica.com/stories/200903040607.html
10. Ibid.
11. Chesa Chesa (Abuja), Chinwendu Nnadozie (Minna), Sola Shittu (Ibadan) and Lekan Sanni (Lagos), "Bloody Clash at Sallah Prayer in Ibadan." http://odili.net/news/source/2005/jan/21/418.html

12. Mary Pat Fisher, *Living Religions* (Upper Saddle River, NJ: Prentice-Hall, 2002), 467.
13. Johan Galtung, "Religions, Hard and Soft." *Cross Currents*, http://www.crosscurrents.org/galtung.htm
14. "Tackling Communal Violence in Nigeria," http://www.findarticles.com/p/articles/mi_m0KZH/is_5_17/ai_n6332992
15. Ibid.
16. Saliba Sarsar, "Palestinian Christians: From Visions to Reality," forthcoming publication.
17. For more information on how religious associations can contribute to the peaceful political climate in Nigeria, see Deji Ayegboyin, "Religious Associations and the New Political Dispensation in Nigeria," *Studies in Interreligious Dialogue*, Vol. 15, Issue 1, 2005, 101-113.
18 United States, Library of Congress, Federal Research Division, 304.
19. Dickson Adeyanju, "Christian Leaders Plan Joint Service Feb. 12" http://odili.net/news/source/2005/feb/2/15.html, February 2, 2005.
20. "Cleric asks Leaders not to Ruin Nigeria," *The Guardian*, http://odili.net/news/source/2005/feb/2/23.html, February 2, 2005.
21. "Youth Training Workshop Against Violence," *TakingItGlobal*, www.takingitglobal.org/opps/event.html?eventid=2035 - 19k
22. Ayodele Akinkuotu, "A Dangerous Agenda," *Tell*, No. 12, March 20, 2000, 12-16.
23. Wole Adeyemo, "National Conference Begins Soon," *Tell*, No. 14, April 2, 2001, 22-26.
24. Mustapha Muhammad, "Confab List Causes Uproar in Borno," *This Day*, February 8, 2005. http://allafrica.com/stories/200502080794.html
25. "Strengthening the Structure of Democratic Governance in Nigeria," Address by His Excellency President Olusegun Obasanjo at the inauguration of the national Political Reforms Conference, February 21, 2005 at the Abuja international Conference Centre, The Guardian, February 22, 2005, http://odili.net/news/source/2005/feb/22/42.html
26. Ndidi Okafor and Cajetan Mmuta, "Tobi imposes fast, prayers on members, *Daily Champion*, Vol. 13, No. 44, February 22, 2005, http://odili.net/news/source/2005/feb/22/610.html

Selected List for Further Reading

Awoniyi, H. Olufemi, *Government Subsidy of Christian Pilgrimage is a Bribe* (Ibadan: Centre for Applied Religion and Education, 1998).

Balewa, Balarae Abubakar Tafawa, *Common Law and Sharia in Nigeria: An Unresolved Problem of Coexistence* (Enugu: Fourth Dimension, 2002).

Beckford, James A. (ed), *New Religious Movements and Rapid Social Change (UK:* Sage Publications Ltd. 1992).

Carter, Stephen, God's Name in Vain: The Wrongs and Rights of Religion in Politics (New York: Basic books, 2000).

Chukwulozie, Victor, *Muslim-Christian Dialogue in Nigeria* Berkeley, University of California Press, 1986).

Comaroff, J. L. and J. Comaroff (eds.), *Civil Society and the Social Imagination in Africa* (Chicago: University of Chicago Press, 1999).

Enwerem, Iheanyi M. A Dangerous Awakening: The Politicization of Religion in Nigeria (Ibadan, Nigeria: IFRA, 1995).

Falola, Toyin. Violence in Nigeria: The Crisis of Religious Politics and Secular Ideologies (Rochester, NY: University of Rochester Press. 1998.

Falola, Toyin, and Matthew M. Heaton. *A History of Nigeria* (Cambridge, UK: Cambridge University Press, 2008).

Hackett, Rosalind I. J., ed., *New Religious Movements in Nigeria*, (Lewiston, N.Y.: Edwin Mellen Press, 1987).

Hunwick, John O. ed., *Religion and National Integration in Africa: Islam, Christianity and Politics in the Sudan and Nigeria* (Evanston, IL: Northwestern University Press, 1992).

Kastfelt, Niels, *Religion and Politics in Nigeria: A Study in Middle Belt Christianity* (London: British Academic Press, 1994).

Korieh, Chima J. and G. Ugo Nwokeji, ed., *Religion, History, and Politics in Nigeria: Essays in Honor of Ogbu U. Kalu* (New York: University Press of America, 2005).

Kukah, Matthew Hassan, *Religion, Politics and Power in Northern Nigeria* (African Books Collective, 1994).

Kukah, Matthew Hassan and Toyin Falola, *Religious Militancy and Self-Assertion: Islam and Politics in Nigeria: The Making of Modern Africa* (Avebury, 1997).

Kukah, Matthew Hassan, *Democracy and Civil Society in Nigeria* (Codesria Book Series, Spectrum, 2001).

Laitin, David D. Hegemony and Culture: Politics and Religious Change among the Yoruba (Chicago, IL: University of Chicago Press. 1986).

Ludwar-Ene, Gudrun, ed., *New Religious Movements and Society in Nigeria* (Germany: Bayreuth African Studies, 2001).

Matory, J. Lorand, *Sex and the Empire that is no More: Gender and the Politics of Metaphor in Oyo Yoruba Religion* (Minneapolis: University of Minnesota Press, 1994).

Nzeh, Casimir Chinedu O. From Clash to Dialogue of Religions:A Socio-Ethical Analysis of the Christian-Islamic Tension in a Pluralistic Nigeria (Berlin, GER: Peter Lang Press. 2002).

Oyediran, Oyeleye and Adigun Agbaje, eds., *Nigeria: Politics of Transition and Governance 1986-1996* (Dakar: CODESRIA, 1999).

Paden, John N., *Faith and Politics in Nigeria: Nigeria As aPivotal State in the Muslim World* (United States Institute of Peace Press, 2008).

Paden, P. N., *Religious and Political culture in Kano* (Berkeley: University of California Press, 1973).

Paden, John N., *Ahmadu Bello, Sardauna of Sokoto: Values and Leadership in Nigeria* (London: Hodder and Stroughton, 1986).

Peel, D. Y., *Aladura: A Religious Movement among the Yoruba* (London: Oxford University Press, 1968).

Saliba, John A., J. Gordon Melton, eds., *Understanding New Religious Movements,* Second edition (California: Rowman Altamira Press, 2003).

Turner, H. W., *African Independent Church*, 2 volumes (Oxford: Clarendon Press, 1967).

Umar, Muhammad S. Islam and Colonialism: Intellectual Responses of Muslims of Northern Nigeria to British Colonial Rule (Leiden, the Netherlands: Koniklije Brill NV, 2006).

ARTICLES

Aina, O. I., "Mobilizing Nigerian Women for National Development: The Role of Female Elites," *African Economic History,* No. 21, 1993, 1-20.

Akinyele, R. T. "Ethnic Militancy and National Stability in Nigeria: A Case Study of the Oodua People's Congress," *African Affairs*, Vol. 100, No. 401, 2001, 623-640.

Ayegboyin, Deji, "Religious Associations and the New Political Dispensation in Nigeria," *Studies in Interreligious Dialogue*, Vol. 15, Issue 1, 2005, 101-113.

Barkindo, Bawuro M., "Growing Islamism in Kano City since 1970: Causes, Form and Implication," in Muslim Identity and Social Change in Sub-Saharan Africa, ed., Brenner, Louis (Bloomington, IN: Indiana University Press, 1993), 91-105.

Kalu, Ogbu. "Sharia and Islam in Nigerian Pentecostal Rhetoric, 1970-2003," *Pneuma,* 6. 2 (2004): 242-261.

Kuperus, Tracy, "Building Democracy: An Examination of Religious Associations in South Africa and Zimbabwe,"*Journal of Modern African Studies* 37, 4, 1999, 643-668.

Reynolds, Jonathan, "Good and Bad Muslims: Islam and Indirect Rule in Northern Nigeria," The International Journal of African Historical Studies, Vol. 34, No. 3: 2001, 601-18.

Skinner, Elliott Percival., "Christianity and Islam Among the Mossi," *American Anthropologist,* Vol. 60, No. 6, 1958, 1102-1119.

Warr, Kevin"The Normative Promise of Religious Organizations in Global Civil Society,"*Journal of Church and State* 41, 3, 1999.

Notes on Contributors

Adeboye, Olufunke, Ph.D.: Olufunke Adeboye is a Senior Lecturer in the Department of History and Strategic Studies, University of Lagos, Nigeria. She was a visiting Research Associate at the Harriet Tubman Center, York University, Canada in 2006 and has held visiting research fellowships at the Center of West African Studies, University of Birmingham (UK) and at the University of Massachusetts, Amherst (USA). Her research interests include: precolonial and colonial Nigerian history; nineteenth and twentieth century Yoruba state and society, and Pentecostal history in West Africa. She has published widely in various edited volumes and leading Africanist journals such as the *Canadian Journal of African Studies*, *Nordic Journal of African Studies*, *African Studies Review* and the *Lagos Historical Review*.

Adekunle, Julius O., Ph.D.: Julius O. Adekunle holds a Ph.D. in African History from Dalhousie University, Halifax, Canada. He is Professor of African History at the Department of History and Anthropology, Monmouth University, West Long Branch, New Jersey. His research interests include ethnicity, religion, and politics in Africa. He is the author of *Politics and Society in Nigeria's Middle Belt: Borgu and the Emergence of a Political Identity* published in 2004 and *Culture and Customs of Rwanda* published in 2007.

Adeniran, Lateef, Ph.D.: Lateef Ayinla Adeniran obtained his Ph.D. at the University of Ilorin. He is a lecturer in the Department of History, Emmanuel Alayande College of Education, Oyo, Nigeria. He did his undergraduate at the University of Lagos and Masters degree at the University of Ibadan. He has taught several aspects of African history, but he specializes in the political history of Africa as it relates to the development. He has written many articles.

Afolayan, Funso, Ph.D.: Funso Afolayan is Associate Professor of History and African Studies at the University of New Hampshire, Durham. He has held a number of research and teaching positions, including ones at Obafemi Awolowo University; in the Department of Religions at Amherst College; and in the Department of History and African-American Studies Program at Washington University in St. Louis. In addition to several book chapters and research publications in journals, he is co-author of *Yoruba Sacred Kingship: A Power Like That of the Gods* (Smithsonian Institution Press, 1996) and author of *Culture and Customs of South Africa* (Greenwood Press, 2004).

Akinwumi, Olayemi, Ph.D.: Olayemi Akinwumi is a Professor of History and currently, the Dean, Faculty of Arts, Nasarawa State University, Keffi, Nigeria.He has published extensively both in local and international journals. He has also written a number of books, two of which include *The Colonial Contest for the Nigerian Region 1844–1900: A History of the German Participation* and *Crisis and Conflicts in Nigeria: A Political History Since 1960.* He is a recipient of many international awards, including Deutscher Akademischer Austauschdienst and Alexander von Humboldt. He was recently honored with the fellowship of the Historical Society of Nigeria.

Akpen, Philip: Philip is a Lecturer at the Department of History, Nasarawa State University, Keffi, Nigeria. He has attended many international conferences and has published several journal articles and book chapters. He is a Ph.D. candidate at Bayero University Kano.

Alao, Akin, Ph.D.: Akin Alao is Reader in History and Acting Director Institute of Cultural Studies at Obafemi Awolowo University, Ile-Ife, Nigeria. His book, *Statesmanship on the Bench: The Judicial Career of Sir Adetokunbo Ademola, 1939- 1972* was released by Africa World Press in 2007. Alao is president Nigerian Cultural Studies Network, member of Historical Society of Nigeria and a convener of the Nigerian Society for Legal History.

Booker, Teresa A., Ph.D.: Teresa A. Booker is Assistant Professor of African-American Studies at John Jay College of Criminal Justice. Her doctoral dissertation examined the strategies used to deliver humanitarian relief during Operation Lifeline Sudan. Her research interests include peacekeeping, peacemaking, and restorative justice. Recent publications include: "Babies' Daddies: Can the Masai Community Help Heal the Wrongs of Peacekeeper Fathers?" *The International Journal of Restorative*

Justice 3, No. 1 (2007), 90-99; "Cow Reparations for the Dinka," *The International Journal of Restorative Justice* 4, No. 1 (2008), 101-114; and "Genocide in Sudan: a Look at Three Events" in *The International Journal of Regional and Local Studies* 4, No.1 (2008), 71-88.

Bunza, Mukhtar Umar, Ph.D.: Mukhtar Umar Bunza obtained Ph.D. in History in 2001 from the Usmanu Danfodiyo University, Sokoto, Nigeria and is a Senior Lecturer in History, in the same institution. He won a CRD, Ph.D. Thesis Award in 1999, LEVENTIS Research and Co-operation Program Award, University of London, 2001, ISITA, Research Fellow, Northwestern University, Evanston, USA, 2002 and SACRI laureate for Summer School in Ethnography, pluralism and religious fundamentalism, Cluj-Napoca, Babesbolyai University, Romania, 2005. Bunza is widely published in the national and international academic journals and also contributed chapters in books and is the author of *Christian Missions among Muslims: Sokoto Province, Nigeria, 1935-1990,* published in 2007. He is happily married with children.

Gbadegesin, Olujide: Enoch Olujide Gbadegesin teaches in the Department of Religious Studies Obafemi Awolowo University, Ile-Ife since he joined the Academic staff in 2000. He has published several articles on healing, Christian spirituality, and intersection of religion and culture. He has also written an article on religious language. He is presently working on his Ph.D.

Liman, Sa'adatu Hassan: Sa'adatu is a Lecturer in the Department of History Nasarawa State University, Keffi, Nigeria. She has published several articles in international journals and chapters in book, including "Cross-Gender Relations in the 20th Century Muslim Societies: A Study of the Northern Nigerian Situation," in *Inter-Group Relations in Nigeria during the 19th and 20th Century,* ed. Olayemi Akinwumi, 2006. Sa'adatu's scholarly area of interest is in Islamic Law (Women's Rights).

Oladiti, Abiodun Akeem: Akeem Oladiti has a B.A and M.A. degree in History and African Studies, University of Ibadan. He is about completing his doctoral dissertation in African studies, university of Ibadan. He is currently holding a teaching position in the Department of General Studies, Ladoke Akintola University of Technology, Ogbomoso, Oyo State, Nigeria. In 2006, he was a laureate in Codesria/ Sephis Workshop in Dakar, Senegal. He has contributed essays to edited works and published articles in a number of journals including *Ela*: Journal of African *studies* and journal of *Social* Sciences in Pakistan.

Omotola, J. Shola: J. Shola Omotola, currently a Ph.D. candidate in political science at the University of Ibadan, Nigeria He teaches political science at Redeemer's University, Nigeria. He has attended and presented papers at conferences in the United States of America, Asia, and Africa. He has published extensively in reputable international peer-review journals and contributed chapters to many peer-reviewed books. His latest publication is "From Importer to Exporter: The Changing Role of Nigeria in Promoting Democratic Values in Africa," in Joelien Pretorius, *African Politic: Beyond the Third Wave of Democratisation* (South Africa: Juta Press, 2008). His research interests are in Comparative African Democratisation, Oil and Environmental Politics, and Identity Politics, including Ethnic Minority and Gender Issues.

Onoja, Adoyi, Ph.D.: Adoyi Onoja teaches history at the Nasarawa State University, Keffi, Nigeria. He has contributed articles and chapters in journals and books and co-edited a book on Indigenous Knowledge in Africa. His research interest includes security and minorities in colonial Nigeria and issues in democratization in Africa.

Oyeniyi, Adeyemi Bukola: Oyeniyi teaches African History and International Relations at the Department of History and International Relations, Redeemer's University, Nigeria. He studied Classical Studies at the University of Ibadan. He is doing his doctoral program on "Mobility and Social Conflicts in Yorubaland" at the University of Ibadan. Oyeniyi was, at different times, a laureate of the Nordiska Afrika Institutet, Uppsala, Sweden, the Institute of Security Studies, Pretoria, South Africa, the Omohundro Institute for Early American Slavery, the Council for the Development of Social Science Research in Africa (CODESRIA), South-South Exchange Programme for Research on the History of Development (SEPHIS). In the 2007/08 edition of CODESRIA/SEPHIS Research Methodology Workshop, Oyeniyi emerged as the best and only laureate from Nigeria among the 14 chosen from all over the world.

Umaru, Ibrahim: Ibrahim Umaru teaches economics in the Department of Economics, Nasarawa State University, Keffi, Nigeria. He is a doctoral student of the Ahmadu Bello University, Zaria, Nigeria. He has written and published in both national and international journals.

Usuanlele, Uyilawa, Ph.D.: Uyilawa Usuanlele was born in Benin City, Nigeria. He had his education in Nigeria, Sweden, and Canada. He taught history part time and worked as a Researcher with the National Council for Arts and Culture in Nigeria. He is a recipient of a study award of Swedish International Development Agency (SIDA). He is a founding member and former Coordinator of Institute for Benin Studies, Benin City, Nigeria. He has attended and presented papers at conferences, workshops, and seminars in Africa, Europe, and the Americas and has contributed articles and chapters to learned journals and books. He presently teaches African history at State University of New York, Oswego, New York, USA

INDEX